Adobe Premiere Pro Essentials 2024

Edit Faster, Smarter, and More Creatively with Real-World Workflows, Pro Techniques, and AI-Powered Tools

TABLE OF CONTENT

INTRODUCTION

Adobe Premiere Pro is an amazing platform for video creation! It transforms your raw clips into impressive movies that people will love. Whether you're a professional or just passionate about video editing, Premiere Pro stands out as the top choice. Its user-friendly interface and versatile features make editing a breeze.

One of the best aspects is its ability to handle various video, audio, and image formats without the need for conversion. This efficiency allows you to work quickly and innovate freely. Premiere Pro offers powerful tools that can tackle any editing challenge you face, guiding you seamlessly from the editing phase to production and ensuring everything runs smoothly.

User experience is a priority for Adobe, making Premiere Pro easy to navigate. Its consistent design across all Adobe applications encourages experimentation and creativity.

What's more, even beginners can find it straightforward to use, while also tapping into advanced features for impressive results. Throughout this guide, you'll discover how to make your videos look polished and unique, whether for work, personal projects, or even big productions.

Let's explore Adobe Premiere Pro together and get ready to create videos that truly impress!

Adobe Premiere Pro 2024 Features

For professional video editing, Adobe Premiere Pro 2024 is the latest version and is widely used in the film, TV, and streaming industries due to its extensive range of tools for cutting, color grading, and VFX.

Here are some key features:

The latest update introduces significant enhancements to text-based editing. One standout addition is the Filler Word Detection tool, which identifies and removes filler words like "um" and "uh" from your timeline instantly, resulting in cleaner and more polished audio.

Additionally, managing Motion Graphics Templates (MOGRTs) has been streamlined for better organization. New sequence settings allow for quicker project setup, and accessing previous versions of Team Projects is now easier thanks to improvements in Auto Save. While these updates may seem minor, they significantly enhance the editing experience, enabling editors to work more efficiently and effectively in Premiere Pro.

Filler Word Detection with bulk delete for Text-Based Editing

With Text-Based Editing, you can quickly locate and remove all filler words like "uh" and "umm" from your recordings, enhancing their overall sound quality. Simply click on a filler word in your sequence to delete it, just like you would with a clip. This feature supports all 18 languages available in Speech to Text, making it versatile for various linguistic contexts.

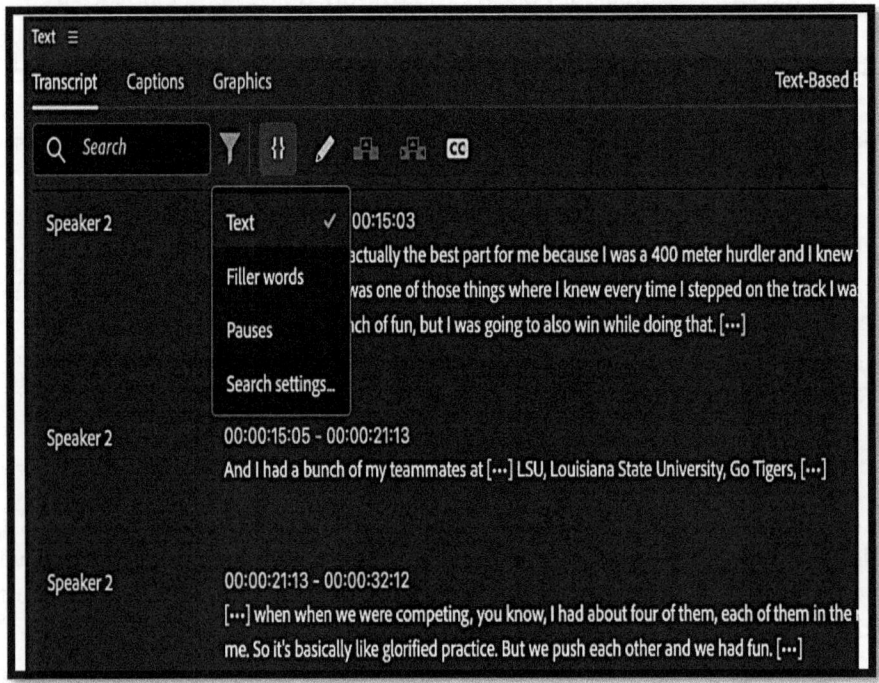

Redesigned MOGRT management

Motion Graphics Templates (MOGRTs) function similarly to After Effects motion graphics but are designed as user-friendly templates with adjustable settings directly in Premiere Pro. Based on user feedback, we've streamlined MOGRT controls for better usability. You can now easily find, view, and organize MOGRT files in various locations, including folders on your hard drive, making your editing process more efficient.

Instead of a dropdown menu, MOGRTs are now displayed as separate rows with check marks, making it easier to browse through collections from various locations. You can explore MOGRTs in two ways: the Browser Tree View, which indicates your current location within MOGRTs, and the MOGRT view below, which showcases miniature layouts from your selected sources. You can adjust the space allocated to each view by resizing the window or toggling the Browser Tree View on and off with the funnel button at the top.

New sequence presets

New sequence settings for HD, UHD, HDR, and social media projects allow you to set up your sequences quickly and efficiently. The most commonly used sequence options have been reorganized for easier access.

To view the new presets, go to File > New Sequence or click the New Item > New Sequence button in the Project panel. You'll find a simplified list of presets, including:

- **HD 1080p**
- **Social** for 4x5, 9x16, and 1x1 timelines
- **UHD (HDR)** for 2160p timelines with HDR color space
- **UHD (4K)** for 2160p timelines with SDR color space
- **Legacy** for all previously included presets

These presets are designed to help you get started quickly, but you can easily modify, delete, or create new ones to streamline your editing process.

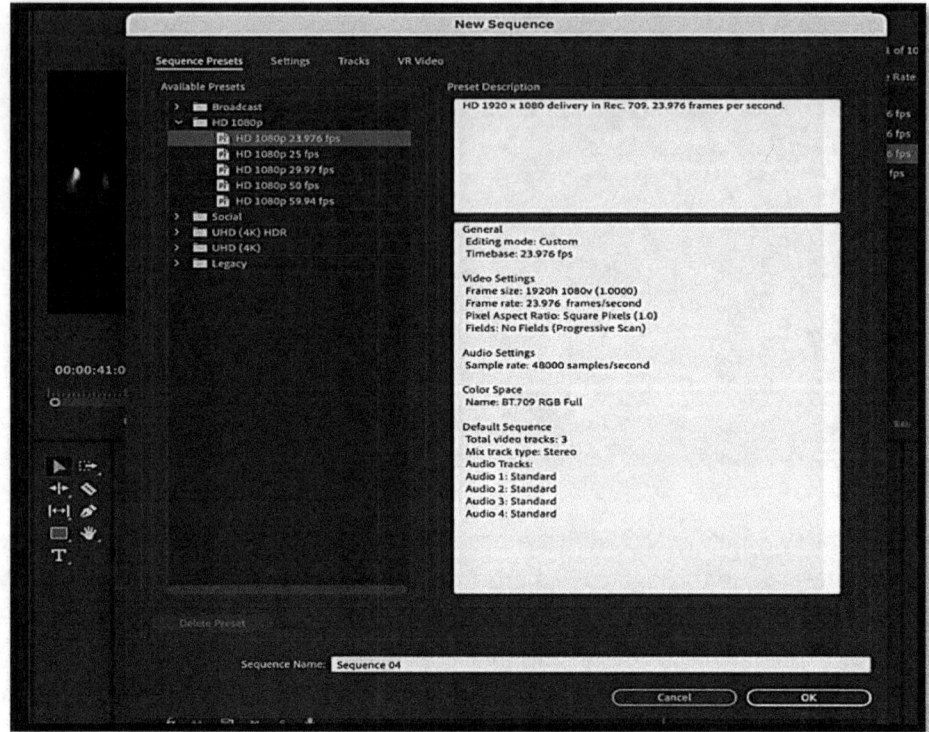

Easier access to Team Projects version history and auto-saves

By clicking on the Team Project name in the top bar of Premiere Pro, you can now access all versions and Auto Save records for that project. This new feature allows you to choose from the following options:

Team Project Settings

You can customize various aspects of the Team Project, including the name, description, collaborators, and additional settings such as color, scratch files, and import preferences.

Version History

Open the Premiere Pro Media Browser and ensure that you've selected the correct version of the Team Project from the list of saved versions.

Auto save History

Launch the Premiere Pro Media Browser and confirm that the latest auto-save of the Team Project is selected. From this auto-save, you can either create a new Team Project or update any existing version.

Trimming and Multicam improvements

A new preference called "Ripple Trim" has been added to the Trim menu. This option, located under "Shift clips that overlap trim points during ripple trimming," ensures that both sides of the trim remain in sync. With this setting enabled, Premiere Pro will adjust clips that cross a cut, cutting new edit points alongside your selected ones. This prevents any clips on either side of the edit from shifting out of place during the trimming process.

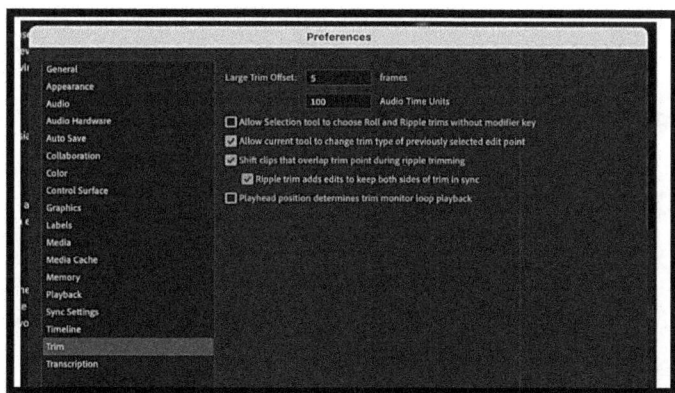

Browse Cloud Locations

Importing media is simple, whether you're using Import mode or the Media Browser, just like you would from a local drive. The Media Browser panel will now display any changes made to files or media in linked Dropbox or OneDrive folders. Locations that are currently connected to your system will be automatically listed in the right column under Cloud while in Import Mode.

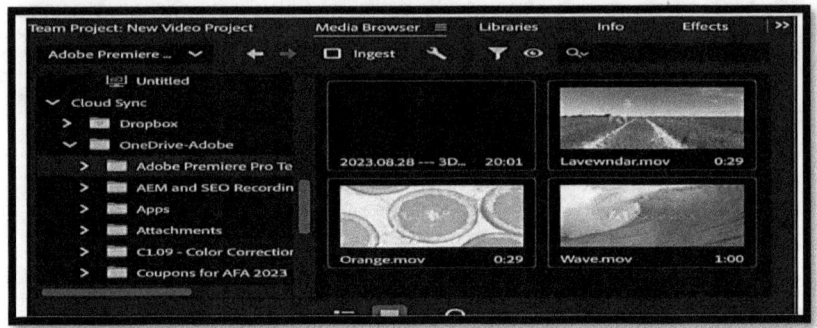

Additional updates

⬚ Support for exporting 16-bit PNG files has been added.

⬚ In Export Mode, destination groups allow you to disable unnecessary elements for a cleaner UI.

⬚ Adobe will discontinue Creative Cloud synced files for all free and paid personal users who aren't part of a Creative Cloud for Enterprise or Teams account starting February 1, 2024.

⬚ All Creative Cloud files will no longer support Sync Settings. You can transfer your personalized preset groups from an older version of Premiere Pro to a newer one on the same computer.

⬚ As of Premiere Pro 24.0, system requirements have changed. Adobe's video and audio tools no longer support Intel versions of Rosetta on Apple M1/M2 devices. Premiere Pro now requires CPUs with AVX2 support on AMD and Intel x86 systems.

Optimizing performance

Having a powerful computer is essential for smooth and efficient editing. A more capable system enhances your creative process by speeding up edits and making them more enjoyable. Premiere Pro is designed to leverage your computer's capabilities, especially with multicore processors and multiple CPUs. Faster, higher-quality processors and additional CPU cores significantly improve editing performance.

For optimal performance, a minimum of 8 GB of RAM is required, but 16 GB is recommended for handling high-definition (HD) media, while 32 GB or more is ideal for ultra-high-definition (UHD or 4K) content. The speed of your storage also plays a crucial role. It's advisable to store your media files on a separate, fast hard drive. For higher-resolution videos or RAW footage, using a RAID array or a fast solid-state drive (SSD) is recommended. Mixing media files with program files on the same drive can lead to slowdowns, so keeping them on separate disks enhances performance.

Utilizing graphics technology, specifically a graphics processing unit (GPU), can further accelerate playback in Premiere Pro. GPU acceleration is beneficial, and most video cards with at least 2 GB of dedicated video memory (VRAM) will perform well; however, 4 GB of VRAM or more is preferred. These improvements can significantly streamline your editing process, especially when working with high-quality video.

Installing Premiere Pro
Installing Premiere Pro2024 on Windows

1. **Download Premiere Pro2024:**
   - Start by downloading the installation file for Premiere Pro2024 for Windows from the official Adobe website or a trusted source.
2. **Wait for the Download to Finish:**
   - Allow time for the download to complete; the duration will depend on your internet speed and file size.
3. **Access the Downloads Folder:**
   - Once the download is complete, navigate to your computer's 'Downloads' folder, where your browser typically saves files.
4. **Locate the Installation File:**
   - Find a file named something like " PremierePro_2024_LS31_win64.exe" in your Downloads folder. This is the installer.
5. **Initiate the Installation:**
   - Double-click the "PremiereElements_2024_LS31_win64.exe" file to start the installation process.
6. **Follow On-Screen Instructions:**
   - An installation wizard will appear. Follow the prompts, which usually include accepting terms, choosing the installation location, and setting preferences.
7. **Internet Connection During Installation:**
   - Keep your computer connected to the internet throughout the installation, as the installer may need to download additional files or updates.

8. **Completion:**
   - Once the installation finishes, Premiere Pro2024 will be successfully installed on your Windows system.

Note: Always download software from reputable sources to avoid security risks. Ensure your system meets the requirements for Premiere Pro2024 for optimal performance.

Installing Premiere Pro2024 on Mac

1. **Download Premiere Pro2024:**
   - Begin by downloading the installation file for Premiere Pro2024 designed for macOS from the official Adobe website or a trusted source.
2. **Wait for the Download to Finish:**
   - Allow time for the download to complete; this can vary based on your internet speed and the file size.
3. **Access the Downloads Folder:**
   - After the download finishes, go to your Mac's 'Downloads' folder, where files are typically saved.
4. **Locate the Installation File:**
   - Look for a file named something like "PremiereElements_2024_MacLBS.dmg" in your Downloads folder. This is the disk image file.
5. **Initiate the Installation:**
   - Double-click the "PremiereElements_2024_MacLBS.dmg" file to mount the disk image and display its contents.
6. **Open the Premiere Pro2024 File:**
   - Inside the mounted disk image, double-click the "Premiere Pro2024" file.
7. **Follow On-Screen Instructions:**
   - An installation window will appear. Follow the instructions to proceed, which typically involve agreeing to terms, choosing an installation location, and setting preferences.
8. **Internet Connection During Installation:**
   - Keep your Mac connected to the internet during the installation, as it may need to download additional files or updates.
9. **Completion:**
   - After the installation process is complete, Premiere Pro2024 will be installed on your macOS system and ready to use.

Uninstall Adobe Premiere Pro
Uninstalling Adobe Premiere Pro on Windows

1. **Access Add or Remove Programs:**

- Click on the Windows search bar, usually located at the bottom left corner of your screen. Type "Add or Remove Programs" and press Enter.
2. **Select Adobe Premiere Pro for Uninstallation:**
   - In the "Add or Remove Programs" window, scroll through the list of installed applications to find "Adobe Premiere Pro." Click on it to select the program.
3. **Initiate the Uninstallation:**
   - After selecting Adobe Premiere Pro, click the "Uninstall" option to begin the uninstallation process.
4. **Save Premiere Pro Settings (Optional):**
   - If prompted by Adobe Creative Cloud, you may have the option to save your Premiere Pro settings before uninstalling. Choose "Yes" or "No" based on your preference, or skip this step if not prompted.
5. **Adobe Uninstall Wizard:**
   - The Adobe Uninstall Wizard will launch to remove Premiere Pro from your device. This process may take some time as it deletes all related files, configurations, and registry entries.
6. **Completion of Uninstallation:**
   - Once the process is complete, you'll receive a confirmation message indicating that Adobe Premiere Pro has been successfully removed from your computer.

Performing nonlinear editing in Premiere Pro

NLE stands for nonlinear editor, and Adobe Premiere Pro is one such program. It functions similarly to a word processor, allowing you to position, modify, and rearrange video, audio, and graphics freely in your final edit. The nonlinear aspect means you can make changes to any part of your project at any time, without following a specific sequence.

In Premiere Pro, you'll create a sequence by combining various media clips. You can edit any part of this sequence in any order, adjusting content, moving clips to change their playback timing, and more. You can blend different video layers, resize images, adjust colors, apply special effects, and mix audio.

Navigating through your clips in Premiere Pro is like sorting files on your computer. The software supports a wide range of media file formats, including XDCAM EX, XDCAM HD 422, XAVC, DPX, DVCPro HD, QuickTime, AVCHD (including AVCCAM and NXCAM), AVC-Intra, DNxHR, ProRes, DSLR video, and Canon XF. It also supports RAW video formats from cameras like RED, ARRI, Sony, Canon, and Blackmagic, as well as ProRes RAW and various 360° video formats and mobile phone camera files.

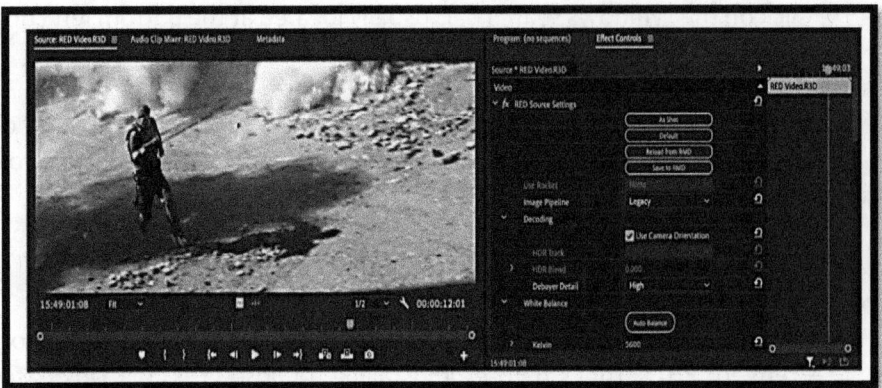

Expanding the workflow

Premiere Pro is a versatile tool that can be used independently but also integrates seamlessly with other software. As part of Adobe Creative Cloud, it provides access to a range of specialized tools that enhance your editing capabilities. By understanding how these different applications work together, you can boost your productivity and expand your creative possibilities.

Including other applications in the editing workflow

Premiere Pro is a powerful tool for video and audio post-production, but it's just one part of Adobe Creative Cloud—a comprehensive suite designed for print, online, and video content. Within this ecosystem, you'll find specialized tools for:

- Creating high-end 3D motion effects
- Generating complex text animations
- Producing layered graphics
- Crafting vector artwork
- Audio production
- Media management

These components can be combined to enhance your projects, ensuring you have everything needed to create professional-quality videos. Here's a brief overview of other key tools in Adobe Creative Cloud:

- **Premiere Rush:** An intuitive video editing app for both mobile and desktop, designed for projects that can be further refined in Premiere Pro.
- **Adobe After Effects:** The go-to software for motion graphics, animation, and visual effects, favored by artists in the industry.

- **Adobe Character Animator:** This tool uses your camera to animate 2D puppets, capturing real-time facial and body movements.
- **Adobe Photoshop:** The industry standard for image editing and graphics creation, allowing you to work with photos, videos, and 3D elements.
- **Adobe Audition:** A comprehensive audio editing tool that offers features for cleaning audio, music production, and creating multitrack mixes.
- **Adobe Illustrator:** A professional program for creating vector graphics for print, video, and web development.
- **Adobe Media Encoder:** This tool allows you to process files for any screen directly from Premiere Pro, After Effects, and Audition.
- **Adobe Dynamic Link:** A cross-product feature that enables real-time collaboration between After Effects, Audition, and Premiere Pro, allowing you to work seamlessly with shared content and sequences.

Exploring the Adobe Creative Cloud video workflow

The workflow in Premiere Pro and Creative Cloud adapts to the specific needs of each project. Here are some examples:

- **Photoshop Integration:** You can edit and apply effects to layered images and stills captured by cameras or scanners in Photoshop, then use these as source media in Premiere Pro. Recent updates have improved this integration.
- **Audio Editing with Audition:** You can send clips directly from the Premiere Pro timeline to Adobe Audition for professional audio cleaning and enhancement, benefiting from the latest features in Audition.
- **Full Sequence Mixing:** Sending an entire sequence to Audition allows you to create a polished audio mix, complete with effects and level adjustments. You can also include video in the session, enabling you to sync audio adjustments with the visuals.
- **Dynamic Link with After Effects:** You can incorporate After Effects compositions into your Premiere Pro projects using Dynamic Link. This allows you to add special effects, animations, and visual elements, with changes in After Effects updating in real time in Premiere Pro.
- **Motion Graphics Templates:** Create motion graphics templates in After Effects that can be easily edited in Premiere Pro. Dedicated controls allow users to modify specific elements while maintaining the original design.
- **Exporting with Adobe Media Encoder:** Use Adobe Media Encoder to export video projects in various resolutions and codecs for web display, social media sharing, or archiving. Premiere Pro also offers built-in presets and effects for seamless uploading to social media platforms.

CHAPTER 1

GETTING STARTED WITH PREMIERE PRO

Understanding the Premiere Pro Interface

Adobe Premiere Pro features a docked, panel-based interface known as a workspace. This setup includes five pre-built workspaces tailored to different workflows and tasks. Most of your editing will occur within the various panels of the user interface. These panels allow you to import and organize your media, as well as preview audio and video clips. The Timeline panel, in particular, is where the majority of your video editing takes place.

Understanding the Default Editing workspace

In the Premiere Pro interface, there are 25 distinct panels available for use. Below are the panels included in the Default Editing workspace:

1. **Source Monitor:** This panel lets you preview and trim clips before adding them to the Timeline.
2. **Program Monitor:** Displays your current sequence, allowing you to see the final output as you edit.
3. **Timeline Panel:** Where you arrange and edit your clips, apply transitions, and manage audio and video tracks.
4. **Project Panel:** Organizes your media assets, such as video clips, audio files, and graphics, in a structured manner.
5. **Effects Panel:** Contains video and audio effects that you can drag and drop onto clips in the Timeline.
6. **Audio Mixer:** Allows for real-time audio adjustments and mixing of different audio tracks.
7. **Essential Graphics Panel:** Used for creating and editing titles and motion graphics.
8. **Lumetri Color Panel:** Provides tools for color correction and grading to enhance your footage.
9. **Media Browser:** Lets you browse and import media files from your computer or connected devices.
10. **Info Panel:** Displays metadata about your clips and sequences, helping you manage your assets.
11. **Markers Panel:** Used to add and manage markers within your timeline for easier navigation and organization.
12. **History Panel:** Tracks your editing actions, allowing you to undo or redo changes easily.

These panels work together to provide a comprehensive editing experience, catering to various aspects of video production.

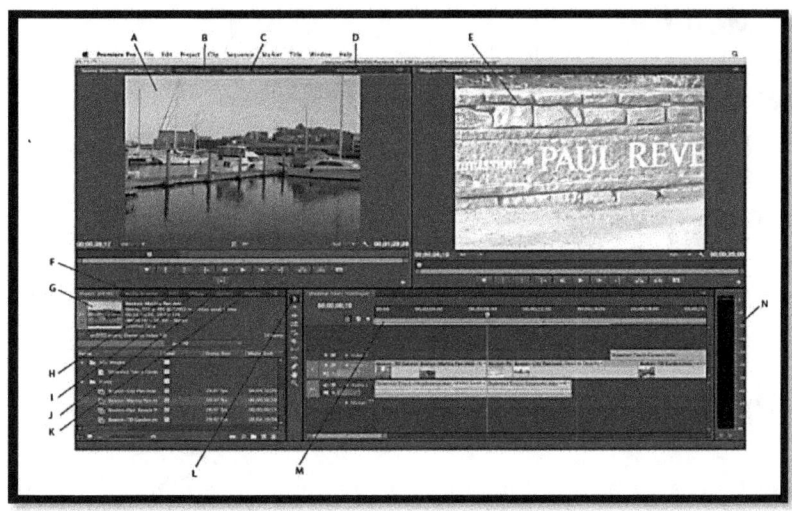

Here's a brief overview of the key panels in Adobe Premiere Pro's Default Editing workspace:

A. Source Monitor

- **Function:** Preview and trim individual audio or video clips before adding them to the Timeline. Set In and Out points, and add markers for efficient organization.

B. Effect Controls Panel

- **Function:** Manage and adjust effects applied to clips. Fine-tune properties like Motion, Opacity, and audio settings for each selected clip.

C. Audio Mixer Panel

- **Function:** Adjust audio settings in real-time, mix audio tracks, and add effects. Useful for fine-tuning the audio aspects of your project while previewing video.

D. Metadata Panel

- **Function:** View and edit metadata for files, including file size, format, and creation date. Helps organize and manage files effectively.

E. Program Monitor

- **Function:** Displays the current sequence as it will appear to viewers. Allows real-time evaluation of edits made in the Timeline.

F. Media Browser Panel

- **Function:** Browse and preview media files stored on your computer. Provides quick access to assets during the editing process.

G. Project Panel

- **Function:** Central hub for all imported media assets, sequences, and titles. Organizes references to files without altering the originals.

H. Info Panel

- **Function:** Displays information about the currently selected item in the Project or Timeline panel, aiding in asset management.

I. Effects Panel

- **Function:** Library of transitions and effects available for clips. Includes visual and audio effects to enhance your project.

J. Markers Panel

- **Function:** Manage markers within clips or sequences, including comments and color codes, to facilitate organization and navigation.

K. History Panel

- **Function:** Records all actions taken during the editing session. Enables undoing of changes but resets when Premiere Pro is closed.

L. Tools Panel

- **Function:** Contains various editing tools (selection, razor, text, etc.) that change the cursor's behavior based on the active tool.

M. Timeline Panel

- **Function:** Main workspace for editing. Arrange clips, modify properties, and apply effects and transitions within distinct timelines for each sequence.

N. Audio Meters Panel

- **Function:** Displays audio levels for clips in the Timeline, providing visual feedback on audio intensity during editing.

These panels work in harmony to streamline the video editing process, enhancing productivity and creativity in Premiere Pro.

Using the Button Editor

The transport controls in Adobe Premiere Pro are key for navigating and examining your footage effectively. Here's a breakdown of their main features:

Transport Controls Overview

- **Location:** Positioned beneath the Source and Program monitors for easy access.

Key Functionalities:

1. **Playback Controls:** Standard playback options allow you to play, pause, and stop video.
2. **Jogging Options:** Frame-by-frame examination lets you scrub through footage precisely for detailed editing.
3. **Marker Placement:** A dedicated button to add markers for important moments in your clips, facilitating organization and navigation.
4. **Comparison View Toggle:** Easily activate or deactivate the Comparison View for side-by-side evaluations of clips.

Source Monitor vs. Program Monitor:

- **Source Monitor:**
  - **Insert and Overwrite Buttons:** These options allow you to add clips to your timeline while controlling how they integrate with existing footage.
- **Program Monitor:**
  - **Lift and Extract Buttons:** These buttons enable you to remove clips from your timeline while keeping the surrounding context intact.

Export Frame Button:

- **Function:** Capture still images from the displayed footage, useful for creating thumbnails or reference images for your project.

These controls enhance the editing experience by providing intuitive ways to manipulate and review footage, streamlining the editing process.

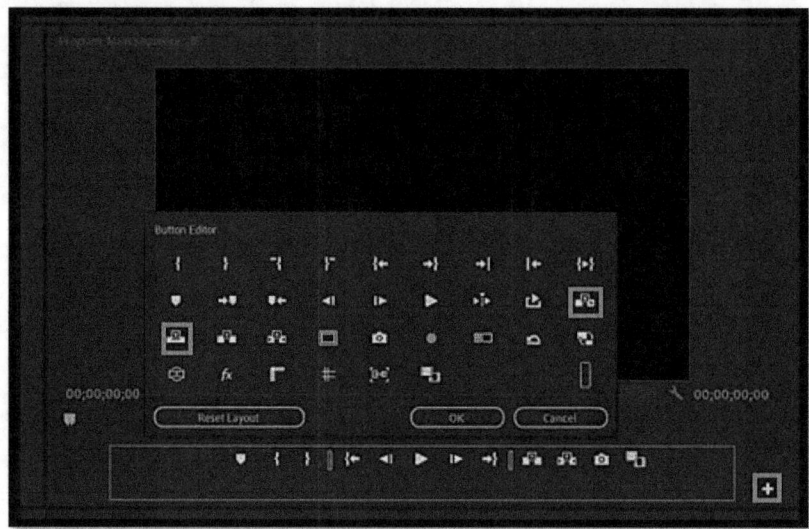

To customize your Adobe Premiere Pro workspace, you can use the Button Editor for a more personalized editing experience. Here's how to do it:

Accessing the Button Editor

1. **Locate the Button Editor:**
   - Click the small "+" symbol in the lower right corner of the screen.

Customizing Your Workspace

2. **Adding Buttons:**
   - When the Button Editor opens, you can drag buttons from the available options directly into the button bar. This allows you to add frequently used tools and functionalities for quicker access.
3. **Removing Unwanted Buttons:**
   - If there are default buttons you don't need, simply drag them back into the Button Editor's option panel to remove them from the button bar.

Finalizing Your Customization

4. **Confirm Your Changes:**
   - Once you've arranged and customized your buttons to fit your workflow, click "OK" to save your settings and continue editing.

This customization capability enhances efficiency by allowing you to tailor your workspace to meet your specific editing needs, making it easier to access the tools you use most frequently.

Premiere Buttons and Keyboard Shortcuts

Here's a list of commonly used buttons in Adobe Premiere Pro, along with their explanations, default keyboard shortcuts, and the order of appearance:

Premiere Pro Buttons Explained

1. **Toggle Proxies**
   - **Shortcut:** Shift + Alt + P
   - **Description:** Switches between proxy and full-resolution media.
2. **Play Around**
   - **Shortcut:** No default shortcut
   - **Description:** Plays a specified range of clips or segments in the timeline, allowing for quick review of a section.
3. **Insert**
   - **Shortcut:** Comma (,)
   - **Description:** Inserts a clip at the playhead position in the timeline without overwriting existing clips.
4. **Overwrite**
   - **Shortcut:** Period (.)
   - **Description:** Overwrites the clip in the timeline starting from the playhead position.
5. **Lift**
   - **Shortcut:** ; (Semicolon)
   - **Description:** Removes the selected clips from the timeline and leaves a gap.
6. **Extract**
   - **Shortcut:** Shift + ;
   - **Description:** Removes the selected clips and closes the gap in the timeline.
7. **Export Frame**
   - **Shortcut:** No default shortcut
   - **Description:** Captures a still image from the program monitor.
8. **Toggle Comparison View**

- o **Shortcut:** No default shortcut
- o **Description:** Allows for side-by-side comparison of clips to evaluate changes.
9. **Toggle Audio Waveform**
   - o **Shortcut:** No default shortcut
   - o **Description:** Displays or hides the audio waveform on audio tracks for easier editing.
10. **Play/Pause**
    - o **Shortcut:** Spacebar
    - o **Description:** Starts or stops playback in the program monitor.

Conclusion

Each button in Premiere Pro is designed to streamline your editing process, and knowing their functions and shortcuts can significantly enhance your workflow. If you hover over any button, you'll see a tooltip with its name and function, helping you become familiar with all available tools.

Here's a concise breakdown of the Premiere Pro functions you mentioned, along with their default keyboard shortcuts:

Premiere Pro Functions and Shortcuts

1. **Mark In (I)**
   - o **Description:** Sets the start point for editing or selection.
2. **Mark Out (O)**
   - o **Description:** Sets the end point for editing or selection.
3. **Clear In (Ctrl + Shift + I)**

- o **Description:** Removes the previously set In point.
4. **Clear Out (Ctrl + Shift + O)**
   - o **Description:** Removes the previously set Out point.
5. **Go to In (Shift + I)**
   - o **Description:** Moves the playhead to the In point.
6. **Go to Out (Shift + O)**
   - o **Description:** Moves the playhead to the Out point.
7. **Go to Next Edit Point (Down Arrow)**
   - o **Description:** Jumps to the next break or edit in the timeline.
8. **Go to Previous Edit Point (Up Arrow)**
   - o **Description:** Jumps to the previous break or edit in the timeline.
9. **Play Video In to Out**
   - o **Description:** Plays the segment between the In and Out points.
10. **Add Marker (M)**
    - o **Description:** Places a visual marker for reference in the timeline.
11. **Go to Next Marker (Shift + M)**
    - o **Description:** Moves the playhead to the next marker.
12. **Go to Previous Marker (Ctrl + Shift + M)**
    - o **Description:** Moves the playhead to the previous marker.
13. **Step Back One Frame (Left Arrow)**
    - o **Description:** Moves the playhead backward one frame.
14. **Step Forward One Frame (Right Arrow)**
    - o **Description:** Moves the playhead forward one frame.
15. **Play-Stop Toggle (Spacebar)**
    - o **Description:** Starts or stops playback.
16. **Play Around (Shift + K)**
    - o **Description:** Plays a specified number of frames before and after the playhead.
17. **Loop Playback**
    - o **Description:** Continuously plays a selected sequence.
18. **Insert (Comma)**
    - o **Description:** Inserts content from the Source monitor into the timeline.
19. **Overwrite (Period)**
    - o **Description:** Replaces existing content in the timeline.
20. **Lift (Semicolon)**
    - o **Description:** Removes selected content and copies it to the clipboard.
21. **Extract (Apostrophe)**
    - o **Description:** Removes selected content and closes the gap.
22. **Safe Margins**
    - o **Description:** Displays title-safe areas on the monitor.
23. **Export Frame (Ctrl + Shift + E)**
    - o **Description:** Captures a still image from the current frame.
24. **Multi-Camera Record On/Off Toggle (0)**

o **Description:** Toggles recording of multi-camera cuts.

25. **Toggle Multi-Camera View (Shift + 0)**
    o **Description:** Switches between different camera angles.
26. **Revert Trim Session**
    o **Description:** Undoes trimming adjustments.
27. **Toggle Proxies**
    o **Description:** Switches between proxy and full-resolution footage.
28. **Toggle VR Video Display**
    o **Description:** Turns VR display on or off for editing VR content.
29. **Global FX Mute**
    o **Description:** Temporarily bypasses all effects in the sequence.
30. **Show Rulers (Ctrl + R)**
    o **Description:** Displays rulers for alignment.
31. **Show Guides (Ctrl + Semicolon)**
    o **Description:** Toggles guides for alignment.
32. **Snap in Program Monitor (Ctrl + Shift + Semicolon)**
    o **Description:** Enables snapping to guides for precise positioning.
33. **Comparison View**
    o **Description:** Compares current frame with a reference frame for color grading and consistency.

Space Entry

- **Description:** Acts as a visual placeholder for organizing buttons or tools in the interface, enhancing layout flexibility.

Each of these functions plays a vital role in streamlining the editing process, enabling precision and efficiency in your projects.

Setting Up Your Workspace

Adobe Premiere Pro offers several standard workspaces that can be customized for various editing needs. Here's a brief overview of some general workspaces and their recommended applications:

1. Editing Workspace

- **Purpose:** Ideal for standard video editing tasks.
- **Applications:** Use this for cutting and arranging clips, adding transitions, and adjusting audio levels. It includes essential panels like the Timeline, Source Monitor, and Program Monitor.

2. Color Workspace

- **Purpose:** Focused on color correction and grading.
- **Applications:** Best for using tools like Lumetri Color for color adjustments, applying LUTs, and refining the visual aesthetics of your project.

3. Audio Workspace

- **Purpose:** Tailored for audio editing and mixing.
- **Applications:** Utilize panels like the Audio Mixer and Essential Sound to adjust audio levels, apply effects, and create a professional sound mix.

4. Effects Workspace

- **Purpose:** Designed for applying and managing visual effects.
- **Applications:** Use the Effects panel and Effect Controls to add, adjust, and manage video and audio effects in your projects.

5. Graphics Workspace

- **Purpose:** Focuses on creating and editing motion graphics.
- **Applications:** Use this workspace for accessing Essential Graphics and creating text, titles, and other graphic elements, enhancing your video with dynamic visuals.

6. Assembly Workspace

- **Purpose:** Ideal for organizing and managing media assets.
- **Applications:** Utilize this for importing clips, organizing project files in the Project panel, and creating sequences before detailed editing.

7. Multi-Camera Workspace

- **Purpose:** Tailored for editing multi-camera sequences.
- **Applications:** This workspace allows you to view multiple camera angles simultaneously and easily switch between them during editing.

Customizing Workspaces

Each workspace can be customized by adding or removing panels according to your workflow preferences. You can save these personalized workspaces for future projects, enhancing your editing efficiency and comfort.

By utilizing the appropriate workspace for your specific tasks, you can streamline your editing process and focus on creativity without getting bogged down by unnecessary tools.

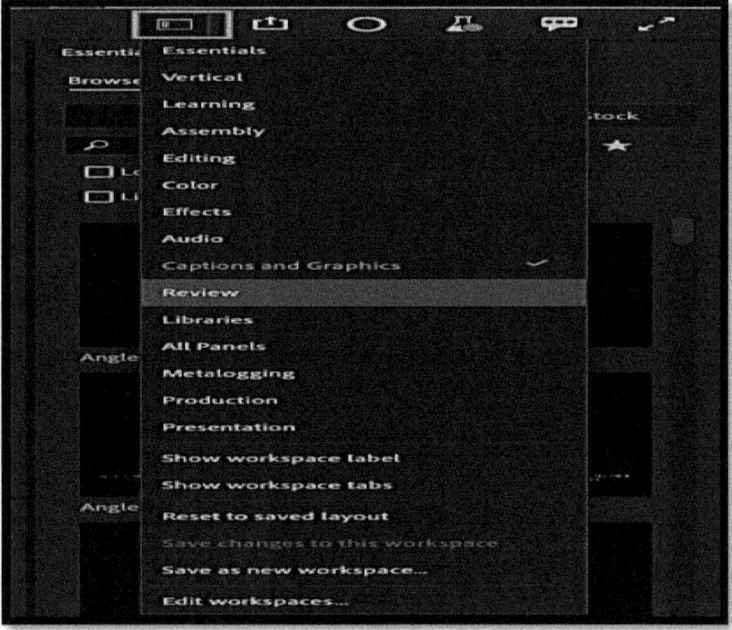

Adobe Premiere Pro features a variety of preconfigured workspaces designed to enhance the editing experience based on specific tasks. Here's a closer look at some of these workspaces:

1. Essentials

- **Description:** A well-organized workspace that provides easy access to essential panels and tools for editing.
- **Best For:** Users with a single monitor, as it ensures a streamlined workflow without clutter.

2. Vertical

- **Description:** Specifically designed for editing vertical video formats.

- **Best For:** Facilitating easy switching between the Source Monitor and Program Monitor, enhancing the editing experience for vertical content.

3. Learning

- **Description:** A workspace tailored for users who want to learn while they edit.
- **Best For:** Beginners taking advantage of in-app lessons, offering a supportive environment for skill development.

4. Assembly

- **Description:** Features a larger Project panel for efficient hover scrubbing and quick rough cuts.
- **Best For:** Rapidly arranging and organizing clips, ideal for the initial stages of video projects.

5. Captions and Graphics

- **Description:** Optimized for working with text, graphics, and captions.
- **Best For:** Effective manipulation of graphic elements and layout components during the editing process.

6. Review

- **Description:** Designed for project reviews and external collaboration (e.g., with Frame.io).
- **Best For:** Facilitating seamless integration with review platforms, making collaboration and feedback more efficient.

7. Production

- **Description:** Suited for collaborative projects involving multiple team members.
- **Best For:** Organizing workflows and managing production pipelines, enhancing collaborative editing efforts.

Customization and Flexibility

Users can easily switch between these workspaces based on their project needs, allowing for a more tailored editing experience. This flexibility helps improve productivity and ensures that editors have the right tools at their fingertips for various tasks.

Change Workspaces

Here's a concise guide on how to access and customize workspaces in Adobe Premiere Pro:

Accessing Workspaces

1. **Dropdown Menu:**
    - Click on the **"Workspace"** menu in the top menu bar.
    - Select the desired workspace from the dropdown list to switch to that configuration.
2. **Window Menu:**
    - Open your project in Premiere Pro.
    - Go to the **"Window"** menu in the menu bar.
    - Choose **"Workspace"** and then select the workspace you want from the list.
3. **Keyboard Shortcuts:**
    - Use keyboard shortcuts to quickly access specific workspaces.
    - Press **Alt + Shift + [number key]** (1 to 9) to open predefined workspaces. For example, **Alt + Shift + 1** opens the first workspace.

Customizing Keyboard Shortcuts

- Premiere Pro allows you to customize keyboard shortcuts for accessing workspaces:
    - Go to the **"Edit"** menu and select **"Keyboard Shortcuts."**
    - In the Keyboard Shortcuts panel, navigate to the **"Workspaces"** section.
    - Assign or modify shortcuts for various workspaces, including any custom ones you've created.

This setup helps streamline your workflow by providing quick access to the tools and layouts you need.

Import a workspace with a project

Adobe Premiere Pro offers a convenient feature that allows you to open projects in the last-used workspace associated with them, which is particularly useful for users who frequently switch between different workspace setups. Here's how to utilize this feature:

Opening Projects in Last-Used Workspace

1. **Before Opening a Project:**
    - Go to the **"Window"** menu in the menu bar.

- o Select **"Workspaces."**
- o Choose **"Import Workspace From Projects."**
2. **Opening the Project:**
   - o After enabling this option, open the desired project. Premiere Pro will load it in the last-used workspace.

If Workspace is Empty

- • If you find that the workspace is empty after importing:
  - o Close the project.
  - o Unselect **"Import Workspace From Projects."**
  - o Re-import the project, ensuring to choose an existing workspace for the project.

This method allows for a more seamless transition between different projects and their respective workspace configurations, enhancing your editing efficiency.

Modify the order of workspaces

You can easily manage and customize your workspaces in Adobe Premiere Pro by following these steps:

Managing Workspaces

1. **Accessing Edit Workspaces:**
   - o Click on the **"Workspace"** menu in the menu bar.
   - o Select **"Edit Workspaces"** at the bottom of the list, or go through **"Window > Workspaces > Edit Workspaces."**
2. **Rearranging Workspaces:**
   - o In the dialog box that appears, you can drag and drop workspaces to change their order.
3. **Hiding or Deleting Workspaces:**
   - o To hide a workspace, uncheck the box next to its name.
   - o To delete a custom workspace, select it and click the **"Delete"** button.
4. **Reverting Changes:**
   - o If you decide not to keep the changes, simply click **"Cancel,"** and your previous settings will remain intact.

This flexibility allows you to tailor the workspace setup to fit your editing style, improving your workflow efficiency.

Create Custom Workspaces

Creating custom workspaces in Adobe Premiere Pro is straightforward and enhances your editing efficiency. Here's how to save your tailored workspace configurations:

Saving Custom Workspaces

1. **Using the Dropdown Menu:**
   - Open the **Workspaces** dropdown menu.
   - Select **"Save as New Workspace."**
   - Name your custom workspace and confirm.
2. **Using the Window Menu:**
   - Go to **"Window"** in the menu bar.
   - Navigate to **"Workspace"** and select **"Save as New Workspace."**
   - Name your custom setup and save it.

Accessing Saved Workspaces

- Your saved custom workspaces will appear in the Workspaces menu for easy access in future projects.

Reverting to Default Workspaces

- If you modify a default workspace and wish to return to its original state, you'll need to delete the workspace configuration file from your **Layouts** folder. This step is crucial for restoring the default layout.

By customizing your workspace, you can optimize your editing environment to better suit your needs and improve your workflow.

Reset a Workspace

To reset the current workspace in Adobe Premiere Pro to its original, saved layout of panels, follow these steps:

1. **Using the Workspaces Dropdown Menu:**
   - Open the **Workspaces** dropdown menu.
   - Select **"Reset to Saved Layout."**
2. **Using the Window Menu:**
   - Go to **"Window"** in the menu bar.
   - Navigate to **"Workspace"** and select **"Reset to Saved Layout."**

This will restore the workspace to its default arrangement, allowing you to start fresh without any customizations.

Creating a New Project

To create a new project in Adobe Premiere Pro, follow these steps:

1. **Using the Top Menu:**
   - Go to the top menu and select **File > New > Project**.
2. **Using the Welcome Screen:**
   - If you're on the welcome screen, simply click on the **New Project** option.
3. **New Project Dialog Box:**
   - This action will open the **'New Project'** dialog box, where you can set various parameters for your project, such as the project name, location, and settings for video and audio formats.

Make sure to configure your settings according to your project requirements before clicking **OK** to create the project.

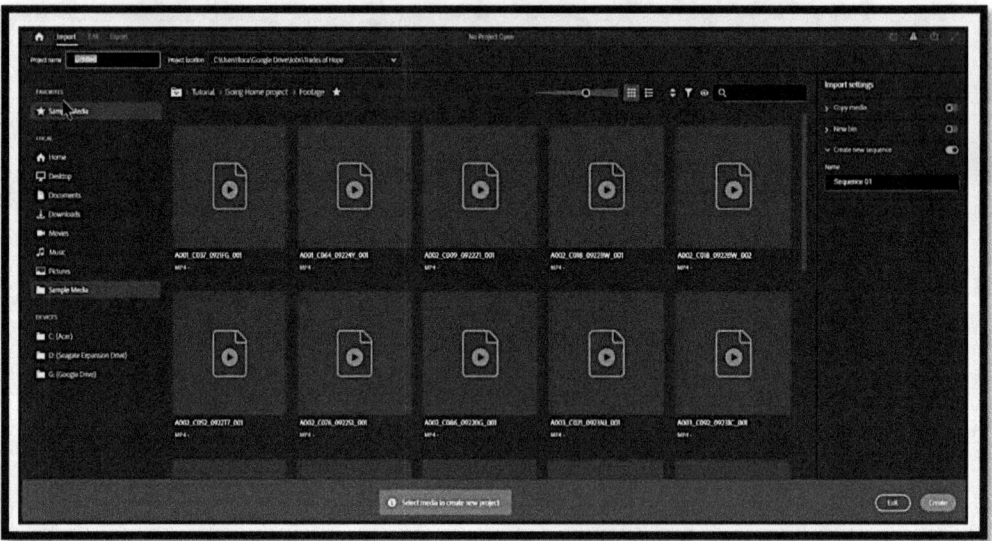

Create Project File

Here's how to set up a new project in Adobe Premiere Pro with a focus on naming and location:

1. **Pay Attention to Screen Fields:** At the top of the screen, you'll find two essential fields ready for your input.
2. **Descriptive Project Name:** In the "Project Name" box, type a clear and descriptive name for your project. This name should reflect the content or purpose of the project, making it easy for anyone to identify.
3. **Picking a Project Location:** Click on the "Project Location" box, then select the "Choose Location" option. This action opens a file browser.
4. **Navigating the File Browser:** Use the file browser to navigate to your desired folder, whether it's your project folder, Desktop, or Documents. Choose a location that suits your workflow and makes it easy to access your project later.
5. **Importance of Naming and Location:** Remember, this file will contain all your hard work. Spend time selecting a meaningful name and a logical location, as this will help you find it easily in the future. Proper organization is key to a smooth editing process!

Importing Media Files
Importing Media Files in Adobe Premiere Pro

1. **Finding Media Files:**
   - Look to the left side of the screen to locate where your media files are saved. This could be your Desktop, Downloads folder, or any other directory where your video files are stored.
2. **Single File Selection:**
   - Navigate to the folder containing your video files. Click on a single file to select it. This action indicates that you've chosen this specific file for import.

This process will help you get your media ready for editing in Premiere Pro!

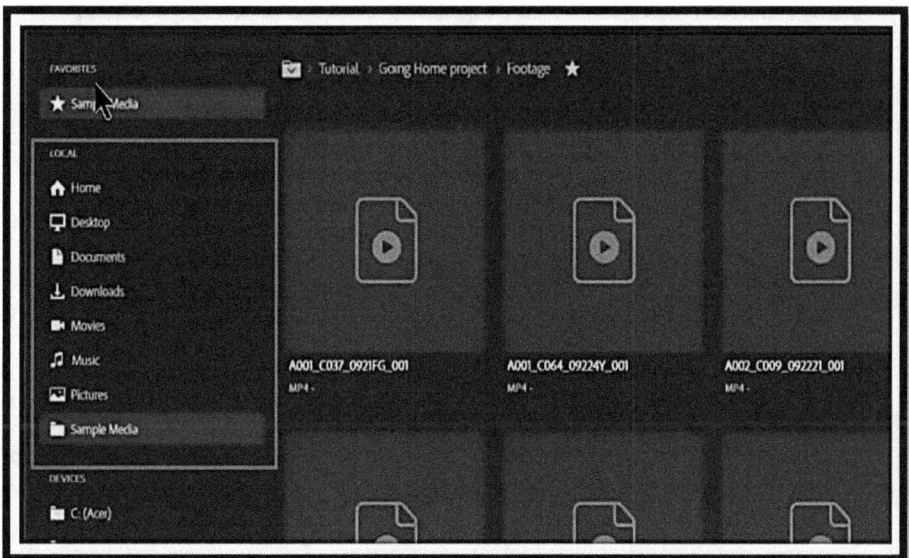

Importing Multiple Files in Adobe Premiere Pro

1. **Picking Out Multiple Files or a Range:**
   - To import several files at once, start by clicking on the first file in your list.
   - Hold down the **Shift** key and then click on the last file in the desired range. This will select all files between the first and last clicked file simultaneously, speeding up the import process.

Using this method allows for efficient selection, making it easier to import multiple assets for your project!

Turn Off Sequence Option
Import Settings in Adobe Premiere Pro

1. **Check Import Settings:**
   - On the right side of the screen, locate the **Import Settings** section.
2. **Create New Sequence Option:**
   - Ensure that the **"Create new sequence"** option is not selected. It should appear gray.
   - If it's blue, click it to deactivate this option.

This step is important to prevent Premiere from automatically creating a new sequence upon import, allowing you to manage your workflow more effectively.

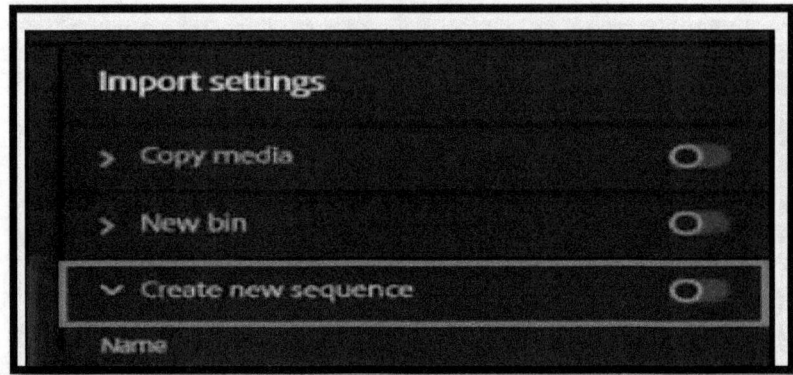

If you have the **"Create new sequence"** option turned on, all your imported files will automatically be added to the Timeline. This can clutter your workspace and disrupt your intended workflow. To maintain control over your project, ensure this option remains off while importing your media files. This way, you can decide when and how to add clips to your Timeline later on.

Confirm

After clicking the **Create** button in the bottom right corner, your project will be initialized. You'll see it appear in the **Project panel**, where you can start organizing and editing your media files. From here, you can create sequences, import additional assets, and begin your editing process. Enjoy diving into your project!

Setting up a Sequence

When you create a new project in Premiere Pro and click **OK**, the **New Sequence** window appears, prompting you to select settings for your sequence. With many categories and options, it can be overwhelming, especially if you're unsure about your project's direction. However, Premiere Pro simplifies this process for you.

Automatic Sequence Creation

If you're uncertain about which settings to choose, Premiere Pro can automatically create a sequence that matches your video clips. This ensures that your sequence settings align with your original footage, optimizing playback performance and maintaining quality.

Tips for Setting Up Your Sequence

1. **Match Settings**: It's best to have your sequence settings closely match the original video's specifications. This improves real-time playback and overall quality.
2. **New Item Menu**: At the bottom of the Project panel, you'll find the **New Item** menu. From here, you can create various elements like sequences, titles, and color mattes.

Creating a Sequence from Clips

- **Drag and Drop**: You can drag a clip or multiple clips from the Project panel onto the **New Item** menu. This automatically generates a sequence with the same frame size and frame rate as the selected clips. The new sequence will take the name of the first clip you selected.
- **Right-Click Method**: Alternatively, right-click on one or more clips and select **New Sequence From Clip** from the context menu. This ensures that your sequence settings perfectly match your clips.
- **Drag to Timeline**: You can also drag clips directly onto an empty Timeline. This will create a sequence that fits the parameters of your video, ensuring compatibility.

By following these steps, you can easily set up a sequence that meets the needs of your project, allowing you to focus on the creative aspects of editing!

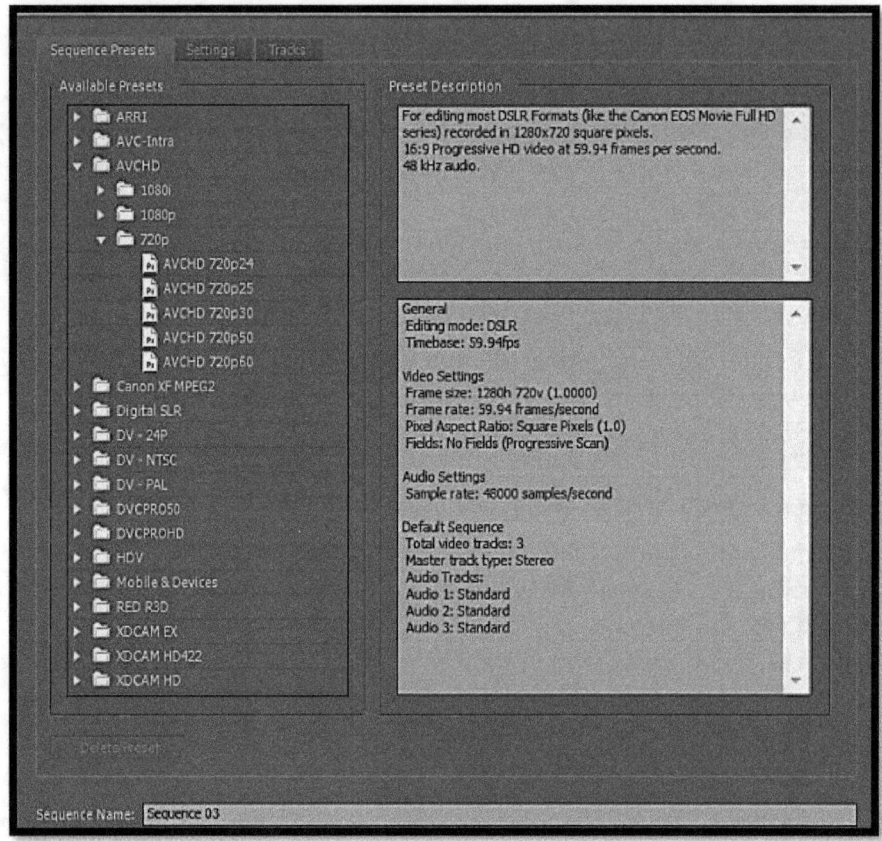

When working with diverse media in Premiere Pro, ensuring that your sequence settings align with your clips is crucial for optimal playback. Here's how it works:

Choosing the Right Media and Settings

1. **Match Settings for Better Playback**: It's beneficial to select sequence settings that closely match the specifications of most of your video files. This helps maintain system performance during playback, resulting in smoother and faster editing.
2. **Automatic Adjustment**: If the first clip you add to your sequence doesn't match the existing sequence settings, Premiere Pro detects this discrepancy. It then prompts you with an option to automatically change the sequence settings to match the characteristics of the new clip.

Benefits of Automatic Adjustment

- **Consistency**: This feature ensures that your project remains consistent, allowing you to work with various media types without stressing over technical details.
- **Streamlined Workflow**: By adjusting the sequence settings automatically based on the first clip you add, Premiere Pro simplifies the editing process, making it easier to incorporate different media without manual adjustments.

Conclusion

Utilizing Premiere Pro's automated adjustment tool helps keep your editing smooth and efficient, allowing you to focus more on creativity rather than getting bogged down by technical settings. This flexibility is particularly useful when dealing with mixed media formats, enhancing your overall editing experience.

Understanding the Makeup of Sequence Presets

Choosing the right sequence settings in Adobe Premiere Pro can significantly enhance your editing experience. Here's a simplified overview of the key components to help you make informed decisions:

Key Sequence Settings

1. **Mode**: This encompasses various technical settings including:
   o **Frame Size**: Determines the dimensions of your video, influencing the overall resolution and aspect ratio.
   o **Pixel Aspect Ratio**: Indicates whether the pixels are square or rectangular, affecting how your video is displayed.
   o **Field Dominance**: Relates to how interlaced video is displayed (either upper or lower field first).
   o **Audio Sample Rate**: Specifies the frequency at which audio samples are captured (commonly 48 kHz).
2. **Frame Size**: The frame size directly affects the visual quality and aspect ratio of your video. Standard options include HD (1920x1080) and 4K (3840x2160), depending on your project needs.
3. **Audio Sample Rate**: Typically set at 48 kHz for video projects, this affects audio clarity and synchronization with video.
4. **Video Preview Files**: These files are generated during editing and can also serve as render files, enabling smoother playback and quicker previews.

Additional Considerations

- **Codec**: While codec isn't explicitly listed, Premiere Pro uses the Mercury Playback Engine to handle various file types efficiently. This feature allows for mixing different formats seamlessly within a project.
- **Sequence Presets**: As your editing setup evolves (for instance, when adding third-party I/O cards), your list of available sequence presets may expand, giving you access to new settings tailored to your hardware.

Performance Enhancements

- **I/O Cards**: Upgrades in Premiere Pro since CS6 have improved compatibility and performance when using I/O cards for video transfer. This allows for better output options and enhanced workflow, especially in professional environments.

Conclusion

Understanding these core settings can help you tailor your projects to achieve the best possible results. By choosing appropriate sequence settings from the start, you can streamline your editing process and enhance playback performance.

The selection processes

Understanding Adobe Premiere Pro's sequence presets is essential for optimizing your editing workflow. Here's a breakdown of how to effectively choose the right settings:

Key Considerations for Sequence Settings

1. **Footage Type**: Knowing the primary type of footage you'll be using is crucial. This informs key settings like:
   - **Frame Size**: Determines resolution and aspect ratio.
   - **Pixel Aspect Ratio**: Affects the display of your footage, ensuring it looks correct on different screens.
2. **Mercury Playback Engine (MPE)**: Introduced in CS6, this technology enhances performance by utilizing MPE acceleration through I/O cards. This allows for smoother playback and faster rendering, significantly improving your editing experience.

Steps to Choose the Right Sequence Preset

- **Identify Your Footage**: Before starting your project, analyze the characteristics of your main video clips (resolution, frame rate, etc.).
- **Select Appropriate Preset**: Use the sequence presets that match your footage to ensure optimal playback and editing performance.
- **Leverage MPE**: If you're using compatible hardware, enable MPE to take full advantage of performance enhancements.

By aligning your sequence settings with your footage, you can create a more efficient and effective editing process in Premiere Pro.

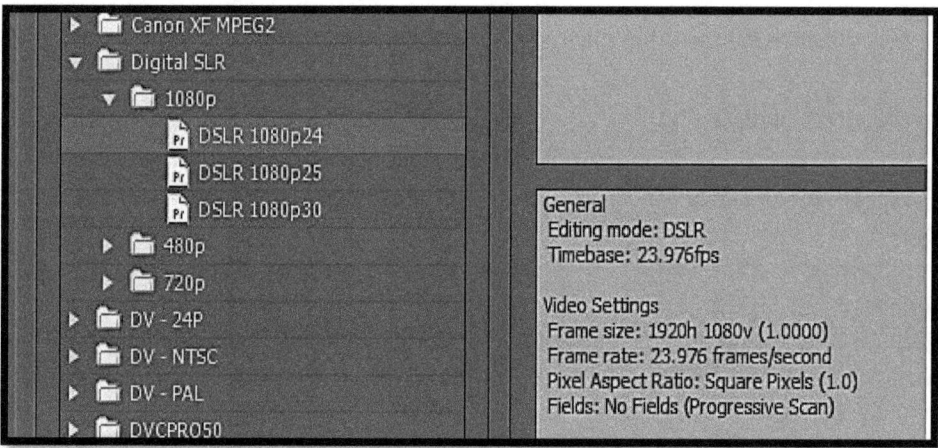

Here's a streamlined guide to selecting a sequence format from presets in Adobe Premiere Pro:

Steps to Select a Sequence Format

1. **Choose the Main Type of Footage**: Start by identifying the primary format of the footage you'll be using, such as XDCAM HD, DVCPROHD, or RED R3D.
2. **Browse Categories**: Navigate through the Category folders in the New Sequence window to find the preset that aligns with your selected footage type.
3. **Set the Frame Size**: After selecting the desired category, choose the appropriate frame size. Decide whether your video will be progressive or interlaced, and select from the options in the "Frame Size" box.
4. **Pick a Frame Rate**: Based on your source footage, select the correct frame rate that matches your clips for optimal playback.
5. **Name and Create the Sequence**: Enter a name for your sequence and click "OK." This will create a new sequence with the chosen settings in the Project panel.

Adjusting Sequence Settings

If you need to modify the sequence settings later, follow these steps:

- **Open New Sequence Dialog**: Go to the **File** menu and choose **File > New > Sequence** to revisit the New Sequence window and make any adjustments as needed.

By following these steps, you can ensure that your sequence settings are tailored to your project's requirements, enhancing your editing workflow.

Adjust the clip length

Here's a concise guide on managing playback and editing clips in Adobe Premiere Pro:

Playback and Viewing

1. **Play/Pause Sequence**: In the Program Monitor, press the **spacebar** to start and stop playback.
2. **Navigate to Specific Points**: You can drag the blue playhead to move to any point in your video.
3. **Fit Video to Monitor**: If the video appears too large or small, right-click (Windows) or Control-click (macOS) the clip in the Timeline panel and select **Set to Frame Size** to adjust it to fit the viewing area.

Trimming Clips

- **Trim Clips**: To shorten a clip, hover over the edge of the clip in the Timeline and drag it inward. This will allow you to keep only the desired parts of the clip.

Managing Gaps

1. **Identify Gaps**: After adjusting your clips, check for any spaces between them. Click on any gap in the Timeline to select it.
2. **Remove Gaps**: Press the **Delete** key to eliminate the gap, ensuring a smooth transition between clips in your sequence.

By following these steps, you can effectively manage playback and maintain a seamless flow in your video project.

Explore the Project Settings

Here's how to access and manage the Project Settings in Adobe Premiere Pro:

Accessing Project Settings

1. **Open Project Settings**:
   - Go to the **File** menu.
   - Select **Project Settings**.
   - Click on **General**.

Key Options in Project Settings

In the Project Settings dialog box, you'll find several important options:

- **Renderer**: Choose the rendering engine, like Mercury Playback Engine, to optimize performance.
- **Video Rendering and Playback**: Set the playback settings for smooth editing.
- **Capture**: Configure capture settings if you're working with live video input.
- **Audio**: Adjust audio settings, including sample rates and playback options.

Importance of Project Settings

- **Performance**: Correct settings help ensure smooth playback and editing.
- **Compatibility**: Adjust settings based on the types of media you'll be using.
- **Quality**: Optimize for the best visual and audio quality in your project.

Make sure to revisit these settings if you notice performance issues or if your project requirements change!

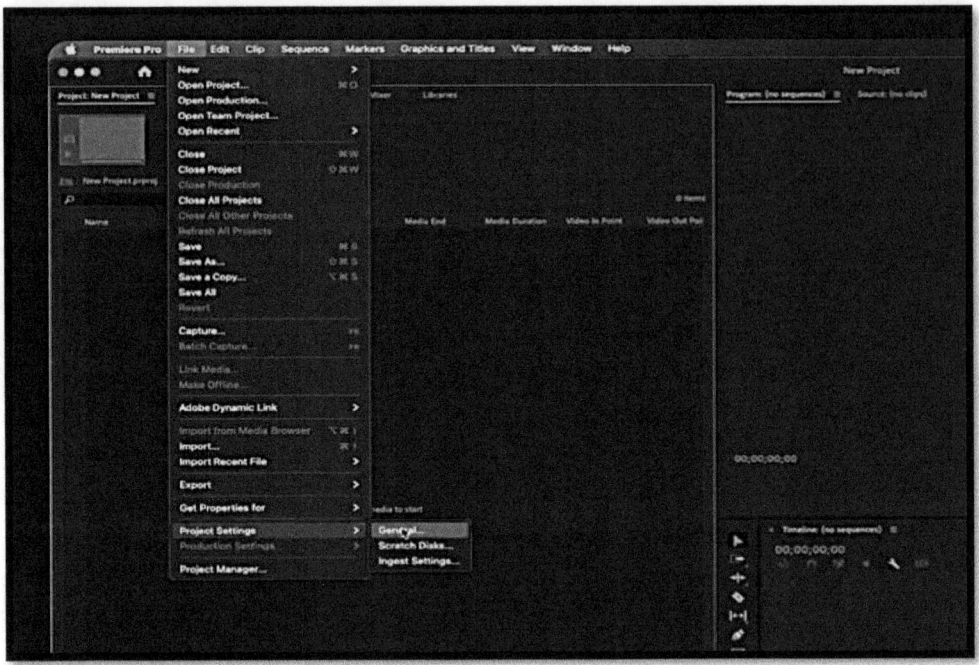

Here's how to manage playback settings and formats in Adobe Premiere Pro to enhance your editing experience:

Managing Playback Settings

1. **Real-Time Playback**:
   - Real-time playback is crucial for assessing how effects alter your clips. However, heavy effects can lead to frame drops.
2. **Dropping Frames**:
   - If you notice dropped frames during playback, consider rendering the timeline to ensure smoother viewing. You can do this by going to **Sequence > Render In to Out**.

Adjusting Display Formats in Project Settings

1. **Access Project Settings**:
   - Navigate to **File > Project Settings > General**.
2. **Change Video Display Format**:
   - Under **Video Display Format**, you can select how time is displayed (e.g., Timecode, Frames) to best suit your workflow.
3. **Change Audio Display Format**:

o In the **Audio Display Format** section, choose how audio time is displayed (e.g., Samples, Timecode) to align with your audio editing needs.

Tips for Optimal Performance

- **Use Proxies**: If working with high-resolution footage, consider using proxies for smoother editing.
- **Optimize Effects**: Use effects that are optimized for real-time playback, and render effects-heavy sections when needed.
- **Regularly Check Settings**: Revisit your project settings as your project evolves to ensure optimal performance and workflow efficiency.

These adjustments help maintain a smooth editing experience and ensure your artistic choices are accurately reflected during playback!

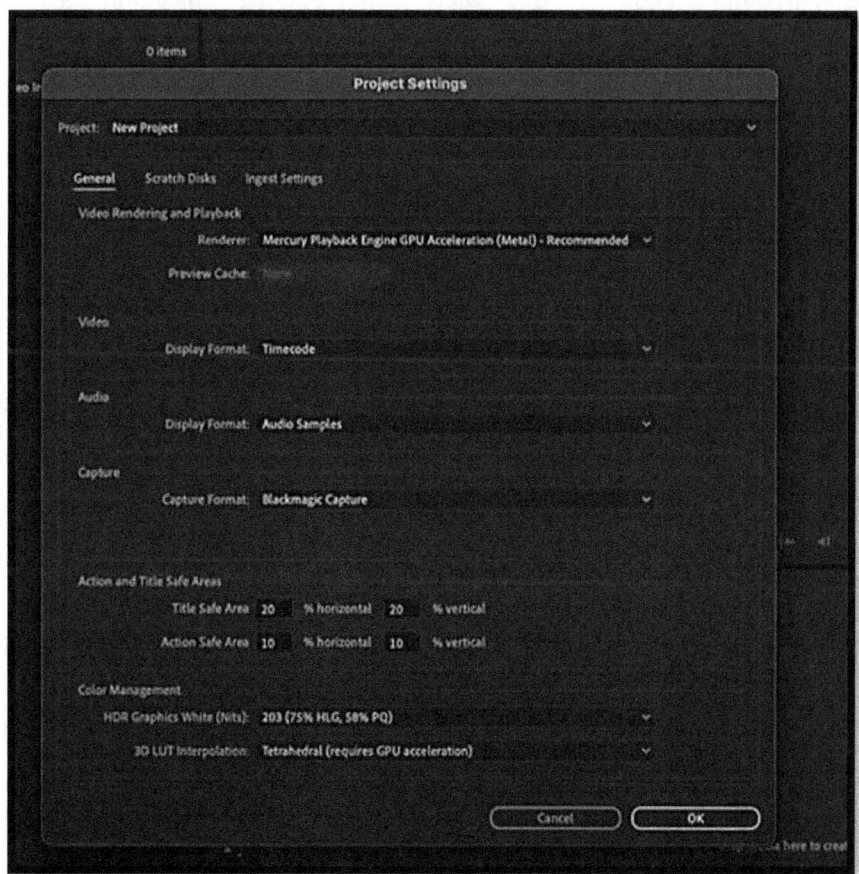

Absolutely! Keeping the default settings—**Audio Samples** for the Audio Display Format and **Timecode** for the Video Display Format—provides clarity and consistency in how you view and edit your project. These settings don't affect playback performance but simply alter how time is represented visually within Premiere Pro.

Key Points:

- **Audio Samples**: This setting is useful for precise audio editing, allowing you to see and work with audio at a granular level.
- **Timecode**: Using timecode helps you maintain synchronization between audio and video, making it easier to reference specific moments in your project.

Flexibility in Settings:

- **Adjust Anytime**: Feel free to adjust these settings during your editing process to better suit your workflow or project requirements. It's all about finding what works best for you and your project!
- **Consistency**: Sticking with standard settings helps avoid confusion, especially when collaborating with others or when revisiting projects later.

By using these settings effectively, you can streamline your editing process and enhance your overall efficiency in Premiere Pro!

The Video Display Format menu

In Adobe Premiere Pro, the **Video Display Format** section in the Project Settings allows you to customize how time is represented in your project, depending on your source material. Here's a concise breakdown of the options:

Video Display Format Options:

1. **Timecode**:
   - **Default Option**: This is the standard setting, used globally to represent time in hours, minutes, seconds, and frames. Ideal for most video projects, especially when working with digital cameras and editing software.
2. **Feet + Frames (16mm or 35mm)**:
   - **For Film Projects**: These options are tailored for projects using celluloid film. They are essential for filmmakers looking to process film negatives and achieve a final image. Use this if your footage comes from 16mm or 35mm film.
3. **Frames**:

- **Animation Focused**: This option counts frames directly, making it suitable for animation projects where precise frame counts are critical. It provides a straightforward view of your footage in terms of individual frames.

Project File Management:

- **Project File**: This file serves as the backbone of your project, storing details about sequences, assets, and editing parameters. It does not alter the original media files; rather, it keeps references to them. If you move, rename, or delete any source files, Premiere Pro may prompt you with a "Where Is the File" dialog upon reopening the project.

Project Panel and Organization:

- The **Project Panel** is where all clips related to your project are stored. It enables easy organization through **bins**, allowing you to manage multiple sequences and their respective environments efficiently.
- You can create multiple sequences within a single project, making it possible to work on different segments separately and combine them for your final output. This feature is particularly useful for managing revisions or various versions of your work.

By understanding these settings and organizational tools, you can streamline your workflow and enhance your editing efficiency in Premiere Pro!

Using the standard digital video workflow

As you gain expertise in video editing, you'll develop a preferred workflow tailored to your projects. Each stage of post-production requires specific focus and tools, and you might spend varying amounts of time on different steps. Here's a breakdown of the key phases you will likely encounter:

Editing Workflow Steps:

1. **Obtain Your Media**:
   - Gather original footage, create animations, or select stock media and other assets necessary for your project.
2. **Ingest the Video**:
   - Import media files into Premiere Pro directly from your camera or storage. Ensure you have backups in different locations to protect against potential storage failures. Use fast storage solutions for smoother playback during editing.
3. **Reorganize Your Clips**:

- Organize your footage into **bins**, which function like folders for easy access. You can also add **metadata** (like color labels and descriptions) to help keep track of your assets.

4. **Create a Sequence**:
   - In the Timeline panel, select the video and audio clips you want to combine. A sequence serves as your edited project, where you'll arrange your clips.

5. **Add Transitions**:
   - Incorporate transition effects between clips, apply video effects, and layer graphics using different tracks in the Timeline panel.

6. **Create Titles and Graphics**:
   - Design or import titles, graphics, and captions that enhance your story and provide context to your audience.

7. **Adjust the Audio Mix**:
   - Fine-tune the loudness and mix of your audio clips. Utilize transitions and effects to create a polished audio experience.

8. **Output Your Project**:
   - Export the finished project to your desired file format for sharing or distribution.

Conclusion

Premiere Pro equips you with powerful tools to navigate each of these phases efficiently. Engaging with the broader community of editors can also provide valuable insights and support as you continue to refine your skills. Embrace the learning process, and enjoy the journey of storytelling through video editing!

CHAPTER 2
BASIC EDITING TECHNIQUES

The Timeline

The Timeline Panel in Adobe Premiere Pro serves as your primary workspace for video editing, acting as a visual canvas for your entire project. It organizes and displays your video clips, audio segments, and graphics in a horizontal layout, with the left side representing the beginning of your video and the right side indicating its conclusion.

Key Features of the Timeline Panel:

- **Editing Functions**: You can easily trim, slice, and move clips, as well as add transitions and effects. This flexibility allows you to refine your project efficiently.
- **Audio Management**: Adjust audio levels directly within the timeline, ensuring your sound design complements your visuals seamlessly.
- **Layer Management**: The timeline supports multiple layers of video and audio tracks. Higher tracks correspond to higher layers in your video composition, enabling you to stack elements for complex editing.
- **Comprehensive Overview**: The Timeline Panel provides a bird's-eye view of your project's progression, making it easy to see how everything fits together and identify areas that need adjustment.

Importance

The Timeline Panel is essential for editing, as it combines an overview of your project with hands-on functionality. It allows you to organize and manipulate all aspects of your video content, ensuring you can craft a polished final product. Whether you're adding effects, rearranging clips, or fine-tuning audio, this panel is the hub of your editing journey.

Using the Timeline Panel

To effectively utilize the Timeline Panel in Adobe Premiere Pro, follow these steps:

1. Import Media Files

- **Accessing Files**: Go to the **File** menu and select **Import**, or simply drag and drop your media files directly into the Project Panel.

2. Move Media to the Timeline

- Once your media is imported, drag the clips from the Project Panel into the Timeline Panel. This is where you'll organize and edit your project.

3. Organize and Manipulate Clips

- **Trimming Clips**: To adjust the duration of a clip, hover over its edge until the trim cursor appears, then click and drag to shorten or lengthen it.
- **Splitting Clips**: Position the playhead at the point where you want to make a cut, select the **Razor Tool**, and click on the clip to create a split.

4. Incorporate Effects and Transitions

- **Applying Effects**: Open the Effects Panel, choose the desired effect, and drag it onto the clip in the Timeline. You can adjust effect parameters in the Effect Controls panel.
- **Adding Transitions**: Similarly, drag a transition from the Effects Panel to the start or end of a clip in the Timeline to create a smooth change between clips.

5. Create and Add Titles

- Click on the **T** icon in the toolbar to create a title. Type your text in the Title window, then drag the title to your desired position in the Timeline.

Conclusion

The Timeline Panel is your main workspace for editing, allowing you to manipulate clips, apply effects, and create titles efficiently. Mastering these tools will enable you to craft a polished video project with ease.

Customizing the Timeline Panel

To personalize the Timeline Panel in Adobe Premiere Pro, follow these steps:

1. Open Your Project

- Launch Adobe Premiere Pro and select the project you want to work on. The Timeline Panel is usually located at the bottom of the interface.

2. Customize the Timeline Panel

- **Right-Click for Options**: Right-click anywhere within the Timeline Panel to bring up a drop-down menu with various customization options.
- **Add or Remove Tracks**: Choose options like **"Add Tracks"** or **"Delete Tracks"** to modify the number of video or audio tracks according to your needs.
- **Customize Appearance**: Click **"Customize"** to select specific elements you want to display in the Timeline.

3. Resize Tracks

- Hover over the border between two tracks until the resize cursor appears, then click and drag upwards or downwards to adjust the height of the tracks for better visibility.

4. Save Your Workspace Layout

- After customizing the Timeline Panel to your liking, save your workspace layout. Go to **"Window" > "Workspaces" > "Save as New Workspace."** This allows you to easily access your preferred layout in future projects.

Conclusion

By personalizing the Timeline Panel, you can create a more efficient and comfortable editing environment that suits your workflow, enhancing your overall editing experience in Adobe Premiere Pro.

Basic Editing Tools and Functions
Understanding the tools

In Adobe Premiere Pro, there are eleven distinct tools designed to streamline various aspects of the editing process. Here's a brief overview of each tool and its specific function:

1. Selection Tool (V)

- The primary tool for selecting, moving, and resizing clips in the Timeline.

2. Track Select Tool (A)

- Allows you to select all clips to the right (or left) of a specific point in the Timeline, useful for moving multiple clips at once.

3. Ripple Edit Tool (B)

- Enables you to trim clips while automatically closing the gap left behind, maintaining the overall sequence length.

4. Rolling Edit Tool (N)

- Adjusts the In and Out points of two adjacent clips simultaneously without changing the overall length of the sequence.

5. Rate Stretch Tool (R)

- Changes the speed of a clip while adjusting its duration accordingly, allowing for slow-motion or fast-motion effects.

6. Razor Tool (C)

- Splits a clip into two at the playhead position, enabling you to isolate sections of a clip for editing.

7. Slip Tool (Y)

- Changes the In and Out points of a clip without altering its position in the Timeline, perfect for fine-tuning clips.

8. Slide Tool (U)

- Moves a clip while adjusting the neighboring clips to maintain continuity, useful for repositioning without leaving gaps.

9. Pen Tool (P)

- Allows you to create and edit keyframes on the timeline for precise control over effects and transitions.

10. Text Tool (T)

- Used to create text and titles within the program, offering various formatting options for visual storytelling.

11. Hand Tool (H)

- Enables you to navigate around the Timeline without adjusting clips, useful for zoomed-in editing.

Conclusion

These tools collectively enhance your editing efficiency and precision, making it easier to create professional-quality video projects in Adobe Premiere Pro. Familiarizing yourself with each tool will significantly improve your workflow.

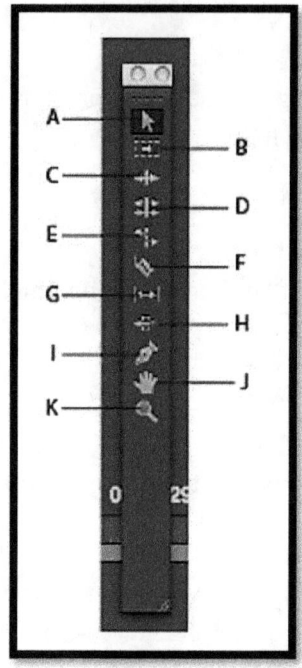

Here's a concise overview of the eleven essential tools in Adobe Premiere Pro, highlighting their functions:

A. Selection Tool

- **Function:** Allows you to select and interact with clips, buttons, and menu items. It's the primary tool for most editing tasks and is recommended as the default option.

B. Track Selection Tool

- **Function:** Selects a clip and all clips to the right in the same track. Holding Shift allows you to select consecutive clips across all tracks.

C. Ripple Edit Tool

- **Function:** Trims the In or Out point of a clip while automatically closing gaps created by the edit, preserving the sequence's continuity.

D. Rolling Edit Tool

- **Function:** Adjusts the In and Out points of adjacent clips simultaneously without changing the total length of the sequence.

E. Rate Stretch Tool

- **Function:** Modifies the length of a clip while keeping its In and Out points the same, changing the playback speed without altering the clip's position.

F. Razor Tool

- **Function:** Splits clips at a specific point in the Timeline. Holding Shift allows for splitting all clips across tracks at that moment.

G. Slip Tool

- **Function:** Changes the In and Out points of a clip simultaneously while maintaining its overall length.

H. Slide Tool

- **Function:** Moves a clip left or right in the Timeline while adjusting neighboring clips to keep the total length intact.

I. Pen Tool

- **Function:** Used for setting or selecting keyframes for clip attributes in the Effect Controls panel, allowing for detailed animations.

J. Hand Tool

- **Function:** Moves the viewing area of the Timeline left or right, providing an alternative to the scroll bar for easier navigation.

K. Zoom Tool

- **Function:** Enables zooming in or out of the Timeline, allowing for greater control over the level of detail shown during editing.

These tools collectively enhance your editing efficiency and precision in Adobe Premiere Pro, making it easier to craft professional-quality videos. Familiarizing yourself with each tool will significantly improve your workflow.

Create a sequence of clips

To get started with your editing in Adobe Premiere Pro, follow these steps to set up your workspace and create a sequence:

1. **Access the Editing Workspace**:
   o Select **Editing** at the top of the screen or go to **Window > Workspaces > Editing**. This will optimize your layout for video editing.
2. **Open the Project Panel**:
   o If you can't find the Project panel, navigate to **Window > Project**. This panel displays all the footage you've imported.
3. **View Thumbnails**:
   o To see your files as thumbnails, click the thumbnail view icon at the bottom of the Project panel.
4. **Create a Sequence**:
   o Choose the first video clip you want to add to your sequence and drag it from the Project panel to the Timeline panel. If the Timeline panel isn't visible, select **Window > Timeline**.
5. **Add Additional Clips**:
   o Continue adding clips to the sequence by dragging them from the Project panel and placing them next to existing clips in the Timeline.
6. **Zooming in and Out**:
   o If your timeline is too long, press the minus (−) key repeatedly to zoom out and see more of your timeline. To zoom in on the area around the playhead, press the plus (+) key multiple times.

Following these steps will help you efficiently organize your clips and begin editing your project in Premiere Pro!

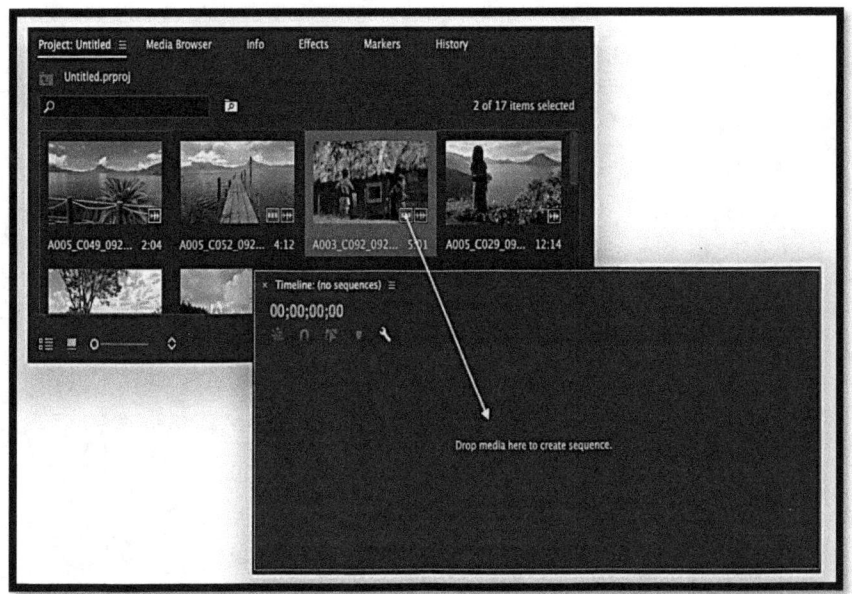

Adjust the clip length

To preview your video in Adobe Premiere Pro, follow these steps:

1. **Playback in the Program Monitor**:
   - Press the **spacebar** to start playback. If the Program Monitor isn't visible, go to **Window > Program Monitor** to open it.
2. **Stopping Playback**:
   - Press the **spacebar** again to stop playback.
3. **Adjusting the Playhead**:
   - Move the blue playhead to the desired starting point for playback.
4. **Adjusting Clip Size**:
   - If a clip appears too large or small in the Program Monitor, right-click (Windows) or Control-click (macOS) the clip in the Timeline panel and select **Set to Frame Size** to fit it properly in the viewing area.
5. **Trimming Clips**:
   - To shorten a clip and display only the desired portion, drag the edge of the clip to adjust its length.
6. **Checking for Gaps**:
   - After adjusting clips, ensure there are no gaps in your sequence. If you find one, click on the gap to highlight it, then press the **Delete** key to close it.

These steps will help you refine your video editing process and ensure a smooth playback experience!

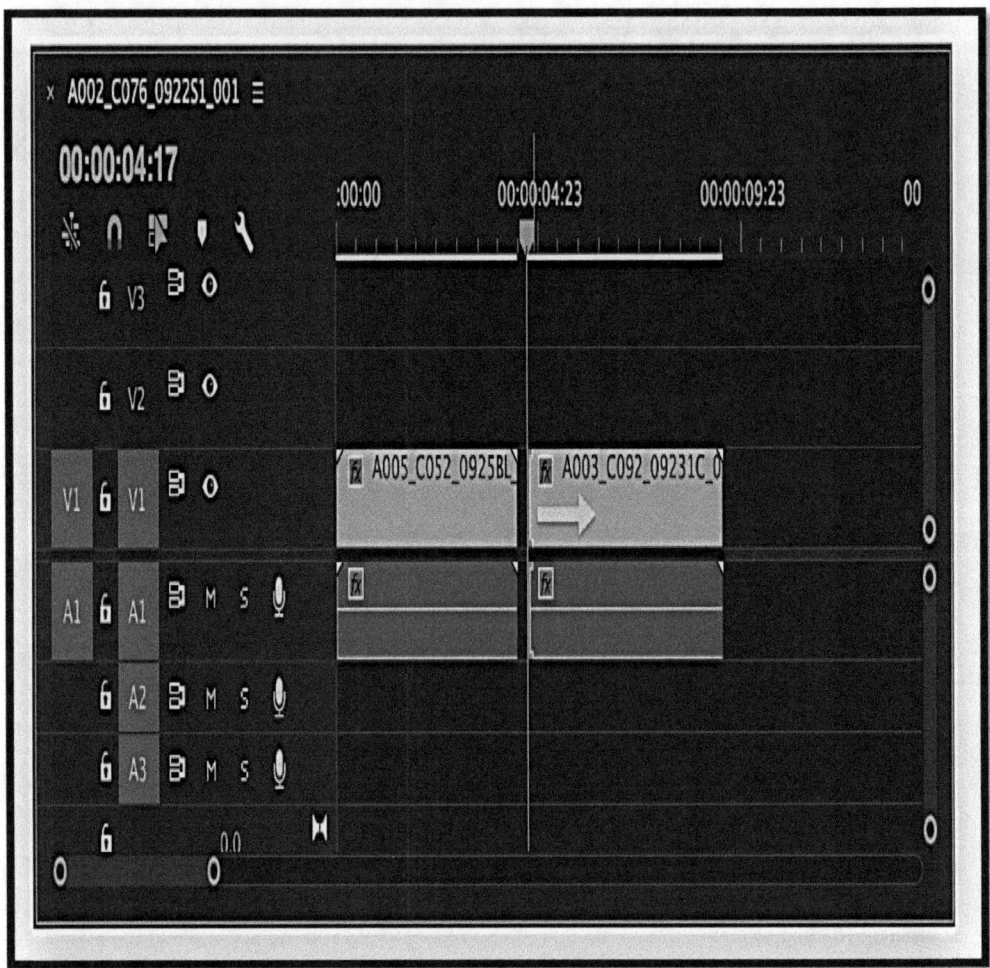

Add transitions between clips

To create transitions between your clips in Adobe Premiere Pro, follow these steps:

1. **Open the Effects Panel**:
   - Go to **Window > Effects** to open the Effects panel.
2. **Locate Video Transitions**:
   - In the Effects panel, navigate to the **Video Transitions** folder and open it. Then, find the **Dissolve** folder.
3. **Apply a Transition**:
   - Drag the **Cross Dissolve** effect from the Dissolve folder and drop it between the two clips in your Timeline where you want to create the transition.
4. **Preview the Transition**:

- Play your sequence by pressing the **spacebar** to see how the Cross Dissolve effect looks in action.
5. **Experiment with Other Effects**:
    - Feel free to try other dissolve effects, such as transitions from black to white or vice versa, by dragging them between adjacent clips.

Enjoy experimenting with different transitions to enhance the flow of your video!

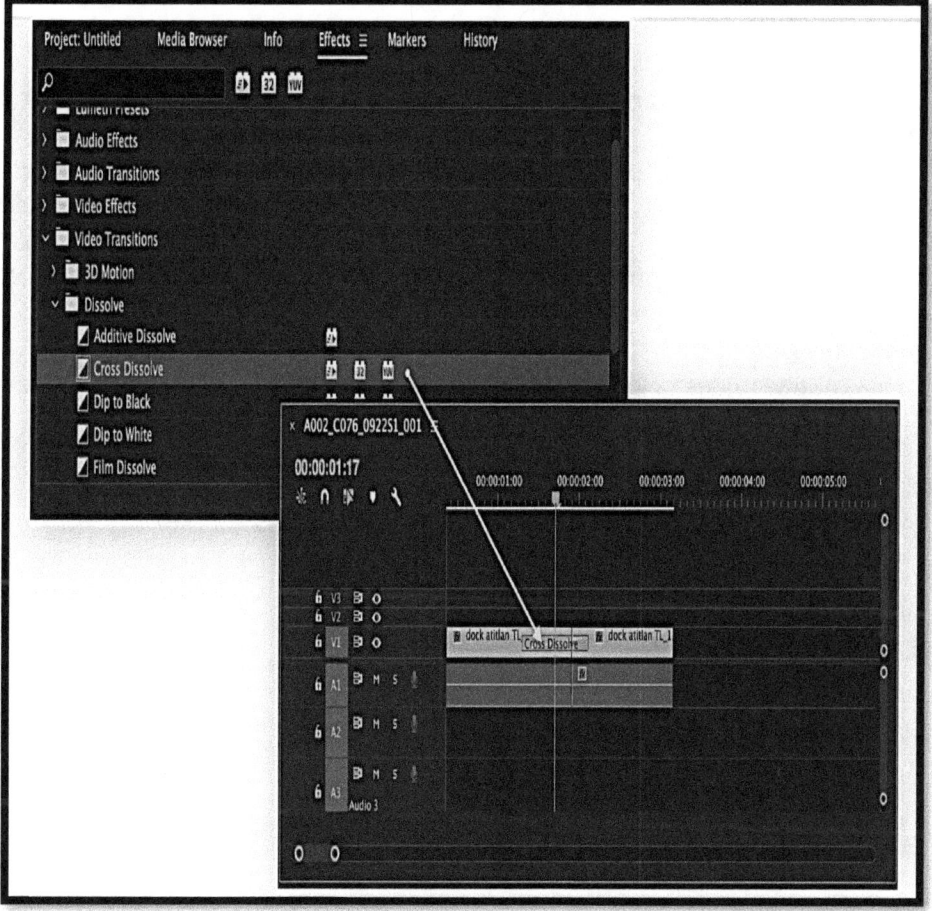

CHAPTER 3
IMPORTING MEDIA

When you import media into Adobe Premiere Pro, you're not creating copies of the files; instead, you're establishing a reference to the original media. This allows Premiere Pro to access and manipulate the media without altering the source files. Here are the four primary methods for importing assets into your project:

1. **Standard Importing:**
   o Go to **File > Import** and navigate to the files you wish to include in your project.
2. **Media Browser Panel:**
   o Use the Media Browser panel to browse local storage, external drives, or networked drives, allowing you to import media directly into your project.
3. **Adobe Prelude:**
   o You can use Adobe Prelude to add and organize video files, which can then be easily brought into Premiere Pro.
4. **Adobe Bridge:**
   o Adobe Bridge helps you manage media, letting you browse, organize, and select files to import into Premiere Pro.

No matter which method you choose, Premiere Pro will create a link to the original media files, whether they're videos, photos, or audio files, allowing for flexible editing without duplicating the source.

Standard Importing

One of the easiest ways to add media to your projects in Adobe Premiere Pro is through standard importing via the File menu. Here's how to do it:

Standard Import Method

1. **Go to the Menu:** In Premiere Pro, select **File > Import**.
2. **Select Files:** Navigate to the files you want to add and click on them to select.

For quicker access:

- On **macOS**, use **Command + I**.
- On **Windows**, use **Ctrl + I**.

This method is ideal for standalone items like music files, graphics, and common video formats like MP4 or MOV. It's especially efficient if you know the exact location of your files.

Note on RAW Media and Complex Structures

For media types that involve more complex folder structures, such as RAW footage or camera files, standard importing may not work effectively. These files often come with associated audio, video, and metadata organized in specific ways.

In such cases, the **Media Browser panel** is the best tool. It simplifies the process of importing and managing footage from cameras with intricate folder systems, ensuring all essential components are handled correctly in Premiere Pro. This panel helps maintain the integrity of your media and its associated data during the import process.

The Media Browser window

The **Media Browser** in Adobe Premiere Pro is a powerful and flexible tool for importing media, often preferred over traditional file import methods. Here are some key reasons why it's highly regarded:

1. Versatility and Information Display

- The Media Browser presents files in a list format, allowing you to view various details about each file, such as metadata, format, and duration. This feature makes it easier to navigate and select from large collections of assets, enhancing your workflow.

2. Accessible Location

- By default, the Media Browser panel is located in the bottom left corner of the Editing workspace. You can quickly access it by pressing **Shift + 8**.
- The workspace is customizable, allowing you to reposition the Media Browser to suit your preferences. You can also access it via the two-sided arrow icon in the panel area.

Overall, the Media Browser streamlines the process of finding and importing media, making it an essential tool for efficient editing in Premiere Pro.

3. Automated Media Examination

- The Media Browser automatically analyzes media assets, simplifying the import process. For instance, if your camera records video in multiple fragmented files, the Media Browser intelligently consolidates these into single clips. This means you can work with complete video and audio components, regardless of the original file organization.

4. Easier Navigation

- The Media Browser enhances your ability to locate specific clips by providing visual previews alongside essential metadata. You can easily access information such as clip length, recording date, and file type, which significantly streamlines the search process in large collections of media assets.

Conclusion

Overall, the Media Browser in Adobe Premiere Pro offers a user-friendly interface that makes it easier to import and manage media files. Its capability to display detailed information and handle complex camera folder structures accelerates your workflow, allowing for a more efficient editing experience.

Ingest Options and Proxy Media
Ingest Settings in Premiere Pro

To optimize your workflow when importing media and creating proxy files, you can configure the settings in the Ingest Settings tab within the Project Settings dialog box. Here's how to do it:

1. **Open Project Settings:**
   - o Go to **File > Project Settings > Ingest**.
2. **Enable Ingest:**
   - o Check the **Ingest** box to enable the feature.
3. **Choose an Ingest Method:**
   - o Select one of the following options:
     - **Copy:** Copies the original media files to the specified location.
     - **Transcode:** Converts the original files to a different format or codec while copying.
     - **Create Proxies:** Generates low-resolution proxy files for easier editing.
     - **Copy and Create Proxies:** Combines the first two options, copying the original files and creating proxies simultaneously.
4. **Set Proxy Presets:**
   - o If you choose to create proxies, you can select a preset that suits your needs (e.g., low-resolution formats). Premiere Pro provides several built-in options, or you can create a custom preset.
5. **Destination:**
   - o Specify where the copied files and proxies will be saved. You can choose to store them in the same location as the original files or select a different directory.

Benefits of Using Proxy Files

- **Improved Performance:** Working with lower-resolution proxies helps reduce strain on your system, enabling smoother playback and faster editing.
- **Flexibility:** Easily switch between proxy and original files as needed. This allows you to edit quickly and preview effects in high quality without hassle.
- **Collaboration:** In collaborative environments, proxies can be shared easily without requiring heavy bandwidth for large files.

Conclusion

Setting up ingest and proxy options in Premiere Pro can greatly enhance your editing workflow, especially when handling high-resolution or RAW footage. By configuring these settings in the Project Settings dialog box, you can ensure a smoother and more efficient editing experience.

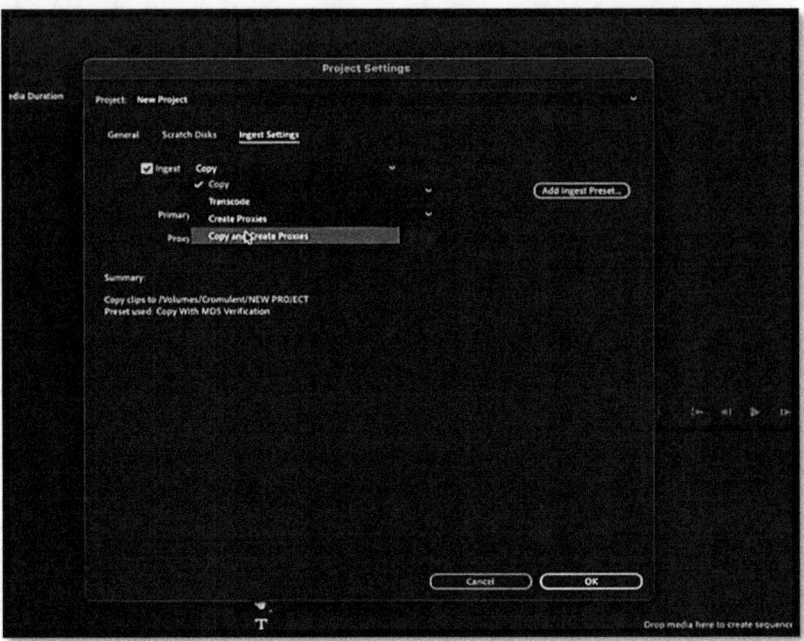

Ingest Settings Options in Premiere Pro

When configuring your ingest settings in Adobe Premiere Pro, you have several options to choose from, each designed to streamline your workflow based on your project needs. Here's a closer look at the options available:

1. **Copy:**
   - **Function:** Copies the original media files to a specified location.
   - **Best Use:** Ideal for importing media directly from a camera's storage. This ensures Premiere Pro has access to the files even if the original storage devices aren't connected.
2. **Transcode:**
   - **Function:** Converts the imported media files to a different format or codec upon import.
   - **Best Use:** Useful in post-production environments that require a standard mezzanine file format for all projects. This ensures compatibility and uniformity in your workflow.
3. **Create Proxies:**
   - **Function:** Generates lower-quality proxy copies of your media files.
   - **Best Use:** Helps improve playback performance on less powerful systems or when dealing with high-resolution footage. Proxies are not suitable for final outputs but facilitate faster editing and collaboration.
4. **Copy and Create Proxies:**

- o **Function:** Copies the original files to a specified location and simultaneously creates proxy versions saved in a different location.
- o **Best Use:** This option combines the benefits of having original media available while working with proxies, offering a flexible editing experience.

Switching Between Original and Proxy Media

To toggle between original and proxy media in your project:

- **Enable Proxy Toggle:**
  - o Go to **Edit > Preferences > Media** (Windows) or **Premiere Pro > Preferences > Media** (macOS) to access the proxy settings.
- **Toggle Visibility:**
  - o Use the **Toggle Proxies** button in the Program Monitor or in the Toolbar. This allows you to switch seamlessly between the high-resolution originals and the low-resolution proxies during your editing process.

Conclusion

By understanding and utilizing these ingest settings effectively, you can enhance your editing efficiency in Premiere Pro. Whether you need to copy, transcode, create proxies, or a combination of these options, configuring the right settings from the outset will ensure a smoother post-production experience.

Importing Still Images File

When adding still photos to Adobe Premiere Pro, it's important to adjust certain settings to ensure they display correctly. Here's a step-by-step guide:

Preparing to Add Still Photos

1. **Check Image Requirements:**
   - o Ensure your photos meet the recommended specifications (e.g., resolution, format).
2. **Access Preferences:**
   - o Go to **Edit** (Windows) or **Premiere Pro** (macOS) in the menu bar.
   - o Select **Preferences** and then click on **Timeline**.
3. **Adjust Timeline Settings:**
   - o In the Timeline preferences, you may want to adjust settings such as:

- **Still Image Default Duration:** Set the default length for how long still images will display in your timeline. The default is usually 5 seconds, but you can change this to suit your project.
- **Video Thumbnails:** Ensure this is enabled to see thumbnails for your still images in the timeline.

Importing Still Photos

4. **Import the Photos:**
   - Use **File > Import** or drag and drop your images into the Project panel.
5. **Add to Timeline:**
   - Drag the imported photos from the Project panel to the Timeline panel where you want them to appear in your sequence.
6. **Adjust Duration (if needed):**
   - If you need to change the duration of a still image, click on the edge of the image in the timeline and drag it to your desired length.

Final Touches

7. **Scale and Position:**
   - Select the photo in the timeline, then use the **Effect Controls** panel to adjust its scale and position if necessary.
8. **Apply Transitions or Effects:**
   - Consider adding transitions or effects to enhance the presentation of your still images.

By following these steps, you can effectively integrate still photos into your video projects in Premiere Pro, ensuring they are displayed as intended.

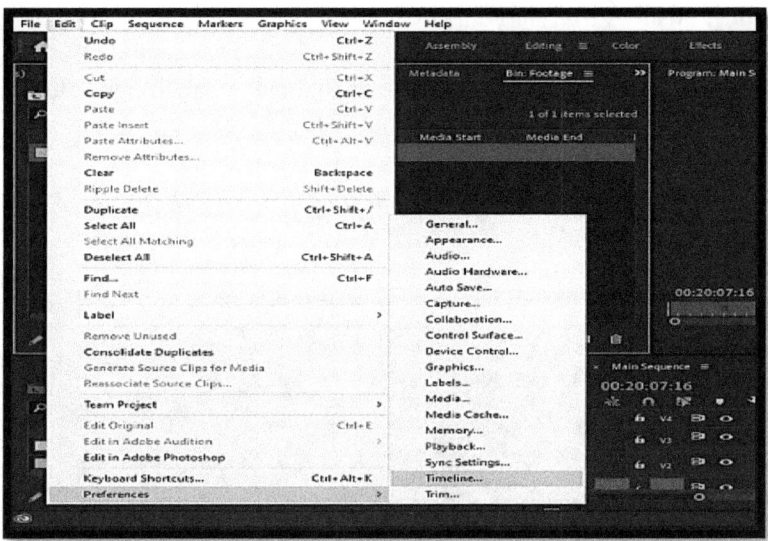

Adjusting the **Still Image Default Duration** in Premiere Pro is a great way to streamline your workflow, especially when working with multiple still images or picture sequences. Here's how to set it up:

Setting the Still Image Default Duration

1. **Open Preferences:**
   o Navigate to **Edit** (Windows) or **Premiere Pro** (macOS) in the menu bar.
   o Select **Preferences** and then go to the **Timeline** section.
2. **Adjust Duration:**
   o Locate the **Still Image Default Duration** setting.
   o Enter your desired duration (measured in frames or seconds) for how long each still image will appear in the timeline.
3. **Import Your Images:**
   o After setting the default duration, import your still images as usual via **File > Import** or by dragging them into the Project panel.
4. **Adding to Timeline:**
   o When you drag your images into the timeline, they will automatically use the new default duration you've set, saving you the need to adjust each one individually.

Benefits of Changing Default Duration

- **Efficiency:** This setting is particularly useful when importing a sequence of images, allowing them to automatically appear for the same duration without manual adjustments.

- **Consistency:** Ensures that all your images have a uniform duration, making the editing process smoother and more cohesive.
- **Time-Saving:** Reduces the repetitive task of changing each image's duration individually, letting you focus on the creative aspects of your project.

By configuring this option, you can enhance your editing efficiency and maintain better control over the timing of your still images in your projects.

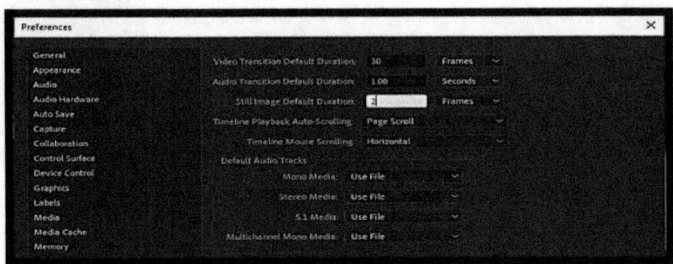

To import still images into Premiere Pro while ensuring they have alpha transparency and are compatible with video color spaces, follow these steps:

Preparing Your Images

1. **Ensure Alpha Transparency:**
   o Use formats that support alpha channels, such as PNG or PSD. Remember that JPEGs do not support alpha transparency.
2. **Check Color Space:**
   o Make sure your images are in a compatible color space, like sRGB or NTSC RGB, to ensure they display correctly in your video project.

Importing Still Images

1. **Open Premiere Pro:**
   o Start your project and navigate to the appropriate bin where you want to import your images.
2. **Importing Method:**
   o Right-click in the bin and select **Import** from the context menu, or use the shortcut **Ctrl + I** (Windows) or **Command + I** (macOS).
3. **Select Your Image:**
   o In the Import window, navigate to the location of your still image, select it, and click **Open**. The image will now appear in your selected bin.

Adding to the Timeline

1. **Drag to Timeline:**
   - Click and drag the imported still image from the bin onto the timeline where you want it to appear.
2. **Adjusting the Image:**
   - Select the image in the timeline and open the **Effect Controls** panel. Here, you can adjust:
     - **Position:** Move the image within the frame.
     - **Scale:** Resize the image to fit your needs.
     - **Opacity:** Change the transparency to blend it with other clips or backgrounds.
3. **Applying Effects:**
   - Just like any other clip, you can apply various effects to your still image from the **Effects** panel to enhance your project.

Final Tips

- **Animate Movement:** You can keyframe position and scale for dynamic movement or transitions.
- **Layering:** Use multiple still images on different tracks to create complex compositions.

By following these steps, you can effectively use still images in your Premiere Pro projects while taking full advantage of their properties and effects.

CHAPTER 4

WORKING WITH AUDIO

Importing and Adjusting Audio
Accessing and Using the Premiere Pro Import Window

Here's a concise guide on how to import files into Adobe Premiere Pro using various methods:

Importing Media into Premiere Pro

1. **Double-Click in the Project Panel:**
   - Quickly open the Import window by double-clicking in an empty space within the Project Panel. This lets you select video files or images to import.
2. **Double-Click in an Open Bin Panel:**
   - If you have a specific Bin panel open, you can double-click in an empty area of that panel to access the Import window.
3. **File Menu Option:**
   - Navigate to the **File** menu at the top of the screen and select **Import**. This will open the Import window for you to choose your files.
4. **Keyboard Shortcut:**
   - Use keyboard shortcuts for efficiency:
     - **Command + I** on Mac
     - **Control + I** on PC
   - This instantly brings up the Import window, speeding up your workflow.

Summary

Using these methods, you can easily import media files into your Premiere Pro project, streamlining your editing process. Choose the method that best fits your workflow!

To add sound files to your Premiere Pro project, follow these steps:

Importing Sound Files into Premiere Pro

1. **Open the Import Window:**
   o Use one of the methods mentioned earlier to access the Import window (double-click in the Project Panel, use the File menu, or the keyboard shortcut).
2. **Select Your Sound File(s):**
   o In the Import window, navigate to the sound file(s) you wish to add.
   o For multiple selections, hold down **Command** (Mac) or **Control** (Windows) while clicking on the files. Alternatively, use **Shift** + click to select a range of files.
3. **Click Import:**
   o After selecting your desired files, click the **Import** button.
4. **Wait for Confirmation:**
   o A brief loading box may appear while your files are being imported. Once it disappears, your sound files will be available in the Project panel.
5. **Add to Timeline:**
   o You can now drag the imported sound file(s) from the Project panel onto your timeline to start using them in your project.

Summary

Using the Import window streamlines the process, ensuring you can easily manage and select multiple sound files for your project. Happy editing!

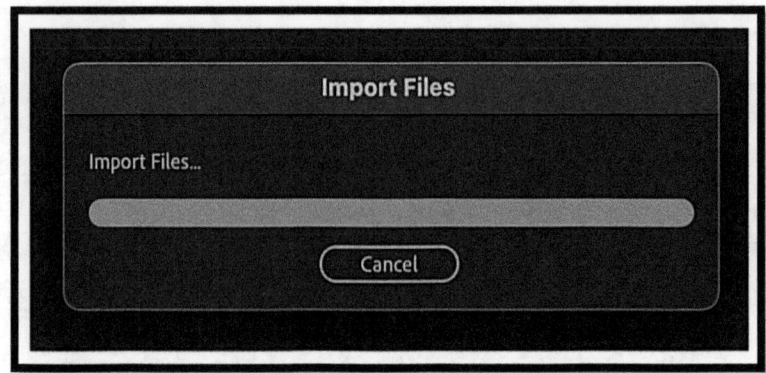

After the Audio is imported in Premiere Pro

Place the music file you just imported into the appropriate bin. Start by double-clicking the file to open it in the Source monitor, where you can set the In and Out Points. After that, drag the file into your timeline to incorporate it into your sequence. Generally, you'll be working with MP3 (.mp3) and WAV (.wav) audio formats, both of which can be added to Premiere Pro without any issues.

Basic Audio Editing
Set Up the Workspace

When working with audio in Premiere Pro, it's beneficial to switch between different workspaces. Premiere offers several built-in workspaces that provide easy access to the tools you need. To access the audio tools, click on the Audio workspace at the top of Premiere Pro. This will give you an overview of your current setup, featuring key screens that are unique to the Audio workspace. The Essential Sound panel will appear on the right, while the Audio Track Mixer is located in the center of the window. These two screens are primarily what you'll use when handling audio in Premiere Pro.

You'll also notice familiar panels from other Premiere workspaces. The timeline panel at the bottom of the application remains the same as the one you used before switching to the Audio workspace. It visually displays how your video and audio clips are arranged in your project.

Adding audio files

The Media Browser is located on the left side of the app. Click on it to add audio to your project. You can use it to locate additional audio clips and easily incorporate them. Just find the files and drag and drop them onto your workspace. If you've already arranged clips in the timeline, you can click and drag the audio clips to align them with your video. Before proceeding, it's a good idea to enlarge the audio track for more detailed editing. You can do this by pulling down the handle beneath the track, which will help you see the audio waveform more clearly.

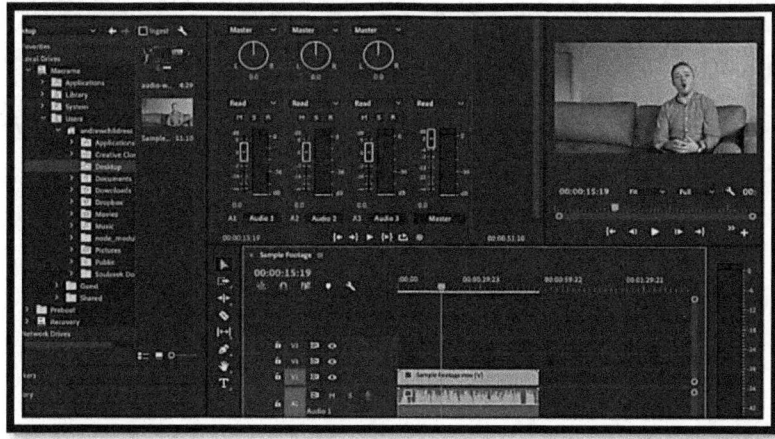

Now that you're familiar with your current layout, let's explore the key panels in this view and how you can use them to adjust the audio. Understanding these panels will enhance your ability to fine-tune your sound effectively.

Changing the Audio Levels

One of the most common tasks when working with audio in Premiere Pro is adjusting the volume. This is crucial for managing multiple audio tracks and ensuring they're balanced. The goal is to find the ideal level that's "loud enough" without being "too loud." Sound levels are measured in decibels, and the numbers to the left of the audio meters indicate these levels.

For your audio clips, aim for the volume to reflect their importance. The main dialogue track should be the loudest and most prominent, while background music and sound effects should be lower so they don't overpower other elements. To adjust the audio levels for a specific track, locate it in the Audio Mixer panel and move the slider up or down. During playback, ensure that the colored lines don't turn red, as this indicates the levels are too high.

You can also adjust audio levels over time using keyframes. To do this, hold down Ctrl (or Cmd on Mac) and click on the waveform in the timeline. This will enable you to set keyframes for volume changes. Simply grab the line running across the track and pull it down to decrease the volume or adjust it as needed.

Next, hold down Ctrl (or Cmd on Mac) and click on another point on the waveform. This will create two keyframes that control the audio levels. You can then adjust these points independently to create changes in volume over time. Just as you can animate visual effects, you can also make the audio gradually rise or fall throughout the clip.

Panning Audio

Next time you're in a movie theater, pay attention to how sounds come from different speakers. Professional audio engineers carefully position sound in specific areas of the soundstage to create a realistic experience. While viewers might be listening on AirPods while watching a video, achieving a balanced sound is still possible. Adjusting the audio tracks in Premiere Pro can help with this, especially when you have multiple tracks.

You can use different methods to manage audio in Premiere. The Mixer panel at the top allows you to adjust a track's overall output. Simply move the slider left or right to modify the audio levels for the entire track.

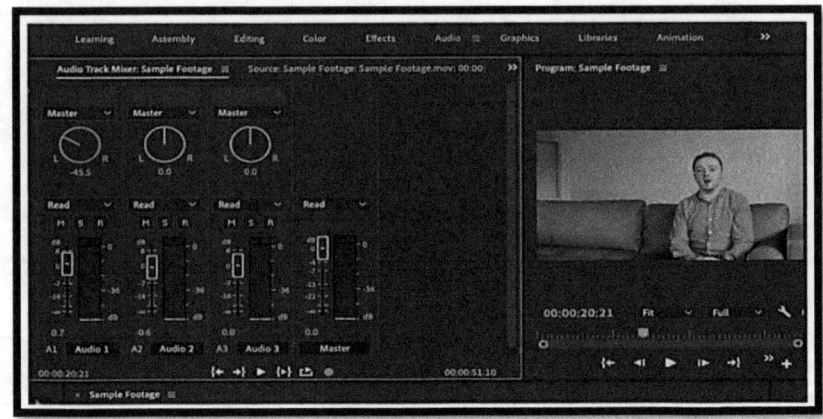

Another way to adjust the audio mix throughout a movie is by using keyframes, just like we did for adjusting volume. Start by clicking on the keyframe button, then select "Track Panner," and choose "Balance." Now you can use keyframes on your clip to control and modify the audio balance over time. If you move the balance back and forth, you'll create an oscillating effect.

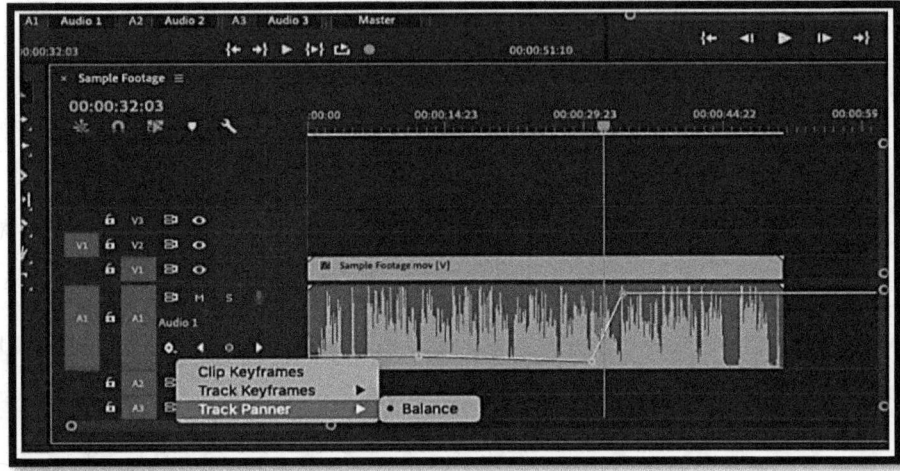

Editing Audio

Working with audio in the timeline is quite similar to working with video. You can adjust where the audio starts and stops by dragging the handles on either end. Additionally, you can easily rearrange clips by dragging and dropping them into position, and use the knife tool to split clips, just like you would with video clips.

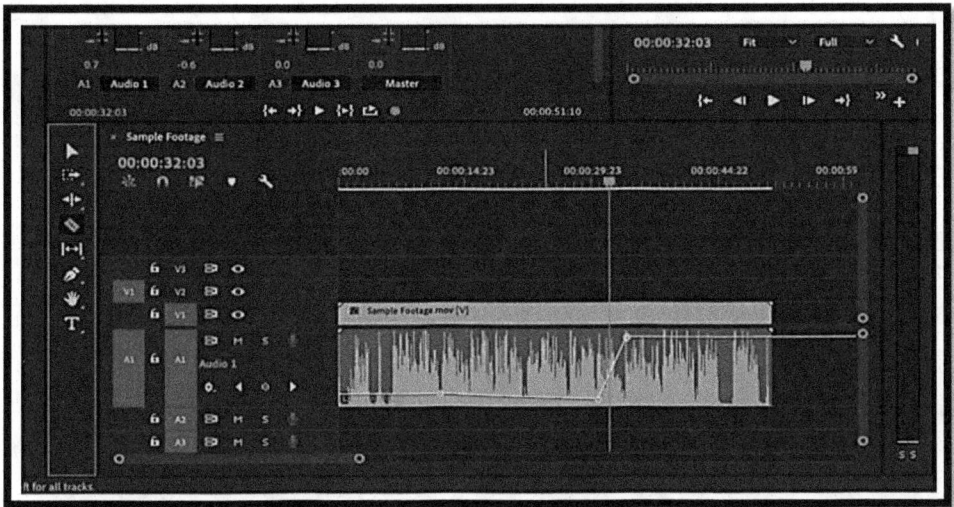

Keep an eye on the waveform while working with audio; it becomes easier to see when you enlarge each track. This will help you identify the best spots for cuts. As you get more familiar with Premiere Pro's audio features, you'll notice that the sound you add to your video clips syncs with their corresponding visuals. If you need to separate audio from a clip, right-click on it and select "Unlink."

In summary, Premiere's audio settings are primarily drag-and-drop. You can find clips in the Media Browser on the left and drag them onto the timeline. You can also rearrange clips by dragging them around. Remember that each project can contain multiple audio tracks, allowing you to stack clips and play several at once. Balancing audio levels will enhance the realism of your sound experience.

Additionally, consider experimenting with audio effects to modify your sound. Open the Audio Effects panel on the left side of the Audio workspace, select an effect you want to use, and then drag it onto the audio clip in your timeline.

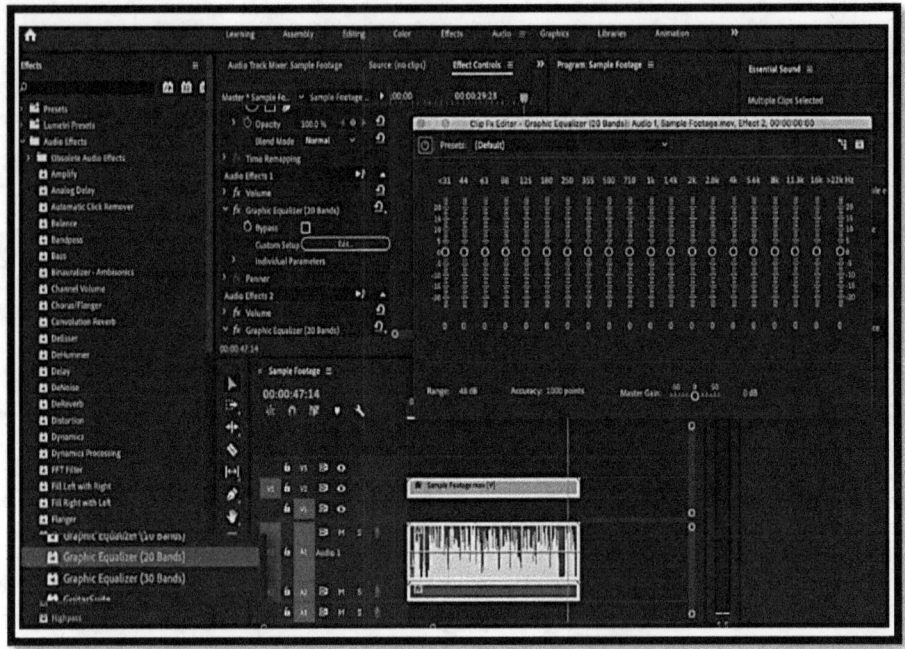

With the movie selected, the Effects Control panel will display more options. For instance, you'll find a section for the Graphic Equalizer (20 Bands). By clicking on "Edit" for this effect, a new adjustment box will appear, allowing you to modify the audio output. Each effect will impact the audio differently, enhancing your existing clip without needing any additional applications.

Using Adobe Stock

Adobe Stock is a versatile service that provides creatives with access to a vast library of millions of high-quality, royalty-free assets, including music, videos, and Motion Graphics themes. Customers can subscribe to various plans for access to multiple assets.

Here's a guide on how to add Adobe Stock audio to your Premiere Pro projects:

1. Accessing Adobe Stock Audio in Premiere Pro:

- Start by selecting the "Audio" workspace in Premiere Pro. Then, go to the "Essential Sound" section and click on "Browse."

2. Browsing and Selecting Tracks:

- Explore tracks by mood or genre. Each genre includes several sub-genres for more specific choices, which you can navigate using the ">" arrow.

3. Searching for Specific Tracks:

- If you have a specific track in mind, enter its name in the Search box at the top of the Essential Sound panel to find relevant results.

4. Fine-Tuning Search Results:

- After making an initial selection, refine your search with filters based on:
  - **Tempo:** Set the pace from 30 to 250 beats per minute.
  - **Duration:** Specify minimum and maximum lengths for tracks, from 0:00 to 5:00.
  - **Vocals:** Choose from music with vocals, instrumental tracks, or a combination of both.
  - **Audio Partners:** Select tracks from a list of available audio partners.

Using these search and filtering options within Adobe Stock's audio library, integrated into the Essential Sound panel, allows you to effectively explore and choose the best music tracks to fit your project's requirements, mood, tempo, duration, and vocal preferences.

Recording a Voice-Over

You can easily create a voice-over while your sequence plays in Premiere Pro. Follow these steps to get started:

1. Ensure Your Microphone Is Set Up Correctly:

- Check that your microphone is properly configured and set as the default input in Premiere Pro's audio hardware settings. On a Windows computer, go to **Edit > Preferences > Audio Hardware > Default Input**. For Mac, navigate to the Premiere Pro menu, select **Preferences**, then **Audio Hardware**, and finally **Default Input**.

2. Prepare for Recording:

- Wear headphones or pause the playing audio before you begin recording. This helps prevent any microphone noise from interfering with the quality of your voice-over.

3. Start Recording Your Voice-Over:

- When you're ready, locate the **Record Voice-Over** button in Premiere Pro and click it. Recording will start from the position of the Timeline playhead.

4. Stop the Recording:

- Once you've finished your voice-over, press the **Stop** button. The newly recorded audio clip will appear in both the sequence area and the Project panel. By default, this audio file will be saved in the same location as your project file, making it easy to find within your project structure.

Change the volume over time

You can dynamically adjust the volume or loudness of audio across your timeline using keyframes, allowing for a more intricate and detailed sound mix. Here's how to effectively use keyframes in Adobe Premiere Pro:

1. Display Audio Keyframes:

- Ensure the **Show Audio Keyframes** option is enabled in the Timeline panel's Settings menu. You can better see keyframes on audio clips by increasing the height of the audio track.

2. Choose the Pen Tool:

- Select the **Pen Tool** from the toolbox. This tool will allow you to create keyframes on the audio clips.

3. Making Keyframes:

- To create a keyframe, click on the thin white line that runs through the audio clip. These keyframes act as markers for settings such as volume levels.

4. Adjusting Volume Levels:

- Drag the newly created keyframe up or down to raise or lower the audio volume at that specific moment. This adjustment lets you modify the audio in real-time.

5. Timing and Placement:

- Move the keyframe left or right along the timeline to adjust when the volume change occurs. This allows you to precisely set when the audio adjustments take effect in your clip.

6. Keyframe Management:

- To delete a keyframe, select it and press the **Backspace** key (Windows) or the **Delete** key (Mac). You can also use the Pen Tool to select multiple keyframes at once, allowing you to move or delete them efficiently.

7. Application to Clips and Tracks:

- Remember that keyframes primarily affect individual clips, but you can also apply them to tracks for broader audio adjustments.

8. Switching Tools:

- Once you're done working with keyframes, switch back to the **Selection Tool** in the toolbox. This tool allows for standard edits without modifying keyframes.

Make the sound better.
Getting Started with the Audio Workspace

- **Access the Audio Workspace:** Navigate to **Window > Workspaces > Audio** to enter the Audio Workspace. Here, you'll find the Essential Sound panel, a powerful tool for enhancing audio quality.

Selecting a Clip to Edit

- **Choose Your Clip:** In the Timeline panel, select the audio clip you want to modify using the Essential Sound panel. This step is crucial, as it determines which audio will be edited.

Identifying the Audio Type in Essential Sound

- **Find the Audio Type:** In the Essential Sound panel, identify the type of audio you're working with. For example, select the appropriate audio group for dialogue or conversations.

Utilizing Essential Sound Settings

- **Enhance Audio Quality:** Activate the settings in the Essential Sound panel to quickly improve sound quality. For instance, enabling the **Loudness** feature will automatically adjust the volume levels to industry standards. You can use EQ to boost certain frequencies, making speech clearer, and the **Enhance Speech** option offers subtle adjustments to improve clarity.

Exploring Additional Options

- **Discover More Features:** The Essential Sound panel offers various adjustments tailored for different audio types. Experiment with these options while listening to the live changes, making it easier to fine-tune your audio.

Finalizing Audio Adjustments

- **Continue Editing:** Once you've used the Essential Sound panel to enhance your audio, switch back to the Editing workspace to continue working on your project. This transition allows you to refine both your edits and audio seamlessly.

How to Use the Essential Sound Panel

Every designer can benefit from the Essential Sound panel, which consolidates some of the most useful audio tools in one location. After selecting a track, you'll find four preset options on the right side of the Audio workspace: Conversation, Music, Sound Effects, and Background. These presets are a great starting point for adjusting audio that fits each category.

When you select a preset, such as Conversation, Premiere Pro will display the tools that are most suitable for that audio type. To optimize your audio, you can enable options like Loudness, Repair, and Clarity to enhance the overall sound quality.

Sometimes, the goal isn't just to fix and balance your audio; you may want to style it and add effects instead. In such cases, utilizing settings from the options list can be very helpful. For example, to create the effect of audio being distant from the action, you can use the **Make Distant** setting. This approach allows you to experiment creatively with audio in your next project, adding depth and interest to your sound design.

In the Essential Sound panel, take advantage of all the available effects to make your audio productions more engaging. For a nostalgic vibe, try the **From the Radio** effect, or use **Over the Intercom** for that classic "principal voice" sound in your next video. These effects can add unique character and enhance the overall experience of your project.

Audio Track vs. Audio Clip Mixer

In Premiere Pro, there are two primary ways to edit audio: the Audio Track Mixer and the Audio Clip Mixer.

The **Audio Track Mixer** is designed to manage entire tracks, allowing you to adjust settings that impact all audio clips within that track. This is useful for applying uniform changes across multiple clips.

In contrast, the **Audio Clip Mixer** lets you modify individual clips currently under the playhead. This allows for more precise adjustments on a clip-by-clip basis, giving you greater control over specific audio elements in your project.

How to Use the Audio Clip Mixer

Let's take a closer look at the Audio Clip Mixer. You can access it in the Workspace by clicking on the **Audio** tab in the top menu bar, or by navigating to **Window > Audio Clip Mixer**.

The Audio Clip Mixer displays the same number of audio channels as the audio tracks in your timeline. As you add more audio tracks, the number of channels in the clip mixer will increase accordingly.

It's important to note that the Audio Clip Mixer affects the audio clips within those tracks, not the tracks themselves. The mixer indicates which clip you're working with based on the position of the playhead. As the playhead moves over a track, you'll see the effects applied to each audio clip within the corresponding channel. Thus, the functionality of the Audio Clip Mixer is entirely dependent on the playhead's position, allowing you to make precise adjustments to the specific clips you're dealing with.

Improve Your Audio with the Audio Clip Mixer

While your audio is playing, the audio meters will fluctuate to indicate the volume levels. If the audio is silent, the meters will remain flat. It's crucial to monitor these levels, as going into the red zone can cause clipping, resulting in lost sound quality.

You can adjust the volume of the audio clips your playhead is currently on by moving the corresponding control up or down. When you make this adjustment, the related clip on the timeline will reflect the change in level.

If you can't see the keyframe indicator, ensure your audio track is tall enough and that audio keyframes are enabled. Right-click on the clip, then select **Show Clip Keyframe > Volume > Level** to make the keyframes visible.

As you adjust the audio scale, you'll notice the blue number changes as well. You can also directly modify this value: simply click and drag the blue number to set a new level, or click it and type in a specific number.

Staying Organized

Understanding how to locate the channel that controls each clip and adjust its volume is crucial for effective audio editing. Equally important is staying organized. However, maintaining organization can be challenging, so grouping similar audio elements on the same tracks can be very helpful.

For example, if you keep all your music on a single track, you'll see all music-related channels in the audio clip mixer together. It's a good practice to label this track clearly—something like "Music" or another descriptive name. This way, as you monitor the audio changes, you'll easily remember the purpose of each channel, making your editing process smoother and more efficient.

Mute, Solo, and Keyframes

In addition to adjusting the volume, there are several other ways to control your audio clips. At the top of the Audio Clip Mixer, you'll find three important icons: **M**, **S**, and a diamond-shaped icon.

- **M (Mute):** Clicking this icon will turn it green, muting the entire track. This allows you to easily silence a track while working on others.
- **S (Solo):** When you click the **S**, it turns yellow, isolating that track so it's the only one playing. All other tracks will be muted, letting you focus on the specific audio you want to hear.
- **Diamond-Shaped Icon:** This icon enables you to create keyframes below the track's playhead, allowing for precise adjustments over time.

Using these controls can greatly enhance your audio editing experience, making it easier to manage complex projects.

Using the Write Keyframes Function

When you use the diamond-shaped icon, it doesn't create standard keyframes; instead, it generates keyframes for the clip currently under the playhead on that track. When you select the **Write Keyframes** marker, a keyframe will be added automatically whenever there's a change in the audio level. As you move the playhead forward and make additional adjustments, new keyframes will be created, allowing the clip's audio level to change over time.

If you need to remove keyframes quickly, you can use the **Pen Tool** to click on them, then press Backspace (Windows) or Delete (Mac). This process is similar when using the **Write Keyframes** feature; as you adjust the scale while the clip is playing, you'll generate multiple keyframes that alter the audio progressively.

It's important to note that changes made while the playhead is positioned over a specific clip only affect that clip, leaving previous clips unchanged. This distinction between the Audio Clip Mixer and the Audio Track Mixer is significant, as the Audio Clip Mixer treats each clip individually, allowing for detailed and unique adjustments.

Controlling the Audio Panning

You can adjust the audio panning—how much sound is outputted from the left or right channels—in the Audio Clip Mixer. This can be done in two ways: using knobs or sliders.

Knobs allow for fine-tuned adjustments to the pan position, while sliders provide a more visual way to control the audio balance between the left and right channels. Both methods enable you to create a more immersive audio experience in your project.

Using the Panel Knob

You can adjust audio panning by moving the knob at the top of the Audio Clip Mixer to the left or right. For instance, if you have a clip of ocean waves coming in from the right side of the frame, adjusting the pan will help ensure that the sound matches its visual source.

Additionally, if the **Write Keyframe** button is active for that channel, you can animate the audio's position over time, shifting it left or right dynamically.

By right-clicking on any track, you can also mark the high and low points of your audio, known as "peaks and valleys." These markers can be static or dynamic, changing every few seconds to reflect the current audio levels. They will only shift if the audio itself causes them to move.

If you enable the color gradient option, it will change how your audio levels are displayed: either as solid colors (green, yellow, or red) or as a gradual gradient that transitions through those colors, providing a visual representation of your audio levels.

Using the Sliders

You can also right-click and select **Show Channel Volume** to manage the left and right audio channels. This action will display two knobs on the audio channel, allowing you to independently adjust the volume for each channel.

Keep in mind that these adjustments can also be animated using keyframes, provided the **Write Keyframe** option is enabled. This allows you to create dynamic changes in volume over time for each channel.

Applying Audio Effects
Applying a Single Audio Effect
1. Accessing Audio Tools

To find audio effects, go to the **Effects** panel. You can either scroll through the list or use the search box to type in the name of a specific sound effect.

2. Selecting and Applying an Effect

- Once you locate the desired audio effect, click on its icon in the Effects panel.
- Drag the effect onto the audio clip in the **Timeline panel**. Alternatively, you can select the clip and double-click the sound effect in the **Effect Controls panel** to apply it.

3. Adjusting Audio Settings

After applying the effect, you can adjust and refine its settings within the **Effect Controls panel** to suit your preferences.

Applying Multiple Effects to a Single Clip
1. Selecting the Audio Clip

Start by selecting the audio clip in the **Timeline** to which you want to apply multiple effects.

2. Group Selection of Effects

In the **Effect Controls panel**, hold down the **Control** key (Windows) or **Command** key (Mac) while clicking on the desired effects to select multiple effects at once.

3. Applying the Grouped Effects

After selecting the effects, drag the entire group to the chosen audio clip in the **Timeline panel** to apply them all at once.

How to Use Auto Ducking in Premiere Pro

Audio that competes with other sounds in your footage is referred to as "audio ducking." This technique involves lowering the volume of one sound to allow another to take precedence. For example, if you want dialogue to be clear over background music, you'd reduce the music volume during conversations and then increase it again afterward.

While this is typically done by manually adding keyframes, which can be time-consuming—especially in longer projects—Premiere Pro offers a more efficient solution through the **Essential Sound Panel**. Here's how to use it:

Steps for Auto-Ducking in Premiere Pro:

1. **Open or Create a Session**: Start by either opening an existing multitrack session that contains your audio clips or create a new one in Premiere Pro.
2. **Tag Your Audio Clips**: Use the **Essential Sound panel** to categorize your clips by type. This tagging helps Premiere Pro recognize and apply the appropriate adjustments. For example, label clips as "Music" or "Ambience."
3. **Select Background Audio**: In your timeline, click on the background clip (e.g., music) and navigate to the **Essential Sound panel**. Assign it the appropriate audio type, such as "Music."
4. **Enable Auto-Ducking**: Check the box labeled "Ducking" for the selected clip. When activated, Premiere Pro automatically applies an Amplify Effect to the clip, generating keyframes via the Auto Ducking algorithm that adjust the gain. You can easily edit or remove these keyframes without affecting your overall sound design.

For auto-ducking to work effectively, ensure that other audio tracks (like dialogue and sound effects) are also assigned audio types in the **Essential Sound panel**. This categorization provides Premiere Pro with the necessary information to implement the ducking feature, ensuring smooth audio adjustments throughout your project.

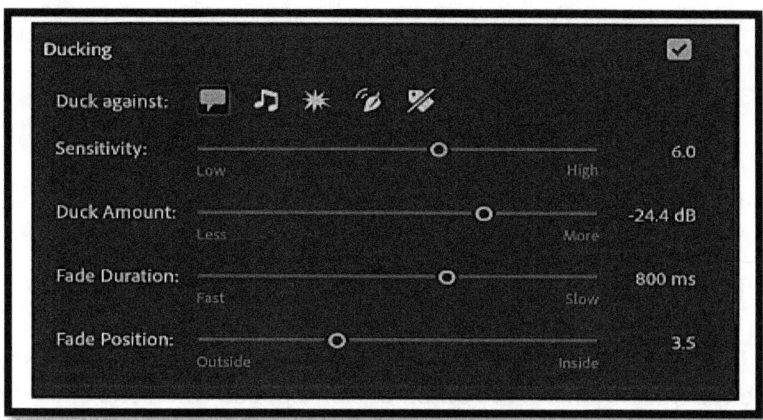

Configuring Auto-Ducking Options in Premiere Pro

To effectively use the auto-ducking feature, you can customize several parameters. Here's how to do it:

1. **Duck Against**:
   o Select the audio content types you want to duck against, such as **Dialogue**, **Music**, **Sound Effects**, **Ambience**, or **Untagged Clips**. This choice dictates which audio tracks will influence the ducking behavior.
2. **Sensitivity**:
   o Adjust the sensitivity setting to control the threshold for when auto-ducking activates:
     ▪ **Higher Sensitivity**: Prioritizes lowering the music volume more aggressively when dialogue occurs.
     ▪ **Lower Sensitivity**: Allows for louder music during dialogue, resulting in fewer adjustments.
     ▪ **Moderate Sensitivity**: Balances the two, providing more dynamic adjustments.
3. **Duck Amount**:
   o Set how much the volume of the music clip is reduced:
     ▪ **Right**: Increases the volume reduction, making the music quieter during dialogue.
     ▪ **Left**: Results in more subtle reductions, allowing the music to remain more prominent.
4. **Fade Duration**:
   o Control the speed of volume adjustments:
     ▪ **Quick Fades**: Ideal for rapid changes between music and speech.
     ▪ **Slow Fades**: Better for gradual adjustments, suitable for voiceovers.
5. **Fade Position**:

- Choose where the fade occurs in relation to the dialogue:
  - **Outside**: Fades occur before and after the dialogue.
  - **Inside**: Fades during the dialogue itself.
  - **Middle**: Fades start just before dialogue and end just after.

Generating Keyframes

Once you've configured your auto-ducking options:

1. Click the **"Generate Keyframes"** button. This will calculate and set the keyframes for the **Amplify** effect that Premiere Pro automatically applied when you enabled auto-ducking.
2. **Note**: If you manually adjust the keyframes after generation, be cautious—clicking "Generate Keyframes" again will overwrite any manual changes. Premiere Pro will display the ducking adjustments on the effect's rubber band in the Timeline, making it easier to visualize and edit these keyframes as needed.

By following these steps, you can create a balanced audio mix that enhances the clarity of dialogue while maintaining an engaging background soundscape.

Add & End with Echo Effects in Premiere Pro (+5 Sound Effects)
Adding Echo Effects in Premiere Pro

Creating a sense of space and atmosphere in your audio can greatly enhance the viewer's experience. Here are two methods to add echo effects to your audio in Premiere Pro:

Method 1: Using Audio Effects

1. **Access the Effects Panel**:
   - Go to the **Effects** panel by navigating to **Window > Effects**.
2. **Locate the Echo Effect**:
   - In the Effects panel, search for "Echo" or browse under **Audio Effects**.
3. **Apply the Echo Effect**:
   - Drag and drop the **Echo** effect onto your audio clip in the Timeline.
4. **Adjust the Echo Settings**:
   - Select the audio clip and go to the **Effect Controls** panel.
   - Here, you can tweak various parameters:
     - **Delay**: Adjust the time between the original sound and the echo.
     - **Decay**: Control how quickly the echo fades away.
     - **Wet/Dry Mix**: Balance the original sound with the echoed sound.

Method 2: Using the Essential Sound Panel

1. **Select Your Audio Clip**:
   - Click on the audio clip you want to modify in the Timeline.
2. **Open the Essential Sound Panel**:
   - Navigate to **Window > Essential Sound** to open the panel.
3. **Tag Your Audio**:
   - Assign a tag that suits your audio type (e.g., Sound Effects) to unlock relevant settings.
4. **Apply Echo Effects**:
   - In the Essential Sound panel, look for the **Reverb** option. Adjust settings to simulate echo-like effects:
     - **Room Size**: Change the size of the virtual space.
     - **Damping**: Control how much high frequencies are absorbed.
     - **Wet/Dry Mix**: Similar to the previous method, balance the original and echoed sounds.
5. **Fine-Tuning**:
   - Play back your audio and make further adjustments as needed to achieve the desired effect.

Tips for Effective Echo Use

- **Context Matters**: Consider the environment of your scene—large, open spaces may require longer delays, while smaller spaces may need shorter echoes.
- **Listen and Adjust**: Always preview your changes in the context of the entire project to ensure they enhance rather than distract from your audio.
- **Combine Effects**: Experiment with combining echo with other effects, like reverb, to create a richer soundscape.

By using these methods, you can effectively add echo to your audio, enriching the immersive quality of your film.

Part 1: Create Quality Echo Effects (Surround Reverb) in Premiere Pro
Tips for Adding Sound Effects in Sync with Camera Movement

When integrating sound effects with your clips, it's essential to consider how camera movement and sound sources interact within the scene. Here are some strategies to help you achieve a more cohesive audio experience:

1. Match Sound Source to Visuals

- **Positioning**: Place sound effects based on where the action is happening in the frame. For example, if a character walks past the camera, ensure the footsteps are panned to match their movement across the screen.
- **Distance**: Consider the distance of the sound source from the camera. Sounds that are closer should be louder and more detailed, while distant sounds should be quieter and more ambient.

2. Sync with Camera Movement

- **Keyframe Adjustments**: Use keyframes to adjust the volume and panning of sound effects dynamically. For instance, if the camera moves away from a sound source, you can lower the volume and increase the reverb.
- **Audio Panning**: As the camera moves, pan the sound effects accordingly. If the camera sweeps to the right, pan the sound effects to the right as well.

3. Consider Room Acoustics

- **Room Size**: Adjust the reverb and echo settings based on the size and type of the room depicted in the scene. Larger spaces will typically have more reverb, while smaller spaces will have tighter, quicker echoes.
- **Sound Absorption**: Think about materials present in the scene (e.g., soft furnishings absorb sound, while hard surfaces reflect it). This can inform your use of effects like reverb.

4. Layering Sounds

- **Use Multiple Layers**: For complex scenes, layer multiple sound effects to create a more realistic soundscape. For example, combine footsteps with ambient sounds of the environment.
- **Adjust Levels**: Balance the levels of each layer to avoid clutter and ensure clarity. Use the audio mixer to fine-tune the mix.

5. Test and Refine

- **Play Back**: Frequently test your audio in the context of the full scene. Listen to how the sound effects complement the visuals and adjust as necessary.
- **Gather Feedback**: If possible, get feedback from others to see if the audio matches their perception of the scene.

By paying attention to these details and practicing regularly, you'll develop a stronger intuition for matching sound effects to camera movements and overall scene dynamics, enhancing the immersion of your projects.

Option 1: Basic Echo Effect
Adding Echo and Reverb Effects in Premiere Pro

To enhance your audio with echo and reverb effects, follow these steps:

1. Using the Basic Echo Effect

- **Select Your Clip**: Choose the audio clip in the timeline where you want to add the echo effect.
- **Apply the Echo Effect**:
  - Go to the **Effects panel**.
  - Search for **Basic Echo**.
  - Drag and drop the effect onto your selected audio clip.
- **Adjust Echo Settings**:
  - Select the clip, then go to the **Effect Controls panel**.
  - Tweak parameters like **Delay**, **Feedback**, and **Wet/Dry Mix** to get the desired echo effect. This works well for sounds like footsteps, gunshots, or dialogue.

2. Adding Surround Reverb

- **Prepare Your Clip**: Ensure your audio and video are edited and ready for the reverb effect.
- **Locate Surround Reverb**:
  - In the **Effects panel**, search for **Surround Reverb**.
- **Apply the Reverb Effect**:
  - Drag and drop Surround Reverb onto your audio clip.
- **Adjust Reverb Settings**:
  - With the clip selected, go to the **Effect Controls panel**.
  - Modify settings such as **Room Size**, **Damping**, and **Wet/Dry Mix** to create a spacious sound that fits your scene.

3. Fine-Tuning

- **Playback**: Continuously play back the audio to hear how the echo and reverb interact with the rest of your project.
- **Adjust as Needed**: Use the sliders in the Effect Controls to refine the sound until it feels natural and fits well within the context of your scene.

Tips for Effective Use

- **Context Matters**: Consider the environment of your scene when applying echo and reverb. A large, open space will require different settings compared to a small, enclosed area.
- **Experiment**: Don't hesitate to try different values to find what best complements your audio.

By carefully adding and adjusting these effects, you can significantly enhance the auditory experience of your project.

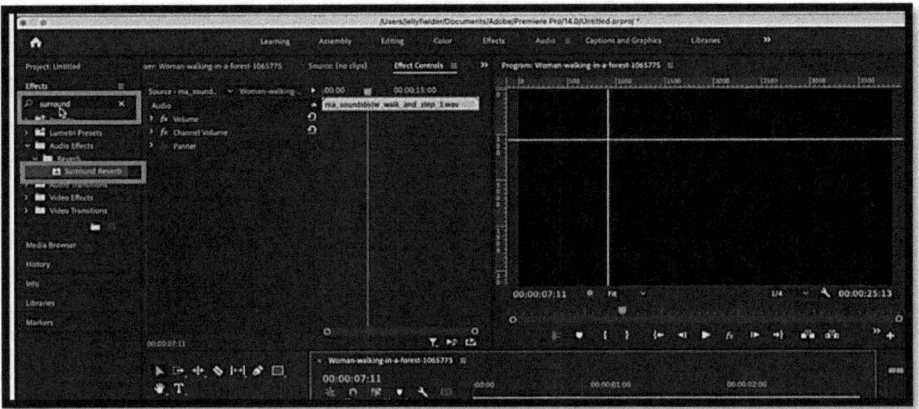

To customize your audio effects further in Premiere Pro, follow these steps:

1. **Select Your Audio Clip**: Click on the audio clip in the timeline that you want to modify.
2. **Open the Effect Controls Panel**: Go to the **Window** menu and select **Effect Controls** if it's not already open.
3. **Locate the Effect**: Find the audio effect you've applied (like Surround Reverb) in the Effect Controls panel.
4. **Edit the Effect**:
   o Click the **Edit** button next to **Custom Setup** for the effect.
   o This will open a detailed settings window where you can adjust various parameters.
5. **Adjust Settings**: Modify settings such as room size, damping, and wet/dry mix to fine-tune the effect to your liking.
6. **Preview Changes**: Play your audio to hear the adjustments in real-time.
7. **Apply and Close**: Once satisfied with your changes, close the settings window to return to your main project.

By using the **Edit** button, you can achieve a more tailored audio effect that fits your project perfectly.

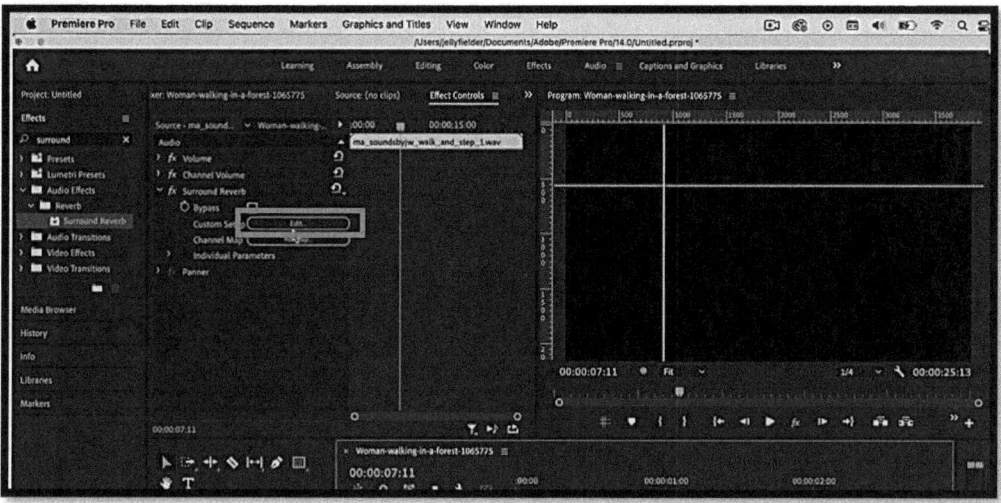

To adjust the audio levels in Premiere Pro, follow these steps:

1. **Select Your Audio Clip**: Click on the audio clip in the timeline that you want to modify.
2. **Right-Click for Audio Gain**: Right-click on the selected audio clip to open the context menu.
3. **Choose Audio Gain**: From the menu, select **Audio Gain**. This will open the Audio Gain dialog box.
4. **Adjust the Gain**:
   ○ In the dialog box, you can raise the **Gain** setting to increase the audio level.
   ○ You can enter a specific value or use the slider to adjust the gain as needed.
5. **Preview Changes**: Click **OK** to apply the changes, then play back your audio to hear the difference.
6. **Fine-Tune as Necessary**: If the levels still need adjustment, you can repeat the process until you achieve the desired sound.

By using the Audio Gain feature, you can effectively control the volume of your audio clips to ensure they sit well in your overall mix.

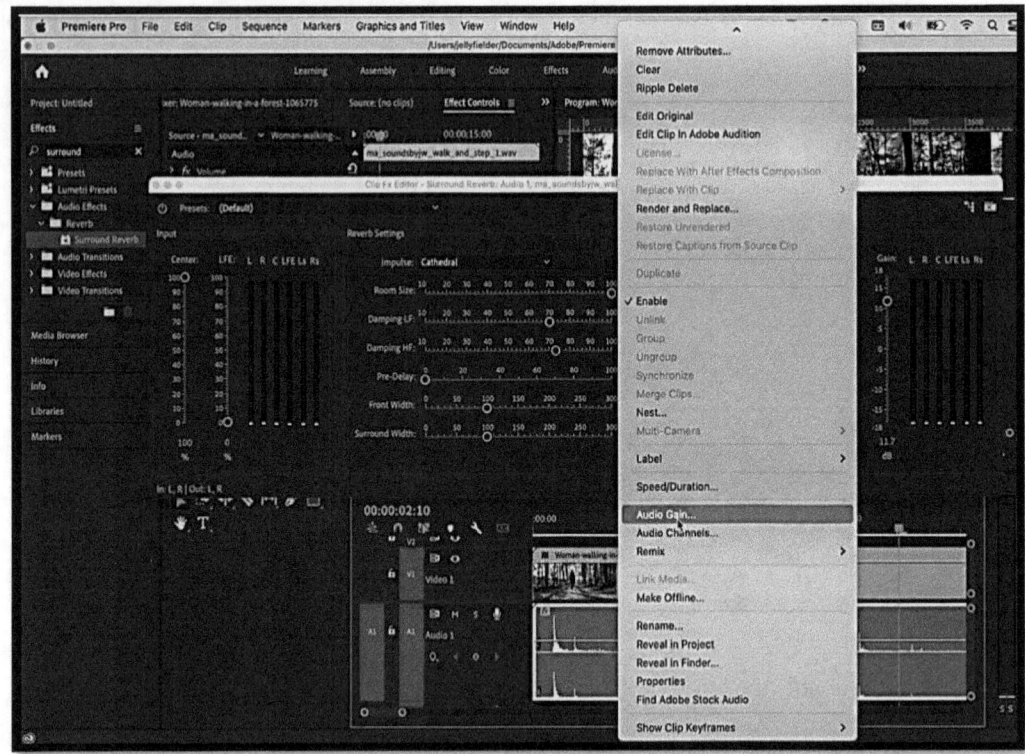

To adjust the audio gain by a specific amount in Premiere Pro, follow these steps:

1. **Select Your Audio Clip**: Click on the audio clip you want to modify in the timeline.
2. **Right-Click and Choose Audio Gain**: Right-click on the selected clip and select **Audio Gain** from the context menu.
3. **Adjust Gain**:
   - In the Audio Gain dialog box, look for the **Adjust Gain by** option.
   - Enter **15** in the box to increase the gain by 15 decibels.
4. **Apply Changes**: Click **OK** to apply the gain adjustment.
5. **Preview Your Changes**: Play back the clip to ensure the audio level is now to your liking.

This adjustment will help balance the audio levels in your project!

To make the room smaller in your audio mix (to create a more intimate sound), you can adjust the reverb settings. Here's how to do it:

1. **Select Your Audio Clip**: Click on the audio clip in your timeline that has the reverb effect applied.
2. **Open Effect Controls**: Navigate to the **Effect Controls** panel.
3. **Locate the Reverb Effect**: Find the **Surround Reverb** effect you added earlier.
4. **Edit Custom Setup**: Click the **Edit** button next to **Custom Setup** to access the reverb parameters.
5. **Adjust Room Size**: Look for the **Room Size** parameter. Decrease this value to make the room sound smaller, which will create a tighter and more focused reverb effect.
6. **Listen and Fine-Tune**: Play back the audio to hear the changes. Adjust the Room Size and other parameters like **Damping** and **Wet/Dry Mix** to achieve the desired effect.
7. **Finalize Your Mix**: Once you're satisfied with how the audio fits within the context of your visuals, make sure to check the overall balance with other audio tracks in your project.

This will help ensure your audio feels cohesive and suits the visuals effectively!

Option 2: End with Echo Effect

To create a fade-out effect with an echoey finish for your music track, follow these steps:

1. **Cut the Music Track**:
    o   In the Timeline, select your music track and use the Razor Tool (or press C) to cut the track at the point where you want it to stop.
2. **Select the Repeat Section**:
    o   Identify the section of the audio clip that you want to repeat for the echo effect. Use the Razor Tool to cut this section as needed.
3. **Move the Echo Section**:

- o Click and drag the cut portion of the audio clip that you want to echo to a different track below the original music track. This will help separate the echo effect from the main music.

4. **Add Transparent Video**:
   - o Right-click in the Project panel and select **New Item > Transparent Video**. This creates a blank video layer that you can use for timing and visual alignment.

5. **Position the Transparent Video**:
   - o Drag the transparent video to your timeline above the audio tracks. This allows you to create a visual cue for where the echo effect begins, if needed.

6. **Apply Reverb Effect**:
   - o Select the section of audio you moved to the new track. Go to the **Effects** panel, search for **Surround Reverb**, and drag it onto the audio clip.

7. **Adjust Reverb Settings**:
   - o In the **Effect Controls** panel, click **Edit** next to the Surround Reverb effect. Adjust parameters like **Room Size**, **Wet/Dry Mix**, and **Decay** to get the desired echo effect.

8. **Fade-Out**:
   - o To create a fade-out, go to the last few seconds of your music track. Select the audio clip, then hold Ctrl (or Cmd on Mac) and click on the audio line to create a keyframe. Drag this keyframe down to create a gradual decrease in volume.

9. **Preview and Fine-Tune**:
   - o Play back your sequence to hear the changes. Adjust the reverb and fade settings as necessary to achieve the effect you want.

This method will give your music track a smooth echo finish while neatly fading out!

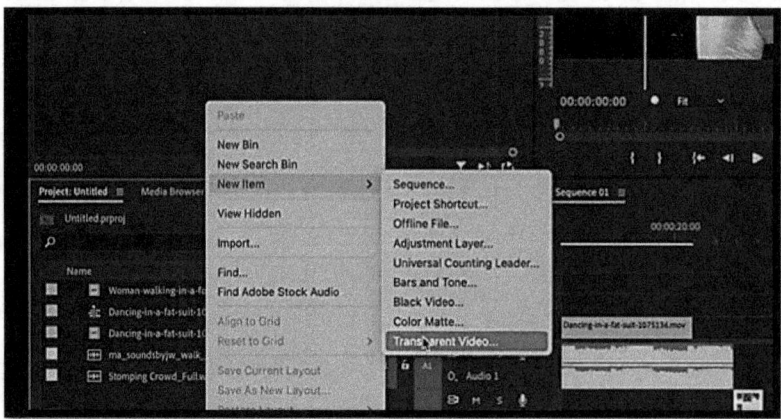

To finish setting up your echo effect and fade-out using the Transparent Video, follow these steps:

1. **Position the Transparent Video**:

- o Drag the Transparent Video to the end of your timeline. This will provide a space for the echo to play after the main audio clip ends.

2. **Open the Audio Track Mixer**:
   - o Go to **Window** in the top menu and select **Audio Track Mixer**. This opens the mixer panel where you can control audio levels for each track.

3. **Select Your Sequence**:
   - o Ensure you select the correct sequence in the Audio Track Mixer that corresponds to the timeline you're working in. This will let you adjust the audio settings specifically for that sequence.

4. **Adjust Audio Levels**:
   - o Use the sliders in the Audio Track Mixer to control the volume levels of your music and echo tracks. You might want to lower the volume of the echo track to create a more subtle effect.

5. **Add Keyframes (if necessary)**:
   - o If you want to further refine the fade-out, you can add keyframes to the audio levels in the Audio Track Mixer. Click on the diamond-shaped icon to enable keyframe writing, then adjust the volume as the timeline plays.

6. **Preview Your Changes**:
   - o Play back the timeline to see how the echo integrates with the rest of your audio. Make any adjustments as needed to ensure a smooth transition.

This process will help you create a polished audio experience in your project!

To add reverb to your audio track using the Audio Track Mixer, follow these steps:

1. **Locate the Audio Track Mixer**:

- o Ensure you have the Audio Track Mixer open and that you're on the correct sequence.
2. **Select the Correct Track**:
   - o Identify the track you want to apply the reverb effect to (in this case, Audio Track 2).
3. **Access the Effects**:
   - o At the end of the Audio Track 2 settings, click the down arrow to open the effects menu.
4. **Choose the Reverb Effect**:
   - o Navigate to **Reverb** and select **Studio Reverb**. This will add the reverb effect to that audio track.
5. **Adjust the Reverb Settings**:
   - o Once the Studio Reverb is applied, you can click the **Edit** button next to it in the Audio Track Mixer to open the settings. Adjust parameters like **Room Size**, **Damping**, **Wet Level**, and **Dry Level** to achieve the desired echo effect.
6. **Preview Your Audio**:
   - o Play your timeline to hear how the reverb impacts your audio. Make further adjustments as needed.

This will help create a more immersive sound experience in your project!

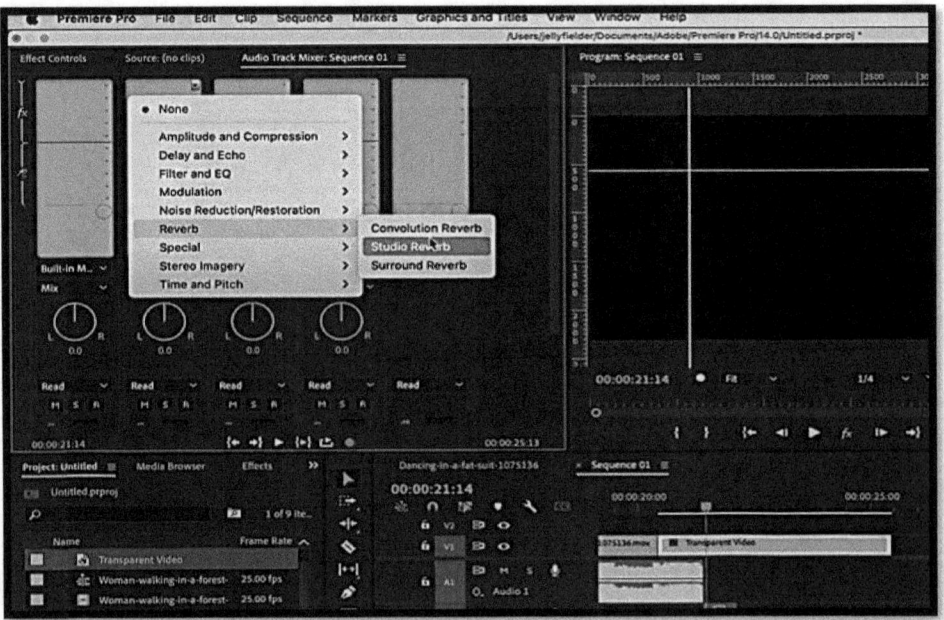

To create a fade-out for your echo effect using keyframes in the Audio Track Mixer, follow these steps:

1. **Open Studio Reverb Settings**:
   - In the Audio Track Mixer, double-click on the **Studio Reverb** effect you added. This opens the settings box.
2. **Adjust Reverb Settings**:
   - In the **Studio Reverb Settings** box, increase the **Decay** and **Wet** settings until you achieve the desired echo effect.
3. **Show Keyframes**:
   - Move to the beginning of **Audio Track 2**. Click on **Show Keyframes** to make the volume keyframes visible.
4. **Select Keyframe Type**:
   - Click on the **Keyframe settings** dropdown and select **Track Keyframes > Volume**. This will allow you to adjust the volume over time.
5. **Add Keyframes**:
   - Position the playhead where you want the fade-out to start, and click the **Add Keyframe** button (the diamond shape) to create a keyframe at that point.
   - Move the playhead to the end of the audio track and add another keyframe.
6. **Adjust Volume Levels**:
   - Drag the second keyframe down to decrease the volume gradually, creating a fade-out effect.
7. **Preview Your Changes**:
   - Play your timeline to listen to the fade-out and adjust the keyframes as necessary for a smooth transition.

This process will give your audio a polished ending with a smooth echo fade-out!

To insert a keyframe for reducing the audio volume using the Pen Tool in Adobe Premiere Pro, follow these steps:

1. **Select the Pen Tool**:
   o   In the **Toolbar**, select the **Pen Tool** (shortcut: **P**).
2. **Locate the Audio Clip**:
   o   Click on the audio clip in the timeline where you want to start the fade-out.
3. **Insert the First Keyframe**:
   o   Click on the thin white line (volume rubber band) where you want the fade-out to begin. This creates a keyframe at that point.
4. **Find the Fade-Out Endpoint**:
   o   Move the playhead to the point in the music where you want the fade-out to end.
5. **Insert the Second Keyframe**:
   o   Again, click on the rubber band at this location to create another keyframe.
6. **Adjust the Volume**:
   o   Click and drag the second keyframe down to lower the volume, creating a fade-out effect over the distance between the two keyframes.
7. **Preview Your Changes**:
   o   Play the timeline to hear the fade-out and make any adjustments to the keyframes as needed for a smooth transition.

This method will effectively create a gradual decrease in volume for your audio clip!

Making changes to the media cache.

To clear the Media Cache in Adobe Premiere Pro, follow these steps:

1. **Access Preferences**:
   - **Windows**: Go to **Edit > Preferences**.
   - **Mac**: Click on the **Premiere Pro Application Menu** and select **Preferences**.
2. **Locate Media Cache Settings**:
   - In the Preferences window, find and select **Media Cache** from the list on the left.
3. **Clear Media Cache**:
   - Look for the **"Delete"** button next to the **"Erase Media Cache Files"** option.
   - Click this button to delete the cached files, freeing up disk space.
4. **Confirm Deletion** (if prompted):
   - Confirm that you want to proceed with the deletion.

By following these steps, you'll successfully clear out old media cache files, helping to optimize Premiere Pro's performance!

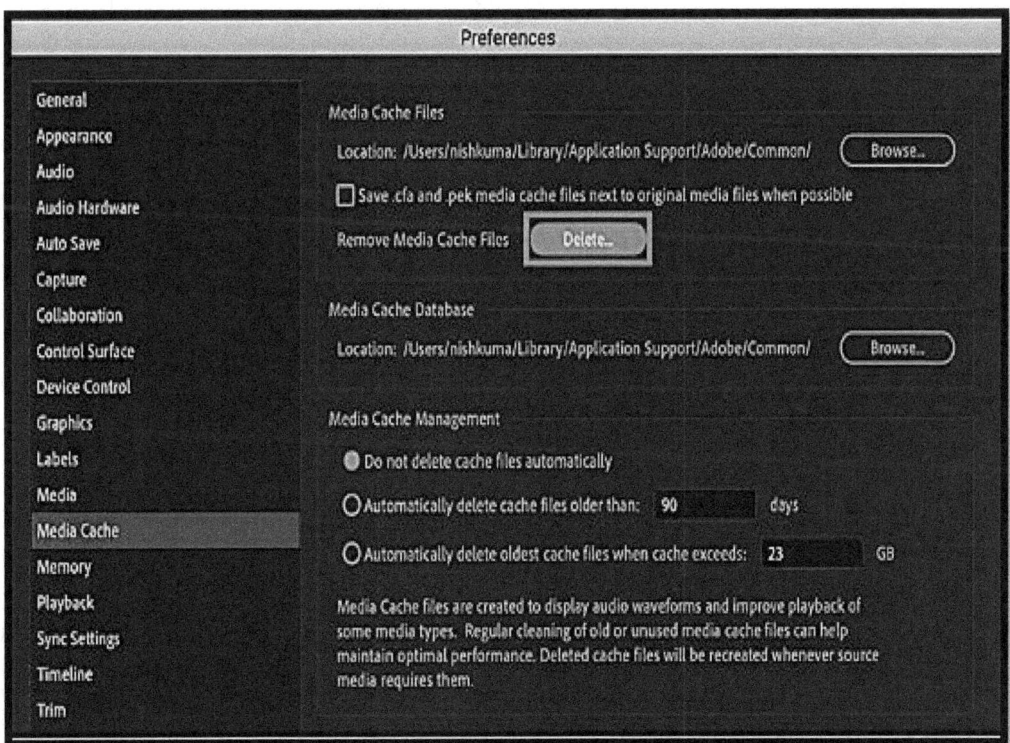

To clear media cache files in Adobe Premiere Pro, follow these detailed steps:

1. **Access Preferences**:
   o **Windows**: Go to **Edit > Preferences**.
   o **Mac**: Click on the **Premiere Pro Application Menu** and select **Preferences**.
2. **Locate Media Cache Settings**:
   o In the Preferences window, select **Media Cache** from the left-hand menu.
3. **Start Clearing Cache**:
   o Click on the **"Delete"** button next to **"Erase Media Cache Files."**
4. **Delete Media Cache Files Dialog Box**:
   o A dialog box titled **"Delete Media Cache Files"** will appear.
5. **Choose Deletion Options**: You'll see three options for deleting cache files:
   o **Delete Unnecessary Media Cache Files**: This option removes cache files associated with source media that is no longer accessible or needed by your current projects, freeing up space without impacting ongoing work.
   o **Delete All Media Cache Files from the System**: Selecting this option will erase all cache files on your system, providing a clean slate for cache management.
   o **Rebuilding Cache Files When Source Media Demands**: After deleting cache files, Premiere Pro will automatically recreate them as needed when you access the source media again. It's recommended to restart Premiere Pro after clearing the cache to ensure this feature functions properly.
6. **Finalize Your Choice**:
   o After selecting the option that best suits your needs, click **"OK"** in the dialog box to initiate the deletion process. This action confirms your choice and removes the selected cache files.

By following these steps, you'll effectively manage your media cache, optimizing Premiere Pro's performance and freeing up disk space!

What location should I save my Media Cache files?

To optimize your Adobe Premiere Pro setup by choosing the right storage for your Media Cache, follow these steps:

Best Practices for Media Cache Storage

1. **Use an SSD or NVMe Drive**:
   o For optimal performance, store your Media Cache files on a fast SSD or NVMe drive. These drives offer significantly higher read and write speeds compared to traditional HDDs, leading to smoother editing experiences.
2. **Dedicated Media Cache Drive**:
   o Ideally, use a separate SSD or NVMe drive solely for Media Cache files. This separation helps manage data more efficiently, as it keeps cache-related activities distinct from other file operations.

3. **Changing Media Cache Location**:
   o Open Premiere Pro and go to **Edit > Preferences** (Windows) or **Premiere Pro > Preferences** (Mac).
   o Select **Media Cache** from the left-hand menu.
   o Click the **"Browse"** button to choose a specific folder or location on your SSD or NVMe drive for storing Media Cache files.
4. **Alternative Storage Solutions**:
   o If a dedicated drive isn't available, you can still store the Media Cache on the same disk as your video files. While this is not as efficient as having a separate drive, it is faster than using an HDD.

Benefits of Proper Storage

- **Improved Performance**: Storing the Media Cache on high-speed SSDs or NVMe drives enhances the program's responsiveness during editing.
- **Faster Access**: Quick access to cache files allows for more efficient playback and smoother editing workflows.
- **Smoother Editing Process**: Overall, these optimizations lead to a more seamless editing experience, enabling you to focus on your creative work without lag.

By following these steps and tips, you can significantly enhance your editing setup in Adobe Premiere Pro, ensuring a faster and more efficient workflow.

Automatically manage your Media Cache files

To effectively manage media cache settings in Adobe Premiere Pro, you can adjust several preferences that control how cache files are handled. Here's how:

Media Cache Management Settings

1. **Do Not Delete Cache Files Automatically**:
   o By default, Premiere Pro retains certain cache files (.pek, .cfa, and .ims) in designated subfolders (Peak Files and Media Cache Files). These files will remain unless you manually delete them, ensuring you have quick access to necessary data without constant rebuilding.
2. **Automatically Delete Cache Files Older Than a Specified Period**:
   o In the Media Cache Preferences, you can set a specific time frame (default is 90 days) after which cache files are automatically deleted. Adjusting this period helps manage disk space by ensuring that older, unused cache files don't accumulate unnecessarily.
3. **Automatically Delete Oldest Cache Files When Cache Exceeds a Certain Volume Size**:

o   This option allows Premiere Pro to automatically delete the oldest cache files when the total size of the cache exceeds a specified percentage of the total volume size. For instance, if the cache grows beyond 10% of the designated volume, the oldest files will be removed, keeping your cache manageable.

How to Access Media Cache Preferences

1. Open **Adobe Premiere Pro**.
2. Navigate to **Edit > Preferences** (Windows) or **Premiere Pro > Preferences** (Mac).
3. Select **Media Cache** from the list on the left.
4. Adjust the settings according to your needs for file retention and deletion.

Benefits of Managing Media Cache

*   **Optimized Storage**: Regularly deleting old cache files prevents unnecessary storage use and keeps your system running smoothly.
*   **Performance Maintenance**: By managing cache size and age, you can ensure Premiere Pro continues to operate efficiently, improving your overall editing experience.
*   **Customizable Control**: Tailoring these settings allows you to balance performance with storage needs based on your specific workflow.

By configuring these settings, you can maintain an efficient editing environment in Adobe Premiere Pro while minimizing clutter from old cache files.

PART II
INTERMEDIATE TECHNIQUES

CHAPTER 5

ADVANCED EDITING TOOLS

Ripple and Roll Edits

Ripple and Roll Edits in Adobe Premiere Pro

Adobe Premiere Pro offers powerful tools like Ripple and Roll Edits that allow editors to manipulate the timing and pacing of their video projects efficiently. Let's dive into how to use these tools effectively.

Ripple Edit Tool

- **Functionality**: The Ripple Edit tool allows you to adjust the length of a selected clip while automatically shifting adjacent clips to fill the gap or accommodate the change. This ensures that your timeline stays continuous without leaving unwanted spaces.
- **How to Use**:
    1. **Activate the Tool**: Press the **B** key or select the Ripple Edit tool from the Tools panel.
    2. **Edit a Clip**: Click and drag the edge of the clip you want to shorten or extend. As you adjust, adjacent clips will automatically move to maintain the flow of the sequence.
    3. **Preview Changes**: You can play back the timeline to hear and see how the ripple adjustment affects the pacing of your project.

Roll Edit Tool

- **Functionality**: The Roll Edit tool enables you to adjust the Out Point of one clip and the In Point of the adjacent clip simultaneously. This allows for fine-tuning of transitions without affecting the overall length of the timeline.
- **How to Use**:
    1. **Activate the Tool**: Select the Roll Edit tool from the Tools panel or press the **N** key.
    2. **Edit Clips**: Click on the edit point (the cut between two clips) and drag left or right. This adjusts the duration of both clips, giving you control over the transition without altering the total duration of the sequence.
    3. **Check the Transition**: After rolling the edit, play the sequence to ensure the transition feels smooth and maintains the desired timing.

Best Practices for Using Ripple and Roll Edits

- **Plan Your Edits**: Before making adjustments, have a clear idea of how you want the pacing to feel in your video.
- **Use in Conjunction**: Combine Ripple and Roll Edits for comprehensive timing adjustments, allowing for both clip length alterations and smooth transitions.
- **Play Back Frequently**: Regularly preview your edits to ensure they enhance the narrative flow and maintain viewer engagement.
- **Keyboard Shortcuts**: Familiarize yourself with the keyboard shortcuts for quick access to these tools, enhancing your editing speed and efficiency.

By mastering Ripple and Roll Edits, you can significantly improve your editing workflow in Adobe Premiere Pro, leading to more polished and professionally timed video productions.

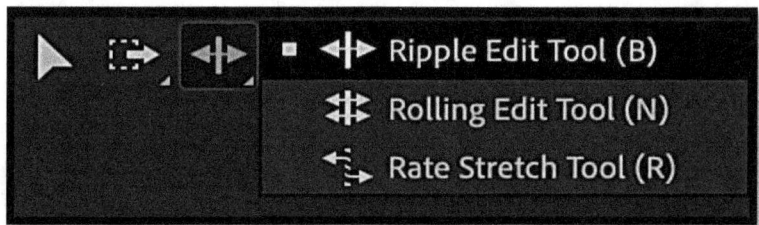

☐ The Ripple Edit tool creates a "ripple effect"—when you trim a clip, it shifts all subsequent clips in your timeline accordingly.

☐ It adjusts the in and out points of the layers and then slides all following clips to align with the new out point.

☐ For example, if you remove 10 frames from the end of a clip, the remaining clips will move forward by 10 frames.

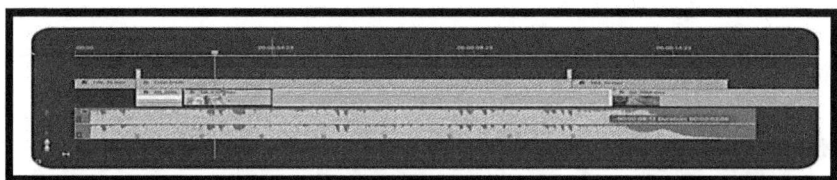

Note: The Ripple Edit tool will not affect any locked video editing tracks. If you have multiple video tracks, be sure to verify which ones are locked and which are not.

How to Ripple Delete in Premiere Pro

The Ripple Edit tool can leave gaps in your timeline, and that's where Ripple Deleting becomes useful.

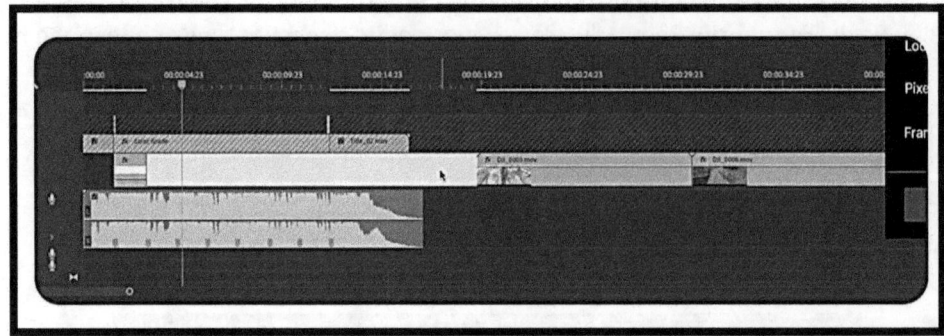

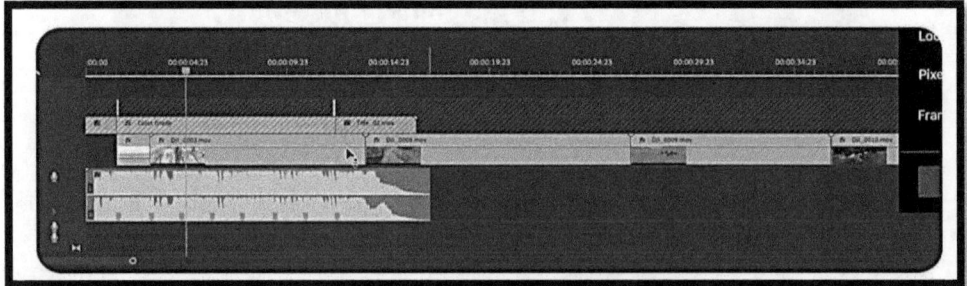

▢ To use Ripple, Delete, just click on the gap between two clips; this will highlight the space in white, indicating what you'll be removing.

▢ Then, press the backspace or delete key on your keyboard. This action will shift your clips to align with the nearest clip's endpoint in the timeline.

▢ Don't forget to lock any tracks that you want to keep unchanged by Ripple Delete.

Roll Edit

The "N" key activates the Roll Edit tool, allowing you to adjust the edit point between two adjacent clips on the timeline. Unlike the Ripple Edit tool, using the Roll Edit tool lets you reposition the edit point without altering the overall duration of the sequence.

Click and drag the cut point, where the in and out points meet between two clips. This will adjust the in and out points without shifting the clips themselves—resulting in one clip becoming shorter while the other becomes longer.

The Rate Stretch Tool

You can adjust a clip's speed using the Rate Stretch tool, eliminating the need to right-click and navigate through options to estimate the percentage for speeding up or slowing down each clip. To activate the Rate, stretch tool, press the "R" key on your keyboard or find it in the Tools window next to the Ripple Edit tool. With this tool, you can modify the playback speed of your footage by dragging either the beginning or ending point of the clip, similar to adjusting its length.

Slip and Slide Edits

You can refine individual clips using the Slip tool, a powerful feature for making adjustments. If you have a clip in your timeline that fits well between two others but could be improved, the Slip tool allows you to modify its In and Out points without needing to delete it and select new clips. This tool lets you make changes without moving or deleting the original clip. To access it, press the "Y" key on your keyboard or click on the Slip Tool in the Tools box. Your cursor will then change to arrows pointing toward vertical bars, indicating the tool is active.

The Slip tool is excellent for making precise adjustments to the visible portion of a clip, which is especially useful when adding transitions between footage. Sometimes, when attempting to add a transition, you might encounter a message indicating there's not enough clip available. This usually happens because the transition requires more frames than are present. With the Slip tool, you can adjust the In and Out points of the clips, allowing you to incorporate the transition without altering the timeline or surrounding clips.

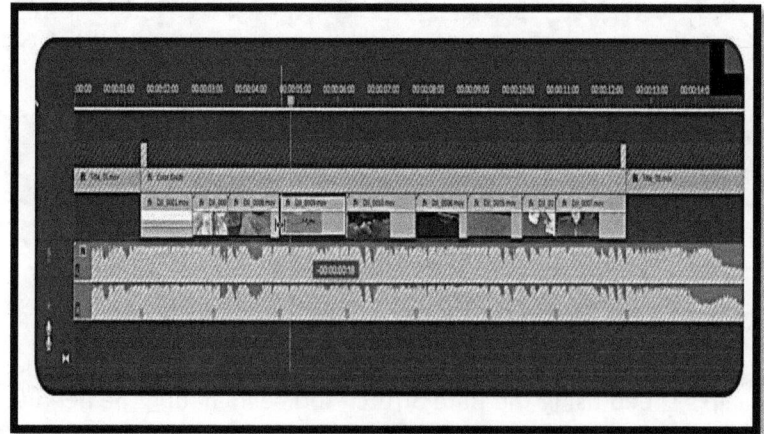

Slide Tool

The Slide tool allows you to rearrange clips on your timeline without needing to cut or reorganize all your footage. This tool lets you move a selected clip while automatically adjusting the clips before and after it to ensure they fit seamlessly. When you use the Slide tool, it considers three clips: the one you want to slide, the one preceding it, and the one following it. For instance, if you want to move a clip earlier in the timeline, the tool will shorten the clip before it and extend the clip after it.

Think of it like film divided into two tracks; moving a clip on the top track affects how the clips below it appears. Similarly, the Slide tool allows changes only within the same track. This makes it particularly useful for editing B-roll, as you can easily reorder and reposition clips to create space for talking-head footage.

Using the Razor Tool

In Premiere Pro, you'll find a small razor blade icon representing the Razor Tool, which is primarily used to cut clips or scenes at specific points. This allows editors to remove unwanted sections or split video for further editing. You can quickly select the Razor Tool by pressing the "C" key on your keyboard, making it convenient to switch between tools while you work.

One of the standout features of the Razor Tool is its precision in making cuts. Editors can zoom in on the timeline for pixel-perfect accuracy, which is especially useful for complex edits like syncing video to music beats or aligning visual elements. Utilizing keyboard shortcuts can significantly enhance your editing efficiency. You can customize the shortcut keys for the Razor Tool in Premiere Pro, and understanding control keys like Alt (or Option on a Mac) can modify how the Razor Tool functions, allowing for actions such as ripple deletes and lifts.

Ripple Edits and Trim Mode

The Razor Tool is frequently used in conjunction with ripple edits, which instantly adjust the timeline when a cut is made, ensuring a smooth and continuous flow in the video without any interruptions. Additionally, the Razor Tool can work alongside Trim Mode to refine cuts by adjusting the In and Out points of clips while maintaining the overall sequence.

Step 1: Select a video clip, then navigate to the Tool menu and choose the Razor Tool. Alternatively, you can quickly access it by pressing the "C" key.

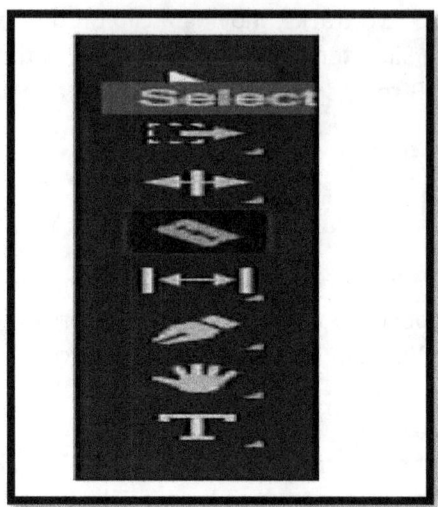

• Step 2: Next, select the portion of the video clip that you wish to trim. You can trim the clip multiple times to create a new segment.

• Step 3: Use the Selection Tool to highlight the section of the video you want to remove. After that, press the "Delete" button to eliminate the selected part.

CHAPTER 6
COLOR CORRECTION AND GRADING

Understanding Color Spaces

Color spaces play a vital role in digital video editing. Premiere Pro, a leading video editing software, offers users a variety of color spaces to achieve their desired aesthetic. To fully appreciate the significance of color spaces in Premiere Pro, it's essential to grasp the basics of color science and how digital devices interpret and reproduce colors.

What is a Color Space?

Certain groups of colors are referred to as "color spaces," which determine how colors are displayed in images and videos. Color spaces define the range and variety of colors that can be represented or stored within the context of Premiere Pro. The most commonly used color spaces are RGB (Red, Green, and Blue) and YUV (Luma and Chroma), each serving a unique purpose in the digital video workflow.

RGB Color Space

In digital media, RGB is the most widely used color model, where colors are created by combining red, green, and blue. Each channel (R, G, and B) can have values ranging from 0 to 255, allowing for a vast spectrum of colors. Premiere Pro supports various RGB color spaces, including sRGB, Adobe RGB, and ProPhoto RGB. When working with photos or videos captured in different environments, selecting the appropriate RGB color space is crucial for maintaining color accuracy and consistency.

YUV color space

YUV separates luminance (brightness) from chrominance (color information), making it more efficient for video compression. Many video broadcasts and streams utilize YUV. In Premiere Pro, users can work with YUV color spaces such as 709 and 2020, which accommodate various video standards. Understanding how YUV color space's function is essential when working with streaming content or creating videos for specific platforms.

Working with Color Management

Premiere Pro offers robust color management tools that ensure consistent color appearance across all platforms and devices. Users can select their preferred working color space and adjust color space settings in the Color Management options. This feature is particularly useful when editing footage from cameras that use different color spaces or when preparing content for specific screen sizes.

Importing and Exporting Color Spaces

Premiere Pro allows users to retain the original color space of imported video or modify how it is interpreted. This capability is crucial when working with footage from various sources, as it helps maintain consistent colors during editing. Additionally, when uploading a video, users can select the appropriate color space and bit depth based on the target device for the final output.

HDR (High Dynamic Range) Color Spaces

Premiere Pro supports HDR color spaces such as Hybrid Log-Gamma (HLG) and Perceptual Quantizer (PQ), which are increasingly popular in HDR video production. These HDR color spaces provide a broader range of brightness and color, enhancing the viewing experience with greater realism and visual appeal. To achieve optimal results when working with HDR footage, it's essential to understand how to properly configure and manage HDR color spaces.

Basic Color Correction

The color of your video content significantly impacts the overall quality and mood of the project. Color grading is a crucial aspect of post-production that can alter emotions and atmosphere. For instance, *Ex Machina* utilized red tones to convey anger and violence, while *The Matrix* employed green hues to symbolize new life and survival.

Coloring encompasses color grading, which enhances the visual appeal of your footage for creative purposes. This process typically occurs after color correction and is performed by a colorist. While many people use "color grading" and "color correction" interchangeably, they refer to different practices. Color correction involves adjusting brightness, contrast, and shadows to fix errors and create a more natural look. Although color grading requires a certain level of expertise, anyone can perform basic color correction, which is a form of color grading. We will guide you through the steps needed to correct colors in Adobe Premiere Pro CC. For example, consider a video recorded with incorrect color temperature, resulting in a blue tint and insufficient brightness.

STEP 1: Import your video into Premiere Pro and create a sequence. Then, open the Lumetri Color panel by selecting **Window** from the top menu and clicking on **Lumetri Color**.

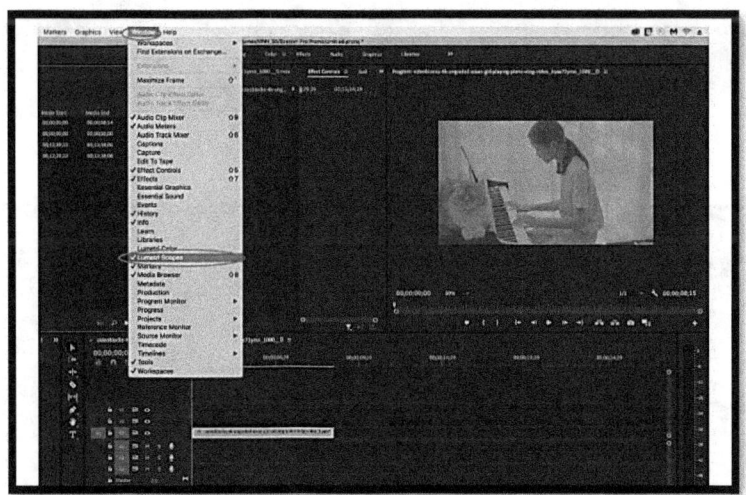

STEP 2: In the Lumetri Color panel, navigate to the **Basic Correction** tab. This section will display all the primary color correction options available.

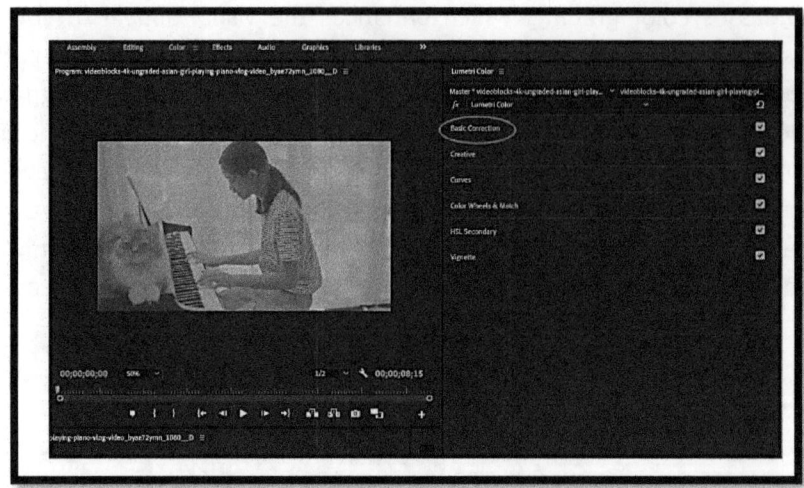

STEP 3: To correct the overall color of the clip, we'll focus on adjusting the blue tint. In the White Balance section, use the WB Selector to click on an area of the frame that is closest to white. Premiere Pro will automatically balance the colors for you.

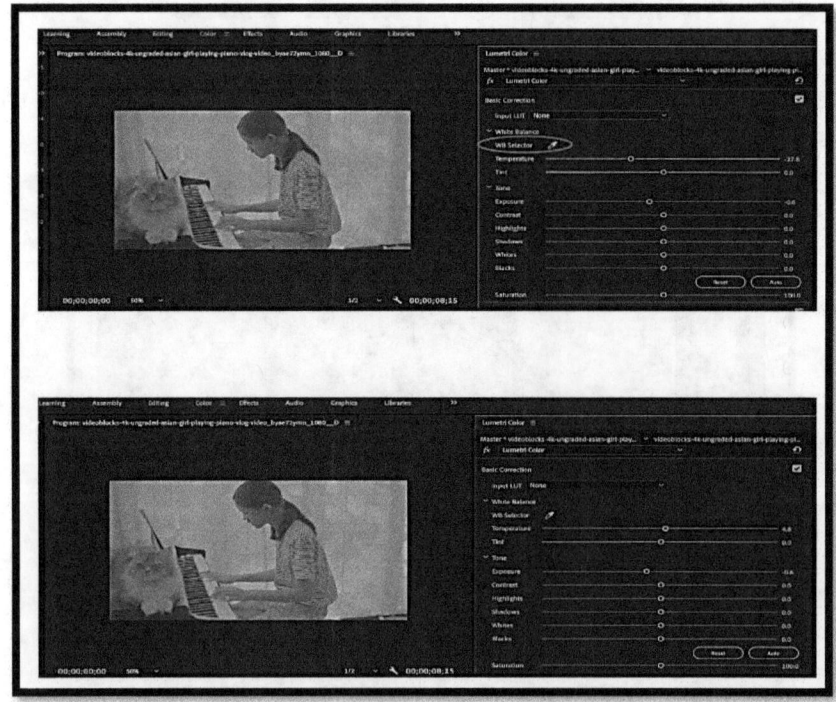

STEP 4: You can further adjust the white balance using the Temperature tool located in the White Balance section. Slide it towards the orange (warmer) side or the blue (cooler) side until the areas in your video that should be white appear pure white.

STEP 5: With the image balanced, let's adjust the Exposure to brighten or darken the overall video. We'll increase the Exposure to 0.7 since this clip is too dark. Now, the bright areas in the video may be slightly less distinct after adjusting the brightness.

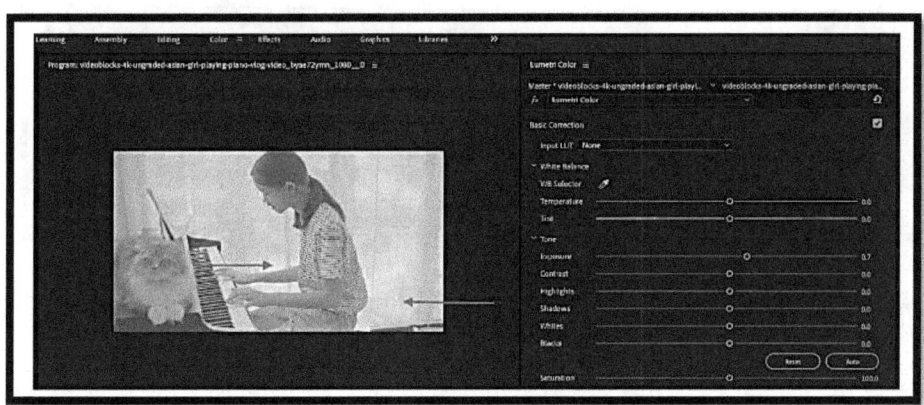

To compensate for this, let's adjust the Highlights scale down to -8.6.

STEP 6: We can enhance the brightness of the darker areas without affecting the lighter parts by adjusting the Shadows setting. By moving the Shadows scale to approximately -20, we've darkened the shadows and intensified the darker regions.

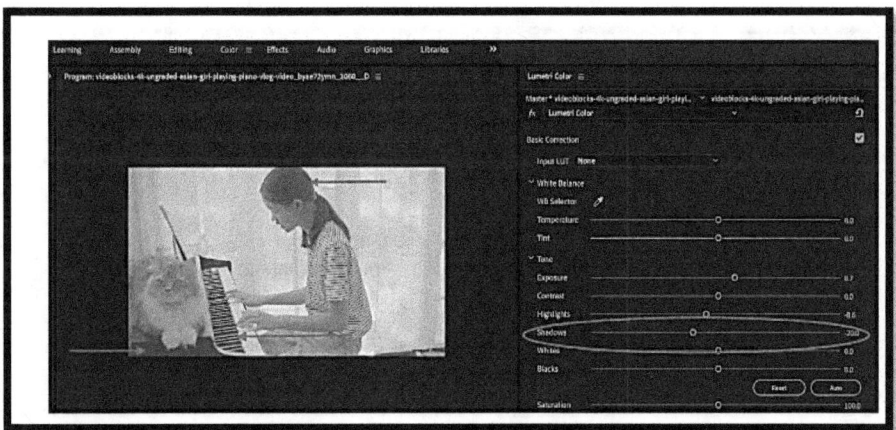

It's recommended not to move the Shadows setting beyond 30 or 40, as doing so can introduce noise and grain into the video.

STEP 7: Next, we'll adjust the Contrast slider. Reducing contrast will wash out the video, making the darker areas much lighter, while increasing contrast will deepen the overall image, making it darker.

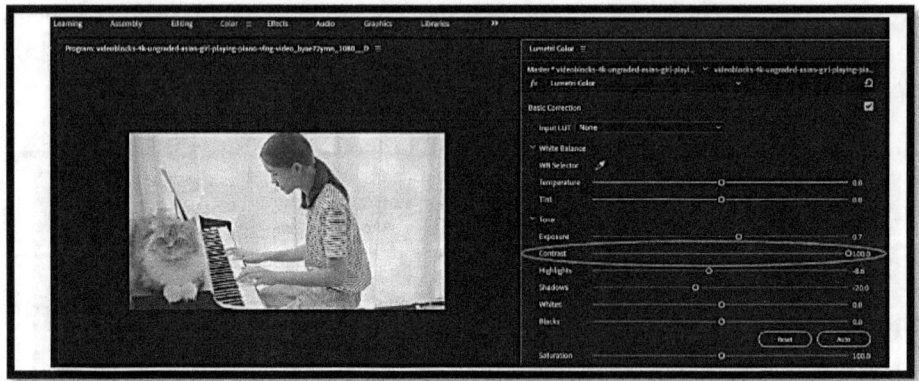

et the contrast to 21 for this clip.

STEP 8: Lower the Whites tool to -13 to maintain clarity in the curtains in the background.

STEP 9: Next, adjust the Blacks scale down to -30 to ensure the darkest areas achieve a rich black level.

STEP 10: Finally, let's adjust the saturation, which will significantly affect the overall appearance of your video. When the Saturation is set to 0, the video will appear black and white, with no color.

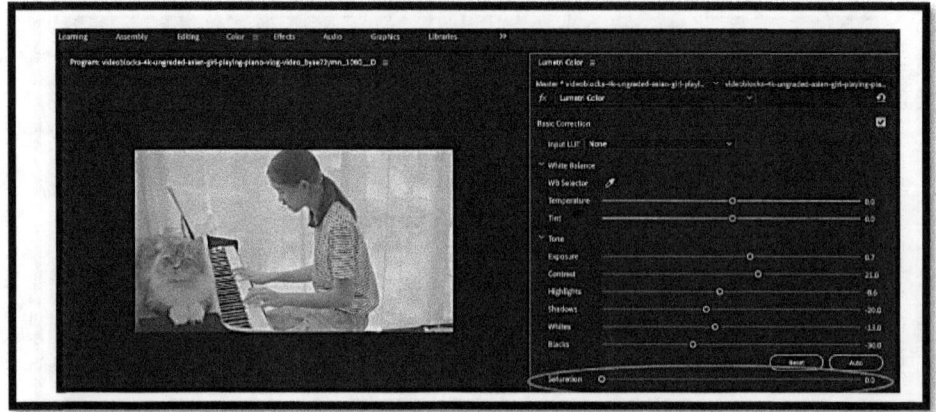

Increasing the Saturation to 200 will enhance the vividness of all colors, but be cautious, as this can also introduce noise and disrupt previous color adjustments. With a saturation level of 200, you might notice a green tint in the clip.

For this clip, set the Saturation to 137. This completes our basic color adjustment.

Color Grading Techniques

Color significantly influences our perception of a scene and the emotions it evokes. In the early days of filmmaking, directors meticulously adjusted color and lighting during shooting, using camera settings, natural light, and various techniques to achieve the desired look. Today, with the help of plugins and effects that enhance color and lighting in post-production, achieving outstanding results is easier than ever.

In this guide, you'll learn the fundamental steps for color grading in Adobe Premiere Pro, which offers some of the best tools for creating visually compelling content. You can adjust lighting, switch to black and white, and perform color grading using the color wheel and curve settings. Additionally, you'll discover innovative effects designed to deliver professional-level color grading results.

The Importance of Color Grading

In post-production filmmaking, adjusting color involves two key concepts: color grading and color correction. While both are related to color management, they serve different purposes.

Color correction is essential when filming in various locations with differing lighting conditions and reflections, especially when using multiple cameras that may produce color discrepancies. This process includes adjusting white balance, temperature, saturation, highlights, and shadows to ensure consistency throughout the film.

On the other hand, color grading is a creative tool that uses color palettes to evoke emotions or physical sensations, such as warmth or cold. This goes beyond mere correction. Adobe Premiere Pro enables you to achieve stunning effects that capture the essence of environments like deserts, tropical islands, or icy mountains, even if your camera struggles to fully convey the natural beauty of these settings during recording.

Preparing Your Color Grading Workflow

To start, you'll want to outline your sequence and master the basics of video editing, including cutting, trimming, and organizing your clips. You don't need to worry about revisiting clips for edits later in the post-production process using this approach.

Step 1: Create an Adjustment Layer

Begin by setting up an adjustment layer. This allows you to modify colors within the adjustment layer itself, leaving the original video footage unaffected.

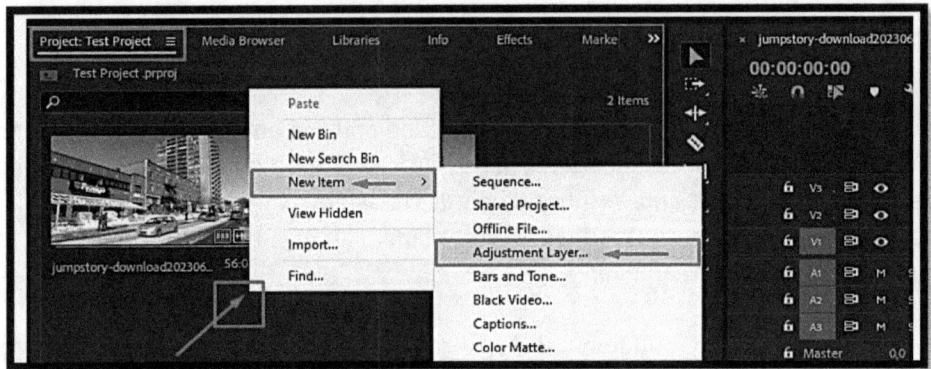

Right-click in the Project area of your workspace and select **New Item > Adjustment Layer** from the dropdown menu. You can maintain the original video settings, which Premiere Pro automatically applies from your sequence. Once you click OK, your new adjustment layer will appear in the Project panel. You can then drag it to the timeline above your sequence and adjust its length to match either the entire sequence or specific clips that require color correction.

Step 2: Color Workspace – The Lumetri Color Panel and Lumetri Scopes

In Adobe Premiere Pro, you can switch between different workspaces to edit video, audio, or color. To grade and correct colors, you'll be using the **Lumetri Color panel** within the Color workspace. To access workspaces, go to the **Window** menu. Select **Color** to transition from the

Editing Workspace to the Color Workspace. In this setup, the Lumetri Color panel will be on your right, the Lumetri Scopes panel on your left, and your video preview will be in the center.

The Lumetri Scopes panel displays waveform graphs that represent your video's color and brightness, serving as a reference while you make adjustments. You can right-click in this area to choose from several scopes:

- **Vectorscope**: Monitors saturation and hue in a circular format.
- **Histogram**: Provides a statistical breakdown of pixel density across color intensities, analyzing shadows, mid-tones, and highlights for tonal adjustments.
- **Parade scope**: Displays individual RGB waveforms, making color comparison and adjustments straightforward.
- **Waveform**: Shows RGB, IRE, luminance, and chrominance from your clips.

In the Lumetri Color panel, you'll find an array of color grading tools, including curves, color wheels, HSL, and vignettes, along with basic correction options. Familiarizing yourself with this panel is essential, as it will be central to your color correction process.

Step 3: Basic Color Correction

Before diving into advanced grading, start with basic correction. At this stage, you can import a look-up table (LUT) to quickly apply a specific style or adjust skin tones using presets. To do this, select the "Input LUT" option and locate the desired LUT on your computer. You can either use a LUT as a foundation and refine your colors further or start from scratch and explore the basic correction options.

Using **Auto Color** can help apply color correction across your entire sequence, giving you a baseline to work from. Afterward, fine-tune each setting to add a unique touch to your video. Here are some key adjustments you can make:

- **White Balance**: Select the whites in your clip to adjust hue and temperature.
- **Tone Tools**: Modify the overall atmosphere—exposure for brightness, contrast for light-to-dark range, and highlights/shadows for specific adjustments.
- **Whites and Black Sliders**: Control the thresholds for highlights and shadows, respectively.
- **Saturation**: Adjust the intensity of colors in your clip. Reducing saturation can create a more muted look.

To maintain consistent color throughout your project, remember to use the Lumetri Scopes as a reference.

Step 4: Advanced Color Grading Tools

In the **Creative Tab**, you can enhance your video's style by applying looks. Within the Effects menu, explore Lumetri Presets for film stocks and camera looks. The intensity slider allows you to adjust the strength of these effects as needed.

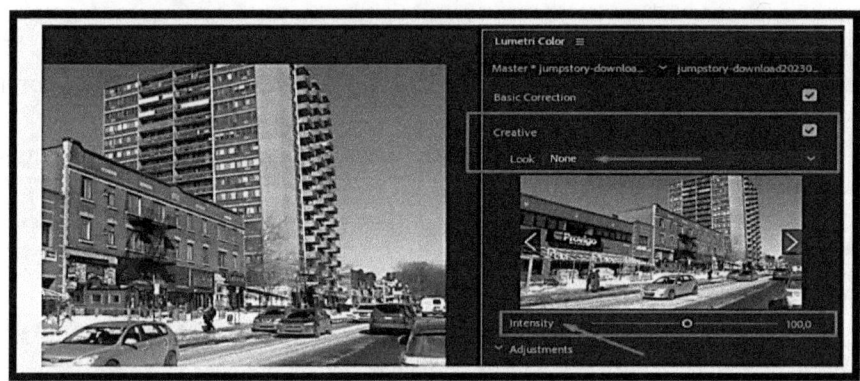

Under the **Creative** tab, you'll find additional modifications like **Faded Film**, which adds an antique look to your video, and **sharpen**, which enhances edge definition. You can experiment with the **Tint Wheels**, **Vibrance**, and **Saturation** to apply blue or green tints to your footage. These tools also allow you to create deeper shadows and enhance highlights for more visual impact.

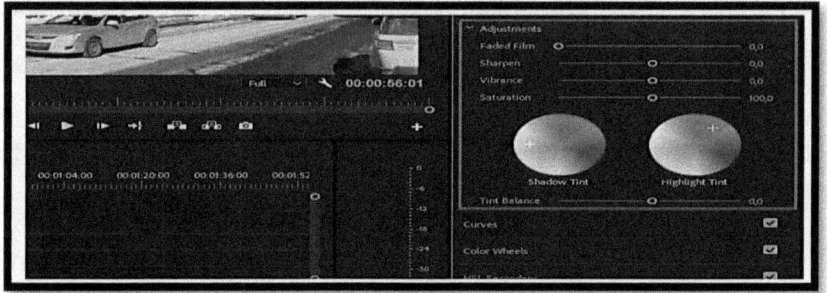

RGB and Hue Saturation Curves

Adobe Premiere Pro offers **RGB curves** and **Hue Saturation curves** for precise color adjustments that create more authentic tones. With RGB Curves, you can modify the luma and tonal ranges of your clips: add highlights by placing a point in the upper-right corner and dragging left, and add shadows using the lower-left corner. For finer color adjustments, use Hue Saturation curves:

- **Hue vs. Saturation**: Adjust the saturation of specific hues, like the sky or skin tones.

- **Hue vs. Hue**: Change the colors of elements in the image, such as plants or clothing.
- **Hue vs. Luma**: Modify the brightness of specific colors.
- **Luma vs. Saturation**: Adjust saturation based on the image's tonality.
- **Saturation vs. Saturation**: Selectively change saturation without affecting similar colors.

Using Color Wheels

The color wheels provide an intuitive way to adjust shadows, mid-tones, and highlights separately. For color matching, you can compare two shots from the same sequence by selecting a scene, clicking the Comparison View button, and using the playhead to choose a reference clip.

HSL Secondary

The **HSL Secondary** tab offers greater control over specific colors, enhancing the main color's prominence in storytelling. Typically applied after basic corrections, use the Key tab to select a color with the eyedropper. Enable **Color/Gray** and refine your selection with H, S, and L adjustments. The Refine tab helps reduce noise and smooth edges. Uncheck **Color/Gray** to modify the selected color using the Correction tab while previewing changes.

Add Vignettes

Vignettes can highlight the main subject by darkening the edges as they lead to a brighter center. You can adjust the center point, size, and the degree of dark or light fade to enhance focus on your scene's focal point.

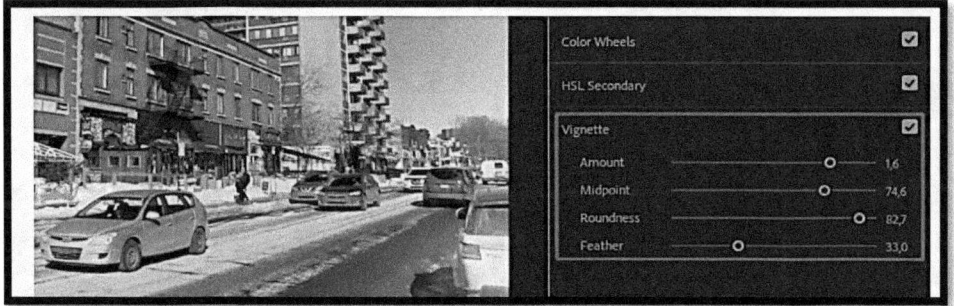

Step 5: Finalizing and Exporting Your Video

Take your time to color grade your video until you achieve the desired look. Once you're satisfied, the final step is to export your video for sharing online. Go to **File > Export > Media**. From there, rename your video, choose a save location, and click **Export** to complete the process.

CHAPTER 7

TITLES AND GRAPHICS

Creating Basic Titles
Creating Titles in Adobe Premiere Pro

When creating titles, you have two options for text presentation, which can be horizontal or vertical:

- **Point Text**: This creates a text box around your text as you type, keeping it on one line until you hit Return or Enter. Adjusting the box size in the Effect Controls panel will also change the Scale property.
- **Paragraph (Area) Text**: The size and shape of the text box are predetermined before typing. Changing the box size alters the displayed text amount but not the text size.

To create titles, use the Essential Graphics panel and the Type tool. In the Graphics workspace, select the Type tool and type your title in the Program Monitor. Use the Horizontal Center button in the Align and Transform tools to center your title.

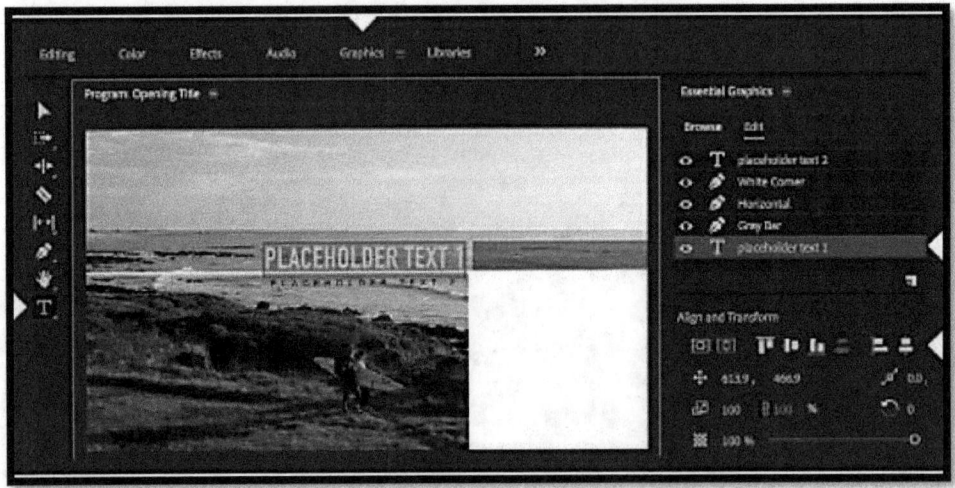

With the Selection tool active, click the gray square and drag its left edge across the screen. If you find that it obscures your title, you can reposition the layer in the Essential Graphics panel. To add a duplicate line, right-click on the layer and select **Duplicate**. To rename the new layer, right-click on it and choose **Rename**. You can adjust its **Position** or **Rotation** settings to move it as needed. Additionally, modify the **Opacity** setting to make the layer semi-transparent.

Zoom out in the Program Monitor and place the playhead at the point where you want the motion to end. Adjust the position, transparency, size, and other attributes of each element to achieve your desired look. Each time you make a change, click the corresponding icon to set a keyframe for that parameter.

Return to the beginning of the Timeline panel and adjust each element's position, transparency, size, and other settings until they're just right. Use the Pen, Rectangle, or Ellipse tools in the Program Monitor to create a shape, which will add a border on top of the existing shapes. To ensure the title appears only inside the new shape, select the **Mask with Shape** option. If you want the title to show only outside the shape, click **Invert**.

Play the sequence to see how the elements move within the mask, completing your opening title design over the video background. If you want to mask only certain layers, you can reposition the mask layer lower in the panel or adjust its settings to affect movement.

Create Title Graphics

You can add shapes, text, photos, and videos to layers, rearranging them using familiar tools from other Adobe Creative Cloud applications. After applying motion or effects, you can export your titles as Motion Graphics designs to share via Creative Cloud Libraries. Simply follow the steps outlined below.

Open the Graphics workspace

Select **Window > Workspaces > Graphics** from the main menu, or click on **Graphics** in the workspace bar at the top of the screen. Ensure your sequence is open in the Timeline panel.

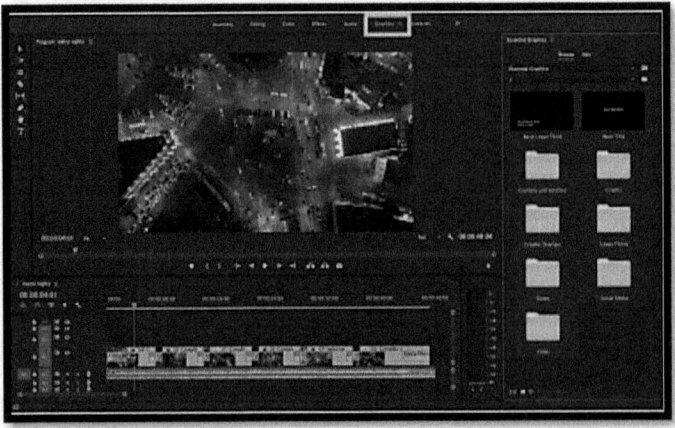

Choose a Motion Graphics template.

In the Essential Graphics panel, double-click to open it. Then, drag the **Film Presents Motion Graphics** template to a video track in the Timeline, where it will appear as a clip with a set duration. Adjust the clip's time and length to fit your film. Consider adding a transition to enhance its appearance in your sequence. Note that some themes may use Adobe Typekit fonts that might not be loaded on your system, so ensure you select the correct font in the **Resolve Fonts** box to avoid any issues.

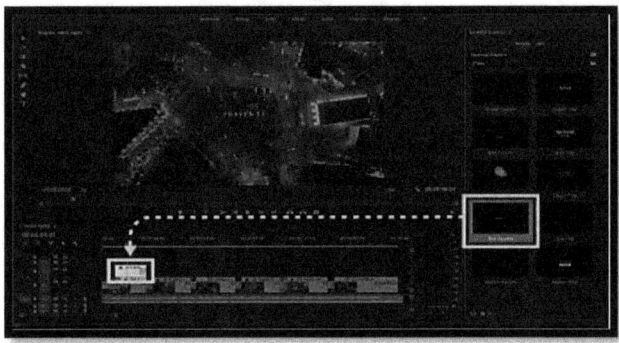

Make a copy of the motion graphic and use it throughout your project.

To add "thanks" consistently throughout your project, use **Alt-drag** (Windows) or **Option-drag** (macOS) the clip to create a copy and place it in a different spot in your sequence.

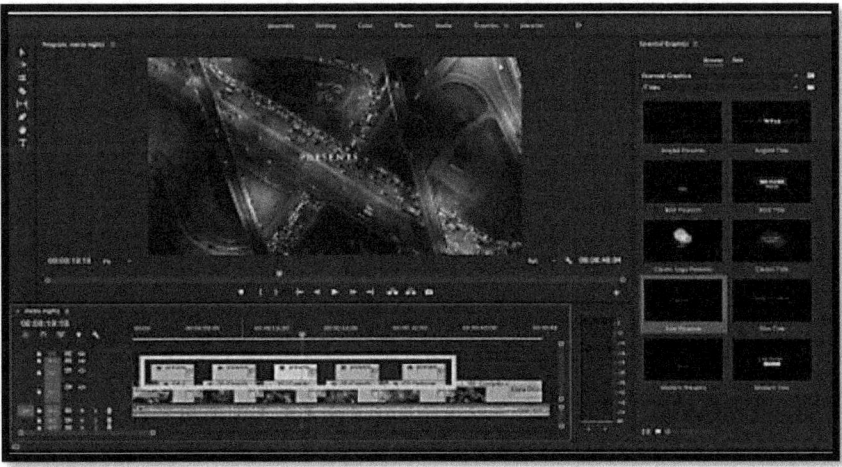

Change the text in the template

Insert a title clip into your sequence, and it will appear in the Program Monitor. Select the Type tool and click on the sample text to create a red outline around it. You can now modify the displayed text. Repeat this process for each of your titles.

Change the template's style

Select the Selection tool and choose a title clip from your sequence. Click on the text in the Program Monitor to create a blue outline around it. To modify the font, go to the Essential Graphics panel and select the Edit tab. In the Text area, you can adjust the font size by dragging the slider up or down. Feel free to customize other text features as needed.

Create or apply a master style

When you're satisfied with your text style, choose "Create Master Text Style" from the Master Styles drop-down menu. Name your new master style and click OK. With the master style created in the Essential Graphics panel, you can now apply it to other title clips in the Program Monitor. Ensure the text is enabled in the Program Monitor to view its properties in the Essential Graphics panel.

Add motion with keyframes

You can adjust the position and size of an effect on a title clip by animating the effect parameters with keyframes. Additionally, applying a cross-dissolve effect at the start or end of a clip can enhance your title's appearance. Premiere Pro offers models like Animated Diagonal Glow, and effects such as Fast Color Corrector (Blue Lens), Gaussian Blur, and Levels, each used in distinctive ways.

Export a Motion Graphics template

Insert a title clip into your sequence. Then, navigate to the main page and select Graphics > Export as Motion Graphics Template. You can rename the template and choose to save it in various locations, such as the Essential Graphics panel, your hard drive, or the Creative Cloud Library. Click OK to save. You can now access this saved template in other projects and share it with others via Creative Cloud Libraries. After saving, you can find the templates in the Essential Graphics panel or your Library under Motion Graphics Templates.

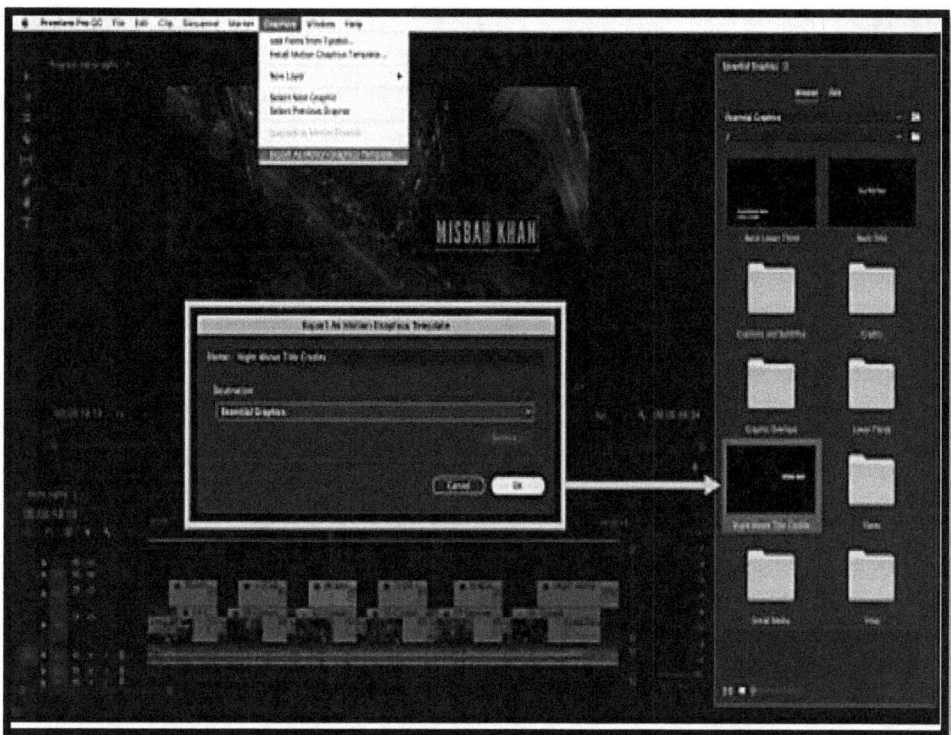

Working with Text Effects

Before diving into effects, familiarize yourself with text editing in Premiere Pro. Use the Type Tool to add text, and utilize the Essential Graphics panel to customize its appearance, including text, size, color, and orientation. Once your main text is set, you can enhance it with effects. Keyframing allows you to create smooth text movements by enabling the Animation setting for the text layer. This feature is great for introducing text, highlighting specific areas, or adding subtle motion to maintain viewer interest.

Adding Text

Step 1: Select the Type Tool (T)

- You can access the Type Tool by clicking on it, using the Essential Graphics panel, or by pressing Ctrl+T (Windows) or Cmd+T (Mac) simultaneously. This will open a new text box for adding text to your video clip. For easier text modifications, it's best to use the Essential Graphics panel.

Step 2: Create a Text Box

- Once the Type Tool is selected, click on the area of the video where you want to add your text to create a text box.

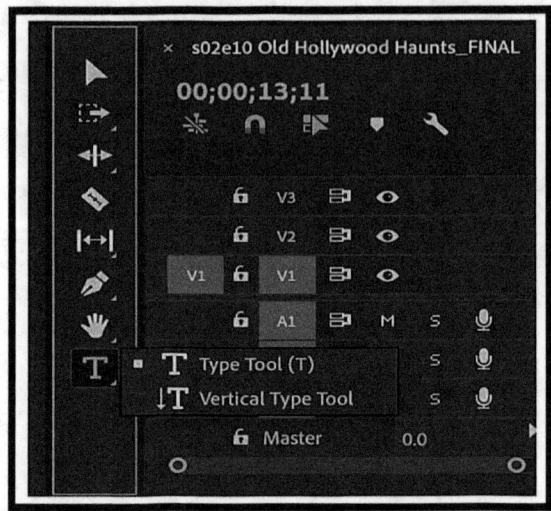

To add text using the Type Tool, locate it in the toolbar. If it's not visible, navigate to **Windows > Tools**, then select the Type Tool. Once selected, you'll see options for both the Type Tool and Vertical Type Tool. To start typing, simply click anywhere in the program panel (viewer). You can also resize the text box by dragging its edges with the Type Tool. Creating a defined text box is useful for containing larger amounts of text.

Step 3: Customize Text Shape, Size, and Color

- In the Essential Graphics panel, you'll find various options to adjust the style, size, and color of your text. Make sure to select the specific text layer you want to modify before making any changes, allowing you to tailor the text to fit your project's needs.

Step 4: Consider Adding a Custom Font

- Think about incorporating a custom font to enhance the visual appeal of your text. This can help your project stand out and align with your creative vision.

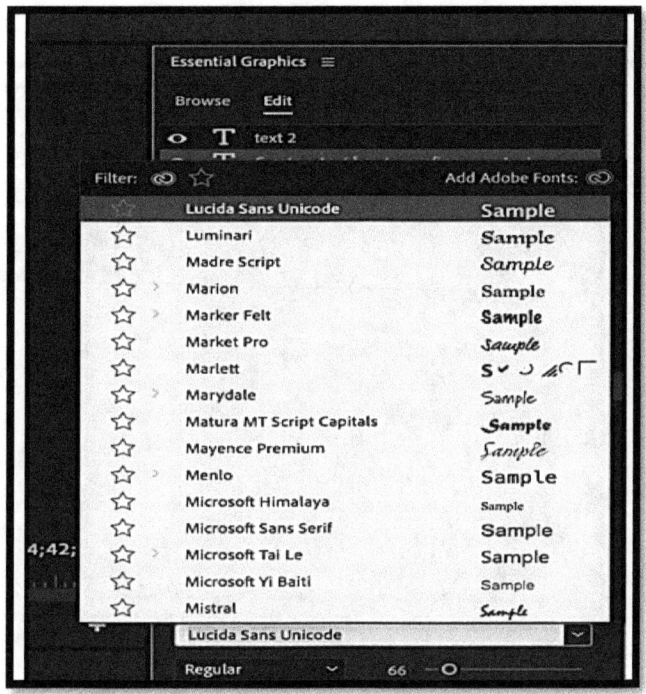

Adobe Premiere Pro includes various font styles, but you can easily add more. Click on the "Add Adobe Fonts" (formerly "Typekit") option in the drop-down font menu in the upper right corner. This will open Adobe Fonts in a new tab, where you can select and activate the fonts you want. Once activated, these fonts will appear in your font options within Premiere.

Additionally, you can access this feature by going to **Graphics > Add Fonts from Adobe Fonts**. If you want to use a font not available in Adobe Fonts, you'll need to download and install it on your computer first. If compatible, it will show up in the font menu. Note that the font may not appear immediately, so you might need to restart the application.

How to Create Text Templates

If you have text you want to reuse, you can save it as a motion graphics file.

1. Select the text and navigate to **Graphics > Export as Motion Graphics Template**. Then, name your file and save it.
2. To use this template later, go to **File > Import** and select the design you want to reuse.

Add a Logo Intro in Adobe Premiere Pro from a Template

Let's start by creating a reveal that highlights your brand using a template called Flat Logo Opener. Ready-made templates make it easy to incorporate your logo. After downloading the file, double-click it to open it in Adobe Premiere. Look for the section labeled "Your Logo." Double-click on this area to access and edit it.

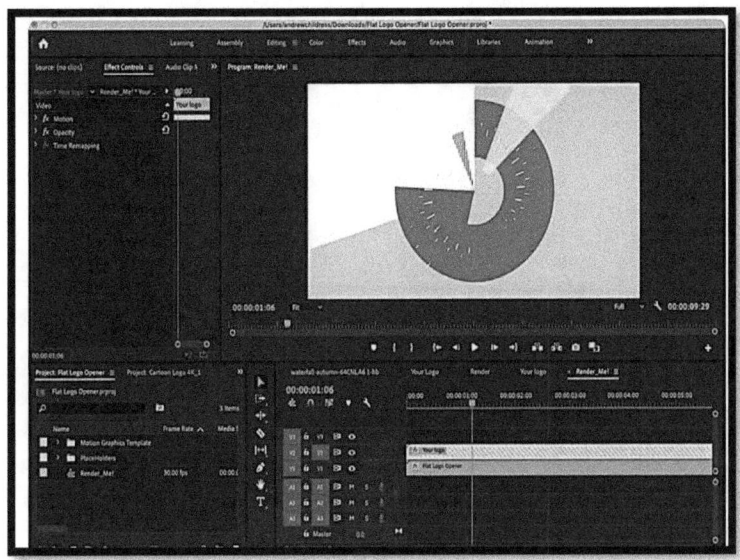

After accessing "Your Logo," add your image to the timeline by selecting your image file and dragging it into place. To align it with the template, grab the right handle and pull it to approximately the 10-second mark.

Tip: You may need to click on the logo and scale it down by dragging the corner to resize it appropriately.

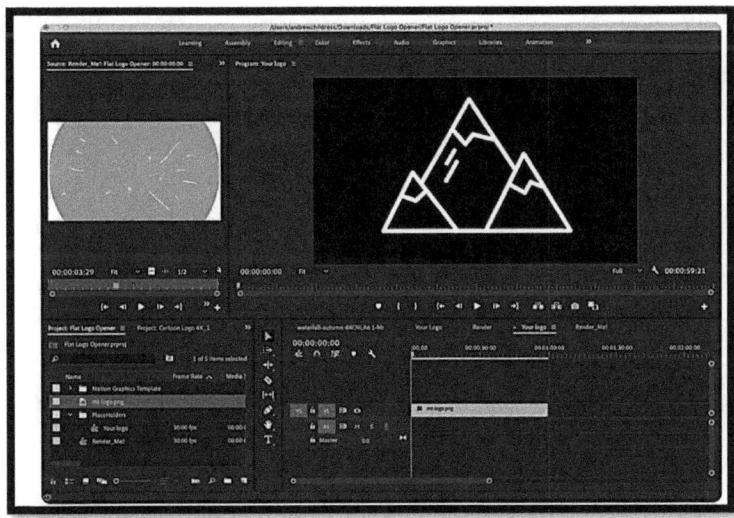

That's it! Now, return to the Render Me! layer and play the preview to see the updated animation featuring your logo.

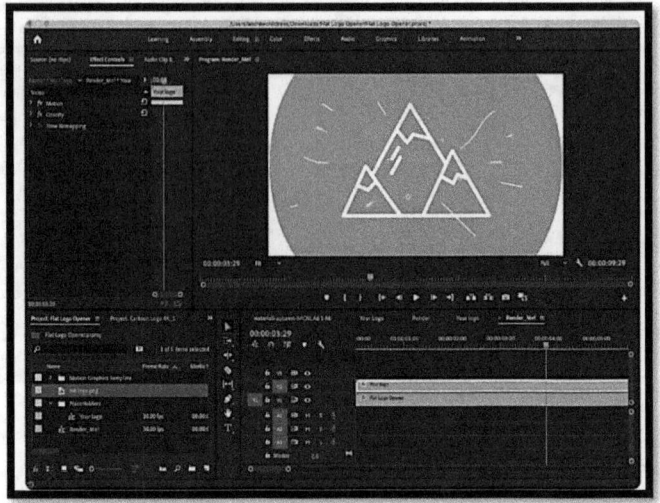

You can make additional adjustments by opening the layer labeled "Flat Logo Opener." At this stage, modifying shapes and colors requires a bit more skill, so if you're a beginner, it's best to choose a template that aligns with your style. Using a template is an efficient way to create a visually appealing introduction, saving you from the lengthy process of starting from scratch.

How to Add a Logo Overlay

The logo layer remains on top of your video throughout the duration, which is ideal for simply adding your logo. Ensure that your brand logo is placed above the video clip to cover the entire video. Then, adjust the logo's handle to the right on the timeline to set the duration as needed.

After placing your logo, you may find that it's too large or not positioned as you envisioned. To adjust this, locate the Effect Controls tab in the upper left corner of the Editing workspace. Here, you can modify the size and position of your logo to fit your design.

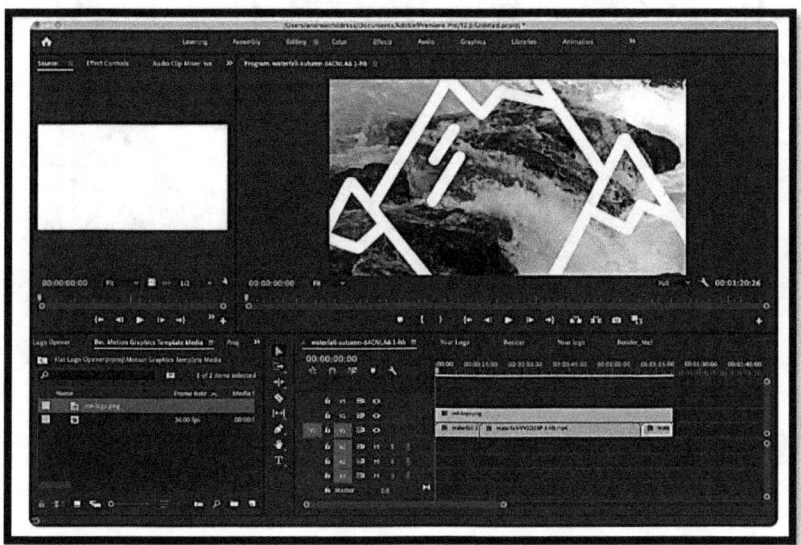

In the Effect Controls panel, begin by resizing your logo to the desired dimensions. Use the scale slider to adjust the size, moving it left to decrease or right to increase the size. Next, use the Position tools to reposition the logo. Click and drag the two numerical values that indicate the pixel coordinates to move the logo around on the screen.

Overview of Text-Based Editing

An easier approach to editing videos is through text-based editing, which utilizes transcriptions of your source media to facilitate the initial edit, or "rough cut." Here are the steps for effective text-based editing:

1. Transcribe Source Media

- Begin by transcribing your source footage, converting spoken dialogue into text.
- Once the transcription is complete, the text will appear in the Transcript box of your editing program.

2. Add Clips

- Use the text in the Transcript box to locate specific content in your source media.
- Identify segments in the transcripts that correspond to the visuals you want to include in your project.
- Select these segments to add the relevant video clips to the Timeline, ensuring the spoken text aligns with the appropriate visuals.

3. Change a Sequence

- In your editing program, switch to the sequence text view. This mode allows you to assemble a rough cut or initial sequence from the recorded material.
- Arrange the video clips in order and make adjustments based on the text-based structure you created, helping to establish a coherent flow.
- After completing the rough cut, transition to regular video editing tools to refine your work further, adjusting transitions, timing, effects, and more.

Text-based editing streamlines the initial phase of video editing by providing a clear guide through transcription. By leveraging this text as a visual reference, editors can efficiently assemble a rough sequence, creating a solid foundation for further enhancements with traditional editing tools.

How to transcribe source media
1. Launch Premiere Pro and Create a New Project

- Open Premiere Pro and start a new project to organize and work with your video footage.

2. Import Media with Automatic Transcription

- When importing your media files, make sure to enable the "Automatic transcription" feature in the Import settings. This allows Premiere Pro to transcribe the audio content of your files automatically.

3. Customize Transcription Settings

- During the import process, you'll have options to customize your transcription settings. You can select your preferred language for the transcription, choose speaker labeling options if needed, and adjust transcription preferences, including accuracy and timing based on your requirements.

4. Review Transcripts in the Text-Based Editing Workspace

- After the transcription is complete and your transcripts are ready, navigate to the Text-Based Editing workspace in Premiere Pro. Here, you can review and access the transcribed text from your source footage.
- The Text-Based Editing workspace is designed for efficient work with transcribed text, allowing you to analyze, select, and utilize the transcriptions to assemble your video edit.

How to transcribe individual source files
1. Open Text-Based Editing Workspace

- Launch Premiere Pro and access the Text-Based Editing workspace within the software.

2. Transcribe Specific Clips

- In the Project panel, locate and double-click the specific video clips you want to transcribe.

3. Access the Text Panel and Start Transcription

- Within the selected clip, navigate to the Text panel and click the blue "Transcribe" button.

4. Configure Transcription Settings

- A dialogue box will open where you can select your preferred language for transcription and decide whether to separate speakers if applicable to your content.

5. Transcription Process and Transcript Window

- Premiere Pro will start the transcription process for the selected clips based on your settings. Once complete, the spoken content will appear in the Transcript window of the Text-Based Editing workspace.

Bottom of Form
How to edit transcripts

To correct the spelling of uncommon words or names, utilize the built-in spell checker or the search and replace tool. If your source file includes multiple speakers, select the Speakers option to add their names to the text for better clarity.

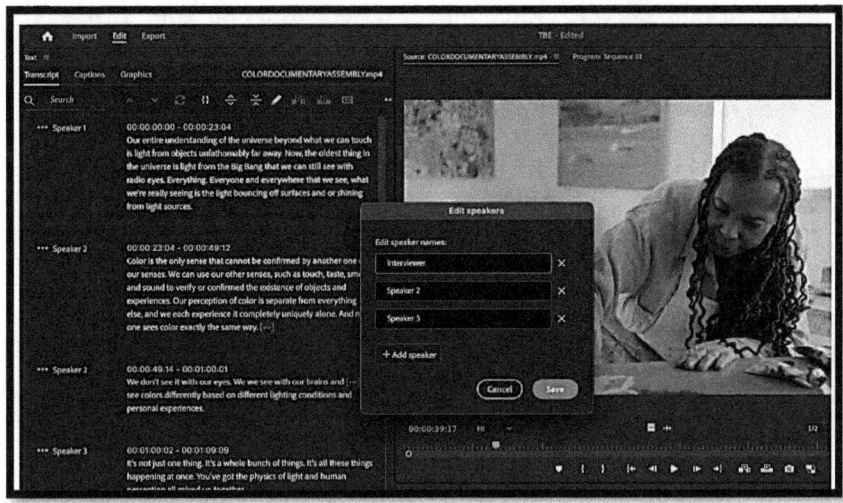

How to add clips to the Timeline

Text-based editing enables you to perform three-point edits to create a sequence on the Timeline:

- In the Transcript box, read through the text or search for the sections you wish to use.
- Highlight the desired text and press the "Insert" button to add it to the main sequence.
- Continue adding clips from the source media to the Timeline until you have included all the clips you want to use.

How to change a sequence

When you add clips to the Timeline, Premiere Pro generates a new sequence transcript, allowing you to refine your rough cut in this updated file.

1. Switch to Sequence Transcript

- In Premiere Pro, navigate to the Timeline panel to access the sequence transcript, which displays your video sequence in text form.

2. Move Clips by Selecting Text

- In the sequence transcript, select the text segments that correspond to the clips you want to reposition.

- Use Ctrl+C (Windows) or Command+C (Mac) to copy and Ctrl+V (Windows) or Command+V (Mac) to paste the clips. Changes in the text will immediately reflect on the Timeline.

3. Remove Clips Using Text Editing

- To delete clips from the sequence, simply select and delete the relevant text in the sequence transcript.
- Premiere Pro will apply a Ripple Edit, automatically adjusting the timeline to fill any gaps left by the removed clips.

4. Transition to Video Editing Tools

- Once you finish your rough cut using the sequence transcript, switch to the traditional video editing tools in Premiere Pro.
- Use these tools to refine your edit further by trimming, adjusting pacing, performing color grading, enhancing audio, and adding titles or graphics to your video.

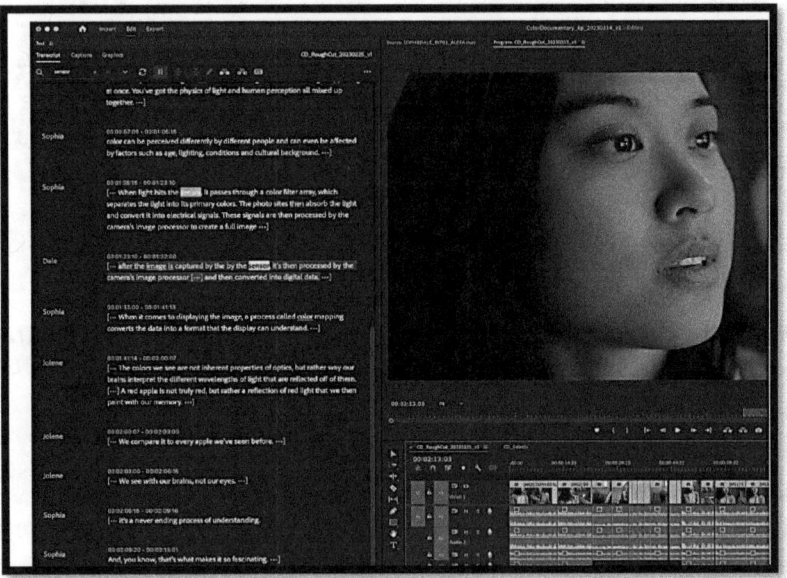

Filler Word Detection with bulk delete

Text-Based Editing allows you to easily identify and remove filler words like "uh" and "umm" from your recordings all at once.

1. Click on the Icon in the Transcript List

- Locate and click the icon in the list of transcripts to access the relevant options.

2. Select Text, Filler Words, or Pauses

- Choose the options for Text, Filler Words, or Pauses to delete multiple instances at once.

3. Remove Instances

- After selecting, you can opt to remove a single instance or all instances of the searched text, spaces, or breaks.

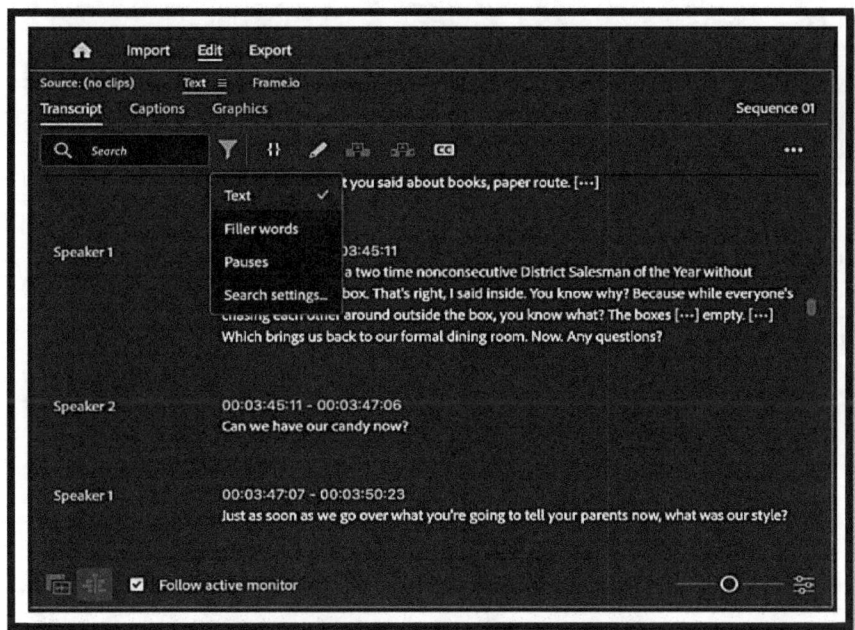

By clicking on the three dots in the upper right corner of the Text panel and selecting **Transcript View Options**, you can adjust the minimum duration that Premiere Pro will wait to recognize a pause or stop in speech.

How to Use Your Logo as a Watermark

A variation of a logo overlay is a watermark, which serves as a more prominent yet faded logo style. Use a watermark to protect your brand's intellectual property or for draft versions. To create a watermark, select your image layer and locate the Opacity dropdown in the Effect Controls panel. Lower the opacity to make the logo less opaque. Watermarks should be clearly visible without being intrusive.

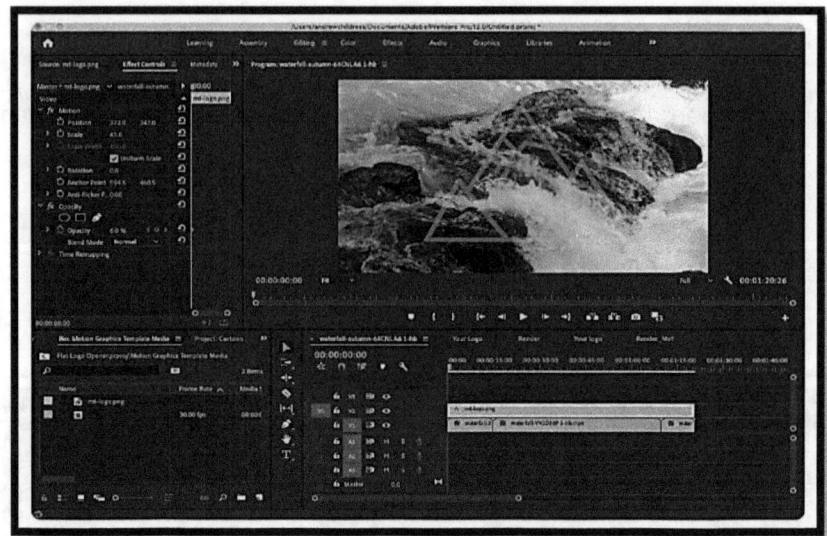

Label patches usually cover the entire area. You can modify the Scale and Position options to enlarge the logo and adjust its placement as needed.

Animating Text and Graphics

Start by selecting Window > Essential Graphics from the menu. Use the Text Tool (T) to create your title. Once you've written it, you'll see a new text layer in the panel under the Edit tab. Select this Text layer to access all its properties and tools.

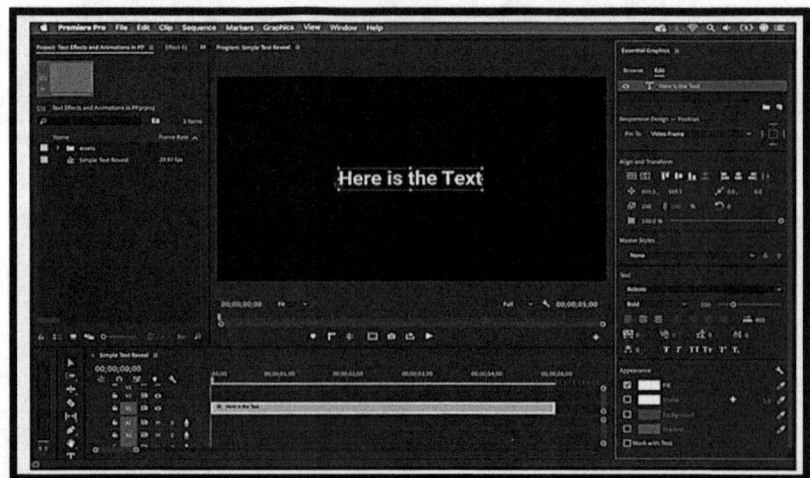

I will use the tools in the Align and Transform section to center my text. In the Text area, I can change the font and style. By going to the Appearance menu, I can modify the color, add a responsive backdrop, drop a shadow, and apply multiple strokes. Next, I'll create two new rectangle layers for the background objects using the "New Layer" button at the top of the panel. I'll make these slightly larger since I'll be applying a mask to crop them. I plan to set one shape to white and the other to red by using the Fill tool in the Appearance section. Finally, I will rearrange the layers, placing the white background at the bottom, the red background above it, and the text at the top.

The Essential Graphics panel now includes masking as a recent feature. To create a mask, I'll first add a new rectangular shape layer. After adjusting its size and position, I'll go to the Appearance area and select the Mask with Shape option. Since the mask will apply to any layers behind it, I'll arrange my layers accordingly. When working on complex projects, I can also organize the layers for better clarity.

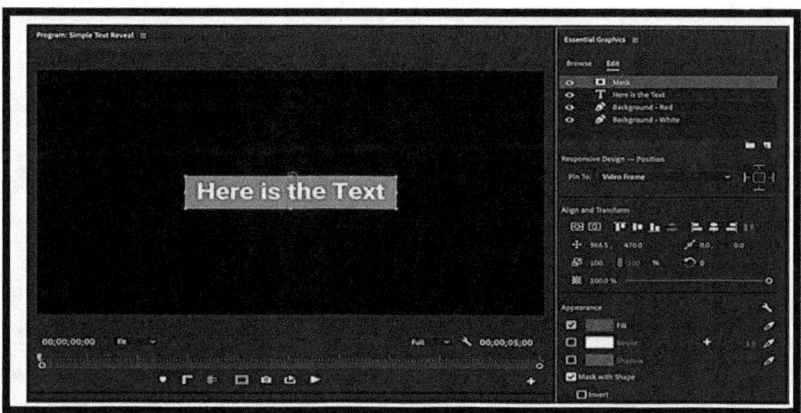

Now that I've completed all the necessary assets, I'm ready to animate the title. The text and backgrounds will enter using a simple Y Position change. I want the first two seconds of the animation to unfold as follows: the white background appears first, followed by the red background, and finally the text element.

To start animating the text layer, I'll move the Playhead to the two-second mark, where I want the animation to finish. Then, I'll select the Text layer and click the Position symbol in the Align and Transform section. This action will add a keyframe at the current time, activating animation for that attribute. The icon will turn blue, indicating that animation is enabled.

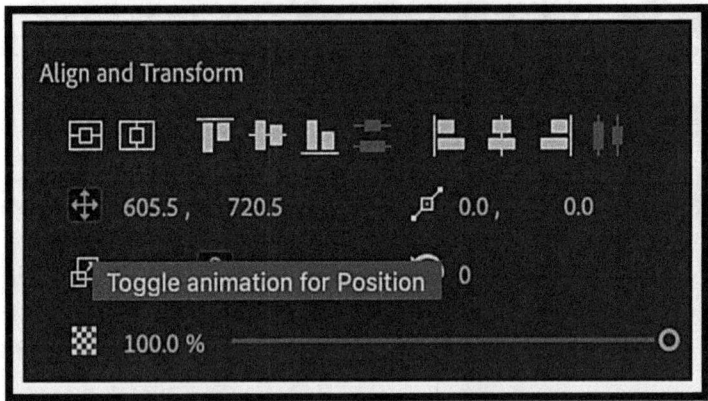

Next, I'll move the Playhead to the one-second mark and adjust the Y property to set the text to its starting position. Each time I modify this attribute, a keyframe will be automatically added.

For the next step, I'll animate both background rectangles using the same process, but I'll offset the timing for each object to create a staggered entrance effect.

Using the Effect Controls tab, I can make precise adjustments to each keyframe to fine-tune the timing of the animation. I'll go to **Window > Effect Controls** to review the keyframes generated by my animation. This panel allows me to see all the effects I've modified in the Essential Graphics panel. When I select a graphic layer in the Essential Graphics panel, it will automatically highlight and reflect in the Effect Controls panel, and the same happens in reverse.

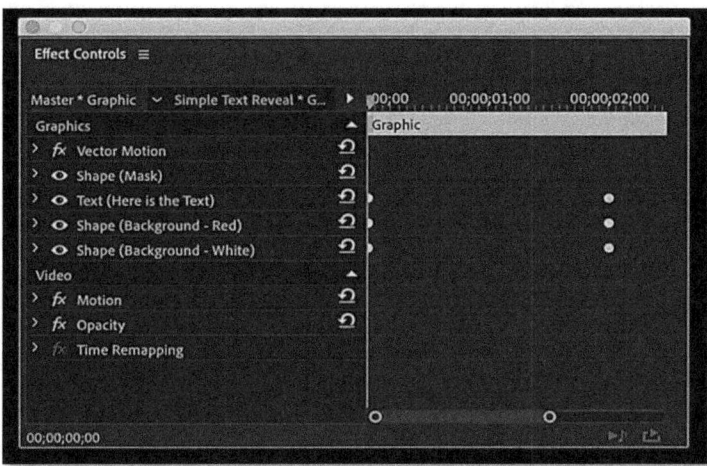

I will apply an ease-out to all the initial keyframes and an ease-in to the end keyframes to ensure smooth animations for each element. Easing can be accessed by right-clicking (or control-clicking) on a keyframe, found under **Temporal Interpolation**.

To further refine the timing of each animation, I can adjust the Speed Curve by selecting the dropdown arrow next to the Position property. From there, I can manipulate each keyframe using a Bézier handle for precise control over the animation's speed.

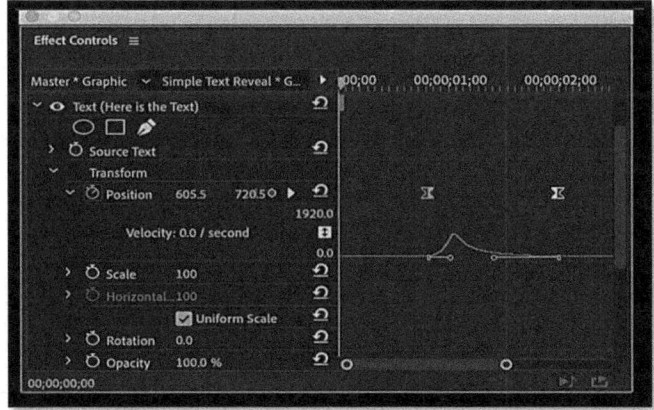

Understanding the Fundamentals of Typography

Understanding how to effectively use type is crucial for creating quality video graphics. Since text often overlays moving images, readability becomes a challenge. It's essential to balance readability with aesthetics, ensuring you convey as much information as possible without creating a cluttered look. Combining functionality with a refined style enhances the professional appearance of your designs. Following typeface norms can also help create text that is easy to read, even against varied and colorful video backgrounds. Strive for clarity while ensuring enough information is displayed, as the amount of text can directly impact readability, especially in motion.

Choosing a Font

Choosing the right font for video editing can be challenging given the wide variety available. To simplify your selection process, consider using a triage approach and evaluate the following factors:

- **Readability**: Is the text legible at the chosen size? Can you easily recognize all the characters? After a quick glance, can you recall key elements of the text?
- **Style**: If you had to describe the font with adjectives, what would they be? Does it effectively convey the intended mood? Choosing the right typeface is as important to your design as selecting the right outfit or hairstyle.
- **Flexibility**: How well does the font integrate with others? Does it offer various weights—such as bold, italic, and semi-bold—that help emphasize important information? Can you establish a hierarchy, such as distinguishing between a speaker's name and title in lower-third graphics?
- **Language Compatibility**: Does the font include all the necessary characters? Some fonts have limited character sets, which could restrict your text.

Answering these questions will guide you toward creating visually appealing titles. Experimentation is key; you may need to try several options to find the best fit. For easy comparisons, modify an existing title or duplicate it for customization. When overlaying text on colorful backgrounds, achieving the right contrast for legibility can be tricky. In such cases, consider adding a stroke or shadow to enhance visibility.

Selecting a Color

Choosing the right colors for a design can be surprisingly challenging, especially given the vast array of combinations available. Only a few colors work well for text while ensuring visibility, which complicates matters further for broadcast television or when adhering to specific branding guidelines. Text placed over busy, dynamic backgrounds often requires careful color adjustments. While black and white are common choices, they may feel conservative; lighter or darker shades with bold, colorful strokes can also be effective. It's crucial that the chosen color stands out against the background, so regularly assess your options based on brand requirements and maintain a consistent color palette throughout your sequence.

Adjusting the kerning

Adjusting the space between letters in a title, known as kerning, is a common practice to enhance the text's appearance and ensure it aligns with the background design. As font size increases, the need for manual adjustments becomes more crucial, making any kerning issues more noticeable. The goal is to create a visual flow that improves both the aesthetics and readability of your content. Professional materials like magazines and posters can provide valuable insights into effective kerning techniques. By adjusting the spacing letter by letter, you can achieve a more visually appealing and cohesive design.

Setting the tracking

Another important text characteristic is tracking, which operates similarly to kerning but applies to larger groups of letters. Tracking controls the overall spacing between characters across a selection, allowing you to either tighten or loosen the spacing.

Here are some common uses for tracking adjustments:

- **Tighter Tracking**: If a line of text is too long (like a lengthy title in a lower third), tightening the tracking allows you to fit more content into the same space without altering the font size.
- **Looser Tracking**: Increasing the spacing can enhance readability, especially with complex fonts or all caps. This technique is often used for large headlines or when text is incorporated into design elements and motion graphics.

You can adjust the tracking for any layer directly in the Text section of the Essential Graphics panel.

Setting the alignment

When aligning text for video, flexibility is key; there are no strict rules. Lower-third titles are often left or right aligned, while centered text is common in rolling titles. The Essential Graphics panel includes alignment buttons to position your text to the left, center, or right based on its anchor point.

If you want to create a text box, use the Type tool to drag and form one, allowing you to fill the width with justification options. Additionally, you can vertically align text within a box to the top, middle, or bottom. Don't hesitate to experiment with different alignments and use the Undo option as needed to refine your design.

CHAPTER 8
MAKING USE OF ESSENTIAL EDITING COMMANDS

Adobe Premiere Pro offers conventional editing features similar to other nonlinear editing systems, with two main editing methods:

1. **Overwrite Edit**: This default method replaces existing content in the timeline with frames from the selected clip, either filling gaps or replacing what's already there. It's straightforward for replacing video.
2. **Insert Edit**: This method shifts existing content to the right to make space for the new clip, preserving the sequence's continuity.

While there are specialized editing techniques like replace edits, understanding these basic methods is crucial for effective footage management and sequence arrangement in your projects. Mastering overwrite and insert edits equips editors to handle most common editing tasks efficiently.

Performing an overwrite edit

Here's a streamlined guide to performing an overwrite edit in Adobe Premiere Pro:

1. **Selecting the Source Footage**: Open your desired clip (e.g., "HS Suit") in the Source Monitor.
2. **Preparing the Timeline Panel**: Position the playhead in the Timeline at the desired start point (e.g., 00:00:04:00).
3. **Changing the Position of the Playhead**: You can either manually enter the timecode in the Source Monitor or use keyboard shortcuts for precision, especially useful when working with camera logs.
4. **Understanding Playhead and Editing Behavior**: The playhead location dictates where new clips are inserted unless In or Out points have been set. When dragging a clip, established In or Out points take priority.
5. **Managing Audio Tracks**: To avoid unwanted audio from the new clip, deactivate the audio track by clicking the A1 source track selection to gray it out.
6. **Configuring Track Headers**: Ensure track headers in the Timeline are correctly set up. Activate or deactivate tracks as needed by clicking the track targeting buttons, focusing on the Source A1 and V1 markers.
7. **Performing the Overwrite Edit**: Click the Overwrite button in the Source Monitor to add the clip to the Video 1 track in your sequence.

8. **Playing the Edited Sequence**: Move the playhead to the start of the Timeline and click the Play button or hit the spacebar to review your edit.

Note: Dragging a clip into a sequence automatically performs an overwrite edit. Holding Command (macOS) or Ctrl (Windows) while dragging allows for an insert edit. Familiarizing yourself with these steps will enhance your editing efficiency and clip management in Premiere Pro.

Performing an insert edit

Here's a concise guide to performing an insert edit in Adobe Premiere Pro:

Insert Editing Overview

Insert editing allows you to add a new clip into the timeline at a specific point, shifting existing clips forward without altering their duration. However, be cautious of potential sync issues between audio and video tracks.

Methods to Perform Insert Edits

1. **Dragging Clips into the Timeline**:
   - Create a sequence with your media.
   - Select a clip from the Source Monitor or Project Panel.
   - Hold down the Control (or Command) key, then drag the clip to the desired location in the Timeline.
   - Release the mouse button to execute the insert, moving subsequent clips forward on the same track and any unlocked tracks.
2. **Using Insert Button Controls**:
   - Create a sequence from your media.
   - Select another clip in the Source Monitor, adjusting the In and Out points as needed.
   - Position the playhead at the intersection point between the clips in the Timeline.
   - Click the Insert button in the Source Monitor's Tools panel to insert the clip, extending the timeline's duration.

Visual Indicator

During the insert operation, the cursor changes to an insert pointer, signaling the action. This process visibly increases the timeline's overall length with the added clip.

By mastering insert edits, you can effectively manage your sequences and enhance your editing workflow in Premiere Pro.

Performing Storyboard – Style Editing

Creating a storyboard is essential for visualizing a film's narrative and ensuring cohesive communication among the production team. Here's a breakdown of the storyboard process:

Storyboarding Overview

- **Definition**: Storyboards are visual representations of a screenplay, often resembling comic strips but including technical details like camera angles, action sequences, dialogue, and sound effects.
- **Purpose**: They help filmmakers convey their vision to the entire crew, facilitating better understanding and coordination.

Storyboard Creation

1. **Drawings**: Create sketches to represent key scenes, focusing on intended camera movements and character actions.
2. **Technical Information**: Include annotations for camera angles, dialogue lines, and sound cues to provide context.
3. **Using Video Thumbnails**: You can utilize video clip thumbnails stored in a bin to visually represent scenes in the storyboard.

Storyboard Edit

- **Rapid Assembly**: By selecting in and out points of clips and arranging them in sequence, you can quickly construct a storyboard edit.
- **Efficiency**: This method allows for a fast assembly of a scene's basic structure, providing a clear roadmap for the production process.

Utilizing storyboards effectively can streamline the filmmaking process and enhance collaboration across the team.

Let's start by making a Storyboard Edit.

Before starting the storyboard editing process in Premiere Pro, it's important to organize your clips effectively. Here's a concise guide to help you set up your workspace:

Organizing Clips for Storyboarding

1. **Create Bins**:
   o Separate clips needed for each scene into designated bins or folders. This will help streamline your editing process.
2. **Open Bins**:
   o Double-click on the bin to open it in its own window. This allows for better visibility and access to your clips.
3. **Workspace Setup**:
   o Expand the bin window to utilize the available workspace efficiently.
4. **Thumbnail View**:
   o Ensure the Thumbnail view is activated for easier visual reference of your clips. You can adjust the icon size to suit your preferences.
5. **User Order Sorting**:
   o In the sort icons' drop-down menu, select the 'User Order' option. This allows you to manually arrange the clips as needed, rather than sorting them alphabetically by name.

Advantages of this Setup

- **Visual Responsiveness**: Premiere's organized interface allows for easier manipulation of clips compared to free-floating icons in other editing software, enabling you to quickly create a storyboard that reflects your vision.
- **Efficient Editing**: Having clips organized and easily accessible facilitates a smoother editing process, helping you focus on the creative aspects of your project.

By taking the time to properly organize your clips, you'll set yourself up for a more efficient and enjoyable editing experience.

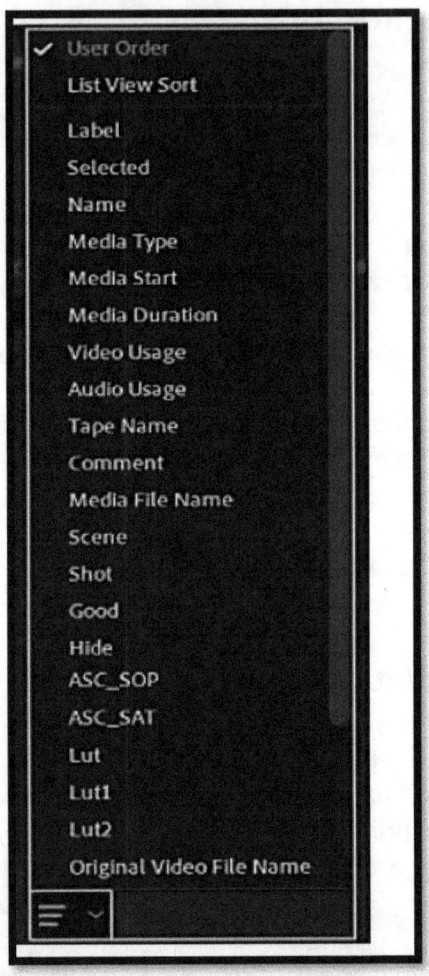

Here's a streamlined guide to organizing and editing your storyboard in Adobe Premiere Pro:

Organizing and Editing Your Storyboard

1. **Arrange Clips:**

o   Drag and drop clips into the desired sequence within your bin. Click and hold on a clip, then move it to the preferred location. Release to drop it in place; a hand icon and white bars will indicate where it will be positioned.

2. **Set In and Out Points**:
   o   For each clip, specify the in-point by pressing **I** and the out-point by pressing **O**. This will help you define the exact portion of each clip to use in your sequence.

3. **Navigating Clips**:
   o   Use the following keyboard shortcuts to control playback:
       - **L**: Play forward
       - **K**: Pause
       - **J**: Play backward
   o   You can also use the spacebar to start and stop playback.

4. **Checking Selections**:
   o   Click on a clip in the bin to reveal a blue bar with a mini playhead. This indicates which part of the clip is currently selected, based on your set In and Out points.

5. **Select All Clips**:
   o   To select all clips in the bin, use the shortcut **CMD+A** (or **Ctrl+A** on Windows).

6. **Create a Sequence**:
   o   Right-click on one of the selected clips and choose **New Sequence from Clip** from the context menu. This action will create a new sequence based on the selected clips.

By following these steps, you can effectively organize your clips and create a coherent storyboard that simplifies the editing process. This setup will help you visualize and arrange your scenes efficiently!

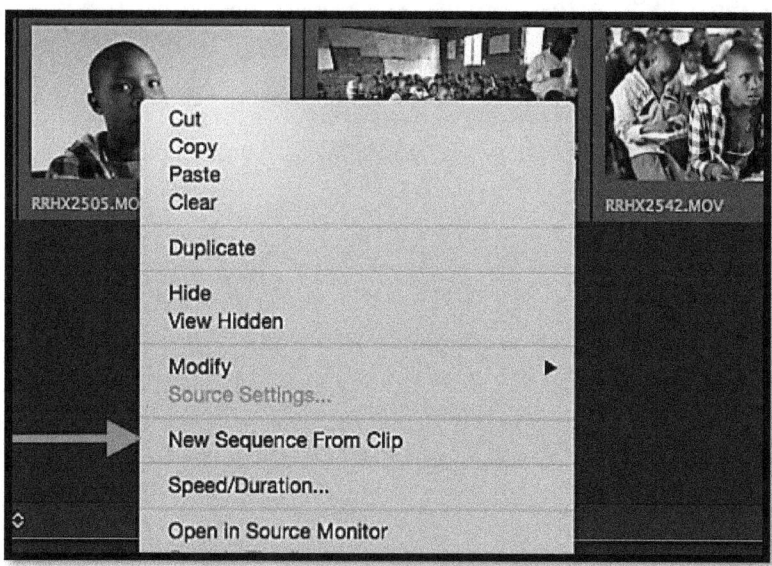

This process will generate a new timeline that mirrors the format and frame rate of your selected clip, along with an edit of your clips arranged in your chosen order. By utilizing this method, you can quickly organize your clips and produce a basic first edit in no time. This approach is especially useful for visualizing the flow of your story and ensuring that all elements are in place before diving deeper into detailed editing.

Three-Point Editing

A three-point edit is a precise technique that allows editors to specify three marks in both the Timeline (or Program Monitor) and the Source Monitor—two In points and one Out point, or vice versa. Adobe Premiere Pro automatically manages the fourth point, making the editing process more efficient.

Steps for a Three-Point Edit:

1. **Open the Sequence**: Start by selecting and opening the sequence you want to edit.
2. **Load the Clip**: In the Source Monitor, load the clip you want to use and identify the section you plan to use.
3. **Select Tracks**: Click on the headers of the tracks in the Timeline where you want the insert or overwrite to occur.
4. **Drag Source Clip Track Indications**: Drag the source clip track indicators to the appropriate track headers for the overwrite.
5. **Set In and Out Points**: Define the In and Out points in either the Source or Program Monitors. You can choose any combination of three marks (two In points and one Out, or two Out points and one In).
6. **Execute the Edit**: Use the buttons in the Source Monitor to perform the insert or overwrite.

This method is especially useful for syncing audio and video, as well as for layering clips effectively. By following these steps, you can ensure that your edits are both precise and efficient.

CHAPTER 9
ADDING TRANSITIONS

Transitions are essential narrative tools in video editing, providing continuity and helping viewers follow the story. They signify changes in location, time, or character perspective, enhancing the audience's understanding of the narrative flow. Techniques like fades, dissolves, and crossfades help signal these shifts, such as moving from indoor to outdoor scenes or indicating the passage of time.

In Adobe Premiere Pro, editors can apply transitions to elevate the professionalism of their projects. While simple cuts are effective, well-placed transitions can reinforce emotional themes and narrative elements. Observing how transitions are utilized in your favorite films and shows can offer valuable insights. By analyzing these techniques, editors can learn to strategically incorporate transitions, enhancing their storytelling and evoking specific audience emotions.

What are Transition Effects?

Adobe Premiere Pro offers a wide range of special effects and preset animations designed to create smooth integrations between clips in a sequence. These tools enable visually seamless transitions between scenes, including options like traditional dissolves, page wipes, and color dips. Transitions serve multiple purposes, such as emphasizing key narrative shifts and ensuring a cohesive flow throughout the video. Essentially, a transition is a visual effect that connects two pieces of content, enhancing their dynamism.

The program features an extensive selection of effects, from simple Cross Dissolve transitions to more intricate ones like glitches and whips. Utilizing these basic transitions can significantly elevate your project's visual appeal, transforming the incorporation of transitions into an art form that enhances storytelling.

Applying transitions is straightforward: simply drag the desired effect from the Effects panel between two clips on the timeline. The impact of a transition depends on various factors, including its placement, duration, and the context in which it's used—such as direction, motion, and starting/ending points. To achieve the desired effect, it's essential to fine-tune these variables. While some transition parameters can be adjusted directly in the Timeline panel, using the Effect Controls panel is often more effective for precise adjustments. Here, editors can select a transition within the sequence and modify its parameters for exact control over its appearance and behavior.

Importance of a Clip Handle

In Adobe Premiere Pro, the extra content found before and after a clip's in-point and out-point is known as clip handles. These handles are crucial for modifying transitions within a clip. When a transition is applied, it appears as a colored overlay on the timeline, indicating its position. Importantly, the transition does not cut or shorten the clip to accommodate the overlapping information; instead, it utilizes the material that extends beyond the in and out points of the clip—this extra content is what we refer to as clip handles.

Having adequate clip handles is essential for creating smooth transitions between two clips. It's important to ensure that there is enough handle after the first clip and before the second clip for a seamless effect. However, if the source material lacks sufficient frames, clip handles may not be present, meaning there's no extra video content to facilitate the transition. In such cases, Premiere Pro will notify users about insufficient material and the potential for repeated frames within the transition. To address this, Premiere Pro can automatically generate clip handles by duplicating the end frames, effectively creating a freeze-frame to fill the gap. In the Timeline panel, this situation is indicated by diagonal warning bars above the transition.

To ensure smooth transitions without interruptions or repeated footage, editors must verify that their source material includes an adequate amount of clip handles.

Using a Transition to Connect Two Clips

To start, adjust your movie in the timeline until you're satisfied with the final result. Next, click on the Effects tab at the top of the screen to switch views. In the Effects Panel, you'll find a folder labeled Video Transitions, which contains both the pre-installed transitions from Adobe Premiere and any you've added yourself. Locate the point on the timeline where the two clips you want to transition between meet, and select your desired transition from the Effects Panel. After selecting it, simply drag the transition to the space between the two clips. If your clip handles are long enough, the transition will be applied successfully.

You can easily adjust the duration of the transition by dragging it along the timeline. This action can lengthen the transition in either direction, as long as you have sufficient clip handles.

Adding Video Transition Effects

In Adobe Premiere Pro, Cross Dissolve is the default transition for video tracks, while Constant Power Crossfade serves as the default for audio tracks. Both transitions can be easily identified in the Effects panel by their blue underlined symbols. If you frequently use a different transition and want to set it as your default, you can easily do so. This change will apply to all future projects but won't affect any transitions that have already been applied to existing sequences.

A key feature in Premiere Pro is the "Automate to Sequence" tool, which allows users to quickly apply the default transition to multiple clips within a sequence. When this command is used, it automatically applies the default transitions for both video and audio to all selected clips. This functionality can significantly streamline the editing process, enabling editors to efficiently apply transitions across sequences and save time by adjusting their default settings.

Create a standard transition

☐ Access **the Transitions**:

- Navigate to **Window > Effects** to open the Effects panel.
- Expand either the **Video Transitions** or **Audio Transitions** folder, depending on which you wish to set as default.

☐ Pick **the Transition**:

- Browse through the available transitions and select the one you want to use for all your projects.

☐ Set **as Default Transition**:

- Right-click on your chosen transition in the Effects panel, or click the Menu button in the panel.
- From the drop-down menu, select **"Set Selected As Default Transition."**

Set the default transition's duration.

Method 1: Using the Edit Menu (Windows) or Premiere Pro Menu (Mac)

☐ Access **Preferences**:

- Go to the **Edit** menu (Windows) or the **Premiere Pro** menu (Mac).

☐ Select **Timeline Preferences**:

- Choose **Edit > Preferences > Timeline** (Windows) or **Premiere Pro > Preferences > Timeline** (Mac).

☐ Adjust **Transition Duration**:

- Find the settings for transition duration in the Timeline preferences.
- Modify the **Video Transition Default Duration** or **Audio Transition Default Duration** as desired.

☐ Confirm **Changes**:

- After adjusting the duration, click **OK** to confirm and apply your changes.

Method 2: Using the Effects Panel

☐ Access **the Effects Panel**:

- Open the **Effects** panel from the navigation bar in Adobe Premiere Pro.

☐ Navigate **to Default Transition Duration**:

- Within the Effects panel, click on the drop-down menu.

☑ Choose **Set Default Transition Duration**:

- Select **Set Default Transition Duration** from the menu options.

☑ Adjust **Duration Values**:

- Modify the values for **Video Transition Default Duration** or **Audio Transition Default Duration** as needed.

☑ Apply **Changes**:

- After adjusting the duration values, click **OK** to confirm and apply the changes.

Apply default transitions between selected clips

Basic audio and video transitions can be applied to any combination of two or more clips. Fixed transitions are automatically placed at every edit point where the selected clips meet, regardless of the current time indicator or track placement. Preset transitions will not be applied if a selected clip is adjacent to a non-selected clip or no clip at all.

- **Select Clips**: Choose at least two clips from the Timeline by either shift-clicking them or drawing a selection box around them.
- **Choose Sequence for Default Transitions**: Decide on the sequence in which you want to apply the default transitions.

Copy and paste transitions
Copying a Transition

☑ Select **the Transition**:

- In your sequence, click on the transition you wish to copy to select it.

☑ Copy **the Transition**:

- Use one of the following methods:
    - Go to **Edit > Copy** from the menu bar.
    - Press **Ctrl+C** (Windows) or **Cmd+C** (Mac) on your keyboard.

Pasting a Transition to a Single Clip

▢ Place **Current-Time Indicator**:

- Move the current-time indicator (playhead) to the cut line where you want to paste the transition.

▢ Paste **the Transition**:

- Use one of the following methods:
  - Go to **Edit > Paste** from the menu bar.
  - Press **Ctrl+V** (Windows) or **Cmd+V** (Mac) on your keyboard.

Pasting a Transition to Multiple Clips

1. **Select Multiple Edit Points**:
   - To copy the transition to several clips, you can:
     - Drag a marquee around the edit points in the sequence to select them.
     - Hold the **Shift** key while using any trim tool to select multiple edit points.
2. **Paste the Transition**:
   - After selecting the desired edit points:
     - Use one of the following methods to paste the transition:
       - Go to **Edit > Paste** from the menu bar.
       - Press **Ctrl+V** (Windows) or **Cmd+V** (Mac) on your keyboard.

These steps allow you to efficiently copy transitions within a sequence in Adobe Premiere Pro and apply them to specific cut lines, whether for a single clip or multiple clips at once. This functionality enhances your editing workflow by enabling quick transitions across different parts of your sequence.

Replace a transition

You can easily change a video or audio transition in the sequence by dragging a new transition from the Effects panel over the existing one. When you do this, the length and orientation of the transition remain unchanged. However, it will reset the parameters of the previous transition to the default settings of the new one.

Using A/B Mode to Fine-Tune a Transition

The A/B editing mode in Adobe Premiere Pro allows you to test transition effects by splitting a single video track into two separate tracks in the timeline. In this mode, two clips that would typically play consecutively on the same track are divided, enabling a transition between them. This setup allows editors to view more details and adjust various transition settings in the Effect Controls panel, including modifying head and tail frames (handles) and other parameters. By separating the components of the transition, editors gain greater control and flexibility to fine-tune the effect, making it easier to achieve precise adjustments for a smooth and professional-looking final video.

Audio Transitions Effects

To switch between audio clips, you can use crossfades, which function similarly to video transitions. A crossfade involves adding an audio transition between two adjacent clips on the same track. For fading in or out, a crossfade transition is applied to both ends of a single clip. In Premiere Pro, you have three options for crossfades: **Constant Gain**, **Constant Power**, and **Exponential Fade**. Each type offers a different way to create smooth audio transitions.

Choose a preset audio transition

- In the **Effects** panel, right-click (Windows) or control-click (Mac OS) on **Constant Gain** or **Constant Power**.
- From the context menu, select **Set Selected As Default Transition**.

Set the length of audio transitions to their default value

☐ On macOS, go to the **Edit** menu and choose **Preferences > Timeline**. On Windows, navigate to **Premiere Pro > Preferences > Timeline**.

☐ In the Preferences box, enter a number for the **Audio Transition Default Duration**.

Crossfade Audio in Adobe Premiere Pro

To sync two audio tracks in Adobe Premiere Pro using crossfades, follow these steps for a smooth transition between pieces, such as background music:

1. **Arrange Your Tracks**: Place the audio clips on the timeline so that they overlap slightly at the point where you want the crossfade.

2. **Apply Crossfade Transitions**: Go to the **Effects** panel and find **Constant Power** or **Constant Gain** under Audio Transitions. Drag your chosen crossfade effect to the overlapping section between the two clips.
3. **Adjust Duration**: Fine-tune the duration of the crossfade by dragging the edges of the transition to create a gradual blend between the audio tracks.
4. **Preview and Adjust**: Play back the audio to ensure a seamless flow. Make any necessary adjustments to the transition duration or positioning to enhance the blend.
5. **Fine-tuning**: Use the **Effect Controls** panel to adjust specific parameters if needed for a more polished sound.

By following these steps, you can ensure that your audio tracks transition smoothly, enhancing the overall viewer experience.

Using the Crossfade Audio Effects

To crossfade audio in Adobe Premiere Pro, start by using the **Selection Tool** to select the two audio tracks you want to crossfade. Then, on Windows, press **Ctrl + Shift + D**, or on macOS, press **Cmd + Shift + D** to apply the default crossfade effect between the selected clips. This will create a smooth transition between the audio tracks.

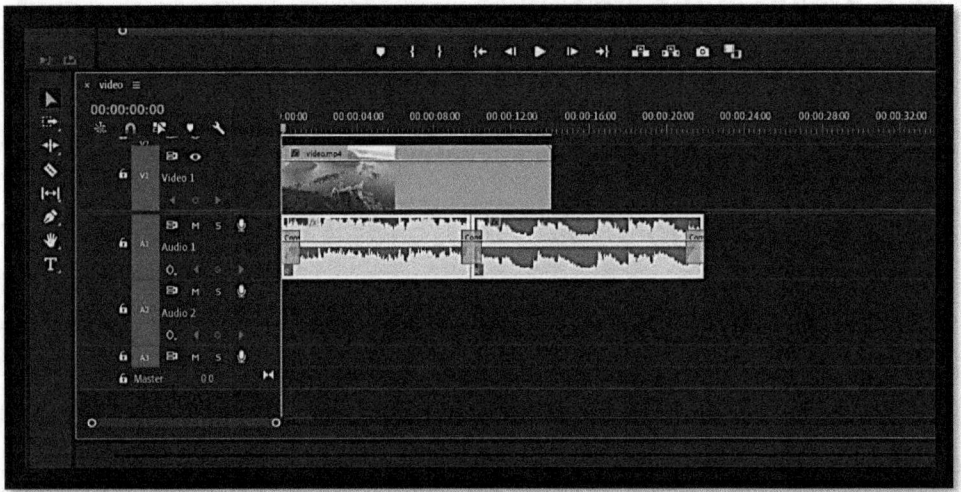

The **Constant Power** effect is applied to the beginning and end (including cuts) of the selected audio tracks using the keyboard shortcut. If you wish to remove the additional effects at the start and end, simply select them and press **Delete**. To apply the effect only at a specific point—such as between cuts—manually select it from the **Effects > Crossfade** tab and drag and drop it to the desired location.

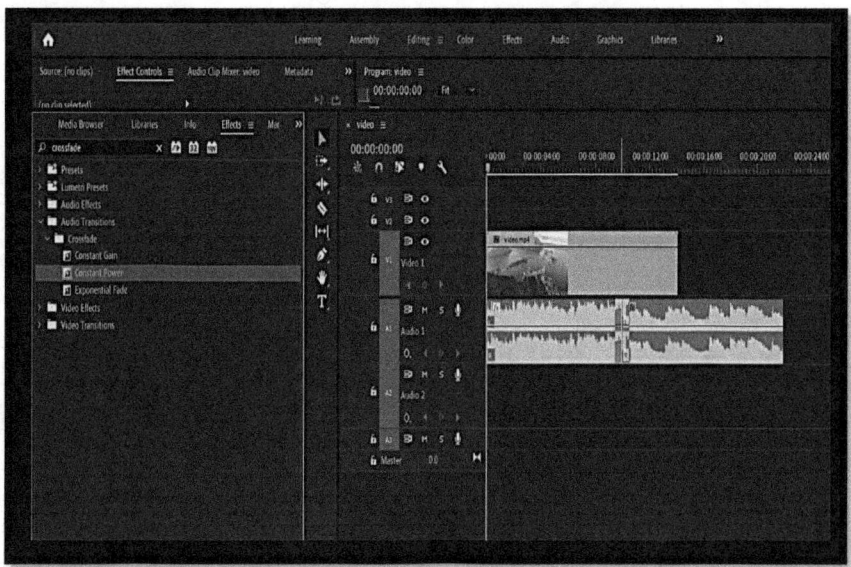

To change the duration of the crossfade effect, click and drag either end of the effect box. If you're familiar with handling effects in Adobe Premiere Pro, you can further customize the crossfade to suit your needs, allowing for more precise control over audio transitions and enhancing your project's overall sound design.

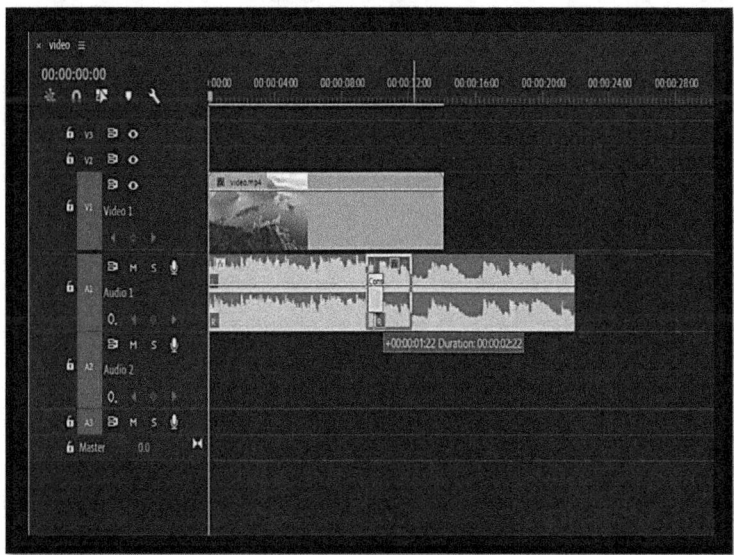

In addition to **Constant Power**, Adobe Premiere Pro offers several built-in effects for crossfading audio tracks. By expanding the **Crossfade** section under **Effects**, you'll find three options: **Constant**

Gain, **Constant Power**, and **Exponential Fade**. Each of these effects provides a different method for blending audio, allowing you to choose the one that best fits your project's needs.

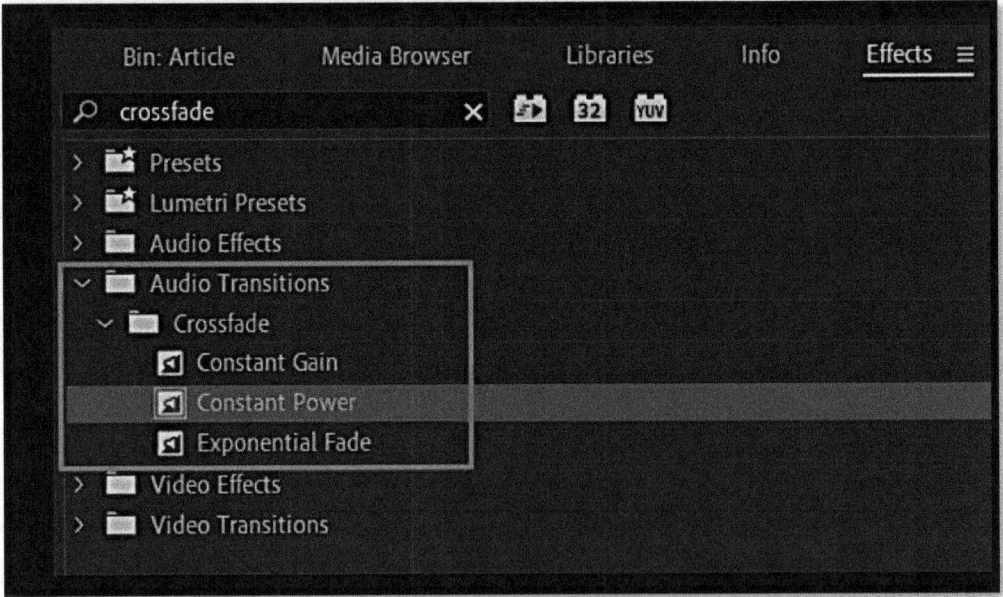

Exponential Gain vs. Constant Gain vs. Constant Power

Constant Power is the default effect applied when you press **Ctrl + Shift + D** on Windows or **Cmd + Shift + D** on Mac. In contrast, **Constant Gain** is the simplest of the three crossfade effects, creating a fading audio effect by adding two keyframes to each track and adjusting the audio levels at a consistent pace. While all three effects achieve the same goal of crossfading audio, they differ in how they manage the volume transitions.

Constant Power and **Exponential Fade** provide smoother and more gradual volume changes compared to **Constant Gain**, which alters audio levels at a constant rate. For a more refined crossfade, it's advisable to use the latter two effects. Experimenting with all three options will help you find the best fit for your project.

To change the default audio effect, expand the **Effects > Crossfade** menu, right-click on the desired audio effect, and select **Set Selected as Default Transition**.

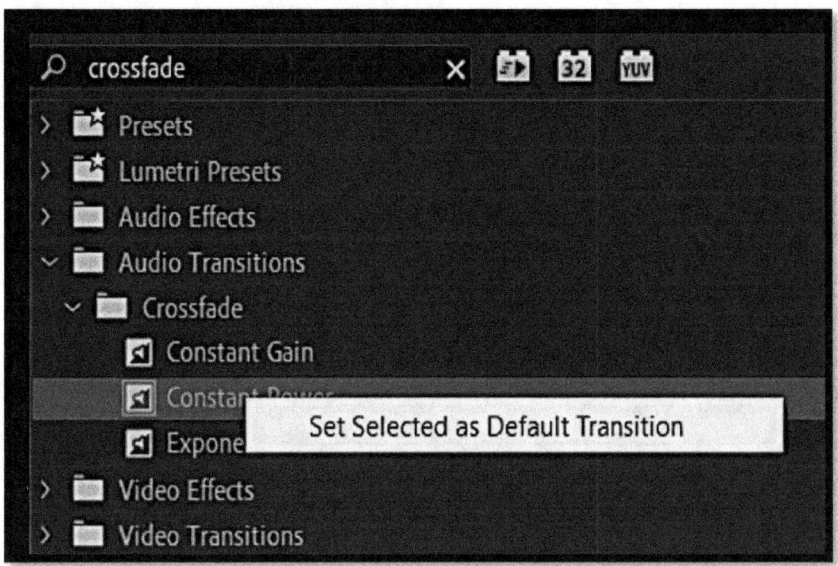

The new default effect will be applied to the clips when you press **Ctrl + Shift + D** (Windows) or **Cmd + Shift + D** (Mac). This allows you to quickly implement your chosen crossfade effect across your audio tracks.

Overlapping Tracks and Crossfading Audio Manually

For greater control over the crossfade effect, you can manually adjust the audio clips using keyframes or the Pen tool. This method is ideal for professionals, as it allows you to modify the volume level at specific timestamps, providing granular control over the audio tracks and enhancing the overall quality of your sound design.

Making Use of the Pen Tool

When experimenting with audio levels or video opacity, the **Pen tool** is incredibly useful. To create a crossfade effect using the Pen tool, start by overlapping the two audio tracks. Apply a fade-out effect to the first audio track while simultaneously fading in the second.

First, move the audio files to separate tracks and ensure they overlap. The duration of the overlap will determine the length of the crossfade effect. Double-click the audio tracks to expand them so that the volume bar becomes visible, allowing you to adjust the levels more precisely.

After you're done setting up your audio tracks, select the **Pen tool** from the tools panel (or press **P**). Identify the timestamp where the second audio track begins, and click on the volume bar of the first audio track to create a keyframe at that point. Then, make another keyframe near the end of the first audio and drag it down to create a fade-out effect.

For the second audio track, create two keyframes similarly. This time, drag the first keyframe down to silence it, effectively fading in the second audio as the first fades out. This technique allows for a smooth transition between the two audio clips.

Using Keyframes to Crossfade Audio in Premiere Pro

Creating a crossfade effect using keyframes is similar to using the Pen tool, but it requires more steps. Start by overlapping the two audio files and determining the duration for the crossfade. Then, in the **Effect Controls** panel, expand the **Volume** option and select the first audio file.

Position the playhead at the timestamp where you want the crossfade to start, and click the Stopwatch button next to **Level** to create a new keyframe. From there, you can add additional keyframes to adjust the audio levels over time, achieving a smooth transition between the two tracks.

Once you create the first keyframe, move it to the end of the first audio track and adjust the **Level** value to **-999 dB**. This will effectively silence the audio at that point. The keyframe will automatically update with this change.

Next, expand the **Volume** option for the second audio track. Position the playhead at the beginning of this audio track and click the Stopwatch button next to **Level** to create a new keyframe. Set this keyframe's value to **-999 dB** as well. This setup will allow for a smooth fade-in of the second audio track as the first fades out.

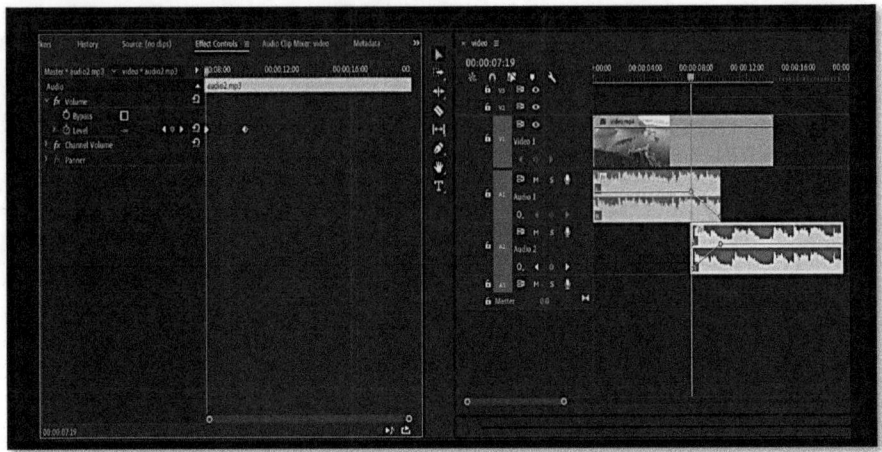

Finally, move the playhead to the timestamp where you want the crossfade effect to end and create a new keyframe by clicking the Stopwatch button again. To streamline the process, you can use markers to indicate important timestamps ahead of time.

When you play back the video, you'll hear the smooth crossfade audio effect you created manually. Now you can continue editing the rest of the video and export it once you're finished. While creating a crossfade effect with keyframes allows for detailed customization, you can also save time by using the **Ctrl + Shift + D** (Windows) or **Cmd + Shift + D** (Mac) shortcuts, or by applying the **Constant Gain** effect from the presets.

Why Crossfade Audio Tracks in a Video?

To ensure a pleasant viewing experience, crossfading two or more audio tracks is essential. Thoughtful audio editing eliminates sudden cuts or transitions that can distract viewers from the video. If you're working on a podcast, it's advisable to use **Adobe Audition** for audio processing instead of doing it directly in Premiere Pro. Adobe Audition is a powerful digital audio workstation that enables you to edit and enhance the quality of your audio tracks more effectively.

Audio clip fade in or fade out

To start, ensure the audio track is larger in the Timeline panel. If necessary, click the triangle to the left of the track name to expand the audio tracks you want to work with.

To create a fade-in effect:

- Drag an audio transition from the **Effects** panel to the beginning of the audio clip in the Timeline panel. Alternatively, you can select the transition in the Timeline. Then, go to the **Effect Controls** panel and choose **Start at Cut** from the Alignment menu.

To create a fade-out effect:

- Drag an audio transition from the **Effects** panel to the Out point of the audio clip in the Timeline panel. You can also select the transition directly in the Timeline. In the **Effect Controls** panel, choose **End at Cut** from the Alignment menu.

These steps will help you achieve smooth audio transitions in your project.

Adjust or customize an audio transition

▢ Access **the Timeline Panel**:

- Open your project in Adobe Premiere Pro.

▢ Double-**Click an Audio Transition**:

- Find the audio transition in the Timeline panel and double-click on it to modify it.

▢ Adjust **the Transition in the Effect Controls Panel**:

- After double-clicking the transition, the **Effect Controls** panel will show the transition's settings.
- Make any desired adjustments to the transition parameters in the **Effect Controls** panel to refine or modify the audio transition's behavior.

Adjusting Audio Volume Keyframe Graph for Fade or Crossfade

1. **Select the Clip with Audio**:
   - Locate the audio clip in the Timeline panel that you want to adjust.
2. **Modify Volume Keyframes**:
   - Instead of using a traditional transition, focus on adjusting the audio volume keyframe graph.
   - Click on the audio clip to reveal the volume keyframes in the **Effect Controls** panel.

o   Modify the volume keyframes graph to control the pace of the fade or crossfade effect. Adjusting these keyframes will change the volume levels at specific points, allowing for a customized audio transition.

These steps provide you with alternative methods to manage audio transitions, giving you greater control over the speed and quality of fades and crossfades in your project.

Professional Transitions and Effects

Premiere Pro offers over 40 video transitions to create smooth transitions between clips. If you need more options, you can use the transition tools in Adobe After Effects and add those effects to your Creative Cloud library.

To apply a transition in Premiere Pro, simply drag and drop it into your desired location. Click on the **Effects** menu located to the left of your timeline and open the **Transition Effects** folder. From there, you can drag the transition to the beginning or end of a clip. Play the video to preview how the transition looks in your sequence.

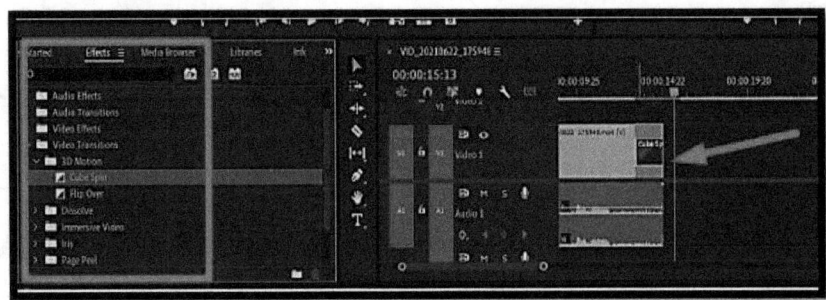

Premiere Pro includes a comprehensive range of video effects to help you address lighting issues, adjust colors, and enhance your footage. In the latest version, Adobe introduced **Warp Stabilize** in After Effects to stabilize shaky video footage. You have various options for correcting videos, including trimming, selecting the desired smoothness, and allowing the software to automatically adjust the edges for optimal results.

CHAPTER 10
ADVANCED AUDIO EDITING

Audio Mixing and Effects
Create an audio mix

Once you've placed your conversation, music, sound effects, and background noise clips on their respective audio tracks in Premiere Pro, you'll need to define each type of audio. To do this, go to the **Audio workspace** (Window > Workspaces > Audio) and select all the clips in a specific track. In the **Essential Sound** panel, click on the appropriate audio type from the list to categorize them correctly.

By categorizing the audio track types, you can adjust levels and add effects more efficiently than if you were modifying each clip individually. For example, in the **Loudness** section, clicking **Auto-Match** will automatically normalize the volume levels for all clips on that track, streamlining your editing process.

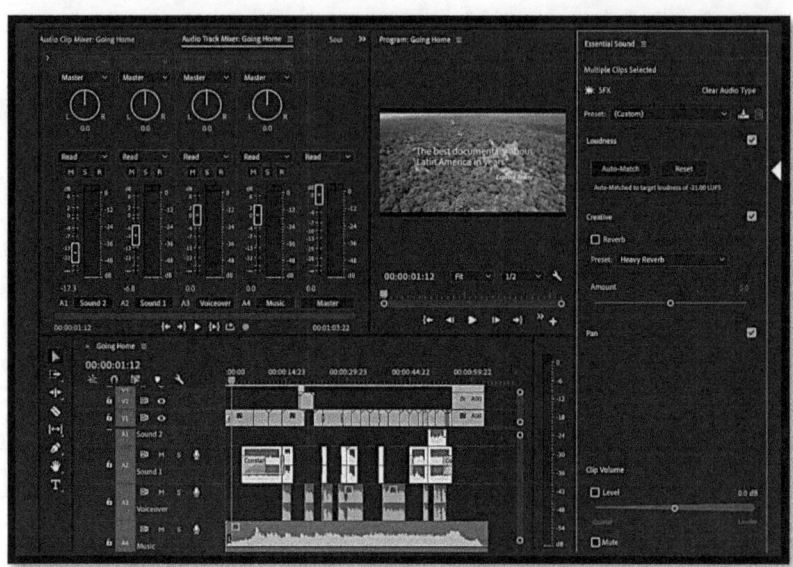

Labeling audio types allows you to adjust how one track interacts with another effectively. One useful technique is "ducking," which helps an audio track stand out from background sounds. Once you've identified the tracks to duck against, click **Generate Keyframes**. You can then fine-tune these keyframes to ensure they sync perfectly with the background music and dialogue in terms of timing and volume.

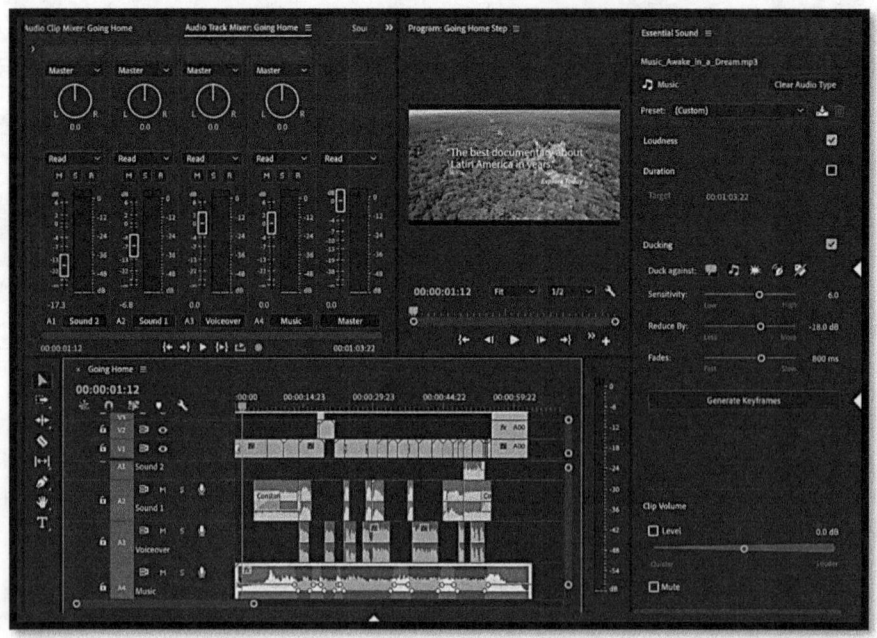

You can enhance your music using EQ settings by adjusting the **Amount** scale to control the strength of the effect. Additionally, in the **Audio Track Mixer**, you can manipulate the vertical sliders while playing your sequence. For instance, lowering a slider will soften all the clips on that specific track, allowing for greater control over your audio mix.

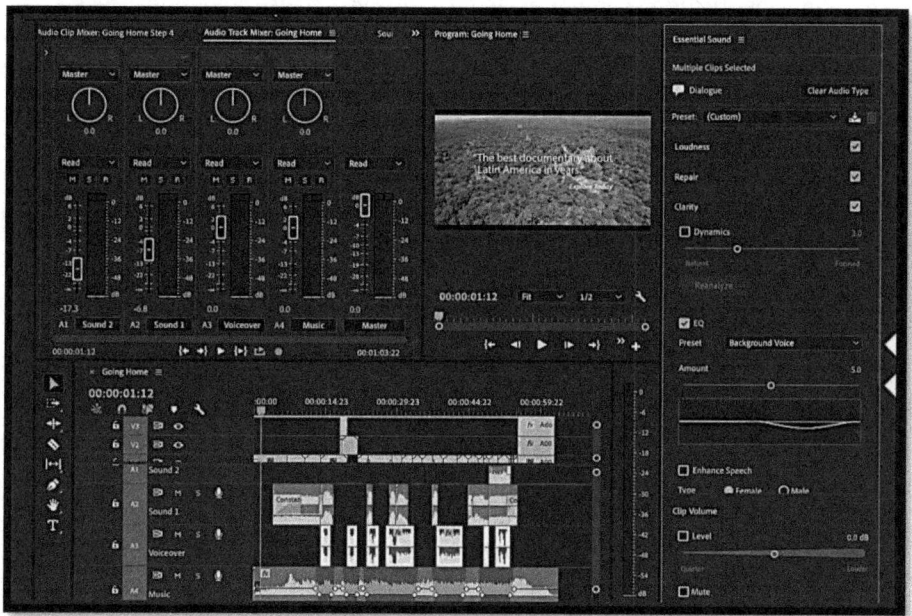

Adjustments in Premiere Pro are nondestructive, allowing you to experiment freely without permanently altering your clips. If you want to revert your changes, simply click **Clear Audio Type** at the top of the **Essential Sound** panel to restore everything to its original state.

Working with Multichannel Audio

Multichannel audio refers to sound recordings with more than two audio channels, unlike traditional stereo audio. Professional-grade cameras can capture up to eight audio channels, even if some are unused in the final file. Adobe Premiere Pro supports up to 32 audio channels, allowing for complex audio editing.

Here are some ways to work with multichannel audio in Premiere Pro:

1. **Review Audio Clips in the Source Monitor:**
   o Open an audio clip in the Source Monitor.
   o Use the **Drag Audio Only** button to focus on the audio waveform.
2. **Modify Clips:**

- o When adding multichannel clips to a sequence, all audio channels are included.
- o To access channel selection settings:
  - ▪ Select one or more clips in the Project panel.
  - ▪ Right-click and navigate to **Modify > Audio Channels**.

3. **Choose Audio Channel Settings:**
   - o Options include using the file's original settings, selecting presets for channel configuration, choosing the clip channel format (mono, stereo, 5.1, or Adaptive), and determining the number of clips to add when editing into sequences.

4. **Match Source Channels to Clips:**
   - o Use checkboxes to assign source audio channels to clips as needed.

5. **Non-Destructive Changes:**
   - o Modifications to clip interpretation settings are non-destructive and can be adjusted at any time.

6. **Review Audio Channels:**
   - o Any changes made to a clip's audio channels will be reflected in the waveform when reviewed in the Source Monitor.

7. **Appropriate Audio Track Types:**
   - o Premiere Pro ensures audio clips are assigned to suitable track types for accurate mixing.
   - o If an appropriate track type is unavailable when editing a clip into a sequence, Premiere Pro automatically creates a new track with the required channel format.

Overall, Premiere Pro provides robust tools for managing and modifying multichannel audio, making it easier to handle complex audio setups while allowing for flexible adjustments within the editing environment.

View audio waveforms

When you play an audio clip in the Source Monitor, the waveforms display immediately, providing a visual representation of the sound. If the clip has multiple audio channels, you can view the waveforms for each channel. To customize the appearance of audio tracks in the timeline, click the **Timeline Display Settings** wrench tool. By selecting **Show Audio Waveform**, the audio will be visually represented as waves in the timeline, making it easier to analyze and edit the audio.

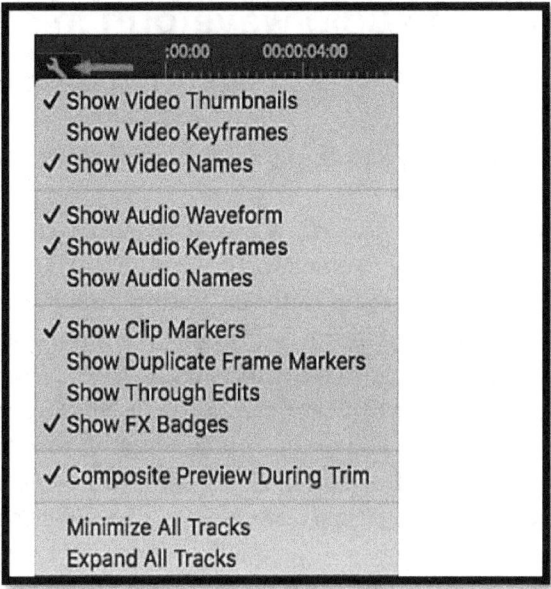

Scrub the audio waveform

"Scrubbing" refers to moving the playhead over an audio waveform, allowing you to quickly navigate through the audio clip. To access the clip in the Source Monitor, simply double-click it in the timeline. When you click on the audio clip, the playhead appears, enabling you to drag it forward or backward for precise movement. If you want to disable audio playback while scrubbing, go to **Edit > Preferences > Audio** and uncheck the **Play audio when scrubbing** option.

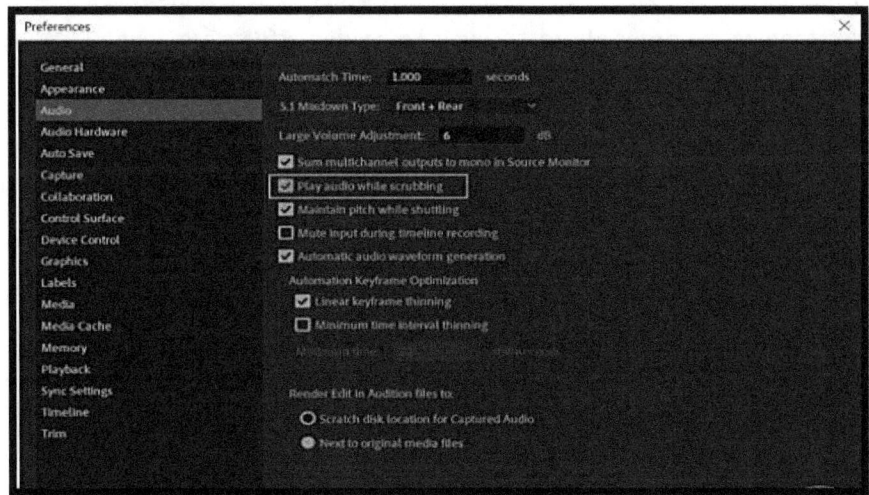

Zoom in or out on an audio waveform in the Source Monitor

To effectively navigate and edit audio waveforms in the Source Monitor:

1. **Open an Audio Clip**: Double-click on the desired audio clip in either the Project or Timeline panel to view it in the Source Monitor.
2. **Horizontal Zooming**: Use the zoom slider below the time bar in the Source Monitor to zoom in or out on the audio waveform by dragging the slider horizontally. This allows you to see more detail in the waveform as it stretches.
3. **Vertical Zooming for Individual Channels**: To focus on a specific channel, locate the vertical zoom bar on the right side of the Source Monitor, next to the decibel scale. Drag this bar up or down to adjust the view of that channel's waveform.
4. **Simultaneous Vertical Zooming**: Hold down the Shift key while dragging the vertical zoom bar to zoom in or out on all channels simultaneously. This ensures that all waveforms adjust together, making it easier to analyze the overall audio structure.

What is an Alpha Channel?

The Alpha channel in Premiere Pro is crucial for managing transparency in images and videos, especially for titles and effects. It allows you to define which parts of a clip are visible or transparent, enabling seamless layering of clips. If a clip lacks an Alpha channel, you can apply effects to create transparency.

Using Blending modes and Channel effects, you can merge visual data from multiple clips into a cohesive collage without losing detail. Higher tracks cover lower ones unless transparency is applied. Understanding the order of processing is key: video effects are applied first, followed by motion effects, and then adjustments to the Alpha channel.

The Alpha Adjust video effect offers advanced opacity control, while the Interpret Footage dialog lets you select how to read the Alpha channel—options like "Invert Alpha Channel" or "Ignore Alpha Channel" allow for fine-tuning transparency based on your project needs.

Mattes and alpha channels

Digital images typically use three color channels—red, green, and blue (RGB)—to represent color data. However, the alpha channel, which stores transparency information, is equally important yet often overlooked. It acts as an invisible map for each pixel, indicating how transparent or opaque it is, with white representing full transparency, black indicating full opacity, and shades of gray indicating varying levels of partial transparency.

In tools like Premiere Pro and After Effects, the alpha channel can be utilized as a matte, where white represents unclear areas and black denotes clear ones. While the alpha channel is commonly used, alternative mattes from different channels or layers can also define transparency more effectively if the source image lacks an alpha channel.

Many file formats support alpha channels, such as Adobe Photoshop, TGA, TIFF, EPS, PDF, and Adobe Illustrator. Additionally, formats like AVI and QuickTime can include alpha channels when saved with high bit levels, enhancing flexibility in image and video editing by preserving transparency data.

About straight and premultiplied channels

Digital files typically store transparency data using either straight alpha channels or premultiplied alpha channels. The distinction lies in how they interact with color channels.

Straight Alpha Channels (or unmatted channels) retain transparency information exclusively within the alpha channel, separate from the color channels (RGB). As a result, the effects of transparency may not be immediately visible unless the software supports this format.

Premultiplied Alpha Channels (or flattened channels), in contrast, store transparency data within both the alpha channel and the RGB channels. In this format, the RGB values are adjusted based on a background color, creating a blended effect that is particularly noticeable in partially transparent areas, such as soft edges. The blending relies on the transparency levels, ensuring that colors appear consistent with the background.

When using premultiplied channels, users may have the option to specify the background color for the premultiplication process, though black or white is typically the default. While straight channels offer better clarity for color information, premultiplied channels are more compatible with various applications, such as Apple QuickTime Player.

When preparing files for editing in software like Premiere Pro or After Effects, it's crucial to decide between straight and premultiplied channels. These programs can detect both types but usually identify only the first alpha channel present in the file. Adobe Flash, on the other hand, specifically recognizes premultiplied alpha channels.

Understanding the differences between these two types of alpha channels is essential for managing transparency effectively across different editing and playback platforms, ensuring the desired visual results.

Making Compositing Part of Your Project

You can elevate your post-production work significantly with compositing effects and settings in Premiere Pro. By leveraging blending effects, you'll discover new creative ways to shoot and edit, making it easier to combine images effectively. Preparing your footage and setting up effects properly can lead to stunning composite results. Here are some key points to consider when compositing in Premiere Pro:

Tips for Compositing Clips and Tracks:

1. **Adjust Clip Transparency:**
   o   To make an entire clip transparent, simply modify the opacity settings in the Effect Controls panel.
2. **Use Source Files with Alpha Channels:**
   o   For making specific areas transparent, import source files that contain an alpha channel. Premiere Pro will retain this transparency, allowing the clip to be displayed accurately in your sequences.
3. **Manually Add Transparency:**
   o   If the source file lacks an alpha channel, you must manually adjust the opacity for each clip instance in your sequence. This can be done through the opacity settings or by applying various effects.
4. **Supported Formats:**
   o   Software like Adobe After Effects, Photoshop, and Illustrator can save clips with or without alpha channels, as long as the file format supports this feature.

By following these guidelines, you can create engaging compositions that enhance the visual storytelling of your project, making the most of the creative possibilities offered by Premiere Pro.

Audio channel mapping

To adjust audio channel mapping in Premiere Pro, follow these steps:

1. **Open Preferences:**
   o   Go to **Edit (Windows) or Premiere Pro (Mac)** in the menu bar and select **Preferences**. Then click on **Timeline**.
2. **Adjust Mapping Settings:**
   o   In the Timeline preferences, you can set how audio channels will be mapped when you import clips. This allows you to customize the routing of audio channels to different tracks based on your project needs.
3. **Modify Audio Channels After Import:**

o   If you want to change the mapping after importing, right-click the audio clip in the Project panel and select **Modify > Audio Channels**. Here, you can manually adjust which audio channels go to which tracks.

This flexibility in mapping is essential for managing complex audio setups, ensuring that each channel is routed correctly for your editing workflow.

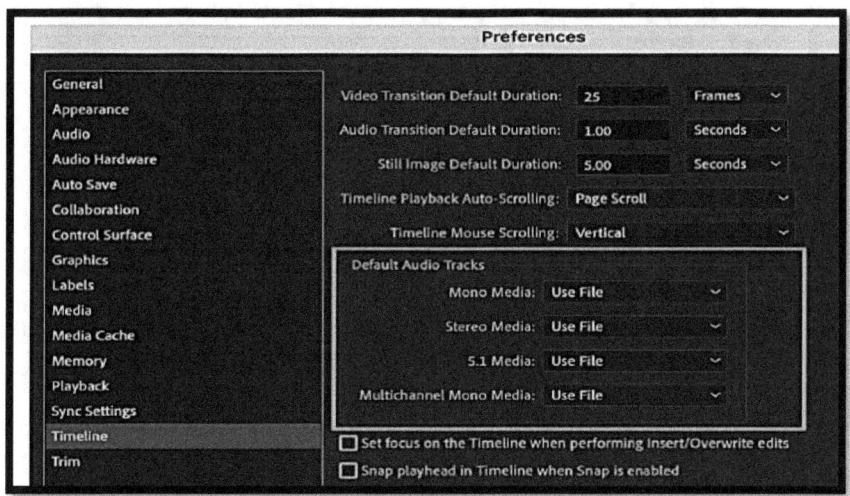

After selecting a file from the list of Default Audio Tracks in the Preferences dialog, click **OK** to confirm your changes. This will ensure that the selected audio tracks are set as the default for future imports, streamlining your workflow when working with multi-channel audio clips.

Change the source audio channel mapping

⬜ In the **Modify Audio Channels** dialog, you can adjust how the audio channels are mapped. You can select options like using the file's original settings or choose a preset for channel configuration, such as mono, stereo, or 5.1.

⬜ Make any necessary adjustments to the channel assignments and track formats as required.

⬜ Click **OK** to apply the changes. This ensures that the audio channels are correctly configured for your selected clips, maintaining consistency across your project.

⏹ After clicking "OK," the audio channels will be mapped according to your selections.

⏹ If you need to revisit or adjust the settings later, simply right-click on the clip again and choose **Modify > Audio Channels** to access the mapping grid.

⏹ Remember, any changes made will apply only to the selected clips, allowing you to customize audio management per your project needs.

Map sequence audio channels to audio output device hardware channels

Mapping audio channels in Premiere Pro allows for customized audio output based on your hardware capabilities, enhancing your audio mixing experience. Here's a streamlined guide to set it up:

1. **Open Preferences**:
   o   Navigate to **Edit > Preferences > Audio Hardware**.
2. **Select Hardware Device**:
   o   In the **Map Output For** menu, choose the audio driver for your desired output device. Premiere Pro defaults to **Desktop Audio** for Windows and **Built-In** for macOS.
3. **Map Sequence Channels**:
   o   Below the **Map Output For** menu, you'll see the available channels for your selected hardware. Use the channel tiles to connect your sequence channels (e.g., stereo, 5.1, or 16-channel) to the appropriate hardware channels.
4. **Confirm Changes**:
   o   Once your mappings are set, click **OK** to save your preferences.

Note: You can map channels to any supported hardware, but the audio will only playback through the device that is currently active. Always ensure your hardware device is on to hear the mappings in effect.

Extract audio from clips

In a project, you can create new audio source clips from existing audio clips while preserving the originals. Any modifications made to the original clips—such as gain, speed, duration, and footage interpretation—are applied to the newly extracted audio clips.

1. In the Project panel, choose one or more audio clips.
2. Go to "Clip," then select "Audio Options," followed by "Extract Audio."

The new audio files generated by Premiere Pro will have "Extracted" appended to their filenames.

Break a stereo track into mono tracks

Using the Breakout to Mono command allows you to convert a clip's stereo or 5.1 surround audio channels into mono audio source clips. When you separate a stereo clip, you create two mono clips, one for each channel. For a 5.1 surround clip, you'll end up with six mono clips, corresponding to each channel. Premiere Pro retains the original source clip, and the Breakout to Mono command generates new source clips with the appropriate channel mapping, rather than creating new files.

1. Select a clip with 5.1 or stereo audio in the Project panel.
2. Navigate to Clip > Audio Options > Breakout to Mono.

The resulting audio source clips will have filenames that begin with the original clip's name, followed by the channel names. For instance, if a stereo clip named Zoom is split, the new clips will be labeled Zoom Left and Zoom Right. Note that the Breakout to Mono command does not link the clips together; use the Source Channel Mappings command for that purpose. Additionally, this command only functions on clips within a sequence in the Timeline panel, not on items in the Project panel.

Break all stereo tracks into mono tracks

Premiere Pro can automatically split stereo and surround channels into individual mono audio clips upon import or capture. Here's how to set it up:

1. Open Preferences and select the Audio tab.

2. In the Source Channel Mapping section, choose Mono from the Stereo Media menu.
3. Click OK to save your changes.

Use a mono clip as a stereo

There are situations where using a mono audio clip as a stereo clip can be beneficial. You can combine a mono clip with a left and right stereo channel through the Modify Clip dialog. Here's how:

1. Select a mono clip in the Project panel.
2. Navigate to Clip > Edit > Audio Channels.
3. In the Modify Clip dialog, set Clip Channel Format to Stereo, then click OK to apply the changes.

Note: The Modify Clip command can only be applied to a mono clip in the Project panel before it appears in the Timeline. You cannot convert a clip to stereo once it's in a mono audio track. Additionally, you can use three audio filters: source clip channel mapping, the Fill Left audio filter, and the Fill Right audio filter. These filters allow you to replace the sound in one channel of a stereo clip with the sound from the other channel.

Link multiple audio clips

A video clip can be linked to multiple audio clips, and audio clips can be linked to each other as well. When you link audio clips in a sequence, only the copies of the master clips are affected; the original audio clips in the Project panel remain unchanged. Moving or trimming linked clips in the Timeline keeps them in sync. You can apply audio effects, like Volume and Panning, to all channels in the linked clips. If you make an edit that only affects one linked clip, you'll see out-of-sync indicators.

In the Source Monitor, you can view and cut a multi-clip link, but it only displays one track at a time, showing markers only for that visible track. The Source Monitor can also display multi-clip links from the Project panel. To place linked clips on different tracks in the Timeline, use the Overwrite or Insert buttons. The Effect Controls panel lists all video and audio tracks in a multi-clip link, allowing you to choose which group to apply effects from the Effects panel to.

Link audio clips

All audio clips must be on separate tracks and share the same channel type. If clips are already linked—such as an audio clip linked to a video clip—you'll need to unlink them first to link multiple clips together.

1. If necessary, select each linked video and audio clip, or highlight several at once, and go to Clip > Unlink.
2. Hold the Shift key and click on each audio clip in the Timeline gallery. You can also shift-click to select a video clip. *Ensure that all audio clips have the same track format, whether mono, stereo, or 5.1 surround.*
3. Finally, navigate to Clip > Link to connect the selected clips.

Change a link between multiple clips in the Source Monitor

1. Double-click on a related file in the Timeline panel.
2. Select a track from the Track menu to view a specific channel.
3. If desired, set the In and Out points for that track.

When you set the In and Out points for a track, the same adjustments apply to the In and Out points of related tracks. If two connected tracks have different lengths, their In and Out points will differ. The In and Out points will only be identical for connected clips if their lengths match.

Keying

When keying a picture, you adjust the transparency based on a specific color value (using a color key or chroma key) or brightness value (using a luminance key). By entering a value, all pixels with similar brightness or color become transparent. This technique simplifies replacing backgrounds, especially when dealing with complex scenes, as long as the background maintains consistent color or brightness.

Bluescreening and greenscreening are common methods for keying out backgrounds with uniform colors. However, you aren't limited to blue or green; any solid color can serve as a background. An alternative approach for defining transparency is difference keying, which allows you to key out any background rather than just a single-color screen.

Color Keying a Greenscreen Shot

What color is the screen? In live-action productions featuring unique backgrounds or Hollywood-style special effects, using a green screen can be transformative. A green screen allows you to film subjects in front of a solid color, which can then be "keyed out" or digitally removed during post-production, enabling you to place the scene against any desired background. This process is known as "chroma keying."

Why use a green background? It's chosen because it can be easily removed without affecting the subject, as it typically doesn't match their skin tone or hair color. However, a blue screen may be preferable when working with low-light conditions or if your project includes green objects, as it minimizes potential conflicts with the background.

Shooting on a green screen can save time and money, but doing it incorrectly can complicate your work. Start by ensuring your green screen is as flat and smooth as possible. Next, focus on proper lighting for the green screen to avoid shadows and uneven color. Lastly, aim for high-quality footage to enhance the effectiveness of your keying process.

Guidelines for lighting your green screen
Preparing your subject for the green screen

Understanding the background, you'll use helps you light the subjects in front of your green screen more effectively. Cameraman Gerry Holtz notes, "What kills a green screen composite is if there's sunshine from the left in the backdrop image, and you lit them from the opposite side." Mismatched lighting like that can create an unconvincing composite, so it's crucial to ensure consistency in lighting direction and quality.

Allow as much distance as possible between the person and the green screen.

Maintaining a safe distance between your subject and the green screen—ideally 10 to 15 feet— ensures proper lighting for the background and prevents green spill on the edges of your subject. Remember that anything green can become transparent in post-production.

Using the Ultra Key tool, even a green tie can create unwanted effects, as it might "rip a hole" in the image. Be cautious of colors with a hint of green, such as khakis, which can make the subject appear semi-transparent. Additionally, be aware of reflections and reversals, and consider using powder to reduce shine on the head or face for a more polished look.

Add a picture to the background of your green screen video.

After filming your green or blue screen video, use green screen software or a video editing tool to remove the background color and insert your new scene. To ensure a smooth edit in Adobe Premiere Pro, follow these steps:

1. **Import Your Footage:** Bring your green or blue screen footage into the Project panel.
2. **Add to Timeline:** Drag the footage onto the Timeline.
3. **Apply Ultra Key Effect:** Go to the Effects panel, search for "Ultra Key," and drag it onto your clip.
4. **Key Out the Color:** In the Effect Controls panel, use the eyedropper tool to select the background color you want to remove.
5. **Adjust Settings:** Fine-tune settings like Matte Generation, Spill Suppression, and Color Correction to improve the keying effect.
6. **Add Background:** Place your new background footage or image on a layer below your keyed footage in the Timeline.

This will help you seamlessly integrate your new scene.

Make sure you lock in your contents before you key out the picture

Perform a rough edit of your footage before investing time in removing the green screen background or color-correcting. This approach ensures you're not spending effort on frames that won't make it into the final edit, as these tasks can be time-consuming. Focus on identifying the best clips first, then proceed with keying and adjustments for the selected footage.

Use what the Ultra Key can do.

After trimming your footage, use Adobe Premiere Pro's Ultra Key tool to remove the background. Find the Ultra Key option in the Effects menu, then use the Eyedropper tool to select a point on the green or blue screen to choose your key color. This step might complete most of the work. If needed, adjust the sliders for Matte Generation, Matte Cleanup, Spill Suppression, and Color Correction to refine the keying effect, as these adjustments will impact how the background is removed.

Change anything you need to about your new background.

Adjust the new video background as necessary. To enhance the depth of field in close-up conversations, consider blurring the background slightly. "Imagine what the background would have appeared like if it had been present during the photo. How can I compensate for that?" Holtz wonders.

To take it a step further, use fancy green screens.

Look for compact, foldable background elements resembling a sphere to use on the green screen. These can help you quickly record keyable footage. Position the pop-up screen in front of the subject you want to capture. In your video editing software, add a basic matte (or "trash matte") between the subject and the edge of the green area, then remove any background that extends beyond the matte line.

Advanced Audio Keyframing

In Premiere Pro, an audio keyframe captures changes in sound at specific moments, similar to animated keyframes. You can keyframe sound effects just like video effects. One common application of audio keyframes is at the clip level, allowing you to reduce audio spikes, balance music with dialogue, or lower the volume of certain audio sections. A key point to remember is to enable the Show Audio Keyframes option in the Timeline panel (wrench icon). The "rubber band," a white line that runs through your audio clips in the Timeline, is where you can create these keyframes. Each keyframe indicates a point where an audio change occurs within the clip.

Here's an interesting tidbit: the rubber band in the Timeline functions similarly to the one in the Effect Controls panel. However, while the Effect Controls panel allows you to view and adjust all audio parameters, the rubber band can only display one at a time. For instance, Maxim recommends using the CMD or CTRL key instead of the Pen tool to create keyframes. By holding down CMD or CTRL and clicking on the rubber band, Premiere Pro will generate keyframes. In the image below, you'll see that the Pen tool is not selected.

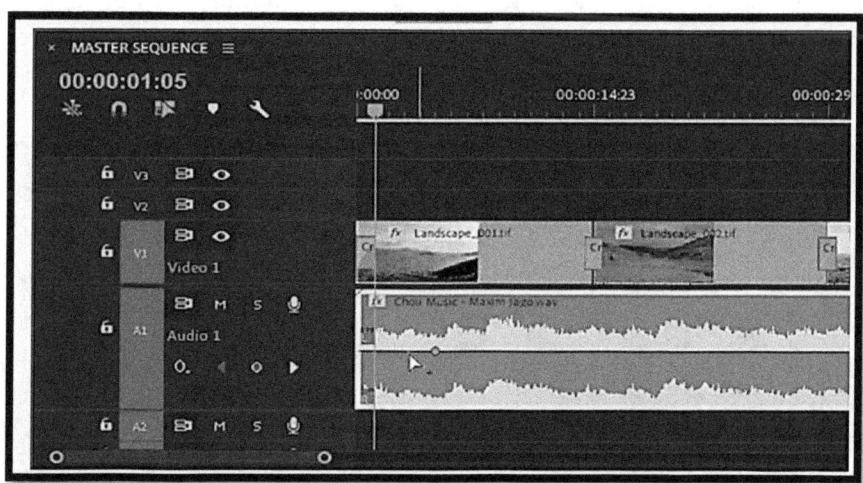

What Are Audio Track Keyframes?

Audio track keyframes are particularly useful in Premiere Pro. These keyframes are added to the audio track (not the music track) and remain intact even when you move or swap audio clips on the track. If you want to view the audio track settings and keyframes, simply double-click the audio track header to expand it. To adjust the volume, click the Show Keyframes button and select "Audio Track Keyframes." Remember that any audio effects you applied in the Audio Track Mixer will also appear here. Going forward, the keyframes on the rubber band will be "pinned" to the track itself rather than to a specific audio clip.

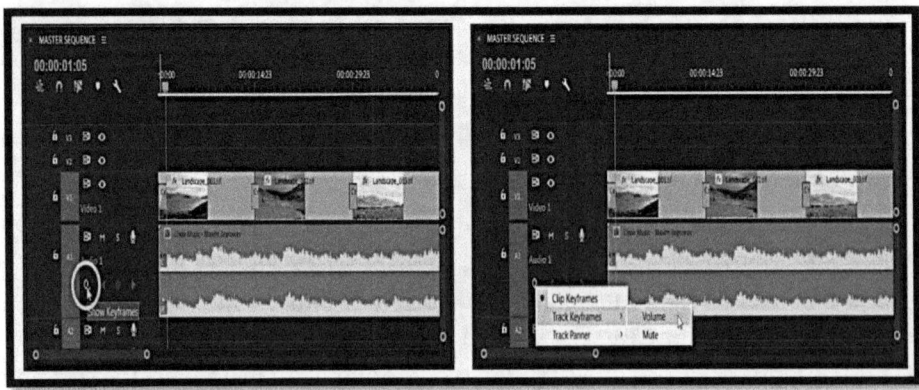

Maxim notes that when you switch to viewing audio track keyframes, the keyframe rubber band extends beyond the clip and down the timeline. In contrast, when using clip keyframes, the rubber band is limited to the area around the clips.

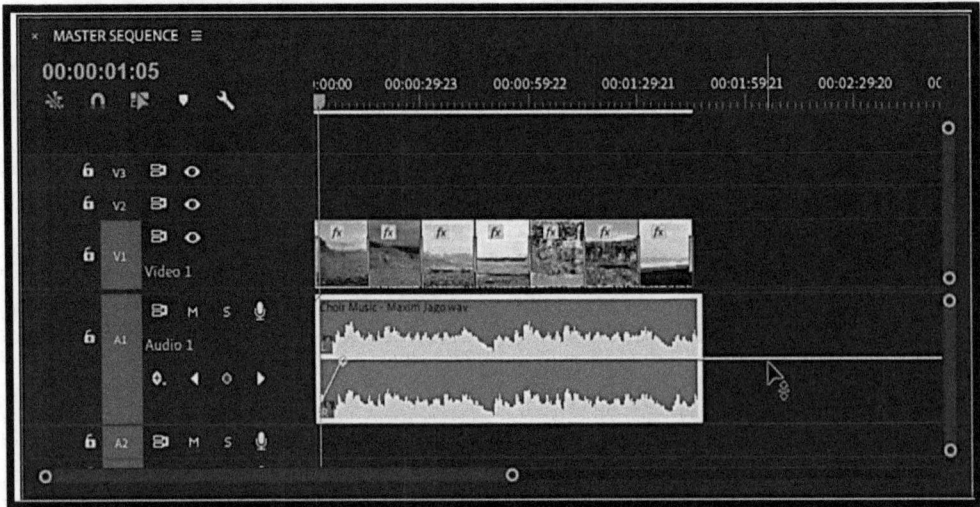

View autosaves and versions of Team Project
View versions of a Team Project

Team Project automatically creates and saves a new version of the project each time a team member makes a change, allowing you to easily view or revert to previous versions. This feature provides a straightforward way to track the project's history.

To access and view different versions of your Team Project, follow these steps:

- In Premiere Pro, click on the Team Project name in the menu bar, then select **Auto Save History** from the dropdown menu.

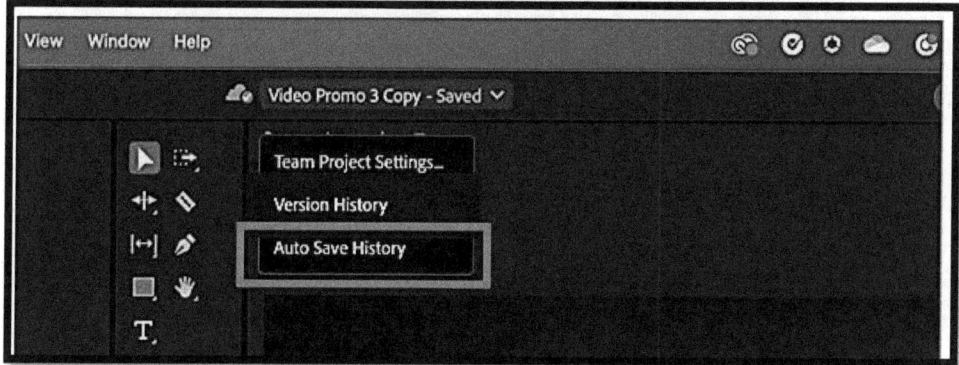

- Navigate to **Edit > Team Project > Browse Versions** to locate the latest version of the project in the Media Browser.

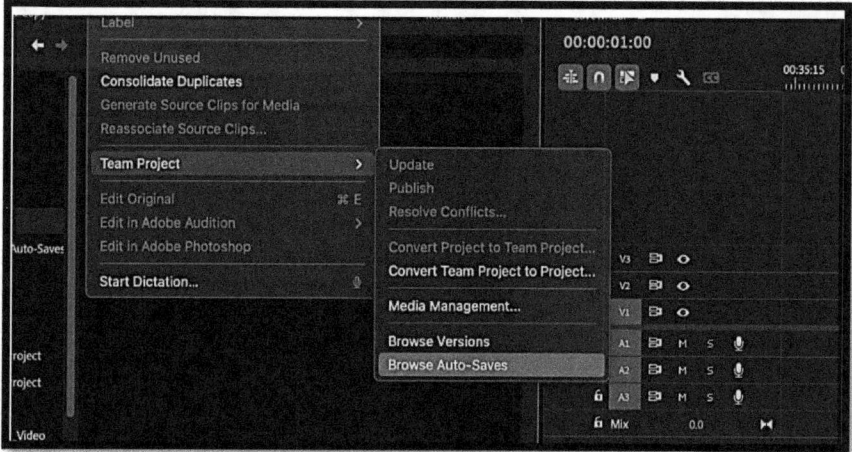

In the Media Browser panel, right-click on the Team Project and select **Team Project Versions**. This will open a dialog box displaying a list of all versions along with details, such as any shared notes that have been made.

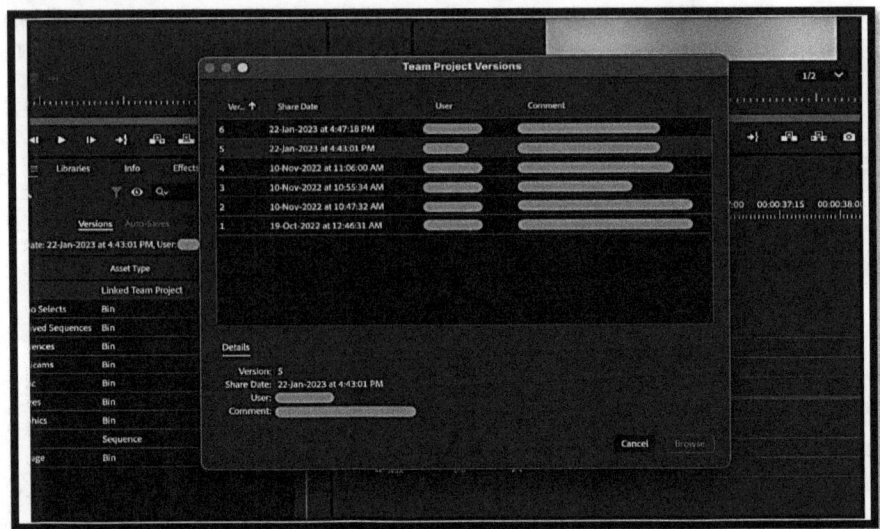

In the Media Browser panel, select the Team Project. Then, use the vertical scale under the **Versions** tab to view the different versions available.

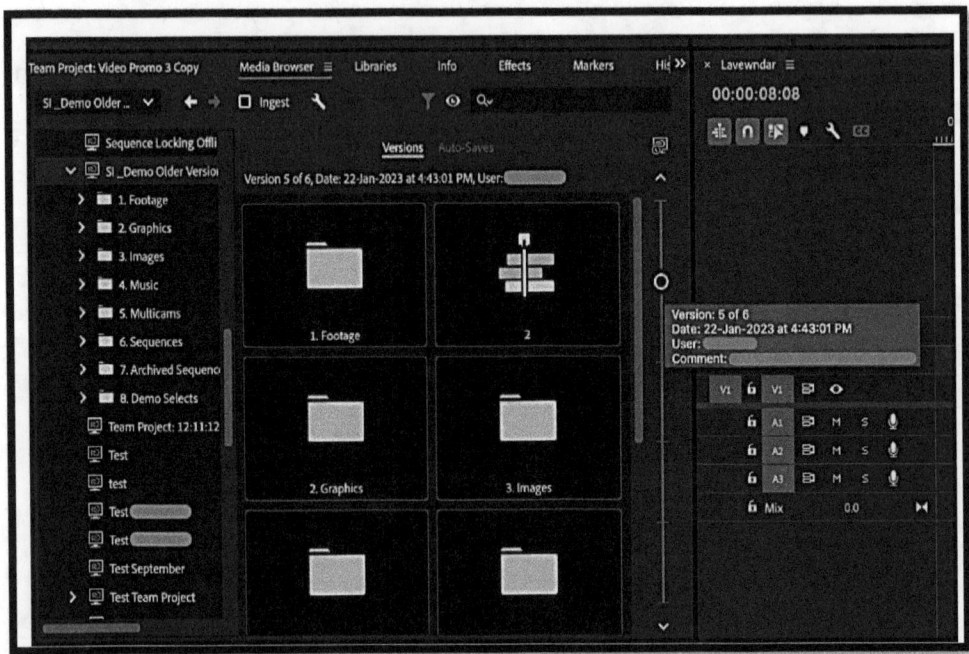

Create a new Team Project from a version

1. Use any of the previously mentioned methods to access the versions in the Media Browser panel.
2. Utilize the vertical slider for versions to navigate to the latest version of the project in the Media Browser, allowing you to view all available versions.
3. In the Media Browser, right-click on the Team Project listed under Creative Cloud and select **"New Team Project from Version."** This will create a new Team Project based on an existing shared version.

A dialog box will appear with the following features:

- The name of the current Team Project will be pre-populated, with "copy" appended to it.
- It will include the same list of collaborators as the original Team Project.

4. Click **OK** to create the new Team Project.

Specify Auto Save cache location

Every edit you make in a Team Project is saved locally and instantly synced with Adobe Cloud. You can also specify where on your local machine to save the Team Project Auto Save files. The project saves in the background as you work and make changes.

Note: For local projects, automatic saves occur at intervals set in the Automatically Save settings. Team Project saves all preferences with each edit, so you don't need to manually save your project after every change, ensuring your work is always preserved.

1. In the menu bar, go to **Premiere Pro** and select **Settings** (macOS) or **Preferences** (Windows). Then, choose **Auto Save**.
2. In the Team Projects section, click **Browse** and select the location on your computer where you want to save the project.

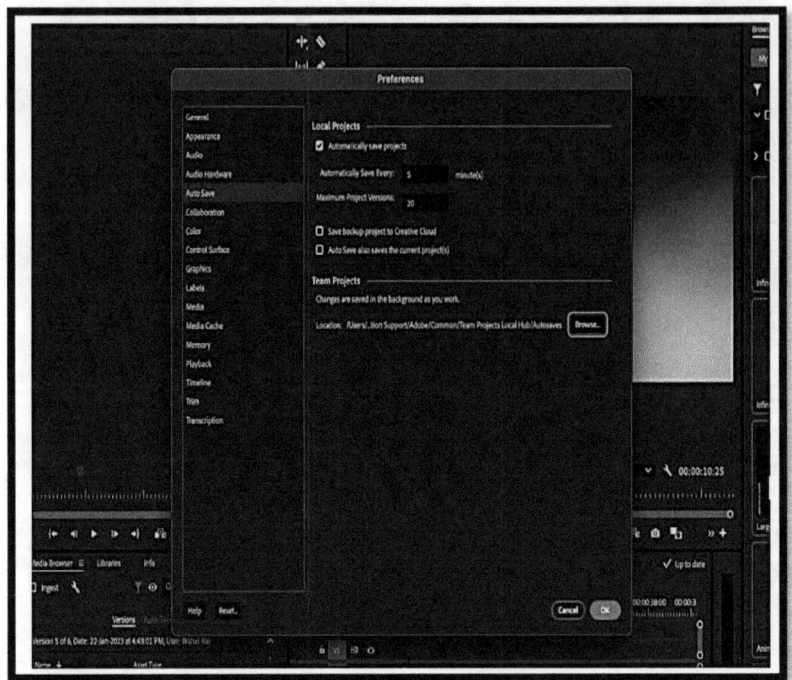

Once you're finished, the changes you've made will be applied to the next Team Project you create.

View auto-saves

You can view all auto saves, check when your changes were automatically saved, revert to an earlier auto save, and even create a Team Project from an auto-saved edit using the Auto Saves tool.

1. Open the Team Project you want to review by going to **Edit > Team Project > Browse Auto-Saves**. Alternatively, you can select the Team Project name from the Premiere Pro menu bar and choose **Version History** from the dropdown menu.
2. Another method is to right-click on the Team Project in Creative Cloud and select **"Team Project Auto-Saves..."** from the menu. This will display a list of all your Team Project auto-saves. You can navigate through the auto-saves using the vertical tool provided for Team Project Auto-Saves.

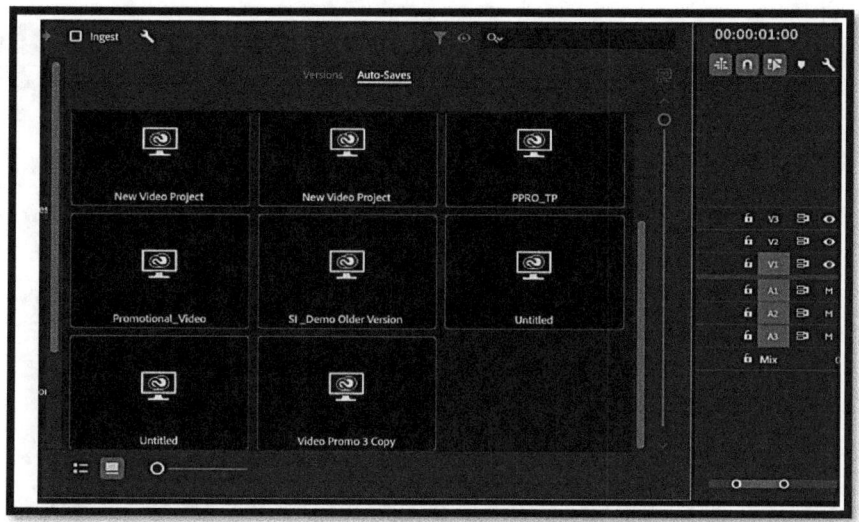

3. Select **"Make Auto-Save the Latest"** to revert the most recent change and restore the last auto-save.

4. Right-click on the Team Project in Creative Cloud, choose **"New Team Project From Auto-Save,"** and then click **"OK."** This will create a new Team Project based on the selected auto-save. A window will appear that:

- Pre-populates the name of the current Team Project.
- Appends "auto-saved copy" to the name.
- Includes the same list of collaborators as the original Team Project.

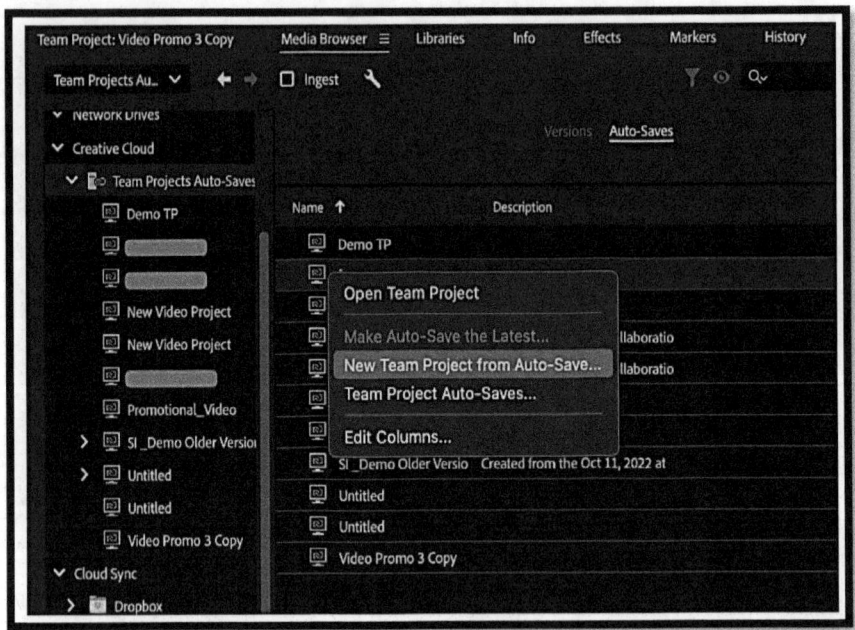

Set Trim preferences
Large Trim Offset

The Trim Monitor Features Large Trim Offset buttons that allow you to adjust trim points by moving them forward or backward. You can customize the number of frames that these buttons shift the trim points in the Trim pane of the Preferences dialog box.

Allow the Selection tool to choose Roll and Ripple trims without the modifier key

Enable this option if you want to edit in Ripple and Rolling mode without having to hold down a control key.

Shift clips that overlap trim point during ripple trimming

Enabling this option will cause overlapping track items to be moved during a ripple removal.

Ripple trim adds edits to keep both sides of trim in sync

To edit clips that span a cut, enable this option. Once you add edit points, they will be cut along with the selected trim points, preventing the clips from shifting out of alignment on either side of the edit.

Playhead position determines trim monitor loop playback

Enabling this option will cause the replay to loop around the playhead position instead of the entire edit point selection.

Set transcription preferences

When using Premiere Pro to transcribe audio clips, you'll encounter the following options and settings for transcription:

- **Automatically Transcribe Clips**: Check this box to enable automatic transcription of clips.
- **Transcription Preferences**: Choose between auto-transcribing all imported clips or only the clips in sequence, depending on your needs.
- **Speaker Labeling**: Select "Yes, separate speakers" for distinct labeling of individual speakers, or choose "No" to keep the labeling unified.
- **Enable Language Auto-Detection**: Activate this option to allow automatic detection of the language during transcription.
- **Default Language**: Pick your preferred language for transcribing clips from the available options.

Noise Reduction and Restoration

Noise reduction is the process of correcting fuzzy areas in your footage. The noise originates from the camera's electronic sensor (CCD), which measures light for each pixel in your image. The monitor displays this information based on your camera settings. In low-light conditions, the camera may not capture enough detail, resulting in less clarity, particularly in the darker parts of the shot.

To effectively reduce video noise, it's best to add more light to your scene. Remember, it's generally easier to darken your footage than to edit out noise afterward. By applying these techniques, the noise in your video will become less noticeable.

Premiere Pro includes a built-in tool for noise cancellation, so you won't need any additional software. This process is quick and easy, making noise reduction an essential part of your editing workflow.

Let's get started!

1. Add Audio to Your Premiere Pro Project

The first step in reducing noise in your Premiere Pro videos is to add audio to your project. Once you open Premiere Pro, familiarize yourself with the layout, particularly the Timeline panel located at the bottom of the interface. This area is central to your project, where you can add video and arrange it as needed. The Timeline controls when the video and audio start, stop, and work in sync. To edit audio, simply drag and drop it onto the Timeline.

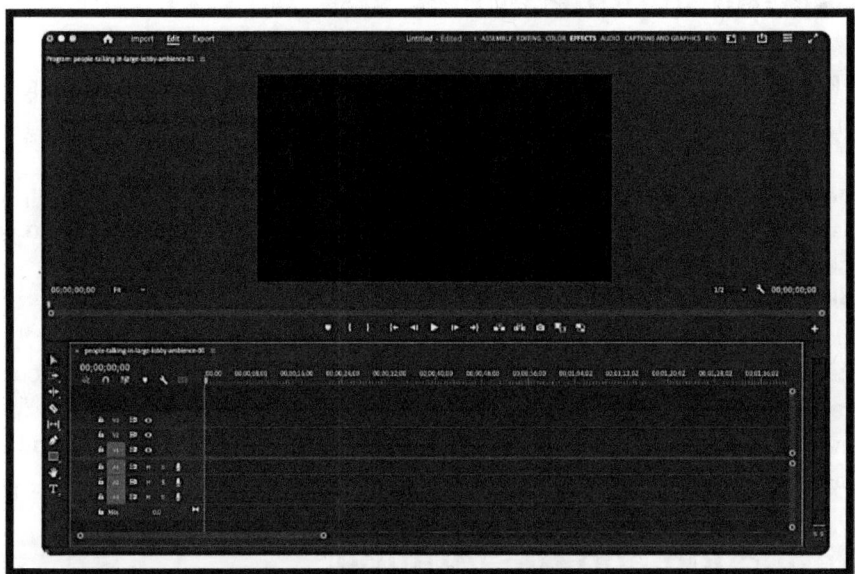

1. Add Audio to Your Premiere Pro Project

The first step in reducing noise in your Premiere Pro videos is to add audio to your project. Once you open Premiere Pro, familiarize yourself with the layout, particularly the Timeline panel located at the bottom of the interface. This area is central to your project, where you can add video and arrange it as needed. The Timeline controls when the video and audio start, stop, and work in sync. To edit audio, simply drag and drop it onto the Timeline.

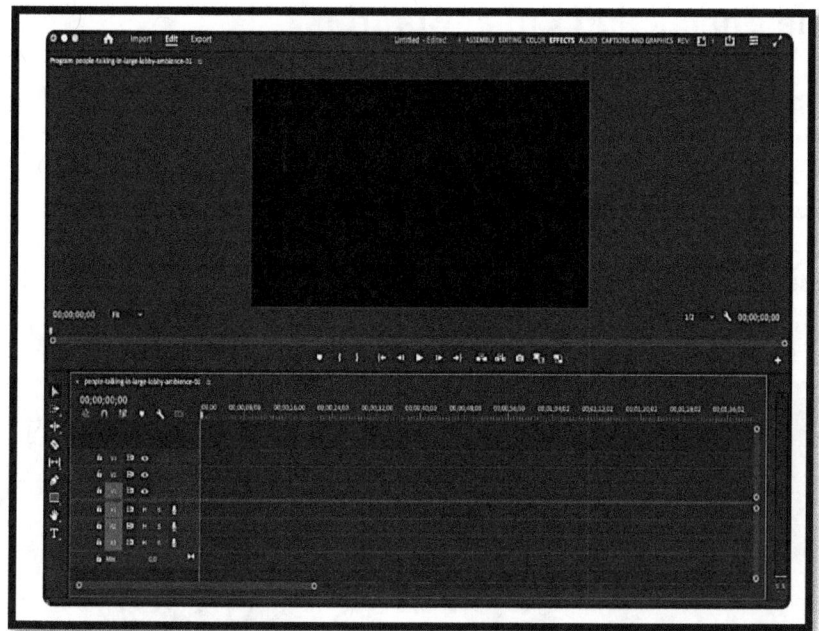

Let's see how to do this. Start by locating an audio file on your computer. Once you find it, click on it to select it. After that, drag the file to your Timeline. The A1 track, labeled on the left side of the Timeline, is a suitable choice for your main audio track. Drop the audio file there to add it to your project.

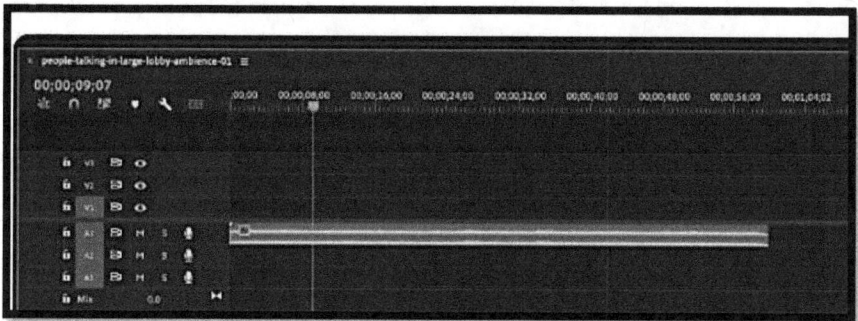

Once you've imported the audio, you're ready to explore Premiere Pro's noise reduction tools. Today, you'll learn how to eliminate background noise from your audio. **Note:** If your video has sound, it will already be on a track labeled "audio."

2. Open the Effects and Effect Controls

To remove background noise, we'll utilize two key sections: the Effects panel and the Effect Controls panel, which are directly linked. In Premiere, you can add effects to clips through the Effects panel and adjust their intensity in the Effect Controls panel. For instance, you'll add a **DeNoise** effect and then use the Effect Controls to determine how much noise to reduce.

To access these panels, go to the top menu of Premiere Pro and click on **Window**. From the dropdown menu, select **Effects** to open the Effects panel.

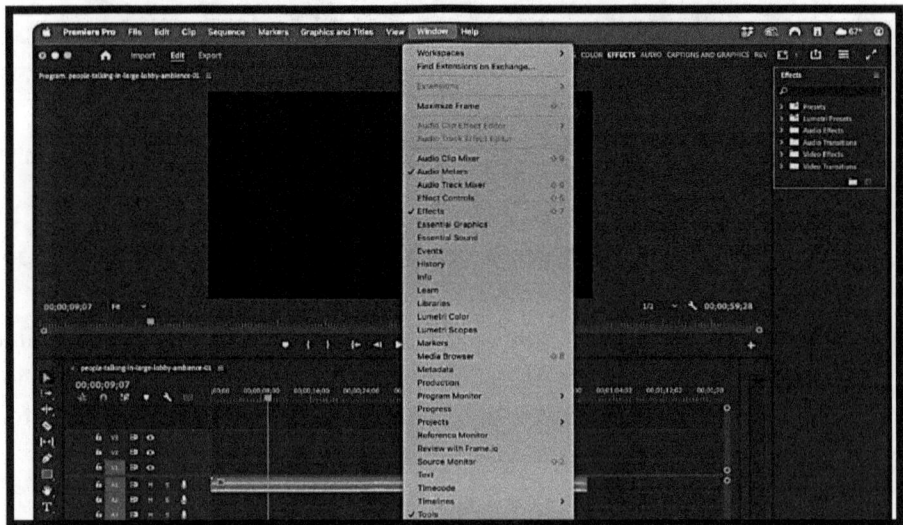

After selecting **Effects**, the panel will open on the right side of Premiere Pro, next to the Timeline. Now, let's open the Effect Controls panel. Go back to the **Window** menu and select **Effect Controls** from the list near the top. This panel will open in the top left corner of your Premiere Pro window.

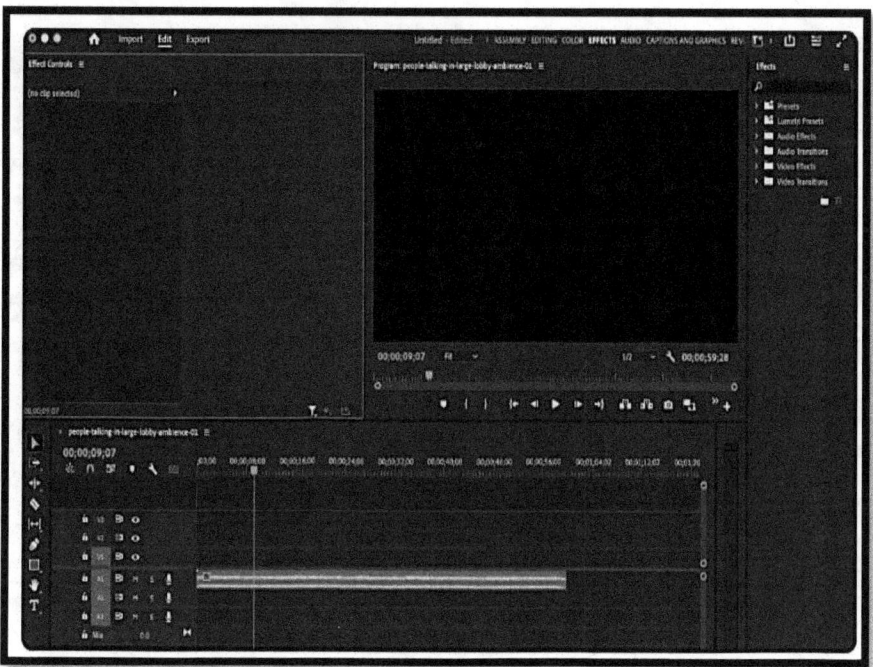

Now we can start removing the background noise in Premiere Pro!

3. Apply a DeNoise Effect in Premiere

As mentioned, DeNoise is an effect specifically designed for Premiere Pro. First, we need to apply it to our audio. Locate the audio clip in the Timeline, which appears as a green bar. Click on it to select it.

Next, go to the Effects panel on the right side of the screen that we opened earlier. Inside the Effects panel, you'll find several subfolders. Look for the **Sound Effects** folder and open it. Then, navigate to the **Noise Reduction/Restoration** folder. In this section, you'll find several effects, including the one we need: **DeNoise**.

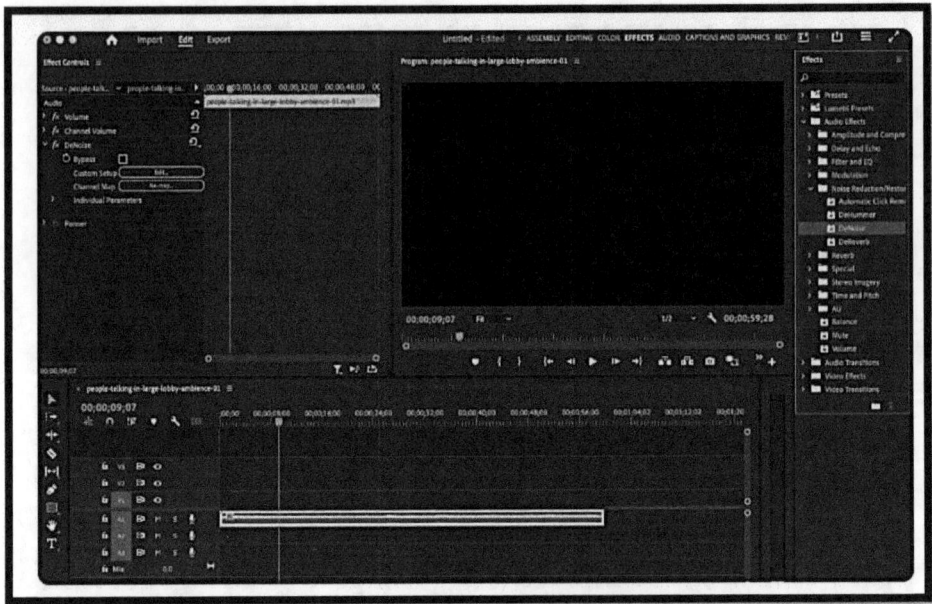

In Premiere Pro, click and drag the **DeNoise** effect onto the audio track you selected in the Timeline. Once you release the mouse, the effect will be applied. And just like that, you've learned how to reduce background noise in your audio!

4. Adjust the Effect

After adding the DeNoise effect, keep an eye on the **Effect Controls** panel in the upper left corner. It will populate with new options, including the **DeNoise** dropdown tool. Here, you can adjust the strength of the DeNoise effect as needed.

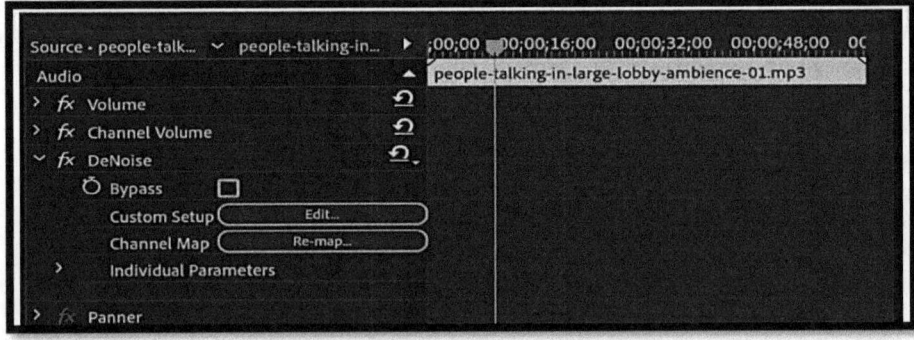

Open the DeNoise menu and click the **Edit** button in the Custom Setup group. This will launch the Clip Fx Editor. You can press the Spacebar on your keyboard to start playing the audio. In the sample box of the Clip Fx Editor, you'll be able to listen to the sound waves as they play back.

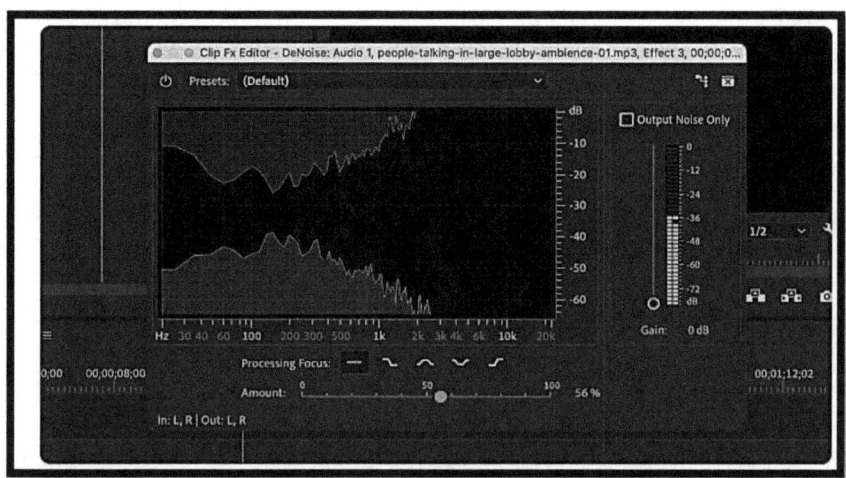

In the Clip Fx Editor, you have several options to adjust your noise reduction. You can start by selecting from the presets available in the **Presets** dropdown, where the Default settings are currently active. By clicking this dropdown, you can choose options like **Light** or **Heavy Noise Reduction**.

At the bottom of the Clip Fx Editor, you have more control over the noise reduction using the **Amount** scale. You can slide it left or right to adjust how much noise is filtered out. Since there isn't a one-size-fits-all setting, it's essential to listen to your audio and make adjustments based on what you hear. You can tweak the strength of the noise reduction as you work, allowing you to retain desired sounds while eliminating background noise.

Once you're satisfied with your adjustments, exit the Clip Fx Editor. The noise reduction settings you configured in Premiere Pro will now be applied to your clip.

More Options: The Essential Sound Panel

You've learned how to reduce noise in Premiere Pro videos using the Effects and Effect Controls. However, there's another powerful option available: the **Essential Sound** panel. This feature can enhance the changes you've already made, or you can use it as an alternative to the Effects panel.

1. Open the Essential Sound Panel

To access the Essential Sound panel, open Premiere Pro and go to the top of the screen. Click on the **Window** dropdown menu, and from the list of options, find **Essential Sound**. Clicking on it will open the Essential Sound panel, which typically appears on the right side of the screen, above the Effects panel we used earlier.

2. Reduce Noise with Essential Sound

With the Essential Sound panel open, you can now proceed to eliminate noise from your audio. Start by selecting your audio track in the Timeline. Next, navigate to the **Key Sound** section, ensuring you are on the **Edit** tab. Under this tab, locate the **Repair** subsection and click on it. New settings and options will appear for you to work with.

Reducing noise should be your first step. To activate this feature, click the checkbox next to **Reduce Noise**. Press the Spacebar to start playing your audio as before. You can then slide the bar left and right during playback to adjust the strength of the noise reduction.

Additionally, if you notice a rumble in the background while recording, you can use the **Reduce Rumble** option. Simply check the box next to it to enable it, and adjust the volume while the audio plays back.

With these tools, you now know how to effectively eliminate background noise in Premiere Pro! You have access to powerful options that can enhance your audio, ensuring it sounds great for your next project. Make noise reduction a regular part of your editing process, and your videos will look and sound fantastic!

CHAPTER 11

MOTION GRAPHICS AND ANIMATION

Introduction to Motion Graphics

Motion Graphics templates (.mogrt) are unique files created in either After Effects or Premiere Pro. These templates are particularly beneficial for Premiere Pro editors, as they leverage After Effects' motion graphics capabilities while being easily accessible and customizable directly within Premiere Pro.

Premiere Pro offers its own Type and Shape tools for creating titles and graphics, which can then be exported as Motion Graphics templates for sharing or future use. Additionally, Premiere Pro comes with a variety of pre-made Motion Graphics templates from both After Effects and Premiere, ready for immediate use.

Furthermore, Premiere Pro allows you to load Motion Graphics templates from various sources, providing editors with greater flexibility:

- **Local Templates Folder**: Editors can save and access Motion Graphics templates locally, making them easy to locate and utilize in Premiere Pro.
- **Creative Cloud Libraries**: Templates stored in Creative Cloud Libraries can be seamlessly used across different projects, ensuring consistency and easy access.
- **Adobe Stock**: Adobe Stock offers a vast collection of professionally designed Motion Graphics templates, providing editors with a wide range of options for their projects.

These import options significantly enhance the availability of Motion Graphics templates for Premiere Pro editors, making it easier to integrate After Effects' motion graphics tools and expand creative possibilities in the editing environment.

Install templates for motion graphics.

In the **Essential Graphics** panel, you can add Motion Graphics templates from your computer to the Local Templates folder. Unlike video files, Motion Graphics designs are not found in the Project panel.

Steps to Add Templates to the Local Templates Folder:

1. **Drag and Drop**: Simply drag and drop one or more templates onto the Essential Graphics viewer. Alternatively, you can click the **Install** button in the bottom right corner to add your MOGRT files.

2. **Select the Template**: Navigate to the folder where your Motion Graphics template is saved and select **Open**.

Once added, the template will be moved to the Local Templates Folder and will be accessible in the Graphics panel.

Note: If a Motion Graphics template with the same name already exists, a prompt will appear asking whether you want to replace the existing template or cancel the installation. Additionally, Premiere Pro will notify you if you attempt to use a Motion Graphics template that is incompatible with your current project version. Templates created in a newer version of After Effects may not work with older versions of Premiere Pro.

The Local Templates folder

The **Local Templates** folder serves as the default location for installing MOGRTs or licensing them from Adobe Stock via the Essential Graphics panel. Here's where you can find it:

*   **macOS**: username/Library/Application Support/Adobe/Common/Motion Graphics Templates/
*   **Windows**: C:\Users\username\AppData\Roaming\Adobe\Common\Motion Graphics Templates\

Note: On macOS, the **AppData** directory is private, and the same applies to the Local Templates folder on Windows. To view these files, you may need to adjust your system settings to make hidden files visible.

If you attempt to load a Motion Graphics template with the same name as one already in Premiere Pro's Local Templates folder, a message will pop up, giving you the option to replace the existing template or cancel the installation.

Premiere Pro will also alert you if you try to install a Motion Graphics template that is incompatible with your current project. If the template was created with a newer version of After Effects, you may encounter issues. Premiere Pro will indicate that the Motion Graphics template is not suitable if it uses features or functions that your current version does not support.

Organize Motion Graphics templates
Create a library

Think of your computer as a vast library, where your files, photos, and videos are the books and items on the shelves. Premiere Pro, a video editing software, allows you to create your own "libraries" to organize and manage your video content. Imagine the **Libraries** panel in Premiere Pro as a special shelf that holds all your curated libraries.

Creating a New Library

1. **Open the Libraries Panel**: To see the libraries panel, go to **Premiere Pro**, select **Window**, and then click on **Libraries**. This opens the panel, similar to visiting a library section to access your books.
2. **Create a New Library**: Click the three-lined "hamburger" icon next to "Libraries." This reveals a menu. Choose **Create New Library**, akin to naming a new shelf in your library.
3. **Name Your Library**: A text box will appear asking for the name of your new library. Type in your desired name and click **Create**. Congratulations! You've just added a new section for organizing your videos.

Adding Graphics to Your Library

If you have an important graphic or image to store in your new library, follow these steps:

1. **Open the Essential Graphics Panel**: This acts like a drawer for your key graphics.
2. **Select Your Graphic**: Right-click on the graphic you wish to add. This is like taking a special item from a box.
3. **Copy to Library**: Click **Copy to Library** and select the library where you want to save it. This is like placing the graphic on the newly created shelf.

Exploring the Essential Graphics Panel

The Essential Graphics panel functions like a gallery for various Motion Graphics styles, allowing you to browse through a collection of options for your videos. Here's what you can do:

*   **Search for Templates**: Type keywords in the search field to quickly locate specific Motion Graphics templates, much like searching for a book by title.
*   **Preview Templates**: Hover over templates to see a preview image, similar to flipping through a catalog.
*   **Sort Your Files**: Organize your templates by title or by "recently used," making it easier to find what you need.
*   **Bookmark Favorites**: Click the star icon next to a template you like to mark it, akin to bookmarking a page in a catalog for easy reference later.
*   **Rename and Tag**: You can rename and tag templates for better organization, similar to adding labels to items in your library.

Just like organizing books in a library makes them easier to find, Premiere Pro's Libraries and panels allow you to efficiently manage your video materials, streamlining your editing process. This organization enhances your ability to quickly access what you need when creating your videos.

Browse and manage Motion Graphics templates

You can easily find and manage Motion Graphics templates in the **Essential Graphics** panel. Here's how to navigate this feature and make the most of it:

Accessing Motion Graphics Templates in the Essential Graphics Panel

In the **My Templates** view, you can perform several useful actions:

- **Search Functionality**: Type keywords or phrases into the search bar to quickly locate specific templates. You can filter results to view templates available in your Libraries or local folders.
- **Preview Animations**: For templates that include video clips, hover over them to see a preview of the animations, allowing you to gauge their suitability for your project.
- **Sorting Options**: Arrange the Motion Graphics files by **Title** or **Most Recently Used** to streamline your workflow.
- **Favorites**: Click the star icon next to any Motion Graphics template to mark it as a favorite. You can quickly access your favorites by using the picks filter next to the search bar.
- **Rename and Tag**: In the **InfoView**, you can change the names of your Motion Graphics templates and add tags to enhance organization and retrieval.
- **Image Size Adjustment**: You can change the size of the images in your MOGRTs for better visibility and selection.

Additional Note

You can also utilize the **libraries** panel to import Motion Graphics templates from **Adobe Stock** or **Creative Cloud Libraries**, expanding your creative options even further.

This organized approach to managing Motion Graphics templates within Premiere Pro allows you to work more efficiently and creatively on your video projects!

Browse Multiple Libraries

You can browse designs from multiple sources simultaneously in the Essential Graphics panel:

- **All Designs**: Click on "All" to view results from all libraries combined.
- **Single Library**: Select a specific library to display only the designs available in that library.
- **Multiple Libraries**: You can choose more than one library at a time to see a broader selection. If you want to reset your selection, clicking "All" will clear any chosen libraries.

This flexibility allows you to efficiently explore a wide range of Motion Graphics templates tailored to your needs!

Manage Extra Folders

You can easily manage custom folder paths in Premiere Pro to access your Motion Graphics templates. Here's how to add new custom folders:

1. **Open the Menu**: Click the hamburger icon next to the Essential Graphics panel.
2. **Manage Folders**: Select "Manage Additional Folders" from the dropdown menu. This will open the Manage Additional Folders dialog box.
3. **Add a Folder**: Click "Add" to create a new group. Select the desired folder and click "Select Folder" to add it to the list.
4. **Remove a Folder**: To delete a folder, click on it in the list and then click "Remove."

This allows you to keep your templates organized and easily accessible!

Drag and drop between locations

You can easily manage your MOGRTs (Motion Graphics templates) by moving or copying them between different locations. Here's how to do it:

1. **Moving MOGRTs**: If you want to move MOGRTs within the same disk, simply drag and drop the templates from one local folder to another.
2. **Copying MOGRTs**: If the folders are on different drives, you can copy the MOGRTs instead. Right-click on the template in the Essential Graphics panel and select "Copy," then navigate to the destination folder and select "Paste."
3. **Moving to Collections**: You can also transfer MOGRTs from a folder on your computer to a collection in your Libraries.
4. **Tracking MOGRTs**: When you select a MOGRT in the Essential Graphics panel, a blue outline will indicate its location in the library, helping you keep track of your templates.

This way, you can easily organize your Motion Graphics templates to enhance your editing workflow!

Adding your local folders from the disk

To manage your MOGRTs (Motion Graphics templates) efficiently within the Essential Graphics panel, follow these steps:

1. **Adding Folders**: Click the plus sign in the top right corner of the Essential Graphics panel. This allows you to add folders from a local drive, cloud drive, or shared network drive to the My Templates window.
2. **Accessing Custom Files**: To locate your custom local files, right-click in the Essential Graphics panel and select "Reveal in Finder/Explorer." This will open the folder where your MOGRTs are stored.
3. **Note on Folder Structure**: If you add a parent folder that contains subfolders with MOGRTs, the templates won't appear in the Essential Graphics panel. Ensure that you add the specific folder containing the MOGRTs.
4. **Using the Context Menu**: The Essential Graphics panel provides a context menu where you can manage your MOGRT files on disk. Options include:
   - **Rename**: Change the name of the MOGRT or folder in the panel.
   - **Remove**: Delete the entry from the Essential Graphics panel (this won't affect the actual folder on your hard drive).
   - **Reveal in Finder/Explorer**: Quickly navigate to the folder containing your MOGRTs.

Remember, renaming or removing an entry in the Essential Graphics panel does not alter the actual folder on your hard drive. This way, you can keep your MOGRTs organized and easily accessible!

Removing default templates

To remove the basic templates provided in the Local Templates Folder in Premiere Pro, follow these steps:

1. **Access the Local Templates Folder**: In the Essential Graphics panel, click on the Local Templates folder in the browser tree.
2. **Reveal the Folder**: Right-click on the Local Templates folder and choose "Reveal" in Finder (macOS) or Explorer (Windows). This will open the folder in your file system.
3. **Delete MOGRT Files**: In the Local Templates folder, delete all the MOGRT files you find there. Make sure to **keep the .txt file** named PrMogrtInstall13-0-0.txt, as this file is necessary for the functionality of the Local Templates.

If you ever want to restore the MOGRTs, simply delete the PrMogrtInstall13-0-0.txt file. The next time you open Premiere Pro, the MOGRTs will be recreated automatically. This allows you to clear out the templates while retaining the option to restore them later!

Using the Essential Graphics panel, look for Motion Graphics templates in Adobe Stock

Choose Adobe Stock from the Browse section in the Essential Graphics panel.

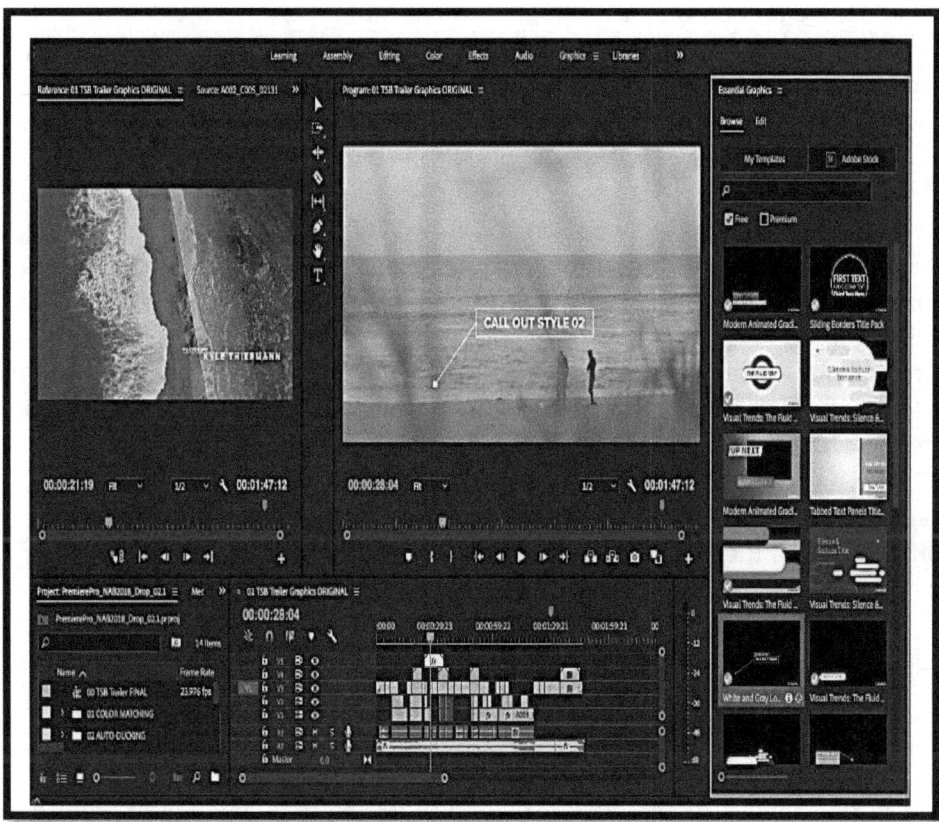

After entering your search term, hit Enter. The stock results resemble pages in a large book, displaying various Motion Graphics templates available for your video projects. You can view a limited number of pages at a time in the browser panel, depending on the themes and image sizes you've selected.

Here's how to effectively navigate and utilize these stock results:

1. **Browsing Methods:**

- o Use the "previous" and "next" arrows to flip between pages, just like in a book.
- o Enter a specific page number in the text box to jump directly to that page.
- o To license a Motion Graphics template, either drag it into your project or click the "License and Download" button.
- o Click the "I" icon below a template's image for more details or to see a preview of its animation.

2. **Licensing and Downloading:**
   - o In this view, click the "License or Download" icon to license the template and save it in your Local Templates folder.

Once you've found a Motion Graphics template you want to use in your video sequence, here's how to add it to your project:

- In the Essential Graphics panel, go to the "Browse" tab to access the store area with these templates.
- Drag and drop your chosen template onto a video track in your sequence, similar to selecting an item from a store and placing it in your workspace.
- Be aware that Premiere Pro might indicate the media is "offline" until the template is fully loaded. If the template requires fonts that aren't installed, you'll need to address those missing fonts.
- After adding the template to your sequence, you can customize its appearance further by clicking the "Edit" tab in the Essential Graphics panel, much like altering features of an item you've selected.

In summary, Premiere Pro allows you to explore a library of Motion Graphics templates, license them, and incorporate them into your video projects, giving you the flexibility to tailor them to your editing needs.

Add Motion Graphic templates to a Sequence

1. Accessing Templates:

- Open the Essential Graphics panel and go to the 'Browse' tab. This section serves as a gateway to a variety of available templates.

2. Adding a Template to Your Sequence:

- Select the desired template and drag it from the Essential Graphics panel onto a video track in your sequence. This action is like picking an item from a shelf and placing it in your workspace.

3. Media Loading Status:

- After adding the template, Premiere Pro may show that the media is 'offline.' This indicates that the template is in the process of loading into your project, similar to having an item prepared for use but awaiting full availability.

4. Fixing Missing Fonts (if necessary):

- If the template requires fonts that are not installed on your system, Premiere Pro will alert you to these missing fonts. You can resolve this by installing the necessary fonts, ensuring the template appears correctly in your project.

5. Customizing Template Appearance:

- Once the template is added to your sequence, you can customize its appearance and attributes. Navigate to the 'Edit' tab in the Essential Graphics panel, which provides tools to adjust and refine the selected template. Here, you can modify various elements to better fit your project's requirements.

Premiere Pro simplifies the process of selecting Motion Graphics templates, incorporating them into your video projects, and customizing them as needed. The Essential Graphics panel is filled with a wide range of templates, allowing you to use it as a toolkit for enhancing your workspace.

Customize your Motion Graphics template

When customizing Motion Graphics templates in Premiere Pro, you can tailor them to fit your project's needs. Here's a step-by-step guide on how to modify these templates:

1. Select Your Template

- Choose the Motion Graphics template you want to customize in your sequence.

2. Access the Essential Graphics Panel

- Open the Essential Graphics panel and click on the "Edit" tab to adjust the design settings to your preference.

3. Edit Template Properties

- In the Edit Template Properties section, you'll find various options depending on the template type:
  - Select from the options provided by the designer to modify colors, source text, and motion settings.
  - Adjust elements like fonts, text size, styles, and more.
  - You can resize features within grouped controls in the themes.
  - Edit data values using worksheet templates that support CSV (comma-separated values) or TSV (tab-separated values).
  - Replace the default media with your own images or videos in replaceable media designs.

4. Real-Time Updates

- Any changes you make in the template settings will be reflected immediately in the template itself.

5. Adjust Template Duration

- To modify how long the Motion Graphics template plays, select it in the timeline and use the red lines at its edges to extend or shorten its duration.

By following these steps, you can effectively customize Motion Graphics templates to enhance your video projects in Premiere Pro.

Regarding updating Motion Graphics templates

- Motion graphics templates created in After Effects can be easily updated in Premiere Pro sequences by swapping them with a newer version.
- To update, simply hold down the Alt (or Option) key and drag the new template over the existing one in the sequence.
- You have the option to update the template for all instances throughout the project or apply the change to just one instance, preserving as many of your edits as possible during the update.

Customizing Motion Graphics templates in Premiere Pro allows you to modify visually striking elements to suit specific project needs. This flexibility enhances the editing process and fosters greater creative freedom.

Creating Animated Lower Thirds
Design your lower third, but don't worry about making it "move" yet.

If you have a vision for how the bottom third of your screen should look, start creating it while the video is paused. Use the square and circle tools (or the pen tool) to create shapes, and employ the text tool to add your content. To ensure everything fits well, use the longest name, title, or location as a reference when designing a template for repeated use.

For more complex designs, you can create images in Adobe Illustrator and import them as .png files. Watching your favorite videos or searching online for inspiration can also spark ideas.

For instance, I found it easy to create my own bottom third, which included my name, title, and a solid color background. The design consisted of two bars, each perfectly sized for the text.

Lock the elements in their final positions first.

At the start, ensure that everything is off-screen or hidden. By the end, all elements should be positioned correctly. Begin by setting the playhead to 2 seconds and making your layers visible. Click the stopwatch icons next to position, scale, and opacity on one of the layers. This will keyframe the properties, locking all objects in place after the 2-second animation is complete.

Animate the elements onto the screen.

There are various methods to bring elements onto the screen, and while these are some options, you can always customize them using keyframes and effects to achieve your desired look. Generally, consider having the shapes animate in the first second and the text in the second. Here's a breakdown of the process:

Animation Steps:

1. **Shape Animation:**
   - Set a position keyframe and drag both rectangles off-screen with the playhead at 0 seconds. This will create an effect of the boxes sliding in from the sides. If you have multiple boxes, stagger their entry points to avoid uniformity.
2. **Unfolding Effect:**
   - To create an "unfold" effect, unlink the "link" icon next to "scale" in the transform options for both rectangles. At 1 second, set the scale to 100% and position them where you want them to be. At 0 seconds, adjust the scale y-values to 0, positioning them so the thin lines start at the desired "top" location.

3. **Text Animation:**
   o To animate the text, search for the "typewriter" effect in the effects panel and drag it onto your text layer. Press the "U" key to reveal the default animation keyframes and adjust their timing so the animation lasts between one and two seconds.
4. **Opacity Fade-In:**
   o Set two keyframes for opacity: one at 0% at 1 second and another at 100% at 2 seconds. This will create a smooth fade-in effect for the text.

Feel free to modify these steps to achieve the exact effect you want!

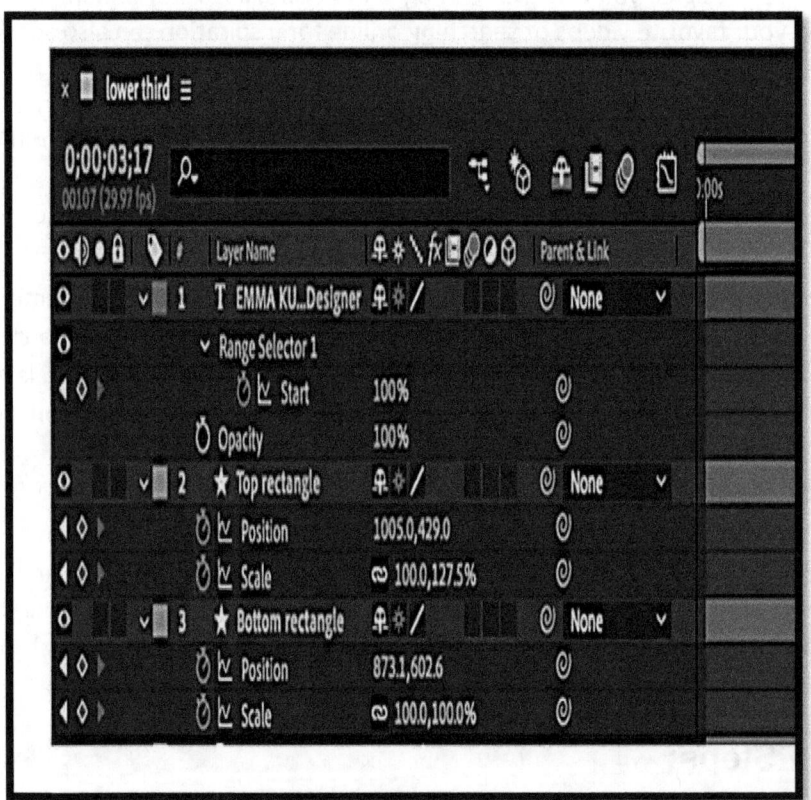

This is an example of the animation I created: it features a typewriter effect where the text appears as both boxes swing in from the left. The video duration has been extended to 3 seconds instead of 2.

Optional: animate the elements off-screen.

When the lower third exits the screen, you can recreate its entry animation by simply copying the same keyframes in reverse at the end of the clip. If you'd prefer not to invest that extra effort, don't worry! Often, it's unnecessary to animate the exit of a lower third, especially in fast-paced interview or b-roll segments. In these cases, drawing too much attention to its appearance and disappearance can be distracting.

Change the timing.

Once your keyframes are in the timeline, right-click on all of them and select "Keyframe Assistant," then choose "Easy Ease." This will smooth out the motion.

Watch the animation in the preview window a few times. Is it moving too slowly or too quickly? Are the elements appearing at the right moments? You can slow down the playback by dragging the playhead with your mouse, which is helpful for closely inspecting your animations.

Connect Premiere Pro and After Effects

When you first open After Effects and Premiere Pro, their interfaces may seem quite similar. Both have a player window, a sequence window, a browser window, and an effects tab. While it might appear that you can make similar changes in both programs, you'll soon notice a key difference in their functionalities.

Premiere Pro: A Quick Overview

Premiere Pro is primarily designed for cutting, editing, and refining video clips, although it also includes features for moving text and transitions. Its timeline is structured to facilitate a flexible and creative editing process, with various editing areas that support a smooth workflow from assembly to final product. You would typically use Premiere for assembling video projects, such as advertisements, music videos, and a wide range of creative editing tasks. Additionally, Premiere excels in audio management, allowing you to mix, edit, and enhance sound within your project.

After Effects: A Quick Overview

For motion graphics, editing, and visual effects, After Effects is the premier tool available. It's much easier to create unique titles and animations in After Effects compared to Premiere Pro, thanks to its extensive range of built-in animation types, each with its own set of customizable options.

However, editing videos in After Effects can be challenging due to its fragmented timeline. Instead of facilitating easy navigation between elements, the After Effects timeline emphasizes keyframing for individual elements. Adding a keyframe indicates the start and end points of an animation. For instance, if you want to create a simulated slow zoom on a clip in Premiere, you'd use keyframes, but finding the keyframing options can be tricky. In contrast, keyframes are central to the workflow in After Effects, making it much more intuitive for motion graphics work.

With its vast array of effects, tools, and third-party support, After Effects is an outstanding choice for motion design and editing tasks.

Using Dynamic Links

In the past, switching between After Effects and Premiere Pro required processing and exporting one project before loading it into the other, which was quite frustrating. If you frequently worked with title sequences created in After Effects, you had to export and import them into Premiere each time, leading to wasted time and multiple copies that took up valuable disk space.

Fortunately, those challenges have been resolved with the Dynamic Link feature. This functionality creates a seamless connection between After Effects and Premiere projects, saving you both time and hassle. Simply put, if you make a change to a title in After Effects, that change will automatically reflect in Premiere. Once you establish a dynamic link between the projects, the selected After Effects compositions appear as clips in the Premiere browser, allowing for a smoother and more efficient workflow.

How to Set Up a Dynamic Link

If you haven't created an After Effects project to link to from Premiere yet, here's how to do it:

1. **Create a New After Effects Project:** In Premiere, go to **File > Adobe Dynamic Link > New...** to start a new After Effects composition.
2. **Name and Save Your Project:** Give your project a name and save it. It's a good practice to save the After Effects project in the same location as your Premiere project for easy access.
3. **Adding More Compositions:** If you want to add another composition, simply repeat the steps. After the first time, it won't prompt you to name the project again, and your compositions will appear in the After Effects viewer.

This streamlined process makes it easy to integrate your After Effects work directly into Premiere.

Linking To an Existing After Effects Project

You can still link your existing motion graphics to Premiere, so don't worry! Just make sure your After Effects files are organized, with properly named comps in the correct locations. Here's how to import them:

1. **Import After Effects Compositions:** In Premiere, go to **File > Adobe Dynamic Link > Import....**.
2. **Locate Your Project:** In the file viewer, navigate to the After Effects project you want to import from.
3. **Select Compositions:** Choose the comps you wish to bring into Premiere and click "OK."

This process allows you to seamlessly integrate your existing After Effects work into your Premiere project.

ADDING & AMENDING YOUR GRAPHICS

After creating your title in After Effects, you can find the Dynamic Link compositions in the browser and add them to your timeline just like any other clip. Once linked, switching between programs to make adjustments to your motion graphics is straightforward. The live link ensures that any changes you make will automatically update in Premiere, allowing for quicker playback and a smoother editing experience.

Tips for Managing Dynamic Links

- Organize **Your After Effects Project:** Ensure your After Effects project is well-managed. It's easy to lose track and forget to name or organize your files, but maintaining order is essential for a clean, easily navigable linked project.
- Keep **Projects Together:** Store your After Effects and Premiere projects in the same location. If you move them after saving, you risk losing the connection, but you can relink them like any other missing clip.
- Familiarize **Yourself with Shared Projects:** If you're using a title project you received from someone else, open it up and familiarize yourself with its layout. Before creating a dynamic link in Premiere, note the names of the compositions you want to import.
- Consolidate **Motion Graphics:** Keep all your motion graphics in one place within After Effects. This allows you to reuse the same text and icon animations across different Premiere projects, streamlining your workflow.

CHAPTER 12
USING MARKERS

Markers allow you to highlight and organize key moments in your clips and sequences. You can use them to indicate important sounds or actions without altering the video itself. Here are the types of markers you can use in Premiere Pro:

- **Comment Markers:** These are used for general notes and reminders, helping you keep track of important information within your project.
- **Chapter Markers:** These markers are ideal for setting up chapters in a video, making it easier for viewers to navigate to specific sections.
- **Segment Markers:** Use these to define segments within a sequence, helping to break down your project into manageable parts.
- **Subclip Markers:** These allow you to mark specific sections of a clip for easy access later.

By utilizing these markers effectively, you can streamline your editing process and enhance your workflow in Premiere Pro.

Marker	Description
Comment	A comment or note about the selected part of the Timeline.
Chapter	Chapter markers in the project allow viewers seeing the finished video use the markers to quickly jump to those points in the video.
Segmentation Marker	Segmentation markers help you define ranges in the video to automate workflows. For example, you can identify certain areas as being leader or as segment where commercials go.
Web Link	Add a URL that provides more info about the selected part of the movie clip.

Markers are likely already integrated into your editing workflow. Many editors use them to quickly locate specific elements within a clip, such as motion or selected sound bites. Others utilize markers to position and align sections in the Timeline. Adobe Premiere Pro features a robust marking system that can even connect to online resources, enhancing your editing capabilities and organization.

Markers panel

By navigating to **Window > Markers**, you can view all the markers in the currently open clip or sequence. The Markers panel provides information such as color-coded tags, In-points, Out-points, and any notes you've added. When you click on a clip thumbnail in the Markers panel, the playhead will jump to the corresponding marker location. The In and Out points are visible on markers within a clip or sequence in the Marker box. You can adjust the marker's position by moving either the In or Out point, allowing it to span multiple frames if needed.

Add markers in the Timeline

You can add markers to the Source monitor, Program monitor, or Timeline in Premiere Pro. Any markers placed in the Program monitor will appear in the Timeline, and vice versa. This flexibility allows you to attach multiple notes or comments to the same clip on the Timeline. Here's how to work with markers:

Steps to Add and Modify Markers:

1. **Position the Playhead:**
   - Move the playhead to the specific point in your timeline where you want to add a marker.
2. **Create a Marker:**
   - Press the "M" key for a quick shortcut or go to **Marker > Add Marker**.
   - Note that markers default to a green color.
3. **Modify the Marker:**
   - Double-click the marker icon to open the Marker dialog box for adjustments.
4. **Choose Marker Options:**
   - In the Marker dialog, you'll find several customization options:
     - **Name:** Assign a name to the marker.
     - **Duration:** Adjust the duration by dragging or entering a new value, which is useful for sequence markers like chapter markers.
     - **Comments:** Add notes for additional context.
     - **Chapter Marker:** Check this option to designate the marker as a chapter marker.
     - **Web Link:** Select this if you want to link the marker to a website.
     - **URL:** Enter the website URL if the Web Link option is selected.
     - **Frame Target:** If using a web link, specify the target frame if applicable.
5. **Navigate Through Markers:**
   - Use the "Prev" or "Next" buttons to cycle through markers, adding comments or adjusting settings as needed.
6. **Confirmation:**
   - Once you're satisfied with your modifications, click the "OK" button to save your changes.

By following these steps, you can effectively utilize markers to enhance your editing workflow in Premiere Pro.

Adding Markers to Clips

Many editors prefer using markers in their workflow. Clip markers can help you add notes or align multiple clips more easily. Here's how to add markers in the Source Monitor and Timeline:

Adding a Marker in the Source Monitor:

1. **Open the Clip:**
   o   Access the clip in the Source Monitor from either the Timeline or the Project panel.
2. **Position the Playhead:**
   o   Move the playhead to the desired location for the marker.
3. **Create the Marker:**
   o   Press **M** or go to **Marker > Add Marker**. This will add a marker to the clip.

Marking a File in the Timeline:

1. **Set Up a Shortcut:**
   o   Go to **Edit > Keyboard Shortcuts** (Windows) or **Premiere Pro > Keyboard Shortcuts** (Mac) to create a shortcut for adding clip markers.
2. **Select the Clip:**
   o   Choose the clip you want to mark and position the playhead where you want the marker.
3. **Add the Clip Marker:**
   o   Press the keyboard shortcut you set for **"Add Clip Marker."** This will add a marker to the clip.
4. **View Marker Details:**
   o   To see the marker's text box, double-click on the marker in the Source Monitor.

Using these steps, you can efficiently add and manage markers to enhance your editing process in Premiere Pro.

Create markers in the Effect Controls panel

You can view all the markers you've created in the Timeline panel within the Effects panel. Additionally, you can add markers to your sequence to indicate where effects should be applied in the Effect Controls panel. Here's how to create and modify markers directly in the Effect Controls panel:

1. **Position the Playhead:**
   o   Move the playhead to the exact spot where you want to add the marker.

2. **Add the Marker:**
    - For Windows, right-click on the timeline marker; for Mac, control-click on it. Then, press **M** or select **Add Marker** from the menu.

By following these steps, you can effectively manage markers to enhance your workflow in Premiere Pro.

Change default marker colors

The default color for markers is green, but you can customize this by setting keyboard shortcuts for each marker color. Here's how to do it:

1. **Open Keyboard Shortcuts:**
    - For Windows, go to **Edit > Keyboard Shortcuts**.
    - For macOS, select **Premiere Pro > Keyboard Shortcuts**.
2. **Customize Marker Colors:**
    - In the Keyboard Shortcuts dialog, find the Command section.
    - Add keyboard shortcuts for each marker color you want to use.

By setting these shortcuts, you can quickly change marker colors to suit your needs while editing.

Navigate between the markers.

To use markers effectively:

- **Select a Marker:** Simply click on the marker you want to use.

- **Navigate Markers:**
  - o To move to the next marker, select **Go to Next Marker > Select Marker**.
  - o To return to the previous marker, choose **Go to Marker > Return to Previous Marker**.

These options make it easy to navigate through your markers while editing.

Move a marker

Here are the options for moving markers:

- **Move a Clip Marker:**
  - o Open the clip in the Source Monitor and drag the marker icon along the time measure. Note that you cannot change clip markers directly in the Timeline panel.
- **Move a Sequence Marker:**
  - o Drag the sequence marker either in the Timeline panel or along the time measure in the Program Monitor.
- **Update Marker Position:**
  - o When you adjust a marker's position in the time measure of the Source or Program Monitor, the associated icon will move accordingly.

These methods allow you to easily reposition markers as needed during your editing process.

Delete markers

Here are your options for removing markers:

- **Remove a Clip Marker:**
  - o Move the playhead to the clip marker, then open the clip in the Source Monitor to delete it.
- **Remove a Sequence Marker:**
  - o Move the playhead over the sequence marker to remove it.

To clear all markers at once, go to **Marker > Clear All Markers**. This option will remove all sequence and clip markers from the selected clips in Premiere Pro.

Display marker comments

In Adobe Premiere Pro, there's a useful feature that allows users to view marker information quickly without opening the Marker dialog box. Simply hover your mouse over a marker, and a tooltip will appear with key details. The tooltip for a sequence marker typically includes up to four pieces of information:

1. **Marker Name (Optional):** If a name has been assigned to the marker, it will display here.
2. **Start Timecode:** This shows the exact timecode where the marker is located in the sequence.
3. **Timeframe:** If the marker has a duration, the tooltip may also include information about its length in the sequence.
4. **Text or Comments (Optional):** Any notes or comments added at the time of creating the marker will be displayed in the tooltip, but only if such details were included.

This feature makes it easier to access important marker information at a glance.

Copy and paste sequence markers

You can include sequence markers when copying and pasting items from the timeline, ensuring that all marker information is transferred seamlessly. This includes the marker's color, notes, length, and type. To enable this feature, navigate to **Markers > Copy Paste Includes Sequence Markers**. This way, all relevant marker data will be preserved during the copy/paste process.

Using Sync Locks and Track Locks

In the Timeline panel, you can use two methods to manage clips on tracks:

- **Sync Locks:** These ensure that clips remain in sync across multiple tracks. When you add or remove clips, the sync lock keeps everything aligned properly.
- **Track Locks:** These prevent any changes to a specific track, keeping it in place and protecting it from accidental edits.

Using these features helps maintain organization and integrity in your timeline while editing.

Using sync locks

In a typical editing project, you'll often work with multiple layers of video clips, and it's essential for them to stay in sync, especially when making ripple edits or inserts. If one track is modified, the others should adjust accordingly. However, there might be instances where you want a specific track to remain unchanged during these edits. In Adobe Premiere Pro, you can prevent tracks from moving by using either **Track Lock** or **Sync Lock**.

When audio and video elements are not properly aligned, it can lead to issues like bad lip sync, where an actor's lip movements don't match the spoken audio. While some synchronization problems are obvious, others may be subtler.

Synchronization generally refers to ensuring that two related actions occur simultaneously. This can involve something as simple as a speaker's name appearing in a lower third or background music that aligns with on-screen action. When these elements are coordinated, they enhance the overall impact of your project.

Using track locks

Track locks, which are different from sync locks, stop anyone from making changes to a track. They're a great way to keep your sequence straight and clips in place on certain tracks while you work. For instance, you could lock your song track while adding different video clips. The music track can't be changed when it's locked, so you don't have to worry about it while you type. Things that are on a locked track are still in the sequence; you just can't change them. You can lock and open a track by pressing the Track Lock button. You can use diagonal lines to draw attention to clips on a locked track. In this case, track locks are more important than sync locks, so moving the audio clips would throw off the timing of the video clips even if the sync locks are turned on.

Source Patch and Target Tracks

A popular method in Premiere Pro is **source patching**, which allows you to specify where to place clips without manually dragging and dropping them. This feature is especially useful for first-time users who want to streamline their editing process. To direct Premiere on how to handle clips, you can use source patching along with **track targeting**.

By setting these options, you can clearly indicate which tracks will receive the clips you're working with, making the editing process more efficient and organized.

What Is Source Patching

When starting with Premiere Pro, many users take a straightforward approach: they simply grab clips and add them to the timeline without much thought. This method works fine for casual projects, but for more complex edits, efficiency and organization become crucial.

Source patching is a key feature that allows you to designate which tracks will be populated when using controls in the Source Monitor, such as overwrite or insert edits. This helps streamline the editing process by clearly instructing Premiere where to place your clips.

For more structured projects, like documentaries, source patching is invaluable. It enables you to layer audio and B-roll effectively, keeping different types of content organized across specific tracks. While the layout of video projects may vary, the principles of source patching can be applied universally, making it a vital tool for editors working on projects with multiple components or those set to music without additional audio.

How Does Source Patching Work?

You might have noticed that you can easily enable or disable audio tracks while editing. This allows you to choose which clips to include in your sequence, helping to dictate where they will be placed when you use commands like Insert or Overwrite, or even when copying and pasting clips.

If you take a closer look at the interface, you'll see two rows of blue-highlighted track options. These rows help you manage which tracks are active and how they interact with your edits, giving you greater control over your audio and video layers during the editing process.

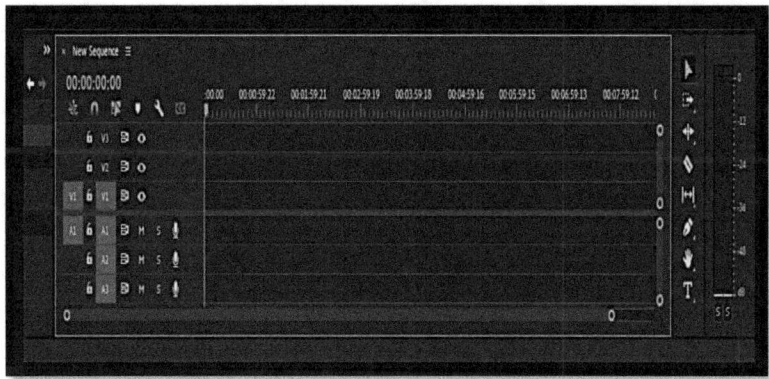

In the second column, each track is clearly labeled, with names like V1, V2, V3 for video tracks and A1, A2, A3 for audio tracks. However, in the first column, you'll notice only two labels: V1 and A1. Even when you select V2 and A2 in the first column, the names remain V1 and A1, which can be a bit confusing since those labels don't reflect the actual tracks you're working with. The original names persist, even as you work with different tracks above and below them.

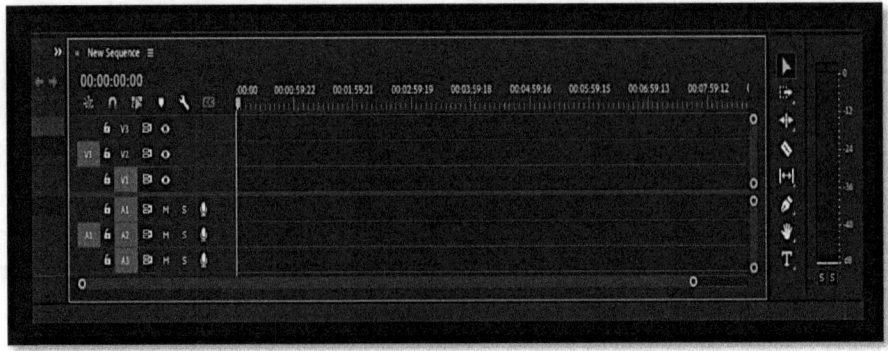

What Is the Difference?

When you're working in the Source Monitor, the first column for source patching becomes essential for precise control over where your clips go. You can select one audio track and one video track at a time, and easily toggle them on or off as needed. The second column is solely for track targeting, allowing you to enable or disable tracks for any automatic media actions, like copying and pasting.

For example, if you copy something to the clipboard, it will paste into the tracks you've targeted in the second column, regardless of what you've selected in the source patching column. However, if you're using drag-and-drop to place clips, the selections in the source patching column are what matter.

Taking the time to understand both source patching and track targeting will streamline your editing process and enhance your workflow, ultimately making your editing experience more efficient and less stressful.

How to Use Source Patching in Premiere Pro

If you're already familiar with source patching, you're on the right track! When both your Source Monitor and timeline have In and Out points set, source patching can seamlessly connect them. For instance, if you've marked your desired segment in the Source Monitor and you want it to land specifically in tracks V1 and A1, ensure that those tracks are selected in the source patching area.

If V3 is currently active but you want your edits to go to V1 and A1, simply click on the buttons for V1 and A1 in the source patching section. You can also use the comma (,) key to insert your selection directly from the Source Monitor into the timeline. This method ensures that your clip is placed exactly where you intend, maintaining a clear and organized workflow.

Exactly! When you're using source patching, the toggles in the first column are the key focus. They determine where your clips will be inserted or overwritten in the timeline. So even if V3 is selected, as long as you have V1 and A1 activated in the source patching area, your clips will go to those tracks instead. This flexibility allows you to control your workflow efficiently without needing to adjust track targeting every time. It keeps everything streamlined and organized!

Exactly! If V1 is left off in your source patching, only the selected audio will be added to the timeline, while the video from the Source Monitor will be ignored. This allows for precise control over what gets added to your sequence, making it easy to manage your audio and video tracks separately. It's a useful feature when you want to layer audio without affecting the video or when you're fine-tuning specific elements in your project.

Absolutely! By turning off the audio track in source patching, you can easily add just the video clips you need without any audio interference. This method is particularly useful when you're focusing on visuals, like creating a montage or aligning specific shots with music, allowing for a more streamlined editing process. It gives you greater control over the final product, ensuring that each element is precisely where you want it.

How to Target Tracks in Premiere Pro

When you press the Lift button (or the semicolon key), Premiere Pro will remove the selected clips from the timeline while leaving a gap where they were. This is useful for reorganizing your edits or creating space for new clips. If you want to maintain the timing of the remaining clips and fill the gap, you can use the Extract function (or the apostrophe key). This way, you can effectively manage your timeline and keep everything aligned as you make changes.

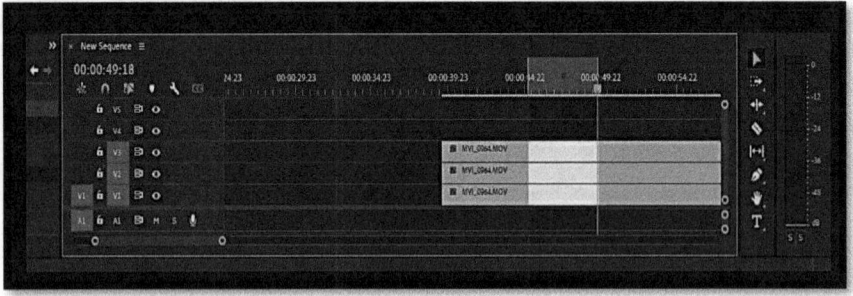

Exactly! When you use the Lift command, the selected clips and their associated In and Out points are removed from the timeline, leaving a gap. This can be a quick way to clear space without affecting the rest of your edits. If you want to remove the clips but keep everything else intact, the Extract command is the better choice, as it fills the gap created by the removed clips. This way, your overall timeline structure remains unchanged.

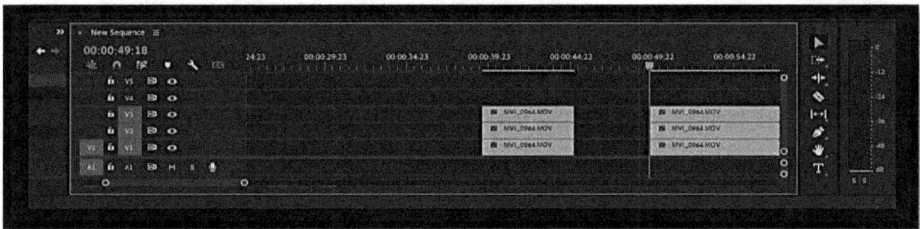

Great approach! By turning off V1 and V2 and focusing on V4 and V5, you can easily reposition your media. When you press Ctrl + V, Premiere will place the lifted content on the selected tracks, allowing for a clean organization of your clips.

If you then decide to only target V3, all the media will stack on that track, ensuring it remains the base layer. This method lets you maintain control over your edit and keep everything neat. Adjusting track targeting like this is essential for managing complex timelines and ensuring your workflow remains efficient. Ready to see how the new arrangement looks?

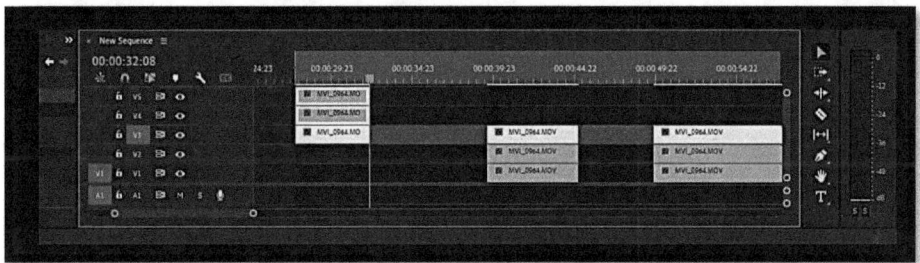

Exactly! Track targeting allows you to manipulate the arrangement of your clips without altering the original selections you made during the Lift, Extract, or copy operations. This means you can maintain the integrity of your content while efficiently reorganizing your timeline. It's a powerful feature that enhances flexibility in your editing process. Just remember, even if some tracks are turned off, any lifted content will still follow the source settings from the original action. This is crucial for maintaining the flow of your project. Do you have a specific arrangement in mind for your clips?

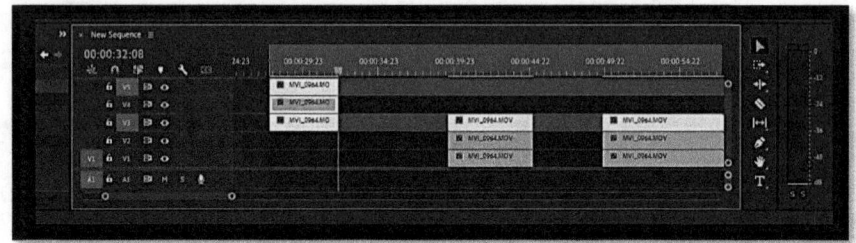

Exactly! By turning off track V2 before performing the Lift, you're ensuring that only the clips from tracks V1 and V3 are affected. This selective approach helps you maintain control over your editing process, allowing you to lift precisely what you need without unintentionally including other clips. It's a great way to keep your timeline organized and focused on the elements that matter most for your project. This method enhances efficiency and reduces the clutter in your edits. Do you often use this technique in your workflow?

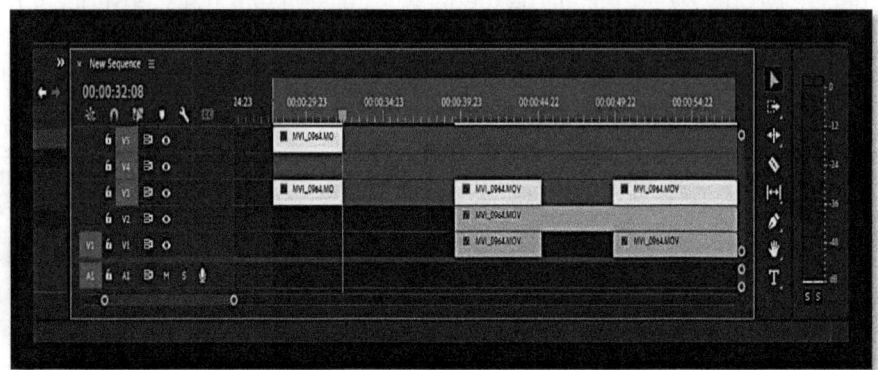

Once again, Premiere allows you to select just the bottom track, rather than requiring you to choose the two tracks containing the clips, including the one in the middle. The Lifted or Extracted portion will be transferred exactly as it is, provided there are enough tracks above the selected one to accommodate everything.

CHAPTER 13

COLLABORATIVE EDITING AND MEDIA MANAGEMENT

Collaborative Workflows

A "shared user workflow" in post-production typically involves using Media Composer or Resolve, allowing multiple individuals to collaborate on the same set of materials or timelines. This setup is especially useful for pairs like an editor and assistant editor, or a director and producer. In contrast, Adobe Premiere and Final Cut Pro have primarily focused on supporting solo filmmakers, enhancing functionality for users working on a single machine while neglecting the collaborative features needed for teams. Following the decline of Final Cut 7, Premiere gained popularity, particularly in social video and marketing, but struggled to penetrate the television and film sectors without better multi-user capabilities.

In scenarios requiring collaboration, previous solutions were often cumbersome. One common method involved sharing. prproj files while ensuring all users had access to the same media across different workstations, leading to significant workload and complexity. Whenever new media was added, it was vital for everyone involved—editors, assistants, directors—to have updated copies. Simultaneously editing the same timelines posed challenges, as there was no way to merge changes effectively. Tracking the "current" version of a project became a major hassle for assistants and post supervisors, complicating collaboration. While multiple users could open a Premiere Pro project file on a shared network, the last person to save would overwrite others' work, requiring constant communication to prevent data loss.

Recently, Adobe has taken steps to enhance multi-user workflows, aiming to penetrate Hollywood's feature film and television markets. This shift has also benefited smaller facilities, where even two users collaborating on a project can save time. For optimal ease of use, all users need to access the same media pool. Currently, working on a shared network provides the most effective solution for multi-user scenarios, with cloud-sharing options anticipated in the near future, which we will discuss below.

Shared Network

Premiere offers users the flexibility to save their media wherever they choose, unlike Media Composer, which functions best when all assets are stored in a designated media folder. Users could theoretically edit directly from a camera capture card, but this isn't always efficient— especially if the card will be formatted soon. As a result, users often store media on various external devices and rarely on their desktops, which complicates collaboration as more users are added. Media Composer can automatically transfer your content to a designated server media drive, and Premiere can achieve similar results if you configure your ingest settings properly. Both programs can effectively manage media migration, but it's essential to store all assets on a central server, commonly known as a Storage Area Network (SAN). Options include hardware solutions from LumaForge, EditShare, Drobo, and Avid, whose Nexis servers are also compatible with Premiere. The key is having a server designed for multiple users to access the same files simultaneously.

We recommend creating a separate folder for each project on your server, including a dedicated "media" folder within it. This approach allows you to transfer the entire master folder—containing all relevant media—when archiving, simplifying the process after project delivery. Premiere can be set to automatically ingest media, moving it to a new location rather than just connecting to the original files. When configuring multiple editors on shared storage, it's crucial to ensure that all media is stored on the shared server, avoiding any reliance on a local editor's internal drive. This helps prevent issues with lost media due to incorrect file paths. One of the biggest frustrations can arise when an editor saves assets to their desktop or an external drive, rendering them inaccessible when they are absent. To mitigate this risk, it's advisable to set up ingest workflows instead of simple connections. You can adjust these settings in the new project start window. If your workflow involves numerous users, consider updating the default settings across all computers in your system to ensure consistency.

Multiple Projects at Once

One of the key features of Premiere for collaborative editing is its ability to have multiple projects open simultaneously. Unlike most editing software that limits users to a single project at a time (with Resolve now allowing quick project switching, though it's resource-intensive and still keeps only one project actively open), Premiere allows for greater flexibility. You can manage your open projects easily using tabs at the bottom of the project window.

This capability is significant for workflows. In the past, users working on a series of episodes might have combined all episodes into one project for ease of navigation, helping to avoid duplication and ensure smooth transitions. However, with the option to open multiple projects, users can now separate episodes into individual projects. This setup allows for quick movement of sequences and assets between projects without the hassle of closing and reopening. It also conserves system memory since you can focus on just one or two episodes at a time rather than all six. For example, you can easily remove text from one project, switch to another, and paste it where needed, streamlining the editing process.

Project Locking

You can enable "project locking" in Premiere by accessing the settings panel for collaborative workflows. When "project locking" is activated, only one person can make changes to a project at a time. This feature is available only when no other projects are open in Premiere. If other editors open the project, they will have "locked" access, meaning they can view all components but cannot make any modifications. A red lock symbol in the bottom left corner of the project panel indicates that the project is locked, signaling that editing is restricted. This is especially useful when multiple people are collaborating on a project.

For instance, if you're working on episode 5 and want to check the current edit of episode 4, you can open it in locked mode without disrupting the editor currently working on it, as long as the project is stored on shared storage.

In addition to locking projects, you can choose to keep a project locked even if you are the only one editing it at that moment. If you know you won't be making any changes and want to allow access for others, or if you want to prevent accidental edits, simply click the clock symbol to lock it. The next person to open the project will have access by default.

Keep in mind that projects only update when they are opened. If another user is working at a different workstation, their changes won't appear on your screen until you close and reopen the project. To optimize system performance, especially memory usage, make sure to close any unnecessary open projects using the file menu or the hamburger menu next to the project tabs.

Project Sharing and Versioning

Tracking the various iterations and modifications made to a project is crucial for collaborative video editing, and this is facilitated by project sharing and versioning. These features allow multiple team members to work together seamlessly. Here's a breakdown of these concepts:

Project Sharing

Project sharing enables team members to access and collaborate on the same project file simultaneously. This functionality ensures that everyone can view the latest updates, making it easier to coordinate efforts and maintain consistency across edits. By using shared storage solutions, editors can easily transfer sequences, media, and other elements without the hassle of sending files back and forth.

Versioning

Versioning involves creating distinct iterations of a project, allowing teams to track changes over time. This feature is essential for maintaining a clear history of edits, making it possible to revert to previous versions if needed. It also provides a way to experiment with different edits without losing earlier work, fostering creativity while ensuring that the team can always return to a stable version of the project.

Together, project sharing and versioning enhance collaboration in video editing, allowing teams to work more effectively and efficiently while minimizing the risk of errors and ensuring everyone is aligned on the project's progress.

Project Sharing

The concept of project sharing involves the ability for multiple team members to collaborate on the same video project simultaneously or at different times. In software like Premiere Pro, this typically means saving project files, media assets, and editing choices in a centralized location or shared storage accessible to all contributors. This setup enhances collaboration and teamwork by allowing team members to access, modify, and contribute to the project as needed.

Here are some key features of project sharing:

- **Centralized Storage**: All project-related content—such as video clips, audio files, graphics, and project files—is stored in a central location or shared server, making it available to everyone involved in the project.
- **Collaborative Editing**: Team members can work on different sections of the project concurrently, enabling simultaneous editing, reviewing, and contributions to various aspects of the video.
- **Real-time Updates**: Changes made by one team member are typically reflected in real-time or through synchronization. This ensures that all contributors see the latest updates, reduces conflicts, and guarantees everyone is working with the most current version of the project.
- **Version Control**: Project-sharing systems often include version control mechanisms that track changes made over time. This feature helps maintain a history of revisions, making it easy to revert to earlier versions if necessary.

Together, these elements make project sharing a vital aspect of efficient video editing workflows.

Versioning

The term "versioning" refers to the management and organization of different iterations or versions of a video project. It involves keeping track of modifications made throughout the editing process, whether by different contributors or at various stages. Each version represents a specific moment in the project's timeline, showcasing a range of changes and adjustments.

Key components of versioning in video editing include:

- **Labeling or Numbering**: Versions are typically labeled or numbered sequentially or with specific IDs, such as v1.0, v1.1, v2.0, etc. This helps distinguish between the various iterations of the project.
- **Documentation and Notes**: Editors often maintain documentation or notes alongside each version, detailing the changes made. These records provide context and insights into what updates or additions were implemented.
- **Retrieval and Archiving**: Older project versions can be archived for reference or safekeeping, allowing editors to revert to earlier iterations if necessary. This is especially helpful when current changes don't meet expectations or require further review.

While project sharing facilitates collaboration among multiple team members, versioning ensures effective management of the project's different iterations. This combination enhances tracking, collaboration, and revision control within video editing workflows.

Media Management Best Practices

To achieve an efficient and organized video editing process in Adobe Premiere Pro, effective media management is crucial. Here are some best practices for managing your media:

Best Practices for Media Management in Premiere Pro

- **Folder Structure**: Create a well-organized folder structure on your computer or storage device before importing media. Organize files by project name and categorize them into folders like "Footage," "Audio," "Graphics," etc. This makes it easier to locate and manage your files.
- **Media Browser**: Use the Media Browser to navigate your media files instead of directly importing them into your project. This tool allows you to preview and select clips before importing, ensuring that you only bring in the clips you need.
- **Consistent File Naming**: Maintain a consistent naming convention for your files. Include relevant details like scene numbers, takes, or timestamps to make it easier to identify and locate assets within Premiere Pro.
- **Metadata and Labels**: Utilize metadata and labels to add descriptive information to your clips. Tagging clips with keywords, descriptions, and other data can significantly improve organization and retrieval within Premiere Pro.
- **Proxy Workflow**: For large or high-resolution files that may slow down your editing, consider using proxies—lower-resolution duplicates that are easier to work with. Premiere Pro allows you to edit with proxies and then relink to high-resolution files for the final output.
- **Trimming Unused Footage**: Remove or trim unnecessary sections of clips during editing to reduce clutter and improve performance. This keeps your project tidy and manageable.

- **Backup and Archive**: Regularly back up your project files and media assets to prevent data loss. Archive completed projects and their associated media to free up storage space and keep your resources organized.
- **Project Management**: Use Premiere Pro's sequences, bins, and markers to manage different aspects of your project. Bins help organize related clips or assets, sequences can organize different edits or versions, and markers can annotate your timeline for easy reference.
- **Offline/Online Editing**: Consider an offline/online editing approach for complex projects. Use lower-resolution files or proxy files during editing, and reconnect to high-resolution files when finalizing your output.
- **Collaboration Tools**: If working in a team, utilize Premiere Pro's collaboration features, such as Shared Projects and Team Projects. These tools allow multiple editors to work on the same project simultaneously while managing versions and changes effectively.

By implementing these best practices for media management in Adobe Premiere Pro, you can streamline your editing process, enhance productivity, and keep your media assets organized and easily accessible.

Replacing Clips and Media

Adobe Premiere Pro offers a range of tools that enable you to replace shots within your project and transfer keyframes and clip attributes between different clips. Utilizing these techniques can significantly expedite your video editing process.

At some point during editing, you may need to modify a clip in your project. This could involve completely replacing a clip, like swapping out an earlier version of an animated logo for a more recent one. Alternatively, you might want to substitute a clip in your Timeline with one from a bin. Depending on your specific needs, there are various methods available for replacing media. Here are a few effective approaches:

Techniques of Replacement

You can modify clips in a Timeline using several methods, depending on how precise you need to be. Regardless of the method chosen, any effects applied to the original clip will carry over to the new one. Here are the options:

- **Option (Alt) Drag**: By holding down the Option (Alt) key while dragging, you can replace any file in the Timeline. To position the new clip correctly, hold the Shift key while dragging it into place. The In point of the new clip will define where the replacement begins.

- **Shift+Option (Shift+Alt) Drag**: If you hold down Shift and Option (Alt) while moving the clip, the original clip's In point will be used instead of the new one. This method is particularly effective when working with footage from multiple cameras that have matching timecodes.
- **Replace Clip Command**: The most straightforward and accurate approach is to use the Replace Clip command. This allows you to swap clips from your bin or Program Monitor, aligning the playhead for precise synchronization, making it highly effective for edits.

Replacing a Clip in a Premiere Pro Sequence

If you need to replace a clip in a sequence while retaining the filters, motion effects, and keyframes, follow these steps to swap out a cutaway shot seamlessly. This method allows you to maintain the overall quality of your film. In my example, I want to preserve the style and the "push-in motion" (animated scale) that I've carefully crafted.

To set an "In" point for a clip in the Project window, make sure to do this first; otherwise, Premiere Pro will default to the clip's first frame. Hold down the Alt key (Windows) or Option key (Mac) and drag the clip from the Source or Project panel onto the clip in the Sequence. Once the clip is selected, release the mouse button. The new clip will inherit the original's features.

Alternatively, you can select the new clip directly in the Project panel. In Icon view, use hover scrub to locate the best In point, then press "I" to set it. To replace a clip in the sequence, right-click on it and choose Replace with Clip > From Bin. This method also ensures that color grading settings from the clip above are applied to the clip below, saving you valuable time!

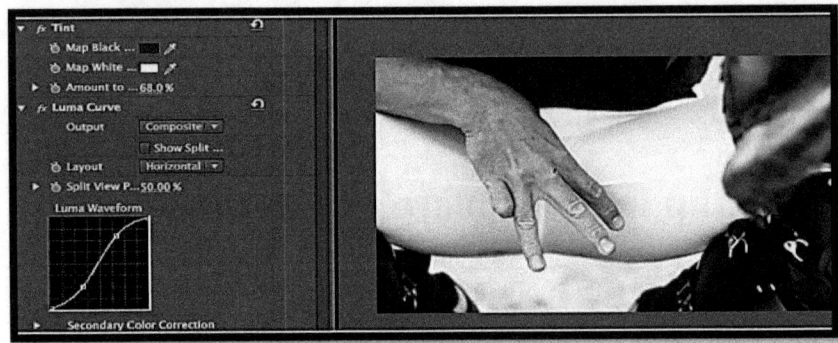

Using Replace Edit to Match Source Frame

This method can be handy when you want to replace a shot in Premiere Pro with a similar one. The Replace Edit feature focuses on the playhead's position in the Source Monitor and the sequence, rather than the In and Out points. For instance, if I wanted to swap one dancer for another performing the same move, this would be ideal. It's also effective for dialogue if both takes sync to the same word.

To use this method, move the playhead to a specific word or action in the sequence, then locate the corresponding point in a different take. Right-click on the clip in the sequence and select Replace with Clip > From Source Monitor, Match Frame. The new clip will retain all the original features, ensuring a smooth transition.

Replacing a Clip in the Project

If you want to use a clip across multiple sequences, this is especially useful when you receive a new file or need to replace a temporary clip. Simply press and hold the clip in the Premiere Pro Project panel, then select "Replace Footage." The new clip will automatically replace the old one in all sequences, while retaining its original features. This makes it a convenient way to update your footage without losing any applied effects or settings.

Changing the Playback Speed of a Clip

The speed of a clip is determined by comparing its playback rate to the original recording speed. The duration for which a clip plays from its "In" point to its "Out" point is referred to as its runtime. You can adjust audio or video clips to fit specific lengths by speeding them up or slowing them down. Here are three options for modifying the speed or duration of a clip:

- **Speed/Duration Command**
- **Rate Stretch Tool**
- **Time Remapping Feature**

Use the Speed/Duration command.

In the Timeline or Project panels, select one or more clips. If you're in the Project panel, hold down Ctrl (Windows) or Command (Mac OS) to select multiple non-adjacent clips. To adjust the speed or duration of a selected clip, go to the menu bar, choose the clip, then right-click to open the context menu.

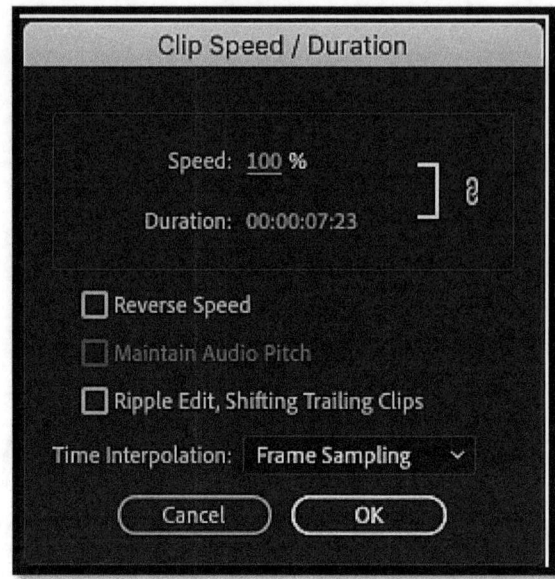

Here are some actions you can take with your selected clips:

- **Change Length Without Speed**: To adjust the length of the clips without altering their speed, click the "gang" button until it displays a broken link. This way, you can also change the speed independently of the duration.
- **Play Clips Backward**: Select "Reverse Speed" to play the clips in reverse.
- **Maintain Audio Pitch**: To keep the audio pitch consistent regardless of speed changes, enable the "Maintain Audio Pitch" option.
- **Shift Trailing Clips**: Use the "Shifting Trailing Clips" option from the Ripple Edit menu to ensure that adjacent clips move accordingly when changes are made.
- **Adjust Speed with Time Interpolation**: If you want to change the speed, select one of the Time Interpolation methods: Frame Blending, Optical Flow, or Frame Sampling.

After making your selections, press the OK button. Clips that have had their speed changed will show a fraction of the original speed.

Use the Rate Stretch tool

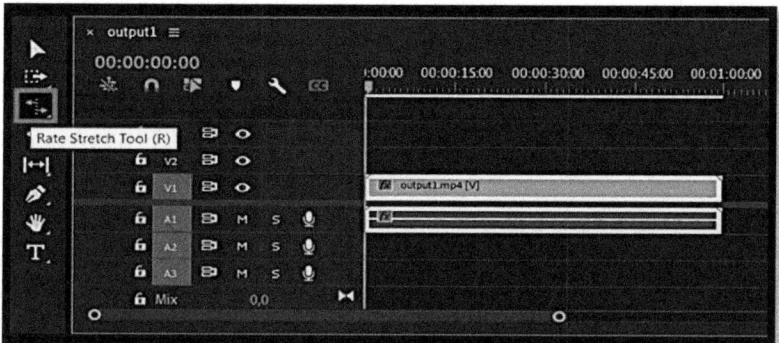

The Rate Stretch tool allows you to easily adjust a clip's length in the Timeline while simultaneously altering its speed to match the new duration. For instance, if you need to fill a specific gap in your sequence with sped-up media, you don't need to worry about the video's original speed as long as it occupies the gap. With the Rate Stretch tool, you can set the speed to any desired level. To use it, simply drag either end of the clip in the Timeline panel to adjust both its length and speed.

Make use of Time Remapping

You can adjust the playback speed of the video portion of a clip using Time Remapping, allowing you to create effects like slow motion and fast motion within the same clip. To get started, right-click on the clip and select **Show Clip Keyframes > Time Remapping > Speed** from the context menu. The clip will be highlighted with a blue tint, and you'll see a horizontal rubber band in the center, which lets you modify the speed.

Just below the title bar, you'll find a white speed-control track. If the clip is difficult to see, zoom in to create more space. You can change the speed by dragging the rubber band up or down, and a tooltip will display the speed adjustment as a fraction of the original speed. As you modify the speed, the length of the video will either expand or contract accordingly. While the audio remains unchanged during time remapping, it is still linked to the video portion of the clip.

Vary changes to speed or direction with Time Remapping

With the time-remapping effect, you can speed up, slow down, reverse, or pause segments of a video clip. For example, imagine a video of someone walking; you could show them moving quickly, then suddenly slowing down, pausing mid-step, or even walking backward before resuming forward motion.

It's important to note that you can only modify the timing of clips within the Timeline panel, not master clips. Additionally, if you change the speed of a linked audio and video clip, the audio will remain synchronized with the video but will play at its original speed, which can result in a mismatch with the visual content.

Vary change to clip speed

To adjust the speed of a clip using time remapping, right-click on the clip to open the context menu, then select **Show Clip Keyframes > Time Remapping > Speed**. The clip will appear with a blue tint, and you'll see a horizontal rubber band in the middle, which allows you to control the playback speed. Above this, in the white speed-control track, you'll find the speed keyframes.

To create a keyframe, press and hold Ctrl (Windows) or Command (Mac OS) and click on the rubber band. Speed keyframes will then appear above the rubber band. When you cut these keyframes in half, you'll create two new ones that mark the start and end of a speed-change transition.

Adjustment handles will show up on the rubber band during the speed change. Here are some options for modifying the speed:

- **Change Speed for a Section**: Move the rubber bands on either side of the keyframe up or down to adjust the playback speed. To limit speed changes to 5% increments, hold down Shift while dragging.
- **Adjust Left of the Keyframe**: To alter the speed of the section to the left of the keyframe, click and drag it left or right. This will change both the speed and length of that section, with parts speeding up becoming shorter and slowing down becoming longer.
- **Make a Speed Change**: Drag the right half of the speed keyframe to the right or the left half to the left to modify the speed.
- **Control Speed Change Dynamics**: By dragging the curve control handles, you can adjust how quickly the speed change ramps up or down.
- **Curve Adjustments**: The shape of the speed ramp's curve influences the acceleration or deceleration of the speed change.
- **Undo a Speed Change**: If you want to remove a change made to a transition, simply select and delete the half of the speed keyframe that you wish to discard.

CHAPTER 14
MANAGING PROJECTS

While it might not seem urgent to stay organized when you first start using Premiere Pro, maintaining organization becomes crucial as you take on more projects. Initially, it's relatively easy to locate your original project files on your storage disk. However, as you dive deeper into multiple projects, managing a variety of media assets from different storage locations can become challenging.

Each project typically contains multiple sequences, each with its own structure. You'll also be working with various graphics, effects presets, and Motion Graphics templates. To navigate this growing complexity effectively, you need a solid organizational framework.

Two key strategies for ensuring your success are establishing a systematic approach to managing your projects and planning for future revisits to older projects. The challenge often arises when these organizational systems are not implemented until they become necessary. For example, while you're immersed in the creative process, you might suddenly need to add a new video clip but find it difficult to keep track of file names or clip locations. This can lead to projects with similar names, misplaced files, and disorganized data.

The straightforward solution is to prepare and establish your organizational structure in advance. Map out your workflow, starting from the collection of source media files through the editing process to the final output, archiving, and future use. Documenting this strategy can be incredibly helpful when you're in the thick of the creative process.

In this section, we will provide insights into Premiere Pro's features that help you maintain control over your creative endeavors while keeping your work organized. We will also explore collaborative techniques that enhance teamwork and streamline project management. By understanding these elements, you'll be better equipped to manage your creative work without losing sight of what matters.

Asset management in Premiere Pro

When working on a project, you might want to adjust how you view your bins. The standard layout provides a comprehensive view of your project's structure, which is helpful. However, there are times when you may prefer to open a bin in a new tab or panel right from the start. This allows you to focus on specific clips within a bin, organize clips in storyboard mode using icons, or use the search box to locate clips within a bin. Some editors prefer bins that overlay the interface, while others like to have them open in new tabs.

To open a bin in a floating panel, in situ, or a new tab, follow these steps:

- **Open a Bin in a New Tab**: Double-click on the bin. This panel can be docked or grouped like any other panel.
- **Open a Bin in Situ**: Use Ctrl-double-click (Windows) or Command-double-click (Mac OS).
- **Open a Bin in a Floating Panel**: Use Alt-double-click on Windows or Option-double-click on Mac OS.

To change the default behavior of the bins in the Project panel, modify the Bins options:

- For Windows, go to **Edit > Preferences > General**. On Mac OS, navigate to **Premiere Pro > Preferences > General**.
- In the Bins section, you can set your double-click preferences. You can also use shortcuts: Ctrl + double-click (Windows), Command + double-click (Mac OS), or Alt + double-click (Windows) and Option + double-click (Mac OS).
- Finally, select **OK** to save your changes.

Using the Project Manager

To explore the Project Manager in Premiere Pro, navigate to the **File** menu and select **Project Manager**. This tool offers several options that streamline the process of consolidating your project. It gathers all media files used in one or more sequences, which is particularly useful for archiving or sharing projects. By using the Project Manager to collect all media assets, you can ensure that nothing is missing or offline when handing the project over to colleagues or storing it for future use, providing you with peace of mind.

When you utilize the Project Manager, it creates a new project file that is independent of your current project. Before deleting the old media or project files, thoroughly review the new project file. It's wise to double-check that all necessary files are present by using a different editing system to verify access. Start by going to the Sequence section of the new project and selecting the sequences you wish to include.

Next, choose from the following options under the "Resulting Project" section:

- **Collect Files And Copy To New Location**: This option creates a duplicate set of media files used in your selected sequences, relocating them to a designated new location. It's especially helpful for archiving, sharing, or backing up projects without altering the original media files.
- **Consolidate and Transcode**: This generates new versions of media files based solely on the clips within the chosen sequences (trimmed clips). Selecting this option opens up various additional settings.

Additional Options:

- **Exclude Unused Clips**: Limits the new project to only include clips used in the selected sequences, removing any unused content.
- **Include Handles**: Adds extra frames to clips, providing flexibility for timing adjustments and trimming later, though it requires more storage space.
- **Include Audio Conform Files**: Incorporates existing audio conform files, saving time by avoiding the need for Premiere Pro to re-analyze the audio. This is especially useful for lengthy projects.
- **Convert Image Sequences To Clips**: Changes imported image sequences into standard video files for easier file management and improved playback quality.
- **Include Preview Files**: If effects have been previously rendered, this option includes those renderings in the new project, saving time on future renderings.
- **Rename Media Files To Match Clip Names**: Renames duplicate media files to correspond with the clip names in the project. This can help with identification but may complicate locating the original source content.
- **Convert After Effects Compositions To Clips**: Replaces dynamically linked After Effects compositions with generated video files, which is necessary when the Project Manager cannot gather dynamically linked compositions or their associated media assets.
- **Preserve Alpha**: When transcoding, this preserves alpha channel information, ensuring transparency in sequences—crucial for sequences that include dynamically linked After Effects compositions with transparency.

By utilizing these options in the Project Manager, you can effectively manage your media assets and streamline your workflow in Premiere Pro.

Edit Videos to the Beat of the Music

Before you start synchronizing video to music, it's important to understand a few key points. This synchronization can be done either manually or automatically. Note that the automatic method is exclusive to Premiere Pro and doesn't work with other editing software like Final Cut Pro or DaVinci Resolve.

Let's start with the automated method that Premiere Pro provides for syncing video to music. However, if you're using a different editing program or prefer to do it manually in Premiere Pro, you can scroll down to see the manual technique.

To effectively synchronize your video to the music, it can be helpful to listen to your music track several times to identify the locations of the beats. This allows you to align video scenes with the musical hits. You'll need to examine the waveform of your audio file and use the arrow keys to pinpoint the exact moments where the rhythm changes. This approach will help you make precise adjustments to the video in relation to the music.

Automatically Sync Videos to the Beat of the Music in Premiere Pro

You can synchronize your video to the rhythm of the music using the **Automate to Sequence** option in Premiere Pro. To effectively sync your video, you'll need to create a few markers. Here's how to get started:

1. Import and Organize Your Media

Begin your video editing project by organizing your media. Creating a well-structured media library will make it easier to manage everything. Once you've imported your audio, drag it to the timeline and position it as desired. You can also adjust the In/Out range of the audio clip to eliminate any unnecessary parts without cutting the original clip.

2. Add Markers

After you've placed your media on the timeline, listen to the audio track and start adding markers to your video. These markers will indicate the locations of the beats, allowing you to align your video scenes with the rhythm effectively.

By following these steps, you'll be on your way to syncing your video seamlessly with the music.

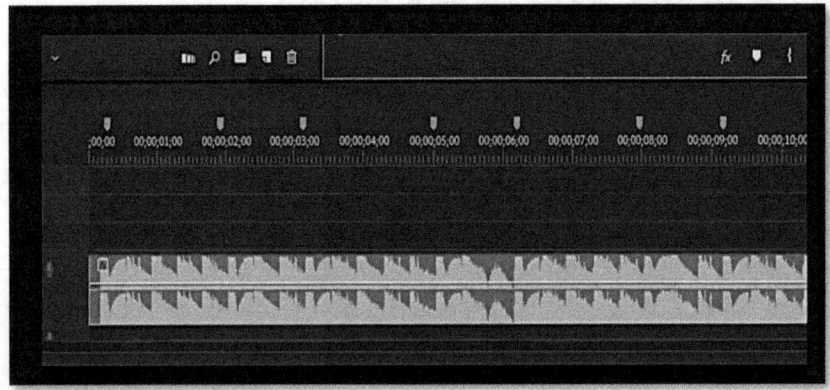

To add markers quickly in Premiere Pro, simply use the shortcut key **"M"** on your keyboard. Whenever you identify a beat in the audio, press the **M** key to insert a marker on your timeline. This method helps you easily keep track of the beats as you listen to the music.

Continue listening to the entire track and add markers as needed. Although it might seem time-consuming at first, adding markers is actually quite straightforward. Just remember that when adding markers, you need to select the entire section of the audio clip, not just a specific part.

3. Add Video to the Timeline

Once you've finished placing markers on the audio track, you can drag your video clips into the timeline. This will allow you to align your visuals with the markers you've set, ensuring a smooth synchronization with the music.

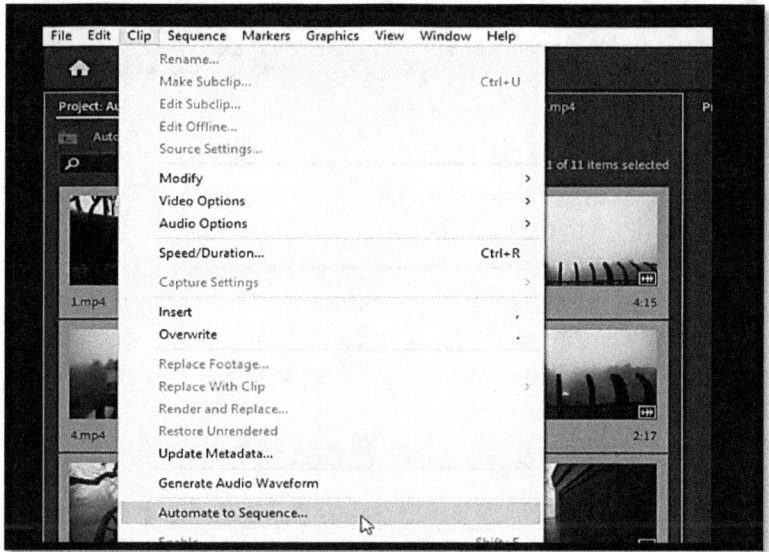

After selecting all the clips in your bin, click on the **Clip** tab in the top menu bar. Then, choose the **Automate to Sequence** option. When prompted to specify your settings, select the following options: **Placement at Unnumbered Markers** and **Selection Order**. This will help you effectively align your clips with the markers you've set, automating the synchronization process with the music.

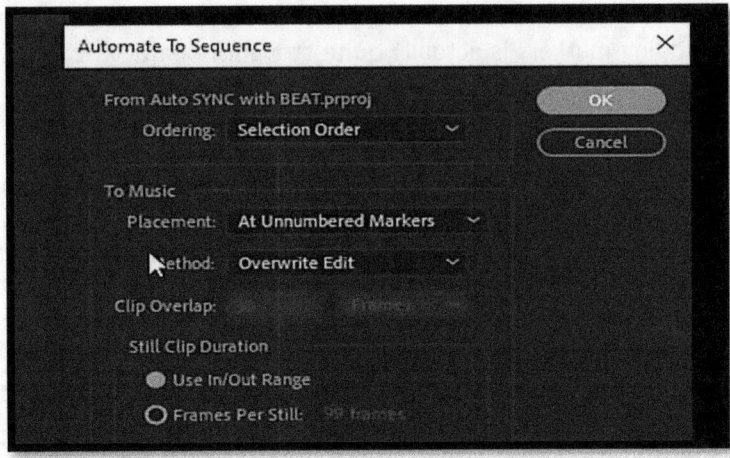

Premiere Pro will automatically add the footage to the timeline, arranging the videos according to the markers you set earlier. Once this process is complete, take a moment to review the project and ensure everything is in the right place.

However, remember that Premiere Pro uses algorithms for this automation, so it may not always align the video clips exactly as you envision. If you prefer a more precise outcome, you can opt for the manual technique, which allows for greater control over the placement of your clips.

Manually Sync Videos to the Beat of the Music in Premiere Pro

While Premiere Pro offers automatic syncing for rhythms, it can be complex, and the results aren't always precise. Thus, a manual approach might be a better option, and this method is applicable in any video editing software.

1. Add Music to the Timeline and Analyze It

Start by opening your preferred video editor and importing the audio clip. Once imported, drag the soundtrack to your timeline and enhance the visibility of the waveforms. Depending on the audio, the waveforms may vary in visibility, so adjust the view until the peaks are clear. These waveforms will help you identify where the music peaks occur and determine the beats.

2. Add Video to the Timeline and Make Cuts

After pinpointing the beats in the audio, drag your video clips to the timeline. Next, edit the video clips to sync them with the rhythm. Pay attention to the transients in the waveforms, as they indicate when the beat starts to change. Make cuts based on the beats, and add clips as needed to ensure everything aligns smoothly.

Eliminating Mistakes

It's a frustrating experience when a client or broadcaster reaches out to inform you that one of your projects is encountering issues. Some problems, like black holes and flash frames, can be particularly embarrassing. Additionally, there may be challenges related to media quality, rights clearances, and other unforeseen complications.

Examining Flash Frames and Gaps

In Adobe Premiere Pro, you can easily find gaps or flash frames by navigating to **Sequence > Go to Gap** in your final sequence. The menu offers four options for this purpose. The first two, **Next in Sequence** and **Previous in Sequence**, allow you to locate gaps either to the right or left of the sequence playhead while ensuring you cover all audio tracks.

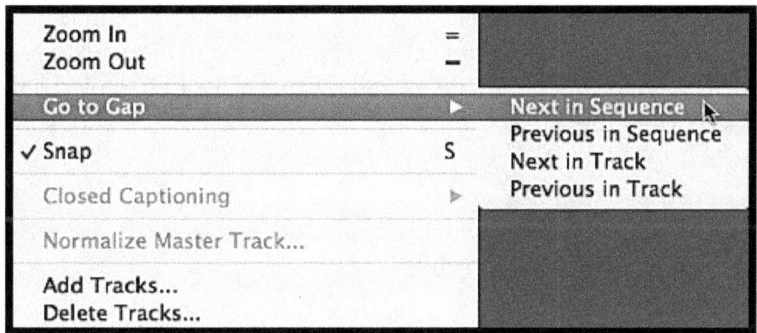

To locate gaps and flash frames on a single track or across multiple tracks in Adobe Premiere Pro, use the **Following in Track** and **Previous in Track** options. These tools focus on the currently selected tracks, whether audio or video. Once you identify a gap or flash frame, follow these steps:

1. **Select the Gap**: Click on the gap in the sequence.
2. **Close the Gap**: Conduct a ripple edit by pressing the **Delete** key on your keyboard. Remember that if Sync Lock is active on the related audio or video track, Premiere Pro will also attempt to move the linked segment.
3. **Check for Obstructions**: If there are clips obstructing the gap, you won't be able to close it. To prevent clips from becoming unsynchronized, consider turning off Sync Lock for those tracks.
4. **Mark In and Out Points**: Select the gap and use the slash (/) key to set In and Out points around it, or go to **Markers > Mark Selection** to do the same.

5. **Extract the Gap**: With the gap marked in the Program Monitor, use the Extract button or press the apostrophe (') key. This will remove the gap and slide all subsequent clips to the left.

Keep in mind that designating a gap will affect every selected audio track. You can participate in the extraction process by clicking the track header to select or deselect a track. Be cautious, as removing tracks from the selection may lead to sync issues with audio and other elements. Note that closing a gap may change the overall duration of your sequence and could result in audio or graphics being out of sync. Additionally, you may choose to clip the clip on one side of the gap as another method of closing it.

Looking for Repeated Shots

During your project, you'll likely start with a large collection of raw media, which you'll then divide into smaller segments. Some editors and producers prefer to avoid reusing the same footage within a sequence, which is common practice. In Adobe Premiere Pro, you can easily check how many times a particular clip is used in a sequence.

To do this, make sure your Project panel is displayed in icon view. If a clip is in use, you'll notice one or two orange icons in the bottom-right corner of the screen. A filmstrip icon represents video clips, while an audio waveform icon indicates audio clips. If a clip contains only video with no associated audio, you'll see the video icon; conversely, if it has only audio, you'll see the audio icon.

If a clip is not currently used, you'll see white icons instead. For video clips that include integrated audio, only the white audio icon will be visible.

Video Legalization

While navigating the legalization of video may seem daunting, it's actually quite straightforward. As an experienced editor, you can confidently handle the licensing process. By employing a few strategies and tools within Adobe Premiere Pro, you can ensure your film complies with legal standards, even if you're not fully familiar with the complexities of the topic.

Legalizing manually

To start the legalization process for video, the first steps involve color correction and grading. A primary objective of color correction is to ensure legal compliance. Consequently, color correcting and grading your footage is akin to manually legitimizing it. We'll explore some Adobe Premiere Pro effects that can help with this process, but it's essential not to rely solely on these effects.

Begin by manually legalizing your footage, and then use these effects to address any miscalibrated pixels you may have overlooked.

Audio Legalization

Legalizing audio is just as crucial as legalizing video. As the saying goes, "audio is half the visual." You've likely encountered frustration with audio that's either too loud or too quiet while watching content. The regulations for audio legalization differ among broadcasters, but understanding a few key techniques can help you create compliant audio.

Here are some essential steps to legalize your audio:

1. **Understand Loudness Standards**: Familiarize yourself with the loudness standards required by your target broadcaster, such as the EBU R128 or ATSC A/85. These standards dictate the average loudness levels and peak limits.
2. **Use Audio Meters**: Utilize Premiere Pro's audio meters to monitor levels in real-time. Keep your average loudness (measured in LUFS) within the acceptable range, typically around -23 LUFS for broadcast.
3. **Normalize Audio Levels**: Apply normalization to ensure consistent audio levels across your project. You can use the Normalize function to set your audio to a specific loudness target.
4. **Limit Peak Levels**: Use a limiter effect to prevent peaks from exceeding the maximum allowed level (often -1 dBTP). This helps avoid distortion and ensures compliance.
5. **Dynamic Range Control**: Consider using compression to manage the dynamic range of your audio. This ensures that quieter sounds are audible while preventing louder sounds from overpowering the mix.
6. **Final Checks**: Before exporting, perform a final check using a loudness meter plugin to ensure your audio meets all specified standards.

By implementing these techniques, you can produce audio that not only enhances your project but also adheres to legal requirements.

Getting to the right levels

Absolutely, getting the audio levels right is critical for producing legal audio. Here's a more detailed breakdown of how to effectively manage audio levels in Adobe Premiere Pro:

Monitoring Levels

1. **Audio Meters**: Use the audio meters in the Audio Mixer for each track to monitor levels. This allows you to see real-time audio peaks and averages.
2. **Master Track Monitoring**: The Master audio track is essential for understanding the overall mix. You can view it in the Audio Mixer or by navigating to **Window > Audio Meters**.

Mixing Guidelines

- **Balance Your Mix**: Ensure that dialogue, music, and sound effects are balanced. Dialogue should typically sit around -12 to -6 dB, while music and effects can vary based on the desired impact.
- **Use Loudness Standards**: Familiarize yourself with loudness standards applicable to your project. For broadcast, a target of around -23 LUFS (Loudness Units Full Scale) is common, but always check specific requirements for the platform.
- **Peak Levels**: Keep peak levels below -1 dBTP to avoid distortion. This is especially important when exporting to ensure no clipping occurs.

Adjusting Levels

- **Normalization**: Utilize the normalization feature to adjust the loudness of clips to a target level, making it easier to maintain consistency across different audio elements.
- **Compression and Limiting**: Use compression to control dynamic range, ensuring that quieter sounds are audible and louder sounds don't overpower. A limiter can help cap the peak levels to maintain compliance.

Finalizing Your Mix

- **Loudness Metering**: Before exporting, use a loudness meter plugin to verify that your overall mix adheres to the required loudness standards. This ensures that your audio is legally compliant and provides a good listening experience.

By paying close attention to these elements, you can achieve a well-balanced and legally compliant audio mix in your projects.

PART IV
SPECIALIZED WORKFLOWS

CHAPTER 15
360-DEGREE VIDEO EDITING

Understanding 360-Degree Video

360-degree videos are an exciting and immersive way to experience storytelling, placing viewers right in the middle of the action. Here's a closer look at how to watch and create 360-degree videos:

Watching 360-Degree Videos

- **Virtual Reality Headsets**: The most immersive way to experience 360-degree videos is through VR headsets like Oculus Rift, HTC Vive, or Meta Quest. These devices allow you to look around in every direction as if you were physically present in the scene.
- **Smartphones**: You can watch 360-degree videos on your smartphone. Simply tilt or rotate your phone to explore the video environment. Some apps support VR viewers, which can enhance the experience.
- **Web Browsers**: Most modern browsers allow you to view 360-degree videos by clicking and dragging your mouse to pan around the scene. Platforms like YouTube and Facebook have built-in support for 360-degree content.

Creating 360-Degree Videos

1. **Equipment**: To capture 360-degree video, you typically need:
   - **Multi-camera Rigs**: These consist of several cameras arranged in a circle or sphere, capturing different angles simultaneously.
   - **360-Degree Cameras**: Single cameras designed with multiple lenses (like the Insta360 or GoPro Max) that capture all angles at once.
2. **Stitching**: After recording, the footage from different cameras or lenses needs to be "stitched" together. This involves:
   - **Software**: Use specialized software (e.g., Adobe Premiere Pro with plugins, Kolor Autopano, or dedicated stitching software) to blend the edges of the clips seamlessly.
   - **Color Correction**: Adjust colors, brightness, and shadows to ensure a uniform look across the stitched footage.
3. **Editing**: After stitching, you can edit the video like any other project:
   - Add effects, transitions, and audio.
   - Ensure the audio is spatially aware, enhancing the immersive experience (consider using ambisonic audio for a true surround sound experience).

4. **Exporting and Sharing**: Once editing is complete, export the video in a format compatible with 360-degree viewing. Upload it to platforms that support 360-degree content, like YouTube or Vimeo, ensuring to select the correct settings for 360 playback.

Conclusion

360-degree video is a powerful medium that allows for an engaging storytelling experience. Whether you're a viewer or a creator, understanding how to watch and produce this type of content can open up new avenues for exploration and creativity.

Introduction to VR Editing

Virtual reality (VR) has transformed our perception and interaction with digital media, including video editing. Adobe Premiere Pro, a widely used video editing software, has introduced advanced tools and features specifically designed for creating VR content. This integration of technologies has given rise to a new specialty known as VR editing, where editors utilize immersive technologies to craft engaging and captivating virtual experiences.

Understanding Virtual Reality Editing

- Immersive **Storytelling:** VR editing transcends conventional narrative techniques by offering artists a three-dimensional canvas. In a 360-degree environment, editors can guide the viewer's focus, enhancing the story's engagement and dynamism. As a result, traditional editing practices must evolve to incorporate more hands-on and experiential approaches.
- Adobe **Premiere Pro Integration:** Adobe Premiere Pro has established itself as a frontrunner in VR editing, featuring tools that streamline the workflow. The software supports various VR file formats, allowing editors to effortlessly import, modify, and export VR content. Additionally, its integration with other Adobe Creative Cloud applications facilitates a more cohesive approach to VR project development.

Key Features in Adobe Premiere Pro for VR Editing

1. VR **Preview:** Editors can preview VR media directly within the Adobe Premiere Pro interface. This feature allows for real-time visualization of how audiences will interact with the immersive environment, enabling precise adjustments to enhance the narrative and visual impact.
2. Spatial **Markers and Annotations:** Editing in VR involves navigating a three-dimensional space, and Adobe Premiere Pro simplifies this with tools for adding spatial markers and

annotations. Editors can strategically place markers in the VR environment to guide viewers' focus and enhance the overall narrative flow.

3. VR **Effects and Transitions:** Adobe Premiere Pro includes a range of effects and transitions tailored specifically for VR video. These tools help editors create engaging media by ensuring smooth transitions between scenes, thereby maintaining viewer interest.

4. Editing **Ambisonic Audio:** Adobe Premiere Pro supports the editing of ambisonic audio, a crucial element for immersive soundscapes in VR. This capability allows editors to craft an enveloping auditory experience, enhancing realism and fostering a stronger sense of presence within the VR environment.

Workflow in Adobe Premiere Pro

⬚ Adding **VR Footage:** Adobe Premiere Pro supports various VR formats, including stereoscopic and monoscopic footage. Editors can seamlessly incorporate VR videos without compromising the quality of the viewing experience.

⬚ Editing **in 360-Degree Space:** Within Adobe Premiere Pro's VR environment, editors can navigate freely to rearrange elements and optimize spatial usage for the best viewer experience. This includes organizing clips, applying effects, and integrating spatial audio features.

⬚ Preview **and Fine-Tuning:** The VR preview tool in Adobe Premiere Pro allows editors to monitor their work in real-time. This iterative approach is essential for refining spatial elements and ensuring a smooth, enjoyable VR experience.

⬚ Exporting **VR Content:** Adobe Premiere Pro offers export options tailored for VR devices. Editors can easily share their projects in formats that preserve the immersive qualities, whether for use on VR headsets, online platforms, or other devices.

Editing 360-Degree Footage

Step 1

Enable VR in Sequence Settings

You can import your 360 videos into Premiere Pro just like any other video. While the software automatically detects VR properties upon loading the media, here are the steps to manually enable VR in the sequence settings:

1. Go to **Sequence** in the menu and select **Sequence Settings**.
2. Look for the **VR Properties** section at the bottom of the settings window.

To enable VR for your sequence, select an image that uses the equirectangular projection, as this is the only projector type currently supported by Premiere Pro.

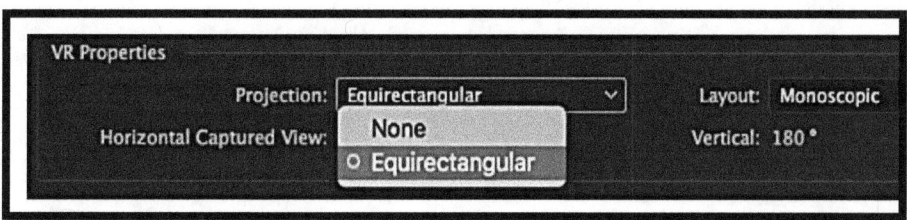

Next, choose the appropriate style based on the camera you used and the type of video recorded. You can select from a monocular view, an over/under view, or a side-by-side view in full stereo. Remember, only one type of video can be played at a time within this sequence. Continue reading to learn more about these settings.

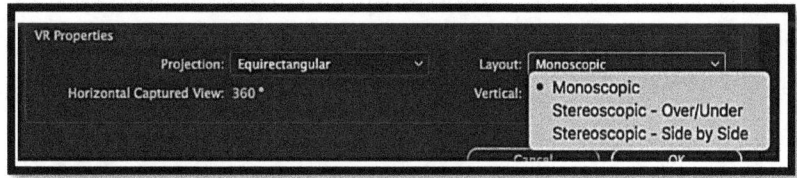

⯀ You can adjust the field of view for your full picture using the Horizontal and Vertical Captured View fields. The default setting of 180 degrees vertically and 360 degrees horizontally is typically suitable, creating a complete spherical view.

⯀ Once you've made your adjustments, click OK to save your changes. You can now utilize the VR video features with your sequence.

What is an Equirectangular Projection?

Imagine a world map: it displays a circular globe flattened onto a surface. In equirectangular projection, the sphere is essentially "unwrapped," where longitude corresponds to the X coordinate and latitude corresponds to the Y coordinate.

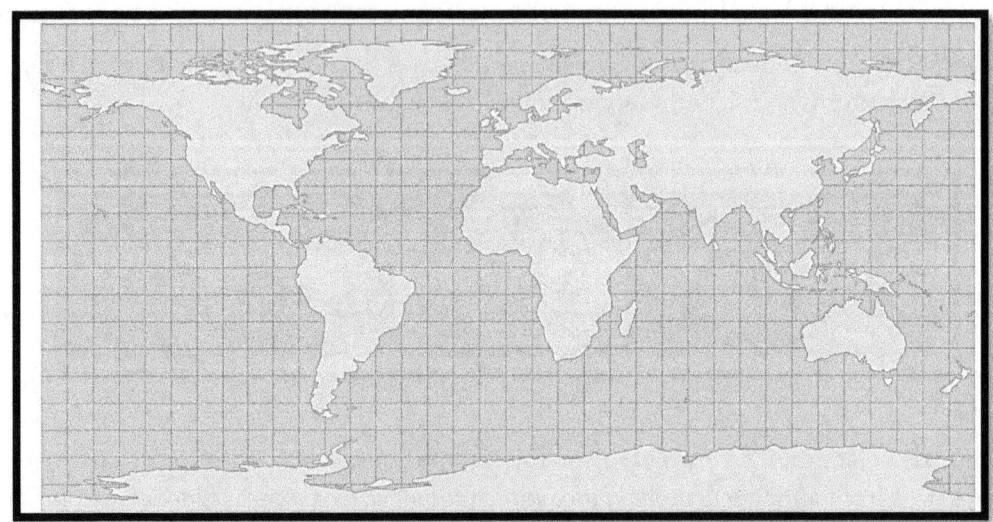

Similarly, equirectangular format is a common file type for 360 video, allowing it to be transformed into a spherical view for a more immersive experience. While it may appear flat, it can also present a distorted landscape. The raw video you assemble will be in an equirectangular format, but you can easily toggle between this format and the VR view while editing in Premiere.

Step 2

Preview the VR Video Display

The next step is to play your clips on the monitor now that VR editing is enabled for your sequence. You can view your video in 360 degrees in two ways:

1. To activate VR video, either right-click on the monitor or click the gear icon (wrench) located on the right side of the screen.

Click the button maker (+) and drag the **Toggle VR Video Display** button to the menu for easy access!

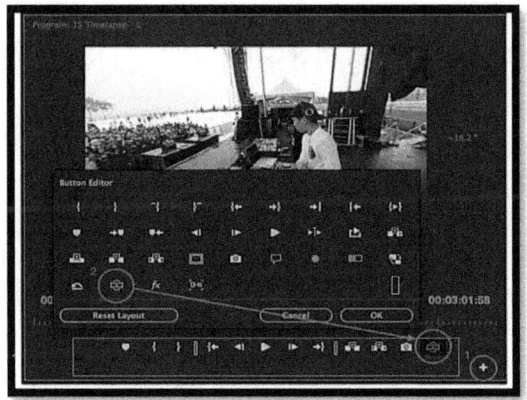

Once the VR Video Display mode is activated, navigate to **VR Video > Settings**. In this mode, the Monitor View areas allow you to select which part of the sphere you want to view, creating various viewing experiences. For example, a setting of 160 degrees by 90 degrees resembles a typical YouTube viewing format. Remember that these choices will influence the size of the view window; in this case, 160 degrees by 90 degrees corresponds to a 16:9 aspect ratio.

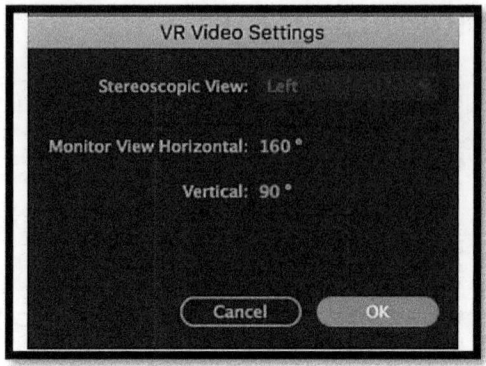

Step 3

Edit Video and Set Center Point

Once you've completed your 360 videos, you can edit it just like any standard video. This means you can trim clips, add images, music, and text, as well as apply color correction and other effects. However, remember that any text you include will remain fixed in one spot; it won't move with the viewer's perspective. When viewed in a circular format, the text may appear somewhat distorted. Additionally, keep in mind that effects like warp adjusters are not compatible with 360 videos.

Example of text distortion in 360 videos

The camera's center point is crucial to consider when working with 360 videos. Unlike a regular camera, you can't adjust where the viewer is looking. However, you can set a central point at the start of your shot to emphasize the subject, ensuring that viewers don't have to turn their heads to see it when you edit your clips together.

To establish the center point in Premiere Pro, use the Offset effect with these steps:

1. Navigate to Video Effects > Distort > Offset in the Effects panel.
2. Apply the Offset effect to your clip in the timeline.
3. Select the clip and open the effects dialog box.
4. To pan the clip horizontally, adjust the first number left or right. Avoid changing the second number, as that will misalign the clip's upright position.

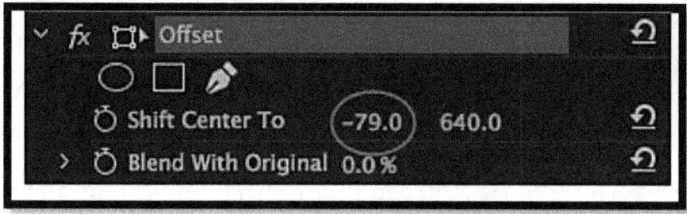

When transitioning between shots in Premiere, remember that the viewer's gaze doesn't automatically return to the center. If the viewer starts looking at the back of the scene in the first shot, they'll likely remain focused there in the second shot, possibly missing your intended focal point.

For exporting your video, select the timeline and press Ctrl/Cmd+M, or navigate to File > Export > Media. This will bring up the export window. After choosing your desired codec, ensure that the "Video Is VR" box is checked at the bottom of the Video tab and confirm that the Frame Layout is correct.

Working with the Bins

Bins function like folders on your hard drive and share the same icon. They allow you to organize your clips into various groups for better efficiency. Just as you can create nested folders on your hard drive, you can place multiple bins inside other bins to create a detailed organizational structure that suits your project. However, it's important to note that bins exist solely within your Adobe Premiere Pro project file and won't be visible as individual project containers on your hard drive.

Creating bins

To create a new bin, locate the "New Bin" button at the bottom of the Project panel and click it. When you first open Adobe Premiere Pro, it automatically generates a new project file with a default name that you can change later. For better organization, it's a good idea to rename your bins promptly. For instance, if you're managing film clips, create a bin named "Theft Unexpected."

There are several ways to create bins: you can go to the File menu and select "New > Bin," or right-click in the Project panel and choose "New Bin" to name it appropriately. For example, you could create a folder called "PSD Files" for those types of files, and another called "Illustrator Files."

To quickly create a new bin for clips already in your project, simply drag and drop them onto the "New Bin" button. You can also use the keyboard shortcut Control+/ (Windows) or Command+/ (Mac) to create a new bin quickly—try naming it "Sequences."

If your Project panel is in List view, clips will be organized by bin names, making it easier to manage your project files. If your panel has many clips and you can't find a clear area to click, try clicking just to the left of the icons to create a new bin in that space.

Opening the bins

⬚ Opening **a Bin in a New Window:** To open a bin in a separate window, double-click the bin. This will create an independent window that you can dock or move anywhere on your screen, providing a focused space for that bin's contents.

⬚ Opening **a Bin in a New Tab:** To open a bin as a new tab, double-click it while holding down the Option (Alt) key. This opens the bin in a new tab within the Project panel, allowing easy access alongside your other tabs without cluttering your screen with additional windows.

⬚ Opening **a Bin In Place:** Hold down the Command (Ctrl) key and double-click the bin to view it in the same space. This allows you to explore the bin's contents while hiding other project elements. To return to the main project view, simply click on the project name or folder at the top of the window.

Customizing Bin and Clip Views

Once you've organized your media into bins, it's important to visualize your clips effectively. Having a thumbnail for each shot makes it easy to navigate and review your footage. Sometimes, you may need to access details about a photo, such as the camera used to capture it. Additionally, you can enhance this information by adding brief descriptions. To explore these options, let's begin by changing your current view.

Changing Views

You can view a bin in either list or icon format. Many editors prefer list view because it allows them to see more clips at once. In contrast, icon view lets you visually browse your clips, scrub through them while hovering, and sort them more graphically. To toggle between list and icon views, use the buttons located in the bottom left corner of the Project panel. You can also switch views using the keyboard shortcuts Command + Page Up (Ctrl + Page Up) and Command + Page Down (Ctrl + Page Down).

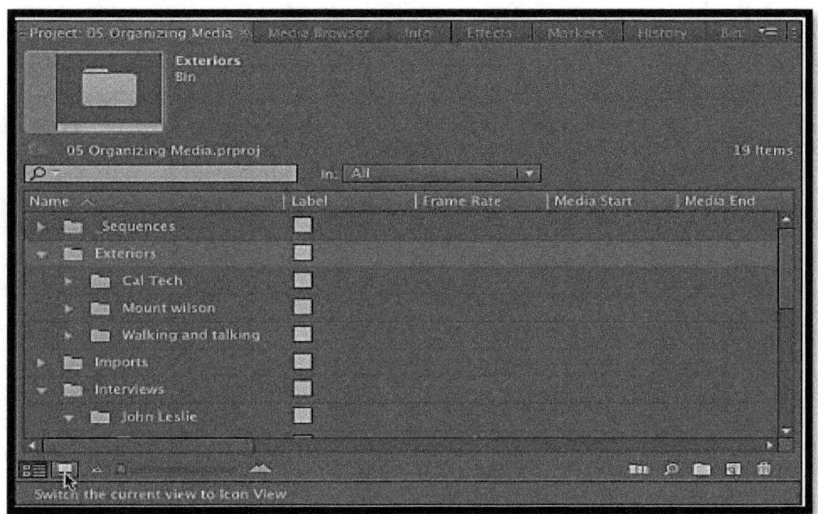

List view

Most editors spend a significant amount of time in list view while working on a project. This straightforward list displays the project name at the top, making it easy to access a lot of information and customize the arrangement.

In list view, you can also preview thumbnails of your clips. To adjust the size and color of the icons, navigate to the Project panel menu and select "Thumbnails." In icon view, you can use the same keyboard shortcuts (Shift + and Shift -) to increase or decrease the size of the thumbnails.

Icon view

"Hoverscrub" allows you to move your mouse over a clip and "scrub" through it interactively, providing a quick way to review your video. This feature has become a favorite, especially for large clips, as it offers a faster way to familiarize yourself with the footage compared to using the Source Monitor—especially when the bin is in full-screen mode.

Here are some benefits of using icon view:

- You can view a clip's title without loading it into the Source Monitor.
- Hoverscrub enables quick skimming through a clip's content by simply hovering the mouse over it.
- It's an excellent way to get to know footage you haven't reviewed yet.
- Many file-based cameras (both still and video) assign clips numerical titles. Icon view allows you to see these clips without needing to rename them.

Reviewing Footage

If your video is interlaced, Premiere Pro needs specific information—such as frame rate, pixel aspect ratio (the shape of the pixels), and the field order—to play the video correctly. While Premiere Pro usually retrieves this information from the file's metadata, you can modify it as needed.

Here's how to get started:

1. **Importing a Video:**
   o Open the Media Browser panel to access your video files, similar to opening a drawer where you keep your footage.
2. **Previewing the Clip:**
   o Double-click on a specific clip to preview it. You'll notice it's in a widescreen format, which is wider than the standard screen.
3. **Adjusting Clip Properties:**
   o To change how the video appears, right-click on the clip in the Project window and select **Modify > Interpret Footage**.
4. **Audio Considerations:**
   o If the video lacks sound, you won't be able to adjust any audio settings.
5. **Understanding Pixel Shapes:**
   o The clip may be set to an Anamorphic 2:1 pixel shape, meaning the pixels are twice as long as they are wide.
6. **Changing Pixel Aspect Ratio:**
   o You can experiment with the pixel aspect ratio by selecting **Conform To** and choosing **Square Pixels (1.0)**, then clicking OK. This may make your video appear squarer.
7. **Aspect Ratio Exploration:**
   o If you want to experiment further, right-click the clip again, choose **Modify > Interpret Footage**, and select **DVCPRO HD (1.5)**. Click OK and check how the video looks in the Source Monitor. This change will make Premiere Pro interpret the frames as 1.5 times wider than they are tall, altering the image to fit a standard 16:9 widescreen ratio.

Adjusting the pixel aspect ratio can lead to significant visual changes, such as circles appearing as ovals. If you notice such distortions, it might be necessary to adjust the pixel aspect ratio to ensure accurate representation.

Freeform View

The Freeform View option in Premiere Pro allows for creative arrangement of your clips. Similar to Icon View, you can explore images, set in and out points, and reorder clips. In Freeform View, clips can be placed freely without a grid, enabling you to edit individual clips or stack them in any layout you desire. This flexibility enhances your project organization and creative thinking. Freeform View was introduced in the spring of 2019 with Premiere Pro version 13.1, so ensure you have the latest version of Adobe Creative Cloud to access this feature.

How to Use Freeform View in Premiere Pro

Here are the steps to start using Freeform View in Premiere Pro:

1. **Access the Project Panel:** Open your project and navigate to the Project panel where your clips are stored.
2. **Switch to Freeform View:** Click on the view options in the top right corner of the Project panel and select "Freeform View."
3. **Arrange Your Clips:** Drag and drop your clips anywhere on the canvas. You can stack them, spread them out, or arrange them creatively.
4. **Set In and Out Points:** Click on the clips to set in and out points as needed for your edits.
5. **Explore Layouts:** Experiment with different layouts to see what best suits your project's needs.

With these steps, you can start customizing your workspace to enhance your workflow.

Getting Started with Freeform View

To access the Freeform View button, navigate to the Assembly workspace in the Project panel. You can adjust the zoom level in your workspace using the scale slider or by using your mouse. To arrange your clips, simply drag and drop them into the designated area. Feel free to stack clips on top of one another for creative layouts! You can also resize individual clips or a group of clips by selecting them, right-clicking, and choosing **Clip Size**.

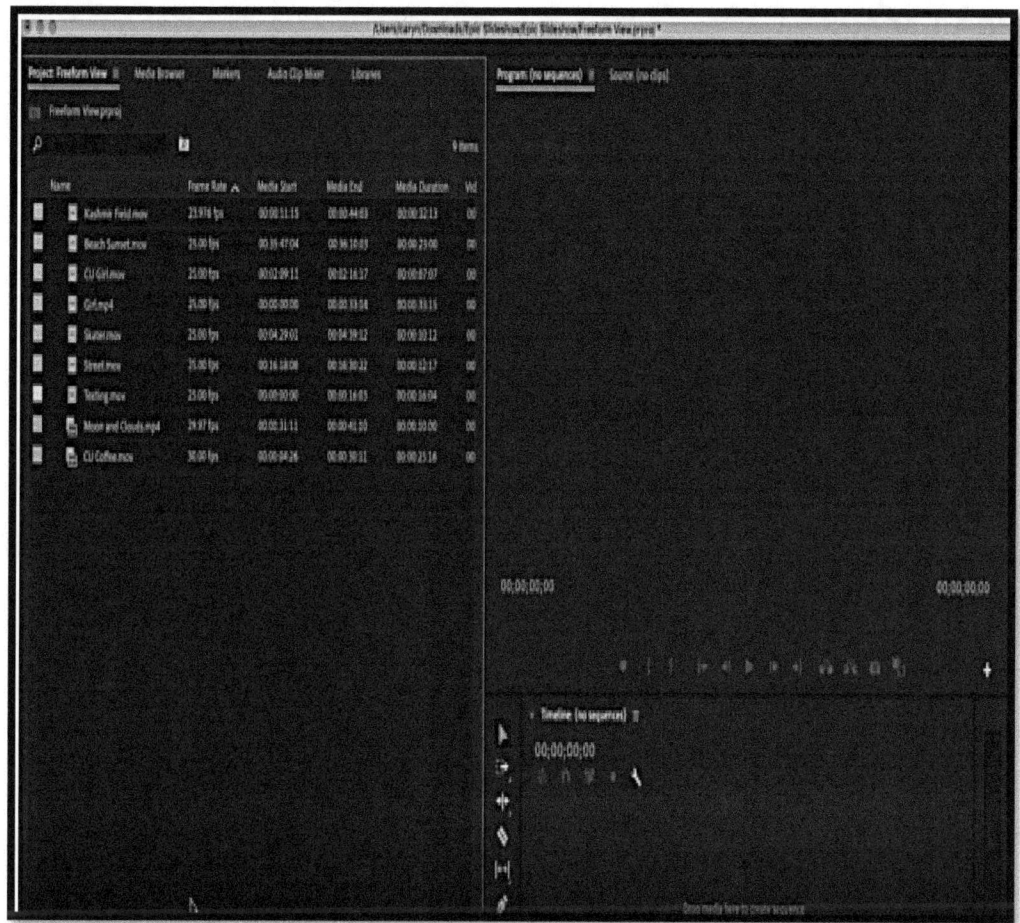

Freeform View Customization
Custom Metadata Display

To customize the information displayed under each thumbnail in Freeform View, go to the panel menu and select **Freeform View Options**. Here, you can choose to display up to two descriptive fields for each clip, allowing you to tailor the information to your needs.

Placing Poster Frames

The small image next to your clip in the Project panel is called a Poster Frame. Choosing an appropriate Poster Frame helps you quickly identify clips. To select a specific frame, hover over the clip, then press Command + P (or Shift + P on a PC) to set it as the Poster Frame.

Assign Labels

Right-click on the clips and select color names from the drop-down menu. These color names will appear on the calendar as well.

Save Layouts in Freeform View

If you've created a layout in Freeform View, experimenting with different storyboards can enhance your workflow. Here's how to do it:

- Right-click in the Project box and select "Save as New Layout."
- Assign a name to your layout.
- In the future, explore various flows and combinations.
- To retrieve a saved layout, right-click and choose "Restore Layout."
- To start fresh with a grid, right-click in the project box and select "Reset to Grid." You can then organize by any criteria you prefer.

Freeform View Editing

In Freeform View, you can manage your videos and begin creating a rough cut. Here's how:

- Hover over each clip and drag it to set in and out points. Press **I** for an in point and **O** for an out point.
- To play or pause clips while in Freeform View, use the spacebar or the J, K, and L keys.
- Start by arranging your clips in a sequence within the Project panel.
- To add the modified clips to your Timeline, select them and drag them over.

Creative Ways to Use the Freeform View

Freeform View allows for great creativity with your footage, and there are two primary ways to approach it:

1. **Sorting Clips by Type**: Grouping clips can streamline your editing process. Unlike List View, Freeform View offers a clearer visual arrangement. Consider these categories:
    - **Shot**: Stack variations of the same shot, then select your favorites.
    - **Angle**: Keep close-ups and wide shots together for coherence.
    - **Character**: For dialogues, group all shots of the same character.
    - **B-Roll**: Organize cutaway shots for easy access during editing.
    - **Action Items**: Group clips needing edits, such as color corrections or effects.

2. **Arranging Clips**: The layout can be tailored to your style, video quantity, and footage type. You can arrange clips in a straight line or layer them over one another to create a visually appealing setup.

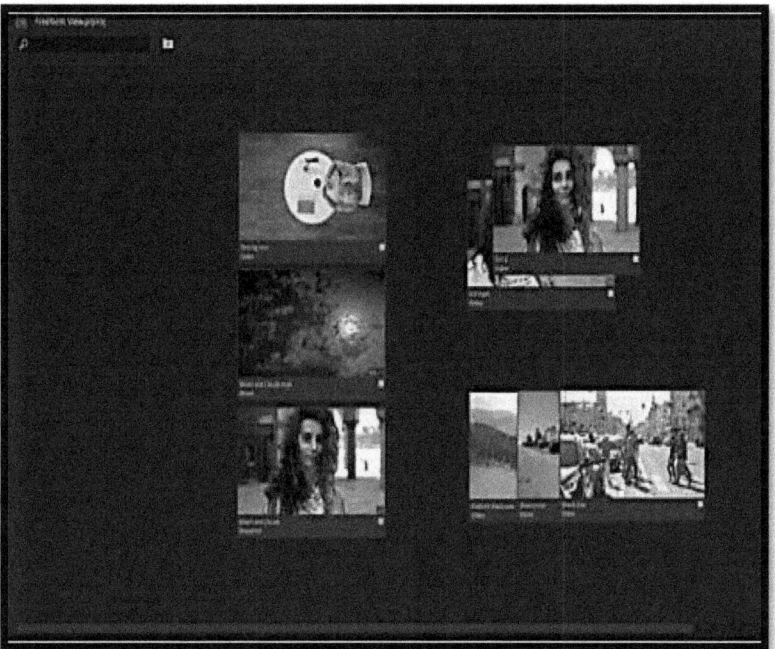

2. Storyboarding in Freeform View

Since video editing is inherently visual, planning your sequence visually is essential. While storyboarding, consider how overlapping or stacked clips in Freeform View can represent the cuts you intend to make in the final edit. You can save your layouts, which is a valuable aspect of storyboarding. Experiment with different cuts and save the successful ones as Layouts. If you're creating various versions of the same video for different platforms, think about how to tailor the design for each. For example, you might save one layout for an IGTV video and another for YouTube. This method helps you organize your clips effectively, allowing you to contextualize your footage and potentially discover new perspectives on your project, ultimately saving you time during editing. The Freeform View in Adobe Premiere Pro provides a clear preview of how new footage will integrate into your project. Explore the Freeform View and share how you've utilized it in your own work!

CHAPTER 16

ADVANCED EXPORTING AND DELIVERY

Export Settings for Different Platforms
Exporting Videos from Adobe Premiere Pro

When exporting videos from Adobe Premiere Pro, selecting the appropriate settings is crucial based on your target platform. Here are guidelines for various platforms:

1. **YouTube**:
   - **Format**: H.264
   - **Preset**: YouTube 1080p HD or 4K
   - **Bitrate**: Target bitrate for the preset or customize as needed
   - **Frame Rate**: Match project frame rate
   - **Audio**: AAC, 320 kbps, 48 kHz
2. **Vimeo**:
   - Same settings as YouTube.
3. **Facebook**:
   - Same settings as YouTube.
4. **Instagram**:
   - **Preset**: Match Source – High Bitrate
   - **Bitrate**: Adjust as needed
5. **Stock Footage Sites**:
   - Same as Twitter, ensuring compliance with site requirements.
6. **Television Broadcast (NTSC)**:
   - **Format**: H.264 or MPEG-2 (confirm with broadcaster)
   - **Preset**: Follow broadcast standard
   - **Bitrate**: Adhere to broadcaster specs
   - **Frame Rate**: Usually 29.97 fps for NTSC
7. **Film Festival Submission**:
   - **Format**: ProRes or DNxHD/DNxHR (check festival guidelines)
8. **Archiving/High-Quality Master**:
   - **Format**: ProRes (Mac) or DNxHD/DNxHR (Windows)

Always verify specific requirements for each platform, as they can vary. Balancing file size and video quality is essential based on your intended use.

Presets and Custom Export Configurations
Export Options in Adobe Premiere Pro

Adobe Premiere Pro offers both preset and custom export configurations, providing users with flexibility for their projects. Here's a breakdown of both options:

1. **Presets**:
   - **Accessing Presets**: After finishing your project, go to "File" > "Export" > "Media."

9. **Choosing Presets**: I
   - Same settings as YouTube.
10. **Twitter**:
    - **Format**: H.264

    - n the Export Settings panel, browse through various presets on the left, categorized by platforms (like YouTube or Vimeo). Click the one that fits your needs.
    - **Adjusting Preset Settings**: After selecting a preset, customize settings like bitrate, resolution, and codec as required.
    - **Saving Custom Presets**: Save your modified preset by clicking the floppy disk icon next to the preset list.
2. **Custom Export Configurations**:
   - **Starting with a Preset**: Choose a preset that closely aligns with your needs for an efficient start.
   - **Fine-Tuning Settings**: Adjust "Basic Video Settings" and "Audio Settings," including resolution and bitrate.
   - **Choosing Format and Codec**: Select your desired file format (H.264, ProRes, etc.) from the "Format" dropdown and choose an appropriate codec.
   - **Saving Custom Configurations**: After adjustments, save your custom settings by clicking "Save Preset," naming it, and choosing a location.
   - **Accessing Custom Presets**: Your saved custom preset will be available in the "Preset" dropdown for future projects.

Additional Tips
Tips for Exporting in Adobe Premiere Pro

- **Experimentation**:
  - Try out various presets and custom settings to discover the best balance between file size and video quality for your needs.
- **Checking Specifications**:

o   Always verify the specifications and requirements of the platform or destination where you intend to share or distribute your video.

Using Adobe Media Encoder
Adobe Media Encoder Overview

Adobe Media Encoder is a vital tool for transcoding and compressing, enhancing the output and release processes in Adobe Premiere Pro. It optimizes files for various platforms, including the Web, DVDs, Blu-ray Discs, and mobile devices. Its 64-bit architecture and multi-core support ensure fast and efficient processing.

Using Adobe Media Encoder:

1. **From Adobe Premiere Pro**: Access the Export Settings by going to "File" > "Export" > "Media." The interface resembles the standalone version, allowing seamless switching between the two programs for an easier workflow.
2. **As a Stand-Alone Application**: Media Encoder can operate independently, allowing you to drop files, source clips, or project files from Premiere Pro or After Effects directly into it. The Watch Folder feature enables automatic encoding when files are added to a designated folder, streamlining the process.

Overall, Adobe Media Encoder offers extensive encoding and transcoding options, integrates well with other Adobe programs, and is essential in the video creation workflow.

Using Adobe Premiere Pro to access Adobe Media Encoder
Exporting with Adobe Media Encoder in Adobe Premiere Pro

Adobe has streamlined workflows within its Creative Suite, enhancing the integration between Adobe Media Encoder and Adobe Premiere Pro. Here's how to leverage this synergy:

1. **Exporting Individual Clips**:
   o   Select a clip in the Project window.
   o   Go to **File > Export > Media** or use the shortcut **Command + M (Ctrl + M)**.
   o   Define specific In and Out points if you want to export a range or the entire clip.
2. **Exporting Sequences**:
   o   To export sequences during review or delivery, select the Timeline panel or the sequence in the Project panel, then navigate to **File > Export > Media**.
   o   You can also drag multiple sequences from the Project panel directly into the Adobe Media Encoder window for exporting.

This integration makes it simple to share individual clips or entire sequences, ensuring a smooth process for preparing projects for various outputs and settings based on user needs.

What Are the Benefits of Using Adobe Media Encoder?
The Importance of Compression in Adobe Media Encoder

Adobe Media Encoder is essential for reducing audio and video file sizes, addressing a significant challenge in post-production: the large size of rendered project files. Compression is crucial for ensuring that projects play smoothly on various devices, especially those with limited processing power, memory, or connectivity, such as mobile devices or older computers.

By compressing media, you enable fast streaming and playback without sacrificing quality, even on less capable devices. In essence, nearly all audio and video content undergo compression at some stage in the production or delivery process. This technique not only reduces file sizes but also enhances accessibility, allowing content to be easily played across a broader range of platforms and network conditions.

Download or Update Media Encoder
Installing or Updating Adobe Media Encoder

1. **Open the Creative Cloud Desktop App**: Launch the Creative Cloud app on your computer to manage your Adobe software and payments.
2. **Check for Updates or New Installations**: In the app, navigate to the "All Apps" section and locate Adobe Media Encoder. If it's installed but outdated, you'll see an "Update" option. If it's not installed, an "Install" option will appear.
3. **Add or Update Adobe Media Encoder**: Click the drop-down menu next to Adobe Media Encoder and select either "Update" or "Install." The app will begin the installation or update process, which may vary in duration based on the update size and your internet speed.
4. **Finishing and Accessing**: Once the update or installation is complete, Adobe Media Encoder will appear in the "All Apps" list. Click "Open" to start using the latest version.

Adding Your Source to the Queue

There are several methods to add items to the Adobe Media Encoder queue, as it integrates seamlessly with the entire Adobe Creative Suite. Here are some of the simplest ways to begin utilizing Media Encoder.

Adding Files to Media Encoder

The "Add Source" feature allows you to easily import files that are already completed and stored on your computer for compression. Additionally, you can include any After Effects composition or Premiere Pro sequence that you've created and saved.

To get started:

1. Open Adobe Media Encoder.
2. Choose a file.
3. Depending on your project, select either "Add Source," "Add After Effects Composition," or "Add Premiere Pro Sequence."

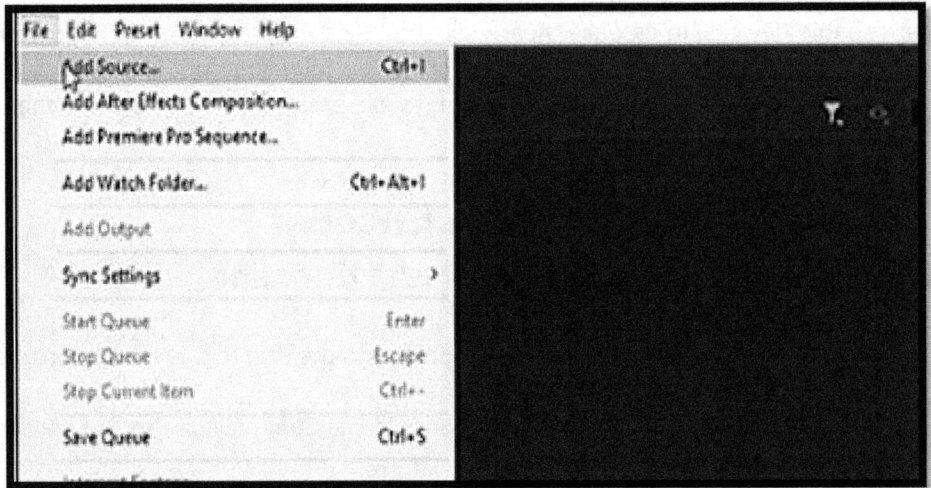

4.

Browsing for Media Encoder Files

The quickest way to add existing files before formatting them is to use the file search option, which allows you to select multiple files at once for the queue.

Here's how to do it:

5. Launch Adobe Media Encoder, a free program for encoding files.
6. Click the plus sign (+) in the Queue panel to add your files.

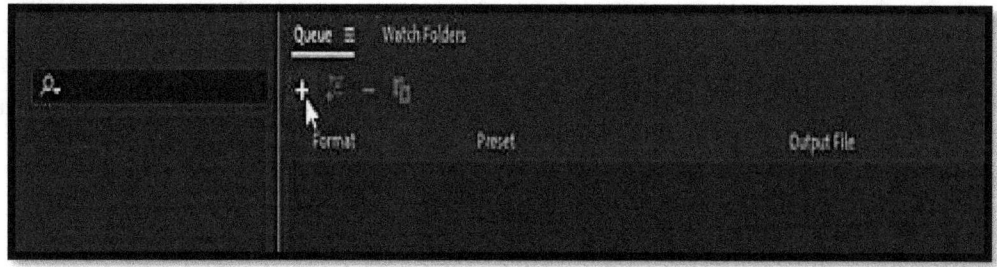

7. Select the file you want to send.
8. Click the OK button.

Importing from After Effects

Adding items to the Media Encoder list from After Effects is straightforward. Here's how to do it:

1. Open your After Effects project.
2. Go to the File menu and select **File > Export**.
3. From the drop-down menu, choose **Add to Media Encoder Queue**.

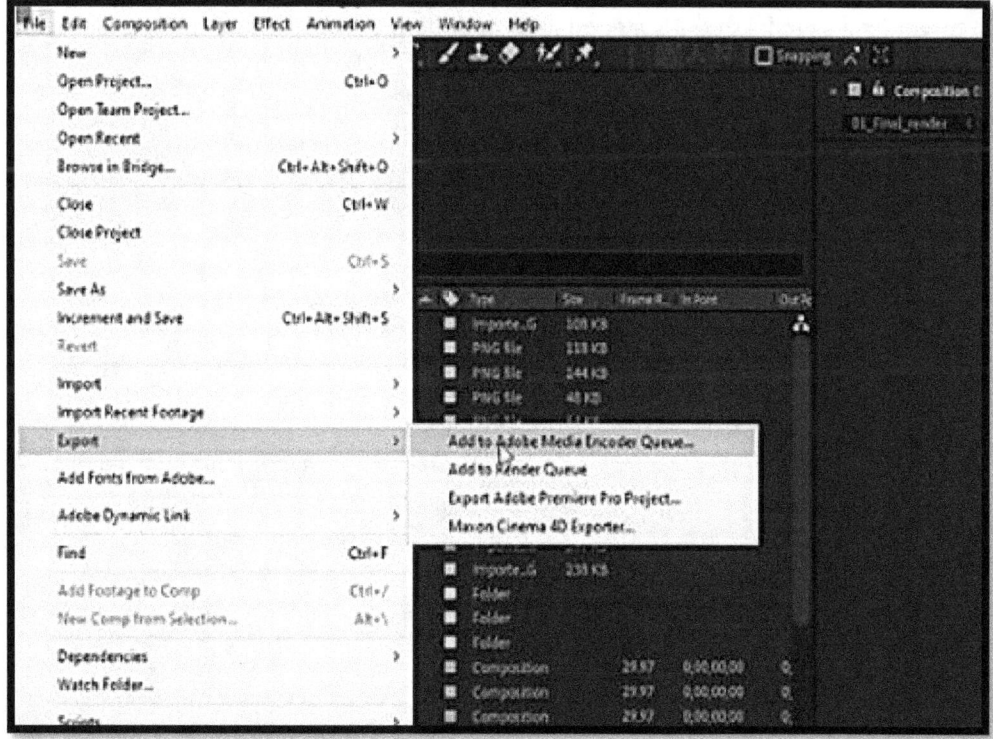

Importing from Premiere Pro

In Premiere Pro, you can easily add your files to the Media Encoder queue with just a single click. This allows you to continue working in Premiere Pro while your project is being encoded. Here's how to do it:

1. Open your project in Premiere Pro.
2. Go to the File menu and select Export, then choose your desired format.
3. When the Export Settings window appears, select Queue.

Changing the Media Encoder's Options

Media Encoder includes pre-configured settings for the most common video formats. By default, it will apply the settings you used for your previous project.

If you need to update those settings, follow these steps:

1. In the Media Encoder Queue, click on the preset text in the Preset box. A pop-up will appear, allowing you to modify the style. Most users select H.264, which has built-in settings for platforms like YouTube, Vimeo, Facebook, Twitter, and more. If you're targeting a specific site, it's a good idea to double-check its requirements before making any adjustments.
2. From the Preset dropdown menu, choose your desired option.

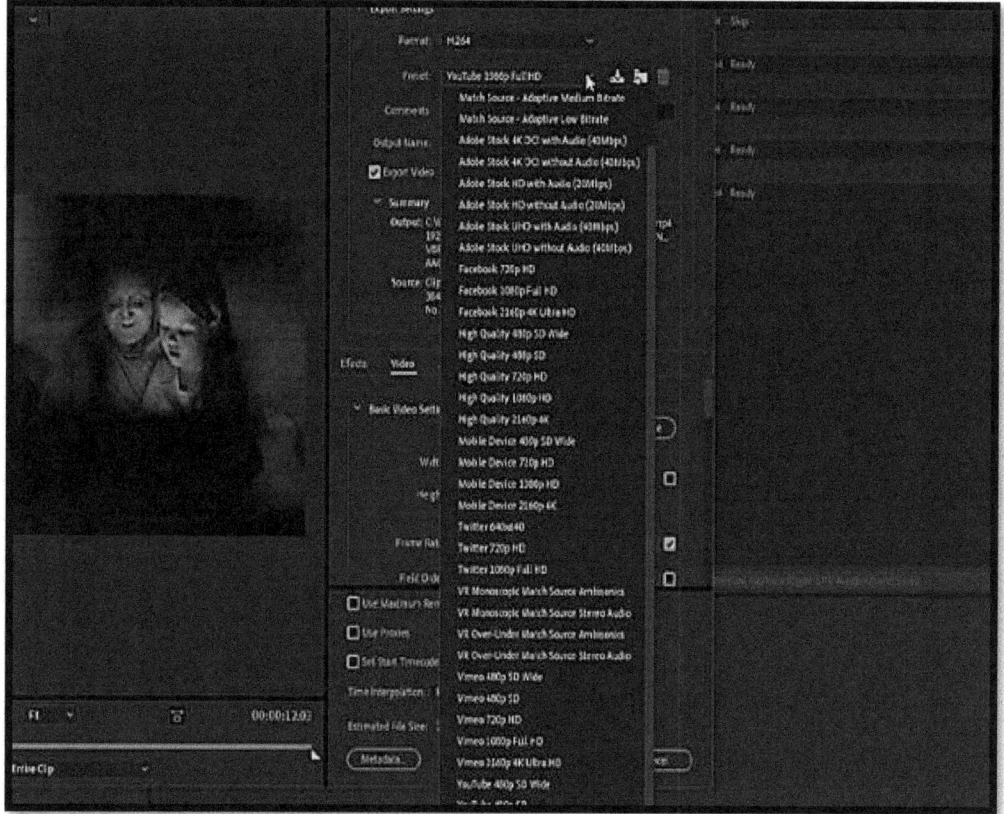

- Select an output name and specify the location for saving the completed files.
- Navigate to the desired folder where you want to save the file. You can also rename the file at this stage.
- Click "Save" when you're finished.

This window offers additional options for customizing settings. If you select the preset for the site where you plan to upload, you typically won't need to make further adjustments.

How to Stop Encoding

If you realize you need to adjust your project or forgot to modify your settings, you might need to halt the encoding process. Stopping it is straightforward and quick. Here's how you can do it:

- To stop the encoding of the current item, navigate to **File > Stop Current Item**. Media Encoder will continue converting the remaining items in the queue.
- To halt the encoding for the entire queue, go to **File > Stop Queue**.

Clearing Your Queue

⬜ Launch Adobe Media Encoder on your computer to view and manage your jobs.

⬜ Select **Files to Delete:** In the Media Encoder interface, locate the jobs or files you want to remove from the queue. You can delete a single file or multiple files at once.

- To select a range of files, hold down the **Shift** key and click the first and last items in the list.
- To select multiple non-consecutive files, hold down the **Ctrl** key (or **Command** key on a Mac) and click each file individually.

⬜ Right-**Click to Remove:** After selecting the files you want to delete, right-click on any of the highlighted items. A context menu will appear.

- Choose the **"Remove"** option from the menu. Clicking this will delete the selected files or jobs from your Media Encoder queue.

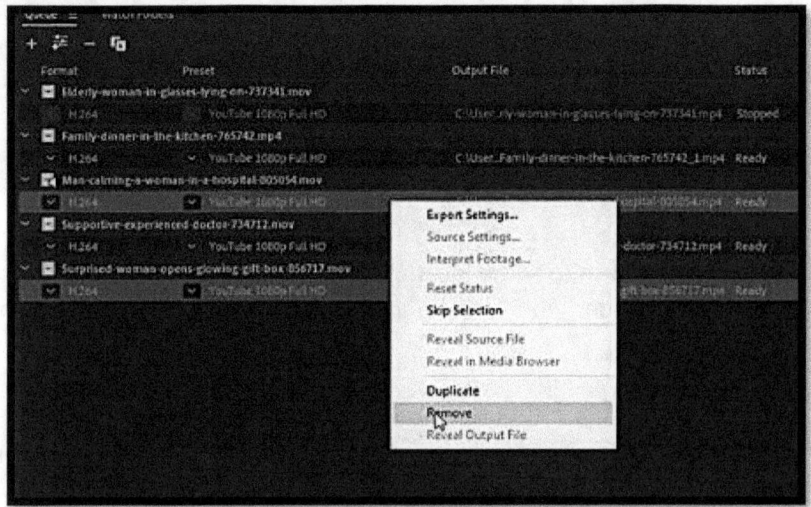

-

Uploading to social media

Once you've compressed your video, the next step is to share or post it. In the Export Settings dialog box of Adobe Media Encoder, you can configure publishing settings to enable automatic posting once the encoding is complete. The Publish options allow you to specify how your video will be sent to various platforms, including your Creative Cloud Files folder, Adobe Stock, Adobe Behance, Facebook, FTP sites, Twitter, Vimeo, and YouTube. This feature is particularly useful because you can save your chosen settings as an export preset. By doing this, you can streamline future social media posts by setting parameters just once. The next time you share media, you can simply select the preset to apply those settings.

Here's how to access these settings in Premiere Pro:

1. Return to Premiere Pro.
2. In the Timeline panel, navigate to **File > Export > Media**. You can also press **Command + M** (macOS) or **Ctrl + M** (Windows) to open the Export Settings dialog box.
3. In the Export dialog, click on the **"Publish"** tab to access sharing options for your video.
4. After making the necessary adjustments, click **"Cancel"** to close the Export Settings dialog and complete the setup.

Keep in mind that each platform has its own requirements for file submission. Generally, you can choose to export a high-quality master file, allowing the tool to create smaller versions as needed. For instance, when uploading to Adobe Stock, generating a high-quality UHD (3840x2160) file allows the server to manage compression and adapt to different video formats and codecs that the platform supports. This approach simplifies the sharing process while ensuring optimal quality across devices.

Exchanging Projects with Other Editing Applications

Premiere Pro supports several common file types for loading and publishing, including EDLs (Edit Decision Lists), OMF (Open Media Framework), AAF (Advanced Authoring Format), ALE (Avid Log Exchange), and XML (Extended Markup Language). These formats are essential for collaborating with writers using different software, as they facilitate the easy sharing of project data. For instance, using AAF as a bridge file simplifies collaboration with Avid Media Composer editors by allowing the exchange of clip information, modified sequences, and specific effects. Similarly, XML serves as a bridge for collaboration with Apple Final Cut Pro editors.

To save an AAF or XML file from Premiere Pro, follow these steps:

1. Select the sequence you want to export.
2. From the File menu, choose **File > Export > AAF** or **File > Export > Final Cut Pro XML**.
3. This action generates the AAF or XML file containing all the necessary project information for sharing or editing in compatible systems.

Additionally, Premiere Pro allows you to save project data into a file that describes the project, enabling it to be recreated using the same media or different editing software. For example, you can export a project as an Edit Decision List (EDL) in the CMX3600 format. Of the various EDL types, CMX3600 is one of the most widely used and effective for transferring files between editing systems. With a broad range of supported import and export formats, Premiere Pro ensures seamless collaboration across different editing platforms, allowing editors to use their preferred tools while still working together efficiently.

Using the EDL files

EDLs (Edit Decision Lists) are best suited for simple projects, typically containing no more than one video track, two stereo audio tracks, and no stacked sequences. They can accommodate common transitions, frame holds, and clip speed changes. For EDLs to function properly, all source content must be recorded and logged with accurate timecode. The capture device, whether it's a capture card or a FireWire port, should be timecode-controllable. Additionally, each recording should have a unique reel number and be set up with a timecode prior to filming to ensure accurate cutting and syncing.

To save a project as an EDL file in Premiere Pro, follow these steps:

1. Open or save the project you wish to export as an EDL.
2. Ensure that the Timeline panel is open in your project.
3. From the File menu, select **File > Export > EDL**.
4. In the EDL Export Settings (CMX 3600) dialog box, choose the video and audio tracks you want to include. You can export one video track along with two stereo audio tracks or up to four audio channels.
5. Specify the location and name for the EDL file.
6. Click **"Save"** to confirm the file's destination and name.
7. Click **"OK"** to initiate the export process.

By following these steps, you can export your project from Premiere Pro in the CMX 3600-compliant EDL format. This method is ideal for simple projects with limited tracks and straightforward edits, facilitating compatibility with editing systems that support EDL imports.

Exporting to OMF

Creating an Open Media Framework (OMF) file in Premiere Pro allows for the transfer of audio data between computers, making it particularly useful for audio mixing. Typically, OMF files consolidate all audio files from a sequence into a single file while preserving the organization of the clips as they appear in Premiere Pro.

Here's a step-by-step guide to creating an OMF file in Premiere Pro:

1. **Select Sequence and Open Export Settings:**
   o Choose the sequence you wish to export.
   o Go to **File > Export > OMF**.

2. **Configure OMF Export Settings:**
   o In the OMF Export Settings dialog, enter a name for the OMF file in the "OMF Title" field.
   o Ensure the "Sample Rate" and "Bits Per Sample" settings match your video specifications. Common defaults are 48000 Hz and 16 bits.
3. **Choose Export Options:**
   o In the "Files" section, select one of the following:
     ▪ **Embed Audio:** This option creates an OMF file that includes all project information and audio files within the sequence.
     ▪ **Separate Audio:** This option splits all audio files (including stereo) into individual mono files, which are saved in the omfiMediaFiles folder, suitable for complex audio mixing.
4. **Select Audio File Format:**
   o If you chose the "Separate Audio" option, pick between AIFF and Broadcast Wave formats. Both formats are high-quality, so ensure they are compatible with your system. AIFF files are often versatile across different platforms.
5. **Configure Audio File Handling:**
   o Under the "Render" section, select either "Copy Complete Audio Files" or "Trim Audio Files" to reduce file size. Adding handles (extra seconds) to the clips allows for greater flexibility during editing and mixing.
6. **Initiate OMF File Creation:**
   o After adjusting all settings, click **"OK"** to begin the creation of the OMF file.

By following these steps, you can successfully generate an OMF file from Premiere Pro, providing a well-organized representation of the audio clips in your sequence. This file format is advantageous for transferring audio projects across compatible systems used for mixing and editing audio.

Exporting Premiere Pro Videos to MP4

Converting movies from Premiere Pro to MP4 format may seem challenging at first since Adobe Premiere Pro doesn't offer a direct "MP4" save option. However, MP4 files are typically encoded with codecs like H.264 or the higher-quality H.265/HEVC, which you can find in the export settings. When exporting to MP4, it's common for the files to appear in a different format due to settings that might not be immediately obvious. MP4 is a versatile format that is compatible with various devices and systems, making this conversion important.

Here's how to convert your Premiere Pro projects to MP4:

1. Open Adobe Premiere Pro and load the project containing the video you want to export.
2. In the timeline, select the video clips you want to include. Selected parts will usually be highlighted in light blue.

3. Go to the **File** menu and select **Export**, or use the keyboard shortcut **Ctrl/Command + M**, or click on the Media icon to access the export options.
4. In the pop-up window, click on the **Format** dropdown menu and scroll to select either the **H.264** or **HEVC** codec that suits your needs.
5. Adjust the video quality settings, name your file, and choose a location to save the exported file.
6. Finally, click on the **Export** button to save your Premiere Pro project as an MP4 file.

By following these steps, you can successfully export your Premiere Pro project as an MP4 file using the H.264 or HEVC codec, ensuring compatibility across a wide range of devices and systems.

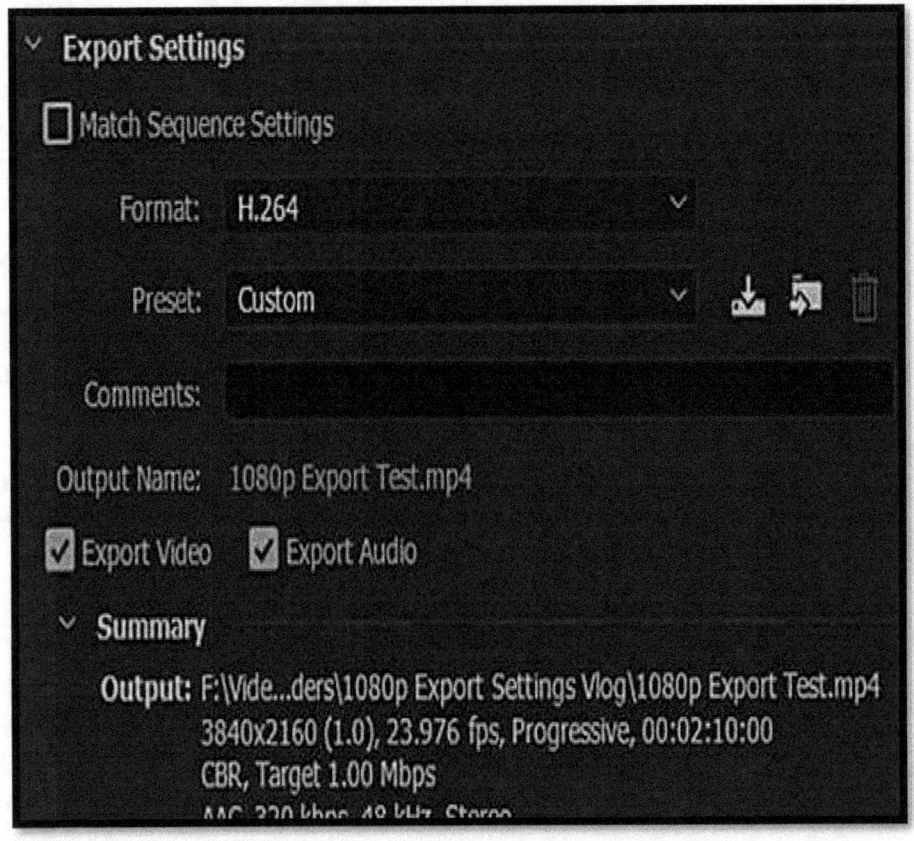

CHAPTER 17
WORKING WITH KEYFRAME INTERPOLATION

In digital video and film, interpolation refers to the method of estimating values between known points or keyframes. This is crucial for creating smooth animations and transitions. For example, if you want a title to move fifty pixels across the screen over 15 frames, you set keyframes at the start and end points, allowing the software to interpolate the intermediate frames for a fluid motion. This process, often called "tweening," generates the frames that fill the gaps between keyframes, enabling seamless transitions in movement, effects, audio levels, visual changes, and colors.

Interpolation can be categorized into two main types:

1. **Temporal Interpolation:** This type focuses on how motion changes over time, indicating whether an object is moving slowly or quickly. However, only a few effects in programs like Premiere Pro fully support keyframe blending over time.
2. **Spatial Interpolation:** This method involves changes in shape, determining whether corners should be smooth or sharp. In Premiere Pro, spatial interpolation can be applied to the keyframes of certain effects to control these variations.

There are two common forms of interpolation:

1. **Linear Interpolation:** This method provides a consistent and smooth transition from one keyframe to the next, with each intermediate frame receiving an equal portion of the change. While it results in smooth movement, it can create abrupt starts and stops.
2. **Bezier Interpolation:** This type allows for variable rates of change, represented by a Bezier curve. It enables a gradual acceleration from the first keyframe to the next and a similarly gradual deceleration, creating a more natural flow.

Depending on your desired outcome, you can choose between linear and Bezier interpolation. Linear interpolation delivers steady, smooth changes, while Bezier interpolation offers more control over the rate of change, resulting in a more organic and fluid animation feel.

Change the keyframe interpolation method

By adjusting keyframe interpolation, you can finely control the speed of changes in your projects. You can modify the keyframe type directly by manipulating the keyframe or its handles, or by selecting an interpolation type from a context menu.

To choose an interpolation method:

- **Right-click** on a keyframe marker in the Effect Controls panel.
- **Right-click** on a keyframe in the Timeline window.

From the context menu, you can select one of the following interpolation options:

- **Linear:** Maintains a constant speed of change between keyframes.
- **Bezier:** Allows you to manually adjust the shape and rate of change on either side of a keyframe, resulting in smooth transitions.
- **Auto Bezier:** Creates a smooth rate of change automatically. When the value of a keyframe changes, Auto Bezier adjusts the direction handles to ensure a seamless transition between keyframes.
- **Continuous Bezier:** Similar to Auto Bezier, this method allows for smooth transitions, but you can manually adjust the direction handles. Changes on one side of a keyframe affect the opposite side, maintaining a smooth shift.
- **Hold:** Instantly changes a property's value without any smooth transition. With Hold interpolation, the graph appears as a horizontal line after a keyframe.
- **Ease In:** Gradually slows down the value change as it approaches the keyframe.
- **Ease Out:** Gradually accelerates the value change until it reaches the keyframe.

Using these interpolation options, you can create more dynamic and nuanced animations in your projects.

Using the Auto Reframe Effects

Auto Reframe intelligently analyzes your video content and automatically adjusts the framing to suit various aspect ratios. This feature is particularly useful for sharing videos on platforms like Instagram, YouTube, or Facebook. You can easily change the aspect ratio of your sequences to square, vertical, or widescreen (16:9), and it supports cropping high-resolution videos, including those up to 4K. Whether you need to resize individual clips or an entire sequence, Auto Reframe makes the process quick and effortless.

Add the Auto Reframe effect to a clip

Here's how to use the Auto Reframe effect in Premiere Pro to adjust your clips:

1. **Apply the Effect:**
   - Hover over **Transform** in the Video Effects menu.
   - Drag the **Auto Reframe** effect onto the clip you want to adjust.
2. **Fine-Tune the Effect:**

- o Go to the **Effect Controls** panel to select the appropriate Motion Tracking option. Premiere Pro will automatically create motion keyframes that follow the action in your video as the effect is applied.
3. **Choose a Motion Setting:**
   - o **Slower Motion:** Ideal for clips where the camera is stationary or moves slowly, such as interviews. This setting results in fewer keyframes, keeping effects more stable.
   - o **Default:** Suitable for most scenarios. The Auto Reframe effect will track movement, but may not perform well with fast action.
   - o **Faster Motion:** Best for fast-paced clips, like action sports or skateboarding videos. This ensures that moving subjects remain centered in the frame and generates more keyframes to keep up with the action.
4. **Adjust Settings:**
   - o If needed, you can modify the **Generated Path**.
   - o Fine-tune other parameters such as **Position, Reframe Offset, Reframe Scale**, and **Reframe Rotation**.
5. **Preview and Adjust:**
   - o Play back the video after applying the effect to see how it looks. You can enhance the results further by copying and adjusting the keyframes in the Effect Controls panel if necessary.

By following these steps, you can effectively use Auto Reframe to adapt your videos for different aspect ratios while ensuring key elements stay in focus.

Resize a Picture

Resizing a landscape image in Premiere Pro is quick and straightforward. Here's how to do it:

1. **Import Your Images:** First, add the images you want to use in your project. You can do this by going to **File > Import**, but it's often easier to simply drag and drop the files into the project panel.
2. **Place the Image on the Timeline:** Drag the image to the timeline where you want it to appear.
3. **Scale the Image:** Right-click (or Control + click on a Mac) on the image in the timeline and select **Scale to Frame Size** from the context menu.

This method will automatically adjust the image to fit the frame of your project.

If the image doesn't fit the frame after scaling, you can adjust its size further using the options below the picture:

1. **Fit:** This option will resize the image to fit within the frame while maintaining its original aspect ratio. It ensures the entire image is visible, but there may be empty space around it if the aspect ratios don't match.
2. **Full:** This setting scales the image to fill the entire frame. While this will remove any empty space, it may crop part of the image if its aspect ratio differs from that of the frame.

Choose either option based on how you want the image to appear in your project.

How to Fit a Portrait Image in Your Video

Resizing a portrait image in Premiere Pro is slightly more complex than with a landscape image, but it's still manageable. Here's how to do it:

1. **Create a Color Matte:**
   o Go to the **Project** panel and click on **New Item** in the bottom right corner.
   o If you can't see the icon, expand your workspace by pressing the three lines on your video and selecting **Panel Group Settings > Maximize Panel Group**.
2. **Adjust the Color Matte:** Once you have created the color matte, you can use it as a background or adjust your portrait image accordingly.

By following these steps, you can effectively handle portrait images within your project.

Before selecting the best color for your color matte, you can specify its size. Here's how:

1. **Choose Size:** When the Color Matte dialog box appears, you'll see options to set the dimensions of the matte. Adjust the width and height according to your project requirements.
2. **Select Color:** After setting the size, choose your desired color.
3. **Click OK:** Once you've made your selections, click **OK** to create the color matte.

This allows you to customize both the size and color of the matte to fit your project perfectly.

To add your color matte and position your portrait image in Premiere Pro, follow these steps:

1. **Add the Color Matte:** Drag and drop the color matte into your project timeline, placing it in a video track above your main footage. This ensures it covers the underlying clips.
2. **Insert the Portrait Image:** Drag and drop your portrait image into a video track above the color matte. If you're experiencing crashes, consider importing the image manually instead of dragging and dropping.
3. **Adjust the Image Size:** Select the portrait image in the timeline and click on **Scale to Frame Size** in the Effect Controls panel. This will resize the image to fit within the color background.

By following these steps, your portrait image should now fit nicely on the screen against the color backdrop.

CHAPTER 18
WORKFLOW OPTIMIZATION

Keyboard Shortcuts and Customization
10 Useful Default Keyboard Shortcuts

Here's a streamlined guide to using keyboard shortcuts and timeline adjustments in Premiere Pro:

1. **Set Default Keyboard Layout:**
   - Ensure you're using the default layout by going to the **File** menu (or **Premiere Pro CC** menu on Mac) and selecting **Keyboard Shortcuts > Keyboard Layout Preset > Adobe Premiere Pro Default**.
2. **Adjust Timeline Size:**
   - Use **Shift + Plus (+)** or **Minus (-)** to zoom in or out of the timeline.
   - **Ctrl + Minus (-)** changes the height of video tracks, while **Alt + Minus (-)** adjusts the height of audio tracks.
3. **Zoom Out Entire Timeline:**
   - Press the **Backslash (/)** key to quickly zoom out and view the entire timeline.
4. **Set In and Out Points:**
   - Mark sections for editing using In and Out points. Clear them with:
     - **Ctrl + Shift + I** (or **Opt + I** on Mac) to clear the In point.
     - **Ctrl + Shift + O** (or **Opt + O**) to clear the Out point.
     - **Ctrl + Shift + X** (or **Opt + X**) to clear both.
5. **Mark Clips:**
   - Press the **X** key to mark the clip under the Playhead.
   - Use the **Forward Slash (/)** key to set In and Out points for all selected clips.
6. **Select Clips:**
   - Press **D** to select the clip under the Playhead.
7. **Deselect Everything:**
   - Use **Shift + Ctrl + A** (or **Shift + Cmd + A** on Mac) to deselect all clips and effects.
8. **Cut Clips:**
   - Press **Ctrl + K** (or **Cmd + K**) to cut a clip at the Playhead.
   - Holding **Shift** while cutting will cut all clips beneath the Playhead.
9. **Ripple Trim:**
   - Use **Q** to trim the clip from the Playhead to the previous edit point, and **W** to trim to the next edit point.
10. **Match Frame:**
    - Press **F** to find the first or master clip in your sequence and open it in the Source Monitor at the current frame.
11. **Reverse Match Frame:**

- o   Press **Shift + R** to find previous occurrences of the frame in your sequence.

These shortcuts and tips can significantly enhance your editing efficiency in Premiere Pro!

Best practices when editing keyboard shortcuts

To ensure a smooth editing experience in Adobe Premiere Pro when customizing keyboard shortcuts, consider the following best practices:

Tips for Efficient Shortcut Management

1. **Avoid Conflicts:**
   - o   When creating new shortcuts, steer clear of key combinations already in use. Conflicts can lead to unintended actions. If you receive a warning while setting a shortcut, try a different combination.
2. **Familiarize Yourself with Existing Shortcuts:**
   - o   Before making significant changes, take the time to learn the default shortcuts in Premiere Pro. Many of these shortcuts are consistent across all Adobe programs and can help streamline your workflow.
3. **Use Mnemonic Associations:**
   - o   Create mnemonic devices to help remember shortcuts. For instance, use "C" for Cut and "V" for Paste. This can make it easier to recall functions as you edit.
4. **Gradually Expand Your Shortcut List:**
   - o   Start by modifying a few shortcuts that are most relevant to your workflow. As you become more comfortable with Premiere Pro, gradually add more customized shortcuts to avoid overwhelming yourself.
5. **Organize and Document Your Custom Shortcuts:**
   - o   Keep a written list of your customized shortcuts along with their functions. This will make it easier to reference them, especially if you work on different computers or collaborate with others.
6. **Backup Your Shortcuts:**
   - o   Save a copy of your custom shortcut set to avoid losing your changes due to software issues or resets. This will ensure that you can quickly restore your personalized setup if needed.

By following these practices, you can enhance your editing efficiency and create a more tailored experience in Adobe Premiere Pro.

Ten Essential Right-Click Commands for Adobe Premiere Pro

In Adobe Premiere Pro, right-clicking on a clip in the Project or Sequence panels opens up a range of useful options that can significantly enhance your editing efficiency. Here are some key features to streamline your workflow:

1. **Speed/Duration Adjustment:**
    o   Quickly modify the speed of your clip or reverse it by selecting "Speed/Duration" from the context menu.
2. **Audio Settings:**
    o   Access audio options to adjust levels, balance, or convert audio channels for better sound quality.
3. **Apply Effects:**
    o   Easily apply effects by right-clicking and selecting from a list of available effects to enhance your clips.
4. **Nest Clips:**
    o   Organize your timeline by nesting selected clips, allowing for easier management and application of effects.
5. **Speed Ramp:**
    o   Create dynamic speed changes within your clip by using the speed ramp option for more engaging edits.
6. **Remove Attributes:**
    o   If you need to delete specific effects or attributes from a clip, right-click to access the "Remove Attributes" option.

These right-click options provide powerful tools for adjusting clip properties and effects, helping you work more efficiently and creatively in your projects.

1. Editing>interpretation of the footage

With many DSLRs recording at 60 frames per second, you can easily create slow-motion clips in Adobe Premiere Pro. To adjust the frame rate of a video clip, follow these steps:

1. **Select the Clip:** Click and hold on the desired clip in the Project panel.
2. **Modify Settings:** Navigate to the menu and select **"Modify" > "Interpret Footage."**
3. **Set Frame Rate:** In the **"Assume this frame rate"** box, choose either **23.94** or **29.97** fps, depending on your desired slow-motion effect.

Once you make this change, the clip's duration will extend, and it will play back more slowly, achieving the slow-motion effect you want.

2. Alter the Audio Channels

You can easily convert the audio in your clips from mono to stereo in Adobe Premiere Pro. Here's how:

1. **Select the Clip:** Press and hold on the clip in the Project panel.
2. **Modify Audio Settings:** From the drop-down menu, select **"Modify."**
3. **Change Audio Format:** You can switch the audio from mono to stereo or vice versa.

This simple adjustment allows you to customize your audio setup to fit your project's needs.

3. Reveal in…

Right-clicking on any file in Adobe Premiere Pro makes it easy to locate it on your hard drive. You can also right-click on a clip in Premiere and select **"Adobe Bridge"** to access additional options. This allows you to rename, play, and rate the clip, enhancing your workflow and organization.

4. Speed and time

Changing the speed of a clip in the Project panel will affect all instances of that clip throughout your project. However, if you adjust the speed of a clip within a specific sequence, it will only modify that instance of the clip, leaving other occurrences unchanged. This allows for more flexibility in your editing process.

5. Blending the frames

To enable smoother motion when changing the frame rate of a clip or output, you should activate **Frame Blend**. Simply select a clip in the Sequence, right-click on it, and choose **Frame Blend** from the context menu. This will help create a more fluid appearance in your edited footage.

6. Remove Effects

Select the clips from which you want to remove effects. A dialog box will appear, allowing you to manage the effects. To eliminate any unwanted effects, simply uncheck them in the list provided.

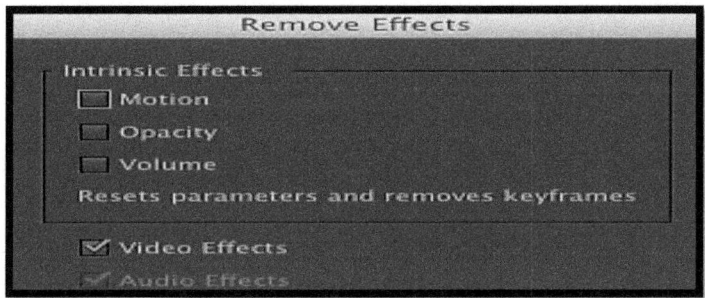

7. Reveal in Project

Right-click on a clip in the Sequence to quickly locate its corresponding file in the Project panel. This will help you easily find and manage the clip's settings and details.

8. Examine the content

Select a clip from the Project panel that you want to analyze for speech or identify faces. For more detailed information and guidance on these features, check out Adobe's website. This can help you achieve better results in your analysis.

9. Edit the Clip in the Audition

This action launches Adobe Audition and transfers the selected clip from the Sequence. Editors can utilize Audition's "Noise Reduction" tool to eliminate background noise from audio files. Once you return to Premiere Pro, it will retain any changes you made in Audition.

10. Replace with After Effects Composition

To change a clip from the Sequence using an After Effects Composition, simply right-click on the clip in Premiere Pro. This method is especially useful for tasks like Motion Tracking in After Effects or applying effects not available in Premiere Pro. If you think you might need the original clip later, it's a good idea to create a copy of the Sequence before proceeding. This approach streamlines your workflow and enhances productivity!

PART VI
ADVANCED TECHNIQUES IN EFFECTS AND ANIMATION

CHAPTER 19

ADVANCED VIDEO EFFECTS

Exploring the Effects Panel

To get started with the Effect Controls panel in Adobe Premiere Pro, follow these steps:

1. Open the Effect Controls Panel

- **Access the Panel:** Go to the menu bar at the top and select **Window > Effect Controls**. This will bring up the Effect Controls panel, typically docked in the upper left corner of your workspace.

2. Select Your Clip

- **Choose a Clip:** Click on the clip you want to edit in the Timeline. This will display its properties in the Effect Controls panel.

3. Explore the Effect Controls Panel

- **View Parameters:** In the Effect Controls panel, you'll see various parameters for the selected clip, such as Motion, Opacity, and any effects you've applied.
- **Real-Time Feedback:** As you adjust settings like position, scale, or opacity, watch the Program Monitor to see changes reflected in real time.

4. Add Effects

- **Access the Effects Panel:** Go to **Window > Effects** to open the Effects panel.
- **Apply an Effect:** Drag and drop an effect onto your clip in the Timeline. It will automatically appear in the Effect Controls panel.

5. Fine-Tune Effects

- **Adjust Settings:** Use the sliders and input fields in the Effect Controls panel to adjust the parameters of the applied effects. For instance, if you added a Gaussian Blur effect, you can control the blur amount here.

6. Keyframing

- **Animate Properties:** If you want to animate a property (like position or scale), click the stopwatch icon next to the property in the Effect Controls panel to create keyframes. Adjust the values at different points in the timeline to create smooth transitions.

7. Preview Changes

- **Real-Time Monitoring:** Continuously play back your sequence in the Program Monitor to preview how your changes affect the overall video.

By following these steps, you'll be able to effectively use the Effect Controls panel in Adobe Premiere Pro, enhancing your video editing process with cinematic effects. Enjoy experimenting with different effects to see how they transform your footage!

2. Use Effect Controls to Transform Clips

Now that you have the Effect Controls panel open, let's dive into how to use it to transform your clips effectively. The Effect Controls panel provides several options for manipulating your video, including **Time Remapping**, **Motion**, and **Opacity**.

A. Motion

- **Position:** Adjust the X and Y values to move your clip horizontally and vertically within the frame.
- **Scale:** Change the size of your clip by modifying the scale percentage. You can also hold the Shift key while adjusting to maintain the clip's aspect ratio.
- **Rotation:** Use the rotation parameter to spin your clip. Enter a value in degrees to set the desired rotation.
- **Anchor Point:** Adjusting the anchor point changes the point around which your clip rotates or scales. It can be useful for creating more complex animations.

B. Opacity

- **Opacity Slider:** Use this slider to control the transparency of your clip. Setting it to 0% makes the clip completely transparent, while 100% keeps it fully visible.
- **Keyframing Opacity:** Click the stopwatch icon next to Opacity to create keyframes. This allows you to animate the opacity over time, fading clips in or out.

C. Time Remapping

- **Speed Adjustment:** Right-click on a clip in the Timeline and select **Show Clip Keyframes > Time Remapping > Speed**. This will allow you to adjust the playback speed of your clip.
- **Creating Keyframes:** Drag the line that appears on the clip to adjust the speed. Add keyframes by Ctrl-clicking (Cmd-clicking on Mac) on the line to create variable speed changes throughout the clip.

3. Accessing More Options

- **Expand Drop-Downs:** Click the small triangle next to each category (Time Remapping, Motion, Opacity) to expand or collapse the options. This gives you access to more specific controls within each category.

4. Real-Time Preview

- **Monitor Changes:** As you make adjustments in the Effect Controls panel, continuously play back your sequence in the Program Monitor to see how your changes affect the overall composition.

Summary

With the Effect Controls panel, you have powerful tools at your fingertips to manipulate clips effectively. Explore these options to create dynamic transitions, control visibility, and adjust timing in your projects. Experimenting with these features will enhance your editing skills and allow for more creative storytelling in your videos!

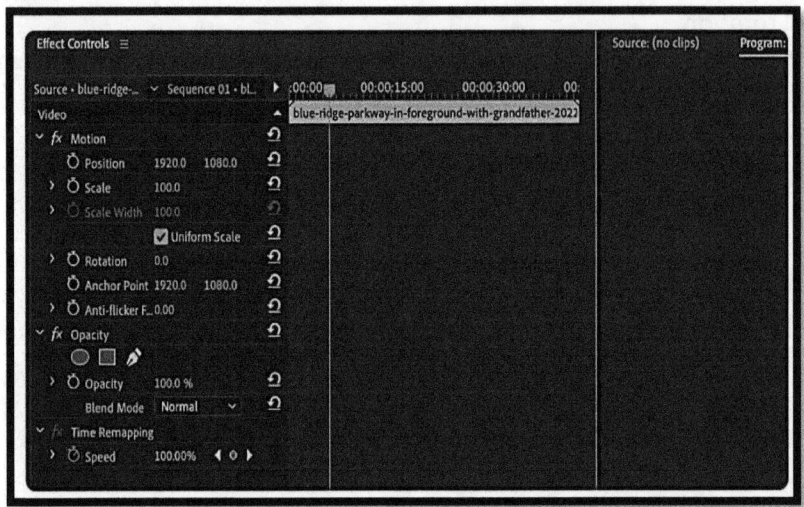

Moving and Scaling Video Clips in Premiere Pro

In Adobe Premiere Pro, adjusting the position and scale of your video clips is straightforward and allows for greater creative control over your composition. Here's how you can effectively use the **Motion** group in the **Effect Controls** panel:

1. Adjusting Position

- **Default Center:** By default, clips are centered in the editing canvas.
- **Changing Position Values:**
  - Locate the **Position** parameter in the Motion section of the Effect Controls panel.
  - The position is represented by two values (X and Y coordinates).
    - **X Value:** Adjust this to move the clip left or right. Increasing the value moves the clip to the right, while decreasing it moves it to the left.
    - **Y Value:** Adjust this to move the clip up or down. Increasing the value moves the clip up, while decreasing it moves it down.

2. Scaling the Clip

- **Zooming In and Out:**
  - The **Scale** parameter acts like a zoom tool.
  - If you set the scale to **125.0**, the clip will zoom in by 25%. Conversely, setting it to **75.0** will zoom out by 25%.
- **Aspect Ratio:**
  - By default, scaling maintains the clip's aspect ratio. Hold the Shift key while adjusting the scale to change width and height independently.

3. Changing Anchor Point

- **Anchor Point Adjustment:**
  - The **Anchor Point** determines the pivot around which the clip rotates or scales.
  - Changing this value can create interesting effects, such as rotating the clip around a specific point rather than its center.

4. Applying Changes

- **Real-Time Feedback:**
  - As you adjust the position and scale, you can view the changes in real time in the Program Monitor.
- **Keyframing:**
  - If you want to animate these changes over time, click the stopwatch icon next to Position or Scale to create keyframes. Adjust the values at different points in your timeline to create dynamic motion effects.

Summary

Using the Motion group in the Effect Controls panel allows you to effectively position and scale your video clips in Premiere Pro. Experiment with these settings to create visually engaging compositions and animations that enhance your storytelling!

Using Effects and Adjusting with Effect Controls in Premiere Pro

The **Effect Controls** panel in Adobe Premiere Pro is not just for basic transformations like position and scale; it also allows you to apply and customize various effects to enhance your video projects. Here's how to add effects and make adjustments using the Effect Controls:

1. Accessing the Effects Panel

- **Open the Effects Panel:**
    - o Go to the top menu and select **Window > Effects**.
    - o This will open the **Effects** sidebar, typically on the right side of your workspace.

2. Adding Effects

- **Browse Effects:**
    - o In the Effects panel, you can browse through various categories such as **Video Effects**, **Audio Effects**, **Transitions**, and more.
- **Applying Effects to Clips:**
    - o To add an effect, simply drag and drop it onto your desired clip in the **Timeline** or directly in the **Program Monitor**.

3. Adjusting Effects in Effect Controls

- **Selecting the Clip:**
  - Click on the clip in the **Timeline** that you just added an effect to. This will display the effects applied to that clip in the Effect Controls panel.
- **Adjusting Opacity:**
  - The **Opacity** parameter allows you to control how transparent or opaque your clip is.
    - Set the Opacity percentage (0% = fully transparent, 100% = fully opaque).
    - Use the **Opacity** settings to create overlays or to blend clips together.
- **Using Time Remapping:**
  - **Time Remapping** enables you to control the playback speed of your clip.
    - Right-click on the clip in the **Timeline** and select **Show Clip Keyframes > Time Remapping > Speed**.
    - You can add keyframes on the rubber band that appears on the clip to create slow-motion or fast-motion effects.
      - Dragging the rubber band up increases speed, while dragging it down slows down the clip.

4. Fine-Tuning Effects

- **Effect Controls for Each Effect:**
  - Each effect you apply will have its own set of controls within the Effect Controls panel.
    - For example, if you apply a **Gaussian Blur**, you can adjust the **Blurriness** and other parameters specific to that effect.
- **Keyframing Effects:**
  - You can animate the properties of effects over time by clicking the stopwatch icon next to any parameter to enable keyframing.
  - Adjust values at different points in the timeline to create smooth transitions and dynamic changes.

Summary

The Effect Controls panel in Adobe Premiere Pro is a powerful tool for not only adjusting basic clip properties but also for enhancing your videos with various effects. By exploring the Effects panel and utilizing Opacity and Time Remapping, you can create visually engaging content that captivates your audience. Experiment with different effects to discover what works best for your project!

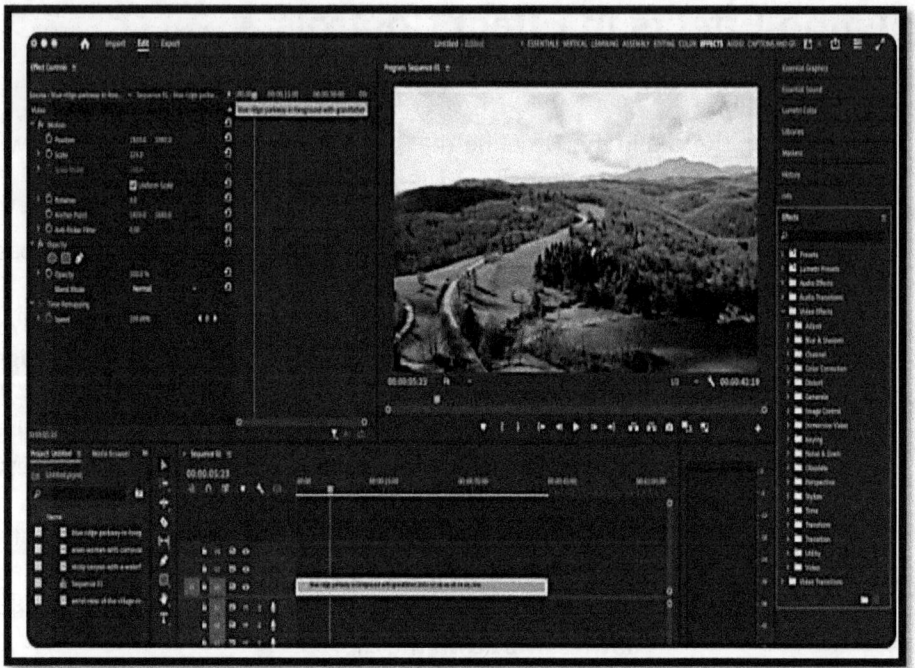

Adding and Adjusting Effects in Premiere Pro

Adobe Premiere Pro provides a wealth of effects that can enhance your videos in various ways. Here's how to add a specific effect, like **Sharpen**, and adjust its properties using the Effect Controls panel:

1. Accessing Video Effects

- **Open the Effects Panel:**
    - ○ Go to **Window > Effects** to display the Effects panel.
- **Navigating to Blur & Sharpen:**
    - ○ In the Effects panel, find **Video Effects** and expand the dropdown.
    - ○ Locate **Blur & Sharpen**, and click to open it.

2. Adding the Sharpen Effect

- **Dragging the Effect:**
    - ○ Find the **Sharpen** effect within the Blur & Sharpen category.
    - ○ Click and drag the **Sharpen** effect onto your desired clip in the **Timeline**.
- **Placement:**

o   Drop the effect on the clip where you want it to take effect. A black bar will indicate the clip has been affected.

3. Adjusting the Effect

- **Viewing in Effect Controls:**
    o   Click on the clip in the Timeline to select it.
    o   Open the **Effect Controls** panel (Window > Effect Controls) if it's not already visible.
- **Adjusting Sharpen Settings:**
    o   In the Effect Controls panel, you'll see a new dropdown for the **Sharpen** effect.
    o   You can adjust the **Amount** parameter to control how much sharpening is applied. Increasing the value will enhance the details in the clip, while lowering it will reduce the effect.
- **Real-time Feedback:**
    o   As you adjust the **Sharpen** value, watch the **Program Monitor** to see the changes in real-time. This helps you find the perfect balance without over-sharpening, which can lead to an unnatural look.

4. Experimenting with Other Effects

- **Exploring Further:**
    o   Feel free to experiment with other effects found in the Effects panel. Each effect can be adjusted in the Effect Controls panel similarly.
    o   Play around with combinations of effects to see how they work together and create unique looks for your video.

Summary

Adding effects like **Sharpen** in Adobe Premiere Pro is straightforward. By using the Effects panel and Effect Controls, you can easily enhance the visual quality of your clips and achieve the desired aesthetic for your project. Don't hesitate to explore the diverse array of effects available to elevate your video editing skills!

Let's set the Sharpen Amount to 30 as an example. Watch the Program Monitor as you make this adjustment; you'll notice the clip becomes clearer. This demonstrates how to add effect controls in Premiere Pro! Using the Effect Controls panel, you can modify the properties of any effect after applying it. Remember, you can apply multiple effects to a clip—it's always the same straightforward process. Simply add an effect to the Timeline, and its settings will appear in the Effect Controls panel. There's a lot you can do, so feel free to experiment for various outcomes. These effects are a simple and quick way to achieve significant changes in your videos using Adobe Premiere Pro. The Effect Controls in Premiere Pro are user-friendly, and with just a few steps, you'll learn how to incorporate them into your projects. A key question to keep in mind is, "Where can I find the effect controls in Premiere Pro?" You'll find these tools invaluable as you dive into editing in Premiere.

Using Masks for Creative Effects

Masking is an essential skill in Adobe Premiere Pro, as it can enhance your projects and resolve various issues with your footage. Typically, masks are used to create vignettes or crop clips into specific shapes. However, once you familiarize yourself with the tools, you'll discover a wide range of additional applications for this effect.

Create a Mask with Shape Tools

In Premiere Pro, the two basic shape masks are the circle and the square, both of which can be added to your clip with a single click. To get started, locate the Crop effect in the Effects panel and apply it to the desired clip. This will hide the other clips in your sequence. You'll find the cropping settings in the Effect Controls panel; simply click on the Crop drop-down to access them. After that, we'll explore the pen tool, but first, let's examine the square and circle tools.

When you click on either shape, the mask will be applied to your clip in the media player. From there, you can adjust the size and style of the mask until you achieve the desired look.

To create the cutting effect, return to the Effect Controls panel and use the Crop percentages to remove sections of the shot. You can decide whether the effect affects the inside or outside of the mask by checking the "Inverted" box.

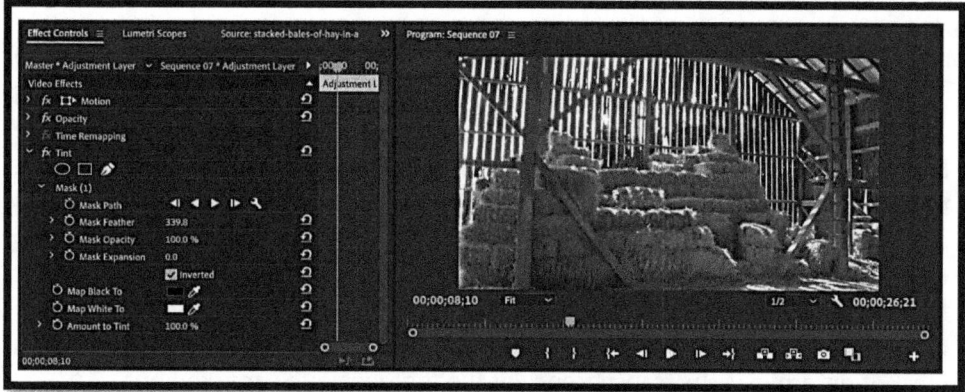

It's easier than you might have expected! Now, let's tackle something a bit more challenging.

Create a Custom Shape Using the Pen Tool

You can use the Pen tool to create shapes beyond just circles and squares. Once you select the Pen tool, you can draw directly on your video in the media player. Clicking on the video adds points to your shape; keep adding points until you're satisfied, then click on the first point to close the shape. A single click will create a corner point, giving your shape a sharp edge. If you click and drag a point, it will develop handles that allow you to create curved lines. Mastering the Pen tool takes practice, especially for achieving balanced shapes, but don't worry—you'll get the hang of it!

How to Modify and Move Masks

Once your mask is complete, you can adjust its points to refine the shape.

- Click anywhere on the mask line to add an additional point to your shape.
- By holding down ALT and clicking on a point, you can add or remove handles for more precise adjustments.

Move Your Mask

By clicking and dragging in the center of the shape, you can reposition the mask anywhere on the screen over your video.

Feather and Adjust Mask Edges

In the Mask Effect options, you'll find three additional settings: Feather, Opacity, and Expansion. Each of these can enhance your mask and add stylish effects to your footage.

- **Expansion** allows you to adjust how close the footage is to the mask's outline. This is particularly useful for complex shapes, as it can help smooth out rough edges without requiring you to perfect every angle.
- **Feathering** enables a gradual fade in or out from the edges of the mask. You can adjust the feathering amount in both the Effects Control panel and the media player.
- **Opacity** functions similarly to how it does in other Adobe programs. When applied to a mask, it determines the transparency of the footage you've masked out.

How to Copy and Paste Masks

Copying a mask from one clip to another is straightforward. In the Effects Control panel, select the clip with the mask you wish to copy. Then, press Cmd+C (Mac) or Ctrl+C (Windows) to copy it.

To paste, select the target clip in the sequence and press Cmd+V (Mac) or Ctrl+V (Windows). While you can copy and paste masks between specific clips, using an adjustment layer is often more efficient if you want to apply changes to the entire sequence.

- To create an adjustment layer, open the Project window and select **New Item**. This will automatically add a new layer to the Project window.
- Drag the adjustment layer into your sequence and place it above the clips you want to modify.
- Follow the same steps to add a mask to the adjustment layer. This time, the effect will apply to all clips beneath it in the sequence.
- You can also copy and paste masks between adjustment layers or between clips and adjustment layers.

Using adjustment layers can save you a lot of time if you need to adjust your masks later. You're already improving your editing skills!

Premiere Pro Masking Tips

You already know how to use masks for cropping, but they can also be applied to nearly any effect that alters the appearance of your clips. Here are a few of our favorites:

Color Effects

You can apply masks to any color effect, allowing you to create more stunning visuals in your films beyond the typical fade-to-black vignette. For example, using the Tint effect can help eliminate colors around the edges of the mask. Additionally, masks can be beneficial for shots with high contrast, enabling you to selectively lighten or darken specific areas of a scene.

Blur Effect

Blurs are an excellent tool for emphasizing key elements in your video. By applying a blur effect, you can selectively blur certain areas of your shot using the same masking options available in the Effects Control panel. This technique is particularly useful when you want to draw attention to a clip's title or other important details.

Color Mattes

While Premiere Pro offers many built-in text boxes, there are occasions when a custom effect is necessary. Masking color mattes is an effective way to introduce color to your videos without needing to use Illustrator, Photoshop, or After Effects.

Troubleshooting Premiere Pro Masks

Masks can be tricky to perfect every time. Let's explore some of the most common mistakes and how to resolve them.

Twisted Handles

You might create a perfect shape and see all the handles, but if one point forms a small, sharp loop, it may be due to the handles being oriented incorrectly. Simply select that point and adjust the handles until the edge appears smooth.

Point Clusters

If adjusting a point doesn't seem to alter the shape as expected, it could be because there are other nearby points affecting it. The video player may appear small unless you're using a large screen, making it hard to see every point on the mask. Use the Zoom feature to check for any extra points. If you find unnecessary ones, you can remove them by holding down Command (Mac) or Control (Windows) and clicking on the point you want to delete.

Playback

When working with masks, you may occasionally encounter playback issues, but don't worry—this is usually due to the effect you're using rather than the mask itself. Always ensure your sequence is properly set up. Knowing how to use masks during editing is invaluable, as they can help you create stunning visuals and correct shooting errors. With the ability to apply color adjustments precisely, you can address specific problems, such as white spots in your footage. While you can rely on built-in effects like the standard Premiere Vignette, mastering masks in Adobe Premiere without additional tools will give you greater flexibility to experiment and solve issues creatively.

CHAPTER 20
PUTTING CLIPS IN MOTION

In video projects that emphasize motion graphics, multiple shots are often layered into complex compositions. These layers are frequently utilized; for instance, a video clip might be scaled down and placed alongside a presenter on camera, or several clips could be displayed in floating boxes. The Motion effect allows you to move, scale, or rotate a clip within the video frame. You can apply the Motion effect to any clip in the Timeline panel, and it will remain accessible. To view and modify the properties of the Motion effect, simply click the triangle next to its name in the Effect Controls panel. Additionally, by setting keyframes for Motion properties, you can create dynamic movement for your clips.

Adjusting the Motion Effects

To view and adjust the features of the Motion effect, click the triangle next to the word "Motion" in the Effect Controls panel. This section provides a reference point indicating the clip's position, size, and rotation. The anchor point for clips is typically located in the center, but you can modify this center point directly on the Effects Control page.

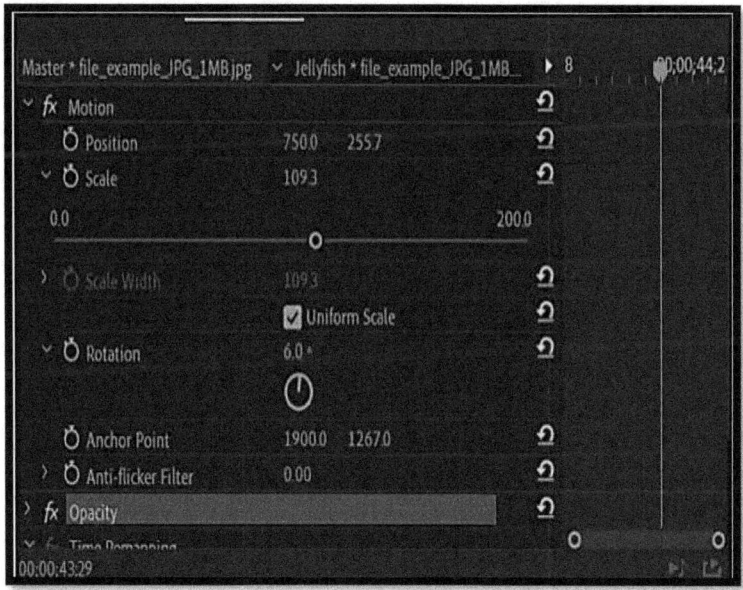

Changing a Clip Position, Size, and Rotation
Scale Clip
Scaling a Clip in Adobe Premiere Pro

1. **Select the Clip in the Timeline:**
   - Open your project in Adobe Premiere Pro.
   - Navigate to the Timeline and select the clip you want to scale.
2. **Access the Effects Control Panel:**
   - Go to the menu bar and open the Effects Control panel. This panel displays various parameters and effects for the selected clip.
3. **Adjust the Scale Parameters:**
   - In the Effects Control panel, find the "Scale" parameter under the "Motion" effect.
   - Click the triangle next to "Scale" to expand the options.
4. **Modify Scale Settings:**
   - To adjust both height and width uniformly:
     - Drag the slider to the right to increase the clip's size.
     - Drag the slider to the left to decrease the clip's size.
5. **Adjust Height and Width Independently (Optional):**
   - If you want to change height and width separately:
     - Deselect the "Uniform Scale" option.
     - Now you can modify height and width values individually for different scaling proportions.
6. **Fine-Tune the Scaling:**
   - Continue adjusting the Scale parameters until you achieve the desired size or proportions for your clip.

Clip Rotation
Rotating a Clip in Adobe Premiere Pro

1. **Select a Clip in the Timeline:**
   - Open your project in Adobe Premiere Pro.
   - Click on the clip in the Timeline that you want to rotate.
2. **Access the Effects Control Panel:**
   - Go to the menu bar and select the "Effects Control" panel.
   - This panel shows various properties and effects for the selected clip.
3. **Adjust Rotation Properties:**
   - In the Effects Control panel, find the "Rotation" property under the "Motion" effect.
   - Click the triangle or disclosure arrow next to "Rotation" to expand its properties.

4. **Apply Rotation Effect:**
   - Enter a specific value in the "Rotation" field to set your desired angle.
   - Alternatively, drag the line within the circular control to visually adjust the rotation.

Adjust Anchor Point
Altering the Anchor Point in Adobe Premiere Pro

1. **Select a Clip in the Timeline:**
   - Choose the clip you want to modify in the Timeline.
2. **Access the Effects Control Panel:**
   - Select the "Effects Control" panel from the menu bar.
3. **Modify the Anchor Point:**
   - Click on the Anchor Point coordinates and enter a new value to update the Anchor Point.

Manipulating Using Clip Handles
Using Handles to Adjust Video Clips in Adobe Premiere Pro

Making adjustments to a video clip within the Program Monitor involves using intuitive handles to modify its position, size, and orientation. Here's a step-by-step guide to effectively create motion effects:

1. **Select the Clip:**
   - In the Timeline panel, choose the specific clip you want to edit by positioning the playhead over it.
2. **Access the Clip in the Program Monitor:**
   - Click on the selected clip in the Program Monitor to ensure it's ready for editing.
3. **Navigate to the Effect Controls:**
   - Open the Effect Controls panel and click on the "Motion" label or the line corresponding to the clip you're modifying.
4. **Utilize Handles:**
   - Hover your mouse over the clip in the Program Monitor to reveal the handles, which indicate where adjustments can be made.
5. **Relocate the Clip:**
   - Click and drag the clip to reposition it on the screen.
6. **Scale the Clip:**
   - To resize the clip, hover near a corner until a resizing handle appears. Drag the handle to adjust the size. To maintain proportions, hold down the Shift key while dragging.

7. **Rotate the Clip:**
   o Position your mouse slightly outside the clip until the cursor changes to a rotation icon. Drag to rotate the clip to your desired angle.

This method offers a user-friendly approach to manipulate video clips in the Program Monitor, allowing for precise adjustments to placement, size, and orientation to achieve your desired visual effects.

Adjusting Size

To crop a movie in Adobe Premiere Pro, first, import the clip you want to work with. Click the **Import** button in the **File** menu. Alternatively, you can simply drag and drop the clip directly into the Timeline.

Open the Effects panel.

You can find the Crop tool in the **Effects** tab, located under the **Transform** category. Click and drag the Crop effect onto your movie clip in the Timeline to apply it.

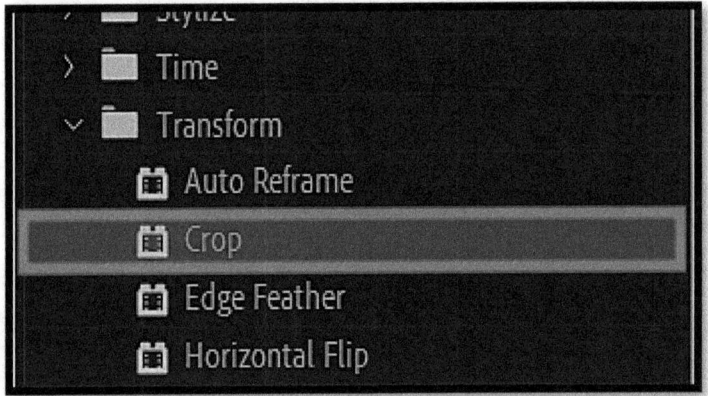

If needed, you can adjust the settings in the Effect Controls panel. You can crop from the Left, Right, Top, and Bottom by changing the respective values. To change the frame size, select the movie clip in the Timeline, then choose **Set to Frame Size** from the dropdown menu.

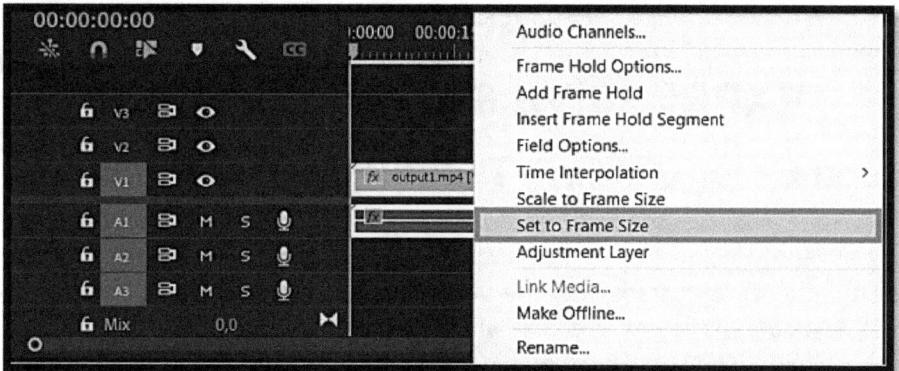

When you right-click on the movie clip, a dropdown menu will appear. Select **"Scale to Frame Size"** to adjust the size of the source clip. This allows you to modify the clip's dimensions instead of relying on previously set settings.

Return to the **Effects** tab to apply the Motion effect. In the Effect Controls panel, locate the Motion dropdown list. For optimal scaling, use the slider to adjust the size of your clip effectively.

A few key factors to consider

☐ By default, a clip appears in the center of the Program Monitor at full size.

☐ The reference point, located in the middle of the clip, is used to determine the position, scale, and rotation values.

☐ The Position, Scale, and Rotation parameters are easier to adjust directly in the Program Monitor, as they are spatial properties.

CHAPTER 21
EXPRESSIVE COLOR GRADING
Advanced Color Grading Techniques

When using advanced color grading in Adobe Premiere Pro, you're engaging in sophisticated techniques to enhance and transform the visual quality of your video project. This intricate process goes beyond basic color correction, allowing you to manipulate colors, tones, and subtle variations to achieve your desired aesthetic. Here are some advanced color grading tips to elevate your visual storytelling:

1. **Look-Up Tables (LUTs):** A fundamental yet powerful tool in advanced color grading is the use of Look-Up Tables. LUTs enable filmmakers to apply specific looks to their footage using preset color profiles or custom maps. You can import third-party LUTs into Premiere Pro, unlocking a wide range of creative possibilities. LUTs provide a quick and efficient way to ensure consistent color grading across multiple clips, whether you're aiming for a dramatic tone, a vintage vibe, or a stylized mood.

2. **Color Wheels and Curves:** Premiere Pro's Color Wheels and Curves offer precise control over color adjustments. With Color Wheels, you can separately fine-tune shadows, midtones, and highlights. This allows for careful enhancement or reduction of specific color ranges, resulting in a more balanced mix. Curves provide a visual representation of tonal distribution, enabling you to accurately control brightness and color intensity.

3. **HSL Secondary Color Correction:** The HSL (Hue, Saturation, and Lightness) Secondary tool in Premiere Pro allows for targeted color correction. Editors can isolate specific colors, adjust their intensity and brightness, and refine particular areas of the image. This is particularly useful for enhancing skin tones, highlighting specific colors in a scene, or adding dramatic effects.

4. **Vignettes and Graduated Filters:** Vignettes and graduated filters are commonly used in advanced color grading to guide the viewer's focus and add depth to a scene. Available in Premiere Pro's effects panel, these tools enable editors to subtly darken or lighten certain areas of the frame. This technique can be used to emphasize specific elements, make subjects stand out, or manage contrast.

5. **Adjustment Layers and Blend Modes:** Creatively using blend modes and adjustment layers is a key aspect of advanced color grading. By adding adjustment layers with various effects and blend modes, editors can experiment with combinations to develop a unique style. This method allows for non-destructive editing, making it easy to adjust changes without altering the original footage.

6. **Keyframing and Dynamic Color Changes:** Keyframing plays a crucial role in advanced color grading, enabling color changes to occur over time. Editors can modify color parameters like hue, intensity, and brightness to enhance storytelling or evoke specific

emotions. This technique is particularly effective in commercials, music videos, and other visually-driven projects.

7. **Filmic Effects and Grain:** To give projects a cinematic quality, filmic effects and grain can be applied. Premiere Pro includes built-in film grain effects and supports third-party tools for further customization. By incorporating subtle film-like elements, editors can create a more traditional video aesthetic, enhancing the overall structure and feel of the footage.

Creating LUTs for Consistent Looks

Steps to Use LUTs in Adobe Premiere Pro

Step   1:   Importing   Your   Footage
Before you can apply LUTs, you'll need to import your video into Premiere Pro. You can either drag and drop your files directly into the project panel or click **"File" > "Import"** to add them automatically.

Step   2:   Accessing   the   Color   Workspace
Once your video is in the timeline, navigate to the **"Color"** workspace. You can find it at the top of the screen or access it by going to **"Window" > "Workspaces" > "Color."** This will open the Lumetri Color panel on the right side of the screen.

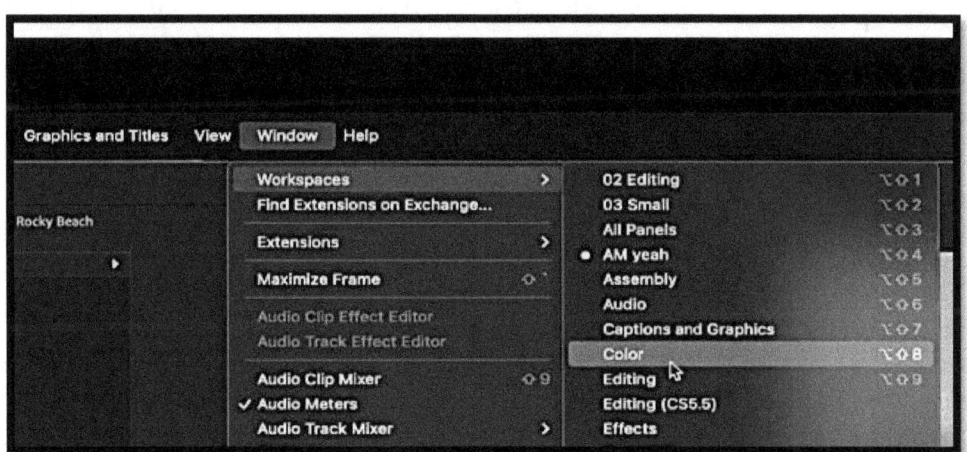

Step   3:   Utilizing   Tabs   for   LUT   Application
On the Lumetri Color panel, you'll find various tabs to explore. The "Input LUT" dropdown is located within the "Basic Correction" tab, which is where you can apply LUTs. Typically, this is where you'd convert log footage to the standard Rec. 709 color space using a LUT.

On the other hand, the "Creative" tab allows you to experiment with the overall appearance of your film. Here, you can apply various artistic LUTs to evoke specific moods or styles in your video.

Step 4: Importing and Applying the LUT
To use a LUT, click "Browse" in the LUT section of either the "Basic Correction" or "Creative" tab. Make sure the LUT file is in the. cube format. Once you've located and selected the desired LUT file, click "Open" to apply it to your footage.

Step 5: Adjusting LUT Intensity
You can also modify the strength or intensity of the LUT to better suit your footage. Adjust this setting by using the "Intensity" slider found under the "Creative" tab in the Lumetri Color panel.

Step 6: Fine-Tuning and Additional Adjustments
Applying a LUT is just the beginning of the color grading process. You'll probably need to refine other parameters like contrast, brightness, highlights, shadows, and colors to achieve your desired look. The Lumetri Color panel is your go-to for making these adjustments. Properly utilizing and tweaking LUTs can significantly enhance your color grading workflow in Adobe Premiere Pro, ensuring a cohesive visual tone across your scenes. Mastering these techniques will greatly improve the overall quality and flow of your video projects.

How to Use the Color Wheels

You can adjust the shadows, midtones, and highlights of your footage using the Color Wheels, which are versatile and powerful tools. Let's dive deeper into how to effectively use the Color

Wheels to achieve the best color grading results. Start by mastering the basics in Premiere Pro before moving on to more advanced techniques. The shadows correspond to the blacks, midtones to the grays, and highlights to the whites, allowing you to adjust each wheel individually to modify the color balance within its tonal range.

To alter the overall warmth or coolness of your footage, use the Temperature tool in the Color Wheels panel. For a natural appearance, ensure the color temperature aligns with the scene's lighting conditions.

The Color Wheels are particularly useful for correcting footage with unwanted color casts. If you notice a tint, identify the dominant color causing it and adjust the opposite wheel to counterbalance. For instance, if your footage has a blue cast, you can warm up the midtones and highlights to mitigate this effect. Adjusting shadows, midtones, and highlights separately can enhance contrast and depth, so make small tweaks to each wheel until you find the right balance. This method is especially effective for improving the overall quality of your footage.

Once you're comfortable with the Color Wheels, you can focus on specific color grading techniques. For instance, you can emphasize or diminish certain colors in specific tonal ranges, helping to draw attention to a subject or create a stylized look. Achieving realistic skin tones is crucial when working with people; use the Color Wheels to adjust the balance of reds and yellows in the midtones for a natural appearance.

The RGB Parade in the Lumetri Scopes panel pairs well with the Color Wheels, as it displays the balance of red, green, and blue channels in your footage. Utilize this tool to identify imbalances and apply precise adjustments using the Color Wheels.

You can also implement keyframing with the Color Wheels to create dynamic color changes over time, adding narrative depth or visual interest to your sequences. Experiment with keyframing to gradually shift color balances for specific scenes or to evoke emotional responses from viewers.

The Color Wheels are just one aspect of the Lumetri Color panel in Premiere Pro. For more complex and refined color grading, consider combining them with other Lumetri effects, such as Curves and Color Correction tools. This integrated approach will enhance your color grading process and produce stunning visual results.

HDR Editing and Display Considerations

The Rec. 709 color space is no longer the sole option for image processing. Premiere Pro is capable of recognizing and working with various color spaces. In the color management section of the Interpret Footage dialog box, users can choose from Rec. 601, Rec. 709, Rec. 2020, Rec. 2100 HLG, and Rec. 2100 PQ. Additionally, there's an option to apply input LUTs to source footage.

In the Sequence Settings dialog box, the Working Color Space dropdown includes both Rec. 709 and Rec. 2100 options. Similarly, the export settings now feature HDR options for select file formats. With the right configurations, you can export H.264 and HEVC files for HDR10 delivery.

Monitoring

Currently, monitoring HDR video can be quite challenging. You want to accurately view how your HDR content appears, but the process involves several steps: the image moves from the software to Windows, then to the graphics driver, and finally over a digital connection to an HDR display. Each of these steps must function correctly for the video to be displayed properly. While HDMI 2.0b can handle the last three steps, the journey through the operating system and graphics driver introduces variables that can be influenced by updates from Microsoft, Apple, Nvidia, AMD, or Intel.

To ensure that you can view your HDR video accurately in Premiere Pro, a dedicated hardware output that supports Adobe's Mercury Transmit is necessary. This provides a direct connection between the software and the HDMI 2.0 (or SDI) output, allowing for standard viewing methods. Currently available hardware options include AJA's Kona cards, Thunderbolt devices, and Blackmagic's DeckLink cards. These devices connect to your HDR display, which can range from a standard HDR TV to a high-end mastering monitor like the Canon DP-V3120, which I used for testing, powered by a Kona 5 card.

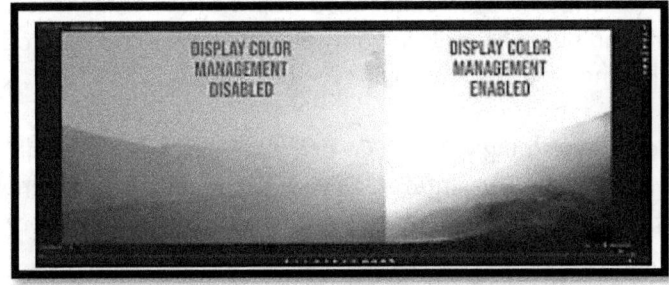

I attempted to connect my HDR display to my Quadro GPU using an HDMI 2.0 adapter, but found that Premiere's output was constrained to the brightness level I had configured for the SDR program in Windows. This limitation applied to both the Program Monitor Panel and the full-screen Transmit output. When I enabled Display Color Management in Premiere's settings, any values above 100 were clipped instead of allowing for peak brightness to reach 100%.

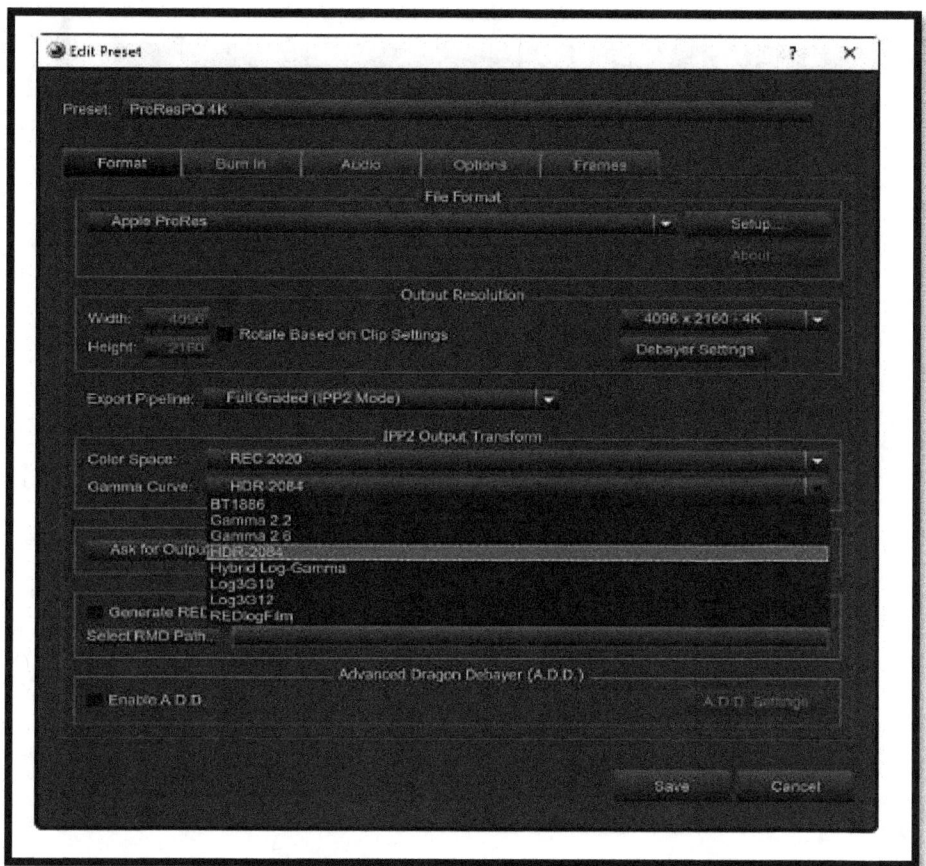

I'm uncertain whether using OS X yields similar results, but currently, neither platform is officially supported by Adobe. Changes to either the operating system or graphics drivers can significantly affect output accuracy. In the future, it should become easier as operating systems and applications improve their user interfaces for HDR displays. Until then, monitoring HDR content on a computer remains one of the biggest challenges, whether you're working with HDR footage or simply watching HDR media.

The first step is to ensure your footage is in an HDR format suitable for editing. Certain cameras, like the Panasonic GH5, which records HLG HEVC files, or Sony models that capture X-AVC in HLG, can directly provide HDR content. Other cameras may record raw images that can be converted into HDR color spaces.

Currently, Premiere Pro cannot directly convert R3D files into HDR. However, RedCineX can transcode R3D files to ProRes in either HLG or PQ formats, allowing you to import those files into Premiere HLG sequences. I hope that in the future, we will be able to edit R3Ds and other raw formats seamlessly within Premiere sequences in HDR without any issues.

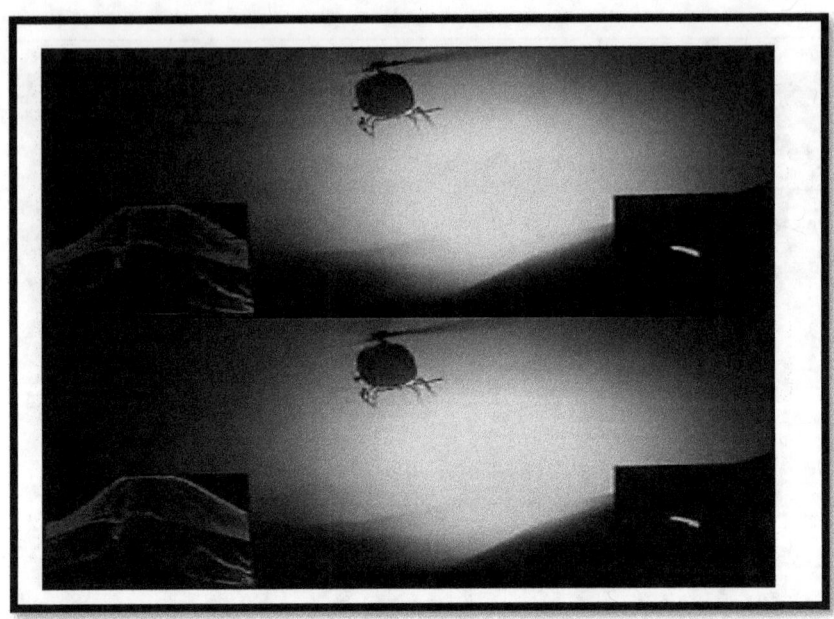

If your video is in the correct format, importing it into Premiere should be straightforward, with new sequences created from it set to HLG by default. You may need to adjust your display settings accordingly and configure your output device to send either HLG or PQ signals, typically done through the Playback Preferences menu.

For HDR media, using a higher bit depth for color is crucial, as Premiere defaults to 8-bit playback. When playback is paused, frames are reprocessed at 32 bits. To maintain this higher bit depth consistently, enable "High-Quality Playback" in the Program Monitor's Wrench menu. While this requires more processing power, it prevents banding, which is a common issue with 8-bit HDR content.

There's also a new Project setting that allows you to select the HDR Graphics White point. The available options are 100 (old SDR standard), 203 (the new de facto standard), and 300 (very bright). Setting it to 203 will help your SDR content align better with your HDR media.

Aside from color adjustments, the editing process remains largely the same. The Lumetri Scopes panel should automatically switch to Rec. 2100, but you may need to adjust the scale in the bottom right corner to HDR for accurate readings.

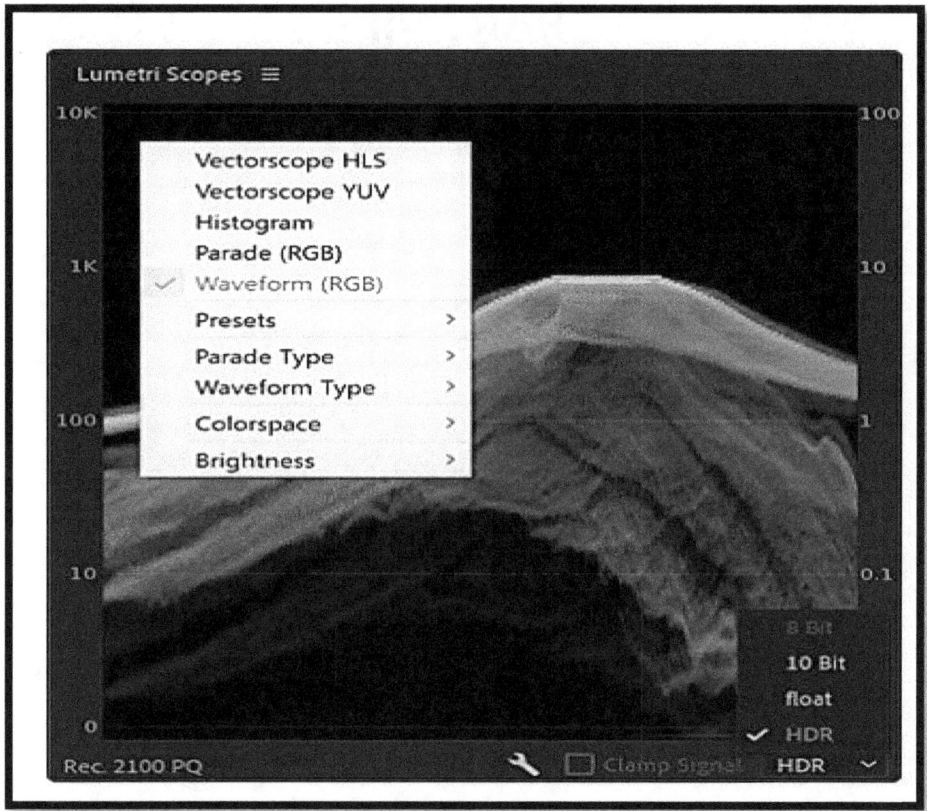

The scale on the right shifts to a logarithmic format. For SDR video, the normal range is 0–100, while most HDR displays can reach a maximum of 1000, and the theoretical maximum for the format is 10,000. Many of the Lumetri Color tools function similarly to how they do with SDR footage, but some settings may need to be adjusted to achieve the same results.

To share your finished work, you'll need to export it in an HDR format. You can share high-quality files using ProRes HQ, ProRes 444, JPEG2000, or X-AVC Intra, but most viewers will access your HDR content via H.264 or HEVC files. While H.264 offers good backward compatibility, HEVC is generally the superior codec for HDR playback on compatible devices.

Regardless of the format you choose, ensure that "Render at Maximum Bit Depth" is enabled, and select the "High10" setting. This will allow you to check the "Rec. 2020 Primaries," "High Dynamic Range," and "Include HDR10 Metadata" options. We hope to see an HLG export option available in the future as well.

PART VII
SPECIALIZED EDITING WORKFLOWS

CHAPTER 22
DOCUMENTARY EDITING TECHNIQUES
Storytelling through Documentaries

Documentaries are a fascinating art form that convey real-life stories in engaging and impactful ways. They combine visual elements, narrative structure, and emotional depth to create a powerful experience. Adobe Premiere Pro serves as a vital tool for filmmakers and documentarians seeking to tell complex stories that resonate with viewers. Its versatile canvas offers a wide array of creative options, allowing editors to arrange clips on the timeline for a coherent and fluid storytelling experience.

Documentaries often incorporate interviews, historical footage, and supplementary images. Premiere Pro's user-friendly design simplifies the integration of these diverse elements. Establishing a strong emotional connection with the audience is key to effective documentary storytelling, and Premiere Pro provides tools to manipulate sound and visuals to elicit specific feelings. With its color editing capabilities, you can create particular moods—whether warm tones evoke nostalgia or cool tones highlight harsh realities. The audio editing features allow for precise control over background noise, music, and dialogue, ensuring that the emotional beats of the story shine through.

An engaging documentary often juxtaposes contrasting elements to convey its message. Premiere Pro's split-screen and multicam editing tools enable the presentation of multiple perspectives simultaneously, enriching the narrative and helping viewers draw connections between different parts of the story. The pacing of a documentary is also crucial for maintaining audience interest. Premiere Pro's robust editing tools, which allow for precise trimming and rearranging of clips, facilitate smooth storytelling. The software's compatibility with various file types and sizes makes it easier to integrate different video sources, resulting in a polished and professional final product.

Documentaries typically unfold gradually, revealing layers of complexity within the subject matter. Premiere Pro's title and graphics features play a vital role in organizing information, providing context, and guiding the audience through the evolving narrative. Its motion graphics capabilities enable the creation of captivating opening sequences that enhance the overall viewing experience.

Collaboration is another essential aspect of documentary filmmaking, and Premiere Pro's seamless integration with other Adobe Creative Cloud applications streamlines the process for directors. The interoperability between Premiere Pro and Adobe After Effects allows for the inclusion of sophisticated visual effects, lending a cinematic quality to the storytelling.

Moreover, Premiere Pro offers a range of export options tailored to the needs of documentary filmmakers, ensuring that the final product meets industry standards for online streaming, television, or film festivals. In summary, Adobe Premiere Pro is a versatile and powerful tool for crafting documentaries that captivate audiences. Its robust features enable creators to weave visually stunning, emotionally resonant, and intellectually engaging narratives. With meticulous editing, skillful layering of elements, and attention to storytelling details, real stories come to life in Premiere Pro, fostering a deeper connection between the audience and the subject matter.

Edit Documentaries in Premiere Pro
Create Vivid Still Photos

Here's a step-by-step guide for animating a photo in your editing software:

1. **Import and Place the Photo**: Bring your image into the editing software and drag it onto the timeline. Adjust its size and position until it's where you want it.
2. **Set the First Keyframe for Position**: Move the playhead about 8 frames before the clip begins. This is where you will set the first keyframe for the photo's Position property.
3. **Set the Second Keyframe and Adjust Position**: Return to the start of your clip and set the second keyframe. Position the photo so it enters from the top of the screen.
4. **Apply Ease In Effect**: Right-click on the last keyframe (where the photo stops) and navigate to **Temporal Interpolation > Ease In**. This will smooth the transition of the movement.
5. **Access the Graph Editor**: Click the downward arrow next to the Position settings to open the Graph Editor, which displays the motion path.
6. **Create a Curve in the Graph**: Adjust the handles of the second keyframe in the Graph Editor. Drag the handle toward the first keyframe to create a curved trajectory for the photo's movement.
7. **Add Gaussian Blur Effect**: Find the Gaussian Blur effect in your effects library and apply it to the image. This will create a soft blur.
8. **Keyframe the Blur Effect**: Create keyframes for the Blur effect at the same points where you set the Position keyframes.
9. **Adjust the First Blur Keyframe**: Set the initial blur level for the first keyframe to around 50 (or a value that suits your vision).
10. **Add Sound Effects**: Include a sound effect, such as an old camera shutter or projector noise, timed to the photo's movement. This will enhance the overall impact of your video.

Match Cut on Text

Here's a step-by-step guide for creating an engaging Match Cut on Text effect in your project:

1. **Gather Text Examples**: Collect at least 12 different images or screenshots of text featuring the word or phrase you want to highlight. Sources can include books, websites, or any written materials.
2. **Ensure Varied Text Positions**: Make sure the target text appears in different locations on the page or within the paragraph across your images. This variation will create a more visually interesting sequence when presented in the video.
3. **Import and Arrange Images in Premiere Pro**: Bring your collected images into Adobe Premiere Pro and arrange them on the timeline in your desired order.
4. **Use Rulers for Alignment**: Go to the "Show" menu and select "Rulers" to help with alignment. Use the blue guide lines that appear in the center of your editing screen for accuracy.
5. **Position Images for Focus**: Adjust each image so that the highlighted word or phrase is centered on the screen. This ensures that the important text captures the viewer's attention.
6. **Adjust Image Duration**: Modify the duration of each image in the timeline. Gradually shorten the display time of each image, transitioning from longer holds to quicker cuts as the sequence progresses.
7. **Add Sound Effects**: Incorporate camera click sound effects at the beginning of each clip, syncing them with the picture transitions. This audio cue enhances the visual impact and makes the sequence more engaging.
8. **Nest the Sequence**: To simplify the editing process, right-click on all your images and select "Nest." This action combines the selected images into a single nested sequence, making it easier to manage.
9. **Easily Adjust Nested Sequence**: If you need to change the size or position of the text or images, you can do so within the nested sequence. This allows for modifications to the entire sequence at once, rather than adjusting each image individually.

Organizing and Structuring Documentary Projects

Using Adobe Premiere Pro's powerful features can greatly enhance your documentary storytelling and streamline your workflow. Here's a step-by-step guide to organizing and structuring your documentary project:

1. Project Setup

- **Create a New Project**: Launch Adobe Premiere Pro and start a new project. Configure project settings, including frame rate, resolution, and scratch disk locations.

2. Media Organization

- **Import Footage**: Use the Media Browser to import your footage into the project. Premiere Pro supports various file formats for flexibility.
- **Organize Bins**: Create bins to categorize your media assets. Organize footage into folders by type, such as interviews, B-roll, and other content.

3. Editing Workflow

- **Timeline Structure**: Arrange your footage on the timeline. Create a rough assembly by dragging clips into chronological order.
- **Labeling and Marking**: Use labels and markers to highlight significant moments or themes, facilitating quick navigation during editing.

4. Storyboarding and Sequencing

- **Storyboard Panels**: Utilize the storyboard panels within Premiere Pro to plan the visual sequence of your documentary.
- **Sequencing Clips**: Organize clips in a logical order to construct a coherent and engaging narrative. Experiment with sequences to discover the most impactful flow.

5. Transitions and Effects

- **Transitions**: Apply transitions between clips to ensure smooth visual continuity. Premiere Pro offers a variety of transition effects to choose from.
- **Effects Panel**: Explore the Effects panel to enhance your story through visual effects, color grading, and adjustments.

6. Audio Management

- **Import Audio**: Import and organize your audio files, including interviews, ambient sounds, and music.
- **Audio Mixing**: Use the Audio Track Mixer to balance and enhance audio elements, ensuring clear dialogue and music that complements the mood.

7. Text and Graphics

- **Text Layers**: Integrate text layers for titles, captions, and graphics. The Essential Graphics panel makes text customization straightforward.
- **Lower Thirds**: Incorporate lower thirds to introduce interviewees or provide context.

8. Multi-camera Editing

- **Multi-camera Sequence**: If applicable, utilize the multi-camera editing feature to sync and switch seamlessly between multiple camera angles.
- **Angle Selection**: Easily switch between different camera angles during the editing process.

9. Collaboration with Other Adobe Apps

- **Dynamic Link**: Use the dynamic link feature to collaborate with other Adobe Creative Cloud applications, such as After Effects and Photoshop, for specialized effects and graphics.

10. Export and Distribution

- **Export Settings**: Choose export settings tailored to your distribution platform. Premiere Pro offers presets for various output formats.
- **Online Platforms**: Directly export and upload your documentary to online platforms or create a high-quality version for film festivals and broadcasting.

11. Project Backup

- **Regular Backups**: Implement regular project backups to prevent data loss. Premiere Pro includes auto-save features, but manual backups are also advisable.

12. Final Review and Feedback

- **Test Screenings**: Conduct test screenings with a diverse audience to gather feedback.
- **Iterative Refinement**: Make adjustments based on feedback, fine-tuning your documentary for maximum impact.

By utilizing Adobe Premiere Pro throughout the documentary production process, you can efficiently organize and structure your project, resulting in a visually compelling and impactful story. The software's intuitive interface and comprehensive toolset empower filmmakers to realize their creative vision with precision.

Balancing Information and Entertainment

Balancing information and entertainment in video content are a nuanced art, and Adobe Premiere Pro serves as a powerful ally in achieving this equilibrium. Whether you're creating educational videos, documentaries, or other informative content, keeping your audience engaged is essential. Here are several tips and techniques to help you strike the right balance in Adobe Premiere Pro:

1. Storyboarding and Planning

- **Start with a Clear Plan**: Outline the key information you want to share and identify moments where entertainment elements can be integrated.
- **Create a Storyboard**: Visualize the flow of your video to allocate time effectively for both informative and entertaining segments.

2. Dynamic Editing

- **Use Varied Editing Techniques**: Keep the visual experience engaging by experimenting with different cuts, transitions, and pacing to maintain viewer interest.
- **Incorporate Transitions and Effects**: Utilize Premiere Pro's built-in transitions and effects to enhance your video without overshadowing the informational content.

3. Effective Use of Graphics

- **Incorporate Graphics and Text Overlays**: Use animations and graphics to highlight key information. Premiere Pro offers robust tools for creating visually appealing titles.
- **Ensure Clarity**: Make sure graphics are clear, concise, and aligned with your overall style.

4. Audio Enhancements

- **Focus on Audio Quality**: A well-mixed soundtrack can significantly enhance the viewing experience.
- **Experiment with Background Music**: Use music or sound effects to create mood without distracting from the information being presented.

5. Engaging Visuals

- **Use Visual Aids**: Incorporate charts, graphs, and relevant B-roll footage to make complex information more digestible and engaging.
- **Enhance Visual Appeal**: Leverage Premiere Pro's color correction and grading tools to improve the visual quality of your footage.

6. Narration and Scripting

- **Craft a Compelling Script**: A well-written script that integrates information and entertainment will set the tone for an engaging video.
- **Use an Engaging Narrator**: The tone and delivery of the narration can greatly impact how the audience receives the information.

7. Interactive Elements

- **Incorporate Interactivity**: Add quizzes or clickable links for further information to enhance viewer engagement.
- **Utilize Plugins for Interaction**: Premiere Pro allows integration of interactive elements through various plugins and external tools.

8. Consistent Branding

- **Maintain a Cohesive Style**: A consistent visual and tonal style throughout your video helps establish brand identity and keeps viewers connected.
- **Organize Your Workflow**: Use Premiere Pro's project management features to streamline your editing process.

9. Test and Gather Feedback

- **Conduct Test Screenings**: Share your video with a sample audience to gather feedback and make necessary adjustments for balance.
- **Leverage Collaboration Features**: Premiere Pro's collaboration tools enable seamless sharing and feedback integration.

10. Accessibility Considerations

- **Ensure Accessibility**: Make your video accessible to diverse audiences by using closed captions and subtitles.
- **Utilize Captioning Tools**: Adobe Premiere Pro offers easy tools for captioning and subtitling your content.

By implementing these strategies in Adobe Premiere Pro, you can effectively balance informative and entertaining elements in your video content, creating engaging and impactful narratives that resonate with your audience.

Post-Production Strategies for Documentaries

Post-production is a critical phase in filmmaking, especially for documentaries, where the cutting methods employed can greatly impact the storytelling. Adobe Premiere Pro stands out as a leading tool in this domain, offering a comprehensive suite of features tailored to the unique needs of documentary filmmakers.

Key Post-Production Features in Adobe Premiere Pro for Documentaries

1. **Logging and Organizing**:
   - **Efficient Footage Management**: Organizing footage is essential in post-production. Premiere Pro's user-friendly bin system allows editors to categorize clips effectively, making it easier to locate specific footage amidst extensive collections.
   - **Metadata and Markers**: Adding metadata, tags, and markers to clips helps highlight significant moments, streamlining the editing process and saving valuable time.

2. **Story Structure and Scripting**:
   - **Crafting the Narrative**: Developing a compelling story is fundamental. Premiere Pro facilitates this by allowing editors to create scripts directly within the project, simplifying the transition from planning to execution.
   - **Experimenting with Storytelling**: Editors can explore various story structures to ensure clarity and impact in the final product.

3. **Advanced Editing Techniques**:
   - **Precision Editing Tools**: The timeline in Premiere Pro serves as a canvas for meticulous editing, enabling seamless cutting, trimming, and rearranging of clips.
   - **Ripple Edit Tool**: This tool ensures smooth transitions between scenes, while multicam editing capabilities allow for dynamic storytelling from multiple angles.

4. **Color Grading and Correction**:
   - **Visual Tone Control**: The visual tone of a documentary significantly influences its emotional impact. Premiere Pro's robust color grading tools, including the Lumetri Color panel, allow for precise adjustments to color, contrast, and brightness.
   - **Creative Control**: Color wheels and curves provide further control over the documentary's visual aesthetic.

5. **Audio Enhancement**:
   - **Comprehensive Audio Tools**: Recognizing the importance of audio, Premiere Pro includes tools for noise reduction, volume adjustments, and spatial audio manipulation.

- - **Seamless Integration of Sound**: Editors can effortlessly add background sounds, music, and voiceovers, ensuring a cohesive audio-visual experience.
6. **Adding Graphics and Animation**:
   - **Incorporating Visual Data**: Documentaries often benefit from graphics and animations to convey facts and context. Premiere Pro simplifies the integration of these elements, allowing editors to enhance their visual storytelling.
   - **Engaging Visual Complexity**: The ability to add text, graphics, and animations elevates the overall production quality.
7. **Collaboration and Versioning**:
   - **Streamlined Teamwork**: Collaboration tools in Premiere Pro, such as project locking and versioning, facilitate efficient teamwork in post-production.
   - **Simultaneous Edits**: Multiple editors can work on different segments concurrently, while version history keeps track of changes for easy reference.
8. **Output and Distribution**:
   - **Flexible Export Options**: After meticulous editing, Premiere Pro provides various output formats suitable for different platforms, ensuring the documentary is optimized for television, online, or theatrical release.
   - **Integrated Media Encoder**: This feature accelerates the export process while maintaining high-quality output.

Conclusion

Adobe Premiere Pro is an indispensable tool for documentary filmmakers in post-production. Its extensive features and intuitive interface enable editors to transform raw footage into powerful visual narratives. By leveraging these techniques, documentarians can elevate their storytelling and create compelling, impactful films that resonate with audiences.

CHAPTER 23
MULTI-CAMERA EDITING

Multicam editing is a powerful technique that allows you to seamlessly cut between different camera angles and perspectives of the same scene, enhancing the viewer's experience. Here's a breakdown of how multicam editing works and its applications:

What is Multicam Editing?

- **Definition**: Multicam editing involves synchronizing and editing footage captured from multiple cameras, all focused on the same scene or subject. This allows editors to choose the most compelling angles during the editing process.

Benefits of Multicam Editing

1. **Variety of Perspectives**: By showing the same scene from different viewpoints, multicam editing keeps the audience engaged and adds depth to the storytelling.
2. **Dynamic Storytelling**: It allows for dynamic cuts that can match the rhythm of the audio or action, making the final product feel more polished and professional.
3. **Improved Narrative Flow**: With multiple angles, editors can more effectively convey emotions, actions, and reactions, enhancing the overall narrative.

Common Applications

- **Music Videos**: Showcasing performances from various angles, capturing the energy and excitement of the music.
- **Soap Operas**: Providing different emotional perspectives of the same scene, making character interactions more engaging.
- **Reality TV**: Presenting contrasting viewpoints on events, highlighting drama or humor through varied angles.
- **Live Performances**: Capturing the energy of an event, allowing viewers to experience it as if they were there.
- **Corporate Videos**: Demonstrating products or services from multiple angles, making presentations more visually appealing.
- **Weddings**: Capturing important moments from various perspectives, ensuring no special moment is missed.

How to Execute Multicam Editing in Premiere Pro

1. **Import Footage**: Start by importing all your camera footage into Adobe Premiere Pro.
2. **Create a Multicam Sequence**: Select all the clips you want to include, right-click, and choose "Create Multi-camera Source Sequence." You can sync by audio or timecode.
3. **Edit the Multicam Sequence**: Once created, open the multicam sequence in the timeline. You can switch between camera angles in real-time while playback is active, making it easy to choose the best shots.
4. **Fine-tuning**: After selecting the best angles, fine-tune your edits, adjusting transitions and adding effects as needed.
5. **Export**: Once satisfied, export your final project in the desired format.

Conclusion

Multicam editing is an invaluable technique for creating engaging and visually dynamic video content. By effectively utilizing multiple camera angles, you can significantly enhance the storytelling aspect of your projects, making them more captivating for your audience. Whether for music videos, documentaries, or corporate presentations, mastering multicam editing can elevate your filmmaking skills to new heights.

Simple Steps to Multi-Camera Editing
Step 1: Create a Multi-Camera Source Sequence

To set up a multicam editing workflow in Adobe Premiere Pro, follow these steps to organize your clips and create a Multi-Camera Source Sequence:

Step-by-Step Guide

1. **Create a Bin**:
    - Open your Project Panel in Premiere Pro.
    - Right-click in the Project Panel and select **New Bin**.
    - Name the bin **Multi-Cam**.
2. **Import and Organize Clips**:
    - Drag and drop all your video clips from different angles into the **Multi-Cam** bin.
    - Ensure you have labeled them appropriately:
        - **Cam 1** (contains the high-quality audio track)
        - **Cam 2**
        - **Cam 3**
3. **Select Audio Sources**:

o It's crucial to have at least one camera angle with high-quality audio for syncing. In your case, **Cam 1** will serve this purpose.

o If you have audio from all cameras, make sure to keep the high-quality track on **Cam 1** and note that the other cameras might have lower-quality audio.

4. **Create Multi-Camera Source Sequence**:
   o Right-click on the **Multi-Cam** bin or press **Ctrl + Click** on a Mac.
   o Select **Create Multi-Camera Source Sequence** from the context menu. This will open the Multi-Camera Source Sequence dialogue box.

5. **Set Sync Options**:
   o In the dialogue box, you can choose how to sync your clips. The options typically include:
      ▪ **Audio**: If all clips have audio, this is a good option to automatically sync based on sound waves.
      ▪ **Timecode**: If your cameras were synced using timecode, select this option.
      ▪ **In Points**: If you've marked specific in points on your clips, you can use this method.
   o Make sure to check that the option to use the audio from **Cam 1** for syncing is selected.

6. **Finalize the Sequence**:
   o After selecting your sync option, click **OK**. Premiere Pro will create a new multi-camera source sequence and place it in your Project Panel.

7. **Editing the Multi-Camera Sequence**:
   o Double-click on the newly created Multi-Camera Source Sequence to open it in the timeline.
   o In the Program Monitor, enable the multicam view by clicking on the **Toggle Multi-Camera View** button (it looks like a camera icon).
   o You can now play back the sequence and switch between camera angles in real-time while editing.

Tips:

- Always ensure your clips are well-organized in bins, especially for larger projects. This will make your workflow much smoother.
- Take some time to familiarize yourself with the multicam editing process; it can be a powerful tool for creating engaging videos.

By following these steps, you'll be able to effectively utilize multicam editing in Premiere Pro, enhancing your project with multiple perspectives and high-quality audio.

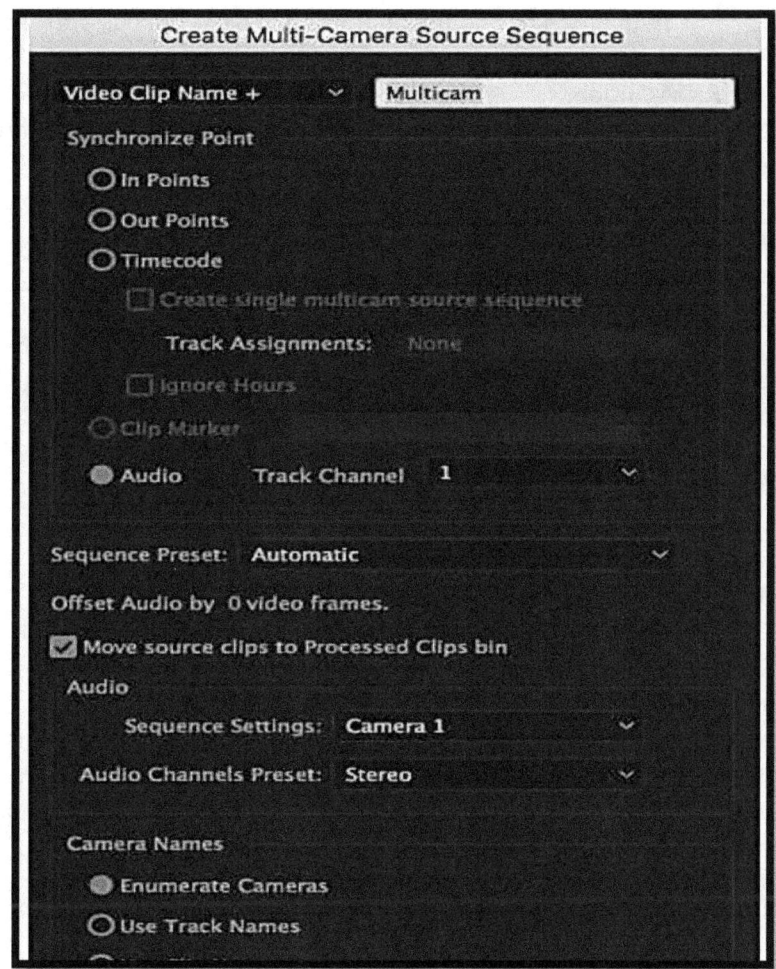

Great choice! Using the "Camera 1" audio option ensures that your multicam edit maintains a consistent and high-quality audio track, which is essential for professional-looking results. Here's a detailed guide to finalize your multicam setup using the audio sync options in Adobe Premiere Pro:

Finalizing the Multi-Camera Source Sequence with Audio Sync

1. **Select Audio Sync Method**:
   - After choosing the **Audio** option in the Multi-Camera Source Sequence dialogue box, you'll see the three audio sync options:
     - **Camera 1**: Sync all clips with the audio from Camera 1.
     - **All Cameras**: Mix audio from all camera sources.

- **Switch Audio**: Use the audio source from the currently selected camera angle.

2. **Choose the Right Option**:
   - Since you want a consistent audio track from Camera 1 throughout your sequence, select the **Camera 1** option.
   - This will ensure that all video clips are synced to the high-quality audio track from Camera 1, giving your final edit a polished sound.

3. **Adjust Audio Sequence Settings** (if necessary):
   - After selecting **Camera 1**, check the audio sequence settings to confirm that they match your project requirements (e.g., sample rate, bit depth). Ensure that your settings reflect high quality for optimal output.

4. **Create the Multi-Camera Source Sequence**:
   - Click **OK** to create the multicam source sequence. Premiere Pro will now process the clips and sync them based on your selected audio option.

5. **Editing the Multicam Sequence**:
   - Open the new multicam source sequence in your timeline. You should now see your different camera angles organized in a single sequence.
   - Enable the **Multi-Camera View** in the Program Monitor by clicking the camera icon. This allows you to see all your angles at once.

6. **Real-Time Editing**:
   - As you play through the sequence, you can switch between camera angles in real-time by clicking on the desired angle in the Program Monitor. The audio will remain consistent from Camera 1, ensuring a seamless listening experience.

7. **Fine-Tuning**:
   - After the initial edits, you can fine-tune transitions between camera angles and adjust the audio levels as needed using the **Audio Track Mixer**.

Tips:

- **Test Your Audio**: Before finalizing your project, do a thorough check of the audio quality to ensure that it meets your expectations.
- **Use Markers**: Consider using markers in your timeline to indicate important moments or transitions, which can help guide your editing choices later.

By following these steps, you'll successfully create a polished and engaging multicam edit that showcases your content effectively while maintaining high audio quality. Enjoy your editing process!

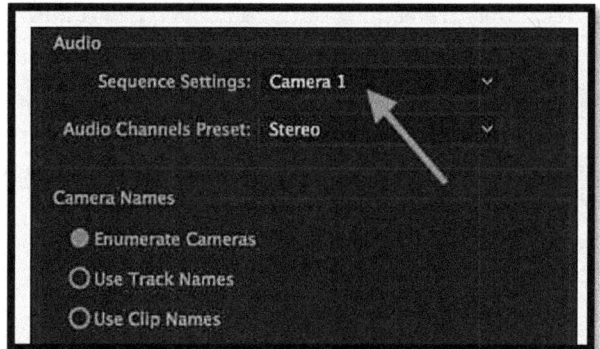

Step 2: Create a Multi-Camera Target Sequence

1. **Access the Multi-Camera Source Sequence**:
   o   In the **Project Panel**, locate the multi-camera source sequence you just created.
2. **Create a New Sequence from the Multi-Camera Source**:
   o   Right-click on the multi-camera source sequence.
   o   From the context menu, select **"New Sequence from Clip."**
   o   This action creates a new target sequence that contains the multi-camera source.
3. **Open the Target Sequence**:
   o   Double-click the new target sequence to open it in the timeline.

Working in the Target Sequence

1. **Enable Multi-Camera Editing**:
   o   Ensure the **Multi-Camera View** is enabled in the **Program Monitor**. You can do this by clicking the camera icon.
2. **Switching Between Camera Angles**:
   o   As the sequence plays, you can switch between different camera angles in real-time. Simply click on the desired camera view in the Program Monitor to change the active angle.
   o   Premiere Pro will automatically cut to the selected camera angle, allowing for seamless transitions.
3. **Editing and Refining**:
   o   Use the **Razor Tool** or the **Cut** function (Ctrl+K or Cmd+K) to make precise cuts if you want to switch angles at specific points.
   o   Adjust audio levels in the **Audio Track Mixer** if needed, ensuring the dialogue and background sounds are balanced throughout.
4. **Final Touches**:
   o   Once you've finished switching angles and making cuts, review the sequence for any adjustments in pacing or audio synchronization.

- You can also apply transitions between cuts if desired for a smoother flow.

Tips for Effective Multi-Cam Editing

- **Markers**: Consider placing markers on the timeline to identify key moments where you want to switch camera angles.
- **Preview and Review**: Always preview your edits to ensure the transitions feel natural and enhance the storytelling.

By following these steps, you'll effectively utilize Adobe Premiere Pro's multicam editing capabilities, making your documentary or video project more dynamic and engaging. Enjoy your editing!

Step 3: Enable Multi-Camera Editing in the Program Monitor

1. **Access the Program Monitor**:
   - Make sure your target sequence is open in the timeline.
2. **Customize the Toolbar**:
   - Click on the **"+" button** (Button Editor) located in the Program Monitor's toolbar.
   - In the Button Editor, find the **"Toggle Multi-Camera View" icon**.
   - Drag this icon into your toolbar for easy access.
3. **Activate Multi-Camera Editing Mode**:
   - Click on the **"Toggle Multi-Camera View" icon** in your toolbar to enable multi-camera editing mode.
   - The Program Monitor will now display all available camera angles.
4. **Keyboard Shortcut**:
   - As a quick alternative, you can enable multi-camera editing by pressing **Shift+0** on your keyboard.

Editing with Multi-Camera Mode

- **View Camera Angles**: You will see all camera angles displayed in the Program Monitor. You can click on any angle to switch views in real-time.
- **Cutting Between Angles**: As your sequence plays, simply click on the desired camera angle to make cuts automatically.
- **Fine-Tuning Edits**: You can go back and adjust the cuts later if needed, using the timeline.

By enabling multi-camera editing, you'll have a powerful tool for creating a dynamic and engaging video that effectively showcases different perspectives! Enjoy your editing process!

Step 4: Understanding the Multi-Camera Editing Interface

Once you're in multi-camera editing mode, the Program Monitor will display two key windows:

1. **Left Window (Multi-Camera View)**:
   - This window shows all available camera angles from your multi-camera source sequence. In your case, you should see the three camera angles (Cam 1, Cam 2, and Cam 3).
   - You can click on any camera angle to switch to that view during playback.
2. **Right Window (Combined Target Sequence)**:
   - This window displays the final output of your edits. As you select different camera angles from the left window, the changes will be reflected in this window, allowing you to see how the edited sequence will look.

Reordering Camera Angles

If you want to reorder the camera views or hide any of them:

1. **Edit Cameras**:

- ○ Click on the **Source Monitor's pop-up menu** (the wrench icon) and select **"Edit Cameras"**.
- ○ A dialog box will open, showing the current order of the camera angles.
2. **Reorder or Disable**:
   - ○ You can drag the camera angles to rearrange them in your desired order.
   - ○ To disable a camera angle, simply uncheck its box. This will hide that angle from the multi-camera view.

Editing Workflow

- **Switching Angles**: As you play your sequence, click on the desired angle in the left window. The right window will automatically update to reflect your selection.
- **Fine-tuning**: After making your selections, you can fine-tune your edits in the timeline if needed.

This setup allows you to create a dynamic viewing experience by seamlessly transitioning between different camera angles, enhancing the storytelling of your project! Enjoy the creative process!

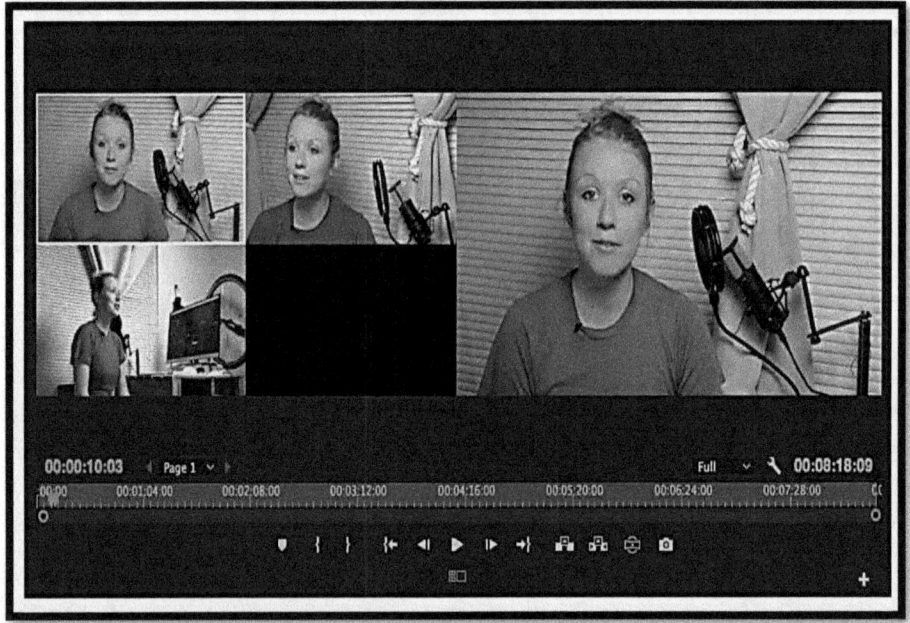

Step 5: Editing and Switching Camera Angles

1. **Play the Sequence**: Press the **spacebar** to start playing your sequence. This will allow you to watch your multi-camera footage in real-time.

2. **Switching Camera Angles**:
   - As the sequence plays, click on the camera view you want to switch to based on the moment you're viewing.
   - Alternatively, you can use the **number keys** on your keyboard:
     - **1** for Camera Angle 1
     - **2** for Camera Angle 2
     - **3** for Camera Angle 3
   - Continue switching between angles until you achieve the desired sequence.
3. **Stop Playback**: When you're satisfied with your edits, press the **spacebar** again to stop playback.

Step 6: Adjusting and Refining Your Multi-Camera Target Sequence

1. **Zoom In**: If you zoom in on the timeline, you'll see that Premiere Pro has created cuts where you switched camera angles.
2. **Using the Rolling Edit Tool**:
   - Select the **Rolling Edit Tool** from the toolbar or simply press **N** on your keyboard.
   - Click on a cut between two clips to select it.
   - You can then **roll the edit** left or right, adjusting the timing of the cut without changing the overall duration of the sequence. This allows for finer control over how the transitions between angles feel.

Additional Tips

- **Fine-Tuning Cuts**: After making your initial angle selections, you can always go back and refine the cuts to improve the pacing and flow of your documentary.
- **Reviewing Changes**: Play back your sequence regularly to ensure the transitions feel seamless and enhance the storytelling.

By utilizing these steps and tools effectively, you can create a dynamic and engaging multi-camera edit that captivates your audience!

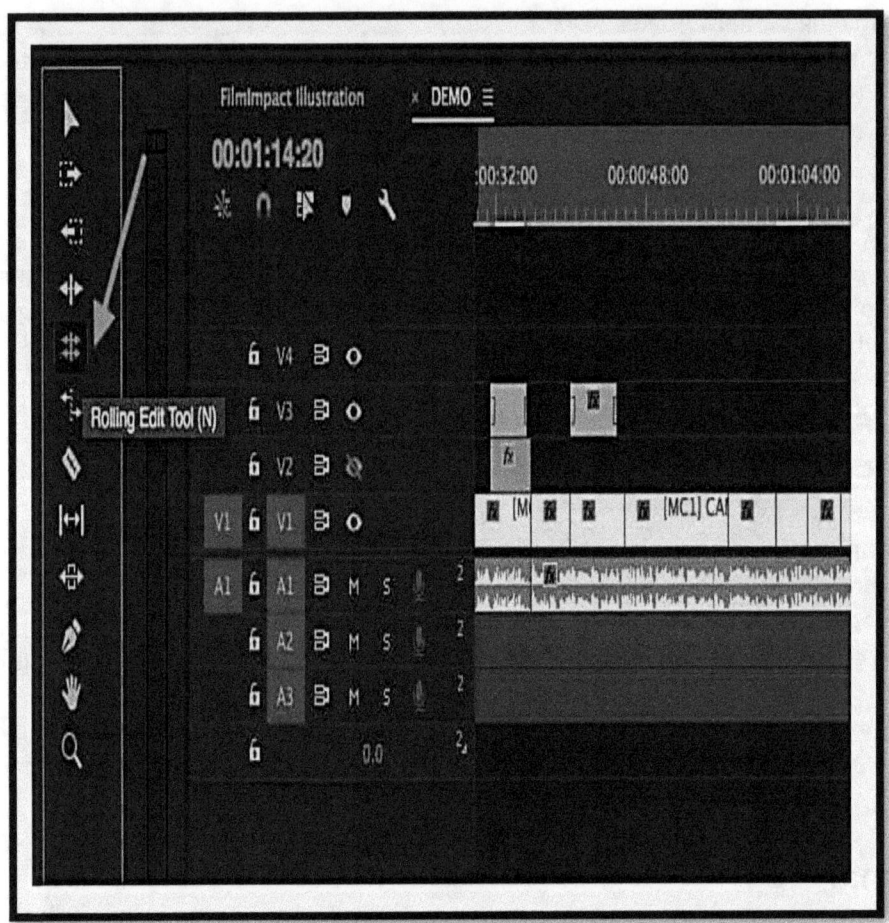

Step 7: Switching Angles During Playback

1. **Switching Angles**: If you want to switch from **Camera Angle 2** to **Camera Angle 3**, simply click on the clip in the sequence where you want to make the change. Then, press the corresponding number key (in this case, **3**) for Camera Angle 3.
   - o This can be done at any point during playback, allowing for real-time adjustments as you review your footage.

Step 8: Adding Effects and Final Touches

1. **Enhancing Your Sequence**:
   - o After you've completed your angle switches, you can apply various effects just like in any other Premiere Pro sequence.
   - o Consider adding:

- **Color Correction**: Use the Lumetri Color panel to enhance the visual quality and ensure consistency across different angles.
- **Music**: Import background music or soundtracks to enhance the emotional impact of your documentary.
- **Transitions**: Add transitions between clips to create smooth visual flows where necessary.

2. **Final Review**:
   - Once you've made all your adjustments, play through your sequence to ensure everything flows well and effectively tells your story.

By following these steps, you can create a polished multi-camera edit that leverages the strengths of each angle, enhancing your documentary's overall narrative and visual appeal!

Synchronizing and Switching Between Camera Angles

Absolutely! Using the number keys for real-time switching is a quick and efficient way to edit your multi-camera sequence. Here's a quick recap:

1. **Real-Time Switching**:
   - While your sequence is playing, press **1** for Camera Angle 1, **2** for Camera Angle 2, and so on.
   - This allows you to seamlessly transition between different views as the action unfolds.

2. **Quick Edits**:
   - This method keeps your editing intuitive and fluid, making it easier to capture the best moments from each angle without interrupting the flow of playback.

It's a powerful feature that enhances your editing efficiency and helps you create dynamic sequences!

Exactly! After you've switched between the camera views and pressed the spacebar to stop playback, you'll see that Premiere Pro has automatically created cuts in the timeline based on your selections. This allows you to construct a dynamic and engaging sequence effortlessly.

Here's a quick summary of what happens:

- **Automatic Cuts**: Each time you switched cameras during playback, Premiere Pro inserted a cut at that point, effectively assembling your multi-camera edit in real time.
- **Timeline Overview**: If you zoom in on the timeline, you can see all the new clips reflecting your camera changes, making it easy to adjust or refine any sections afterward.
- **Fine-Tuning**: You can go back and adjust any cuts or transitions, add effects, or make other edits just like you would with a standard sequence.

This feature really streamlines the editing process and lets you focus on storytelling!

PART VIII
CAREER AND INDUSTRY INSIGHTS

CHAPTER 24

BUILDING A PROFESSIONAL EDITING PORTFOLIO

Selecting and Showcasing Your Best Work

Creating an impressive portfolio using Adobe Premiere Pro is a great way to showcase your skills and creativity. Here's a concise overview of the steps to craft a compelling video reel:

Step-by-Step Guide to Creating Your Portfolio in Adobe Premiere Pro

1. **Organize Your Portfolio**:
   o Curate a diverse selection of your best projects, reflecting various styles and techniques.
2. **Gather High-Quality Footage**:
   o Collect high-resolution clips that highlight your best work. Import them into Premiere Pro using its robust import features.
3. **Create a New Project**:
   o Open Premiere Pro and set up a new project. Organize your workspace with bins for easy navigation.
4. **Set the Tone with an Intro**:
   o Start with a captivating intro that represents your style. Utilize motion graphics templates or custom animations.
5. **Sequence Organization**:
   o Create a master sequence for your showcase. Use nested sequences for individual projects to keep things organized.
6. **Trimming and Cutting**:
   o Trim unnecessary segments using the razor tool and trimming features to keep your reel engaging and concise.
7. **Highlighting Your Skills**:
   o Showcase a variety of editing skills (pacing, storytelling). Use effects and transitions to enhance visual appeal.
8. **Incorporate Audio**:
   o Edit audio carefully to ensure music and voiceovers complement the visuals and enhance storytelling.
9. **Color Grading**:
   o Use the Lumetri Color panel for consistent color grading, ensuring a polished look that fits each project's narrative.

10. **Add Text and Graphics**:
    - Integrate text and graphics for context. Use the Essential Graphics panel for visually appealing titles and annotations.
11. **Review and Refinement**:
    - Regularly review your work for flow and engagement. Seek feedback from peers to make necessary adjustments.
12. **Exporting the Showcase**:
    - Once satisfied, export your video in high-quality formats suitable for different platforms.
13. **Create a Demo Reel**:
    - For a shorter version, craft a demo reel that captures the essence of your work using Premiere Pro's timeline tools.

Final Tips:

- Keep your portfolio dynamic and engaging, reflecting your unique style and technical prowess.
- Update your portfolio regularly with new projects to keep it fresh and relevant.

Using these steps, you can create a standout video reel that effectively showcases your skills as a video maker!

What is a demo reel?

A demo reel is indeed a crucial tool for actors, filmmakers, editors, and animators to showcase their talent and versatility. Here's a more detailed overview of what makes an effective demo reel:

What to Include in a Demo Reel?

1. **Length**:
    - Keep it concise, ideally under two minutes. This ensures that viewers stay engaged and can easily watch the highlights.
2. **Variety**:
    - Showcase a range of your work. For actors, this could include different genres (drama, comedy, etc.). For filmmakers and editors, include clips from various projects that demonstrate different styles and techniques.
3. **Best Work First**:
    - Start strong with your most impressive clips. This grabs attention right away and encourages viewers to keep watching.
4. **Focus on Skills**:

- o Highlight specific skills or unique qualities that set you apart. For actors, it could be emotional range; for filmmakers, it might be editing style or storytelling ability.
5. **Quality over Quantity**:
   - o Choose clips that truly represent your best work. It's better to have fewer, stronger clips than to include everything you've done.
6. **Clear Transitions**:
   - o Edit the clips smoothly together. Use transitions that complement the flow without being distracting.
7. **Professional Presentation**:
   - o Ensure the video is well-edited, with good audio and visual quality. Poor quality can detract from your talent.
8. **Personal Branding**:
   - o Consider including a brief introduction or a title card with your name and contact information. This makes it easier for casting directors and producers to reach out.
9. **Tailor to the Audience**:
   - o If you know who will be viewing the reel, tailor your selections to suit their preferences or the types of projects you're interested in.
10. **Update Regularly**:
    - o Keep your demo reel current by updating it with new work. As your skills grow, so should your reel.

Conclusion

A well-crafted demo reel is an essential tool for anyone in the entertainment industry. It serves not only as a showcase of your talent but also as a reflection of your professionalism and dedication to your craft. By following these guidelines, you can create a compelling demo reel that leaves a lasting impression on casting directors, agents, and producers.

Why are demo reels important?

Absolutely! A demo reel is a vital asset for actors and directors, serving as a visual resume that highlights their skills, versatility, and experience. Here are some key reasons why a demo reel is essential:

Importance of a Demo Reel

1. **Showcases Talent**:
   - o A demo reel provides a platform to showcase an actor's or director's best work, demonstrating their abilities and unique style in a concise format.
2. **First Impression**:

  ○ It's often the first thing casting directors or agents will see. A compelling reel can make a strong first impression and can be the deciding factor in whether you get an audition or job.

3. **Highlights Range**:
  ○ It allows performers to display their range across different genres, styles, and characters, giving a fuller picture of their capabilities.

4. **Essential for Agents**:
  ○ Agents use demo reels to gauge an actor's suitability for specific roles. A well-crafted reel can help you attract the right representation.

5. **Application Requirement**:
  ○ Many casting calls and auditions require a demo reel as part of the submission process. Having one ready can give you a competitive edge.

6. **Networking Tool**:
  ○ A demo reel can be shared easily with potential collaborators, making it a useful tool for networking within the industry.

7. **Tracks Growth**:
  ○ Regularly updating your demo reel allows you to showcase your growth and evolution as an artist, reflecting your most recent and relevant work.

8. **Provides Context**:
  ○ A well-edited reel not only shows what you can do but also provides context about your style, allowing directors to envision you in specific roles or projects.

Tips for Creating an Effective Demo Reel

- **Select Quality Clips**: Choose clips that best represent your work and abilities.
- **Keep It Short**: Aim for around 1-2 minutes to maintain viewer interest.
- **Start Strong**: Open with your best clip to grab attention.
- **Include Variety**: Showcase different roles or styles to highlight your versatility.
- **Edit Professionally**: Ensure high production quality with smooth transitions and clear audio.
- **Regular Updates**: Refresh your reel periodically with new material as your skills and experience grow.

In conclusion, a well-executed demo reel is indispensable for anyone looking to advance their career in the film industry. It effectively communicates your talent and potential, making it easier for agents, directors, and casting professionals to assess your fit for various roles.

Demo reel examples

Here are several examples of what various entertainment professionals might feature in their demo reels:

On-screen actor

A standard demo reel for a television actor typically showcases a range of clips from various acting projects. It's beneficial to include scenes that highlight your ability to perform in different genres, such as drama and comedy. When selecting clips, focus on those that best demonstrate your skills and versatility. This is an opportunity to illustrate your adaptability and proficiency across diverse styles and themes.

Filmmaker

For directors or editors, a demo reel should feature clips from various projects you've worked on. If you specialize in a particular genre, such as science fiction or horror, include scenes that highlight your editing and artistic skills in those areas. You can also incorporate clips from other projects you've directed or edited, such as commercials, advertisements, or videos from special events like weddings.

Animator

If you're an artist, your demo reel should highlight your drawing abilities. Include clips of your standout artworks that best represent your skills. When selecting clips, aim to showcase your versatility as an artist. For example, you might feature work from a highly realistic video game alongside pieces from a more playful, kid-friendly animation project.

Voice actor

Regardless of whether you're a voice actor, your demo reel should highlight your singing skills. You can incorporate voiceovers from commercials, TV programs, documentaries, and films, among other projects. Including actual clips where your voice appears—even if you're not on screen—can be beneficial. This contextualization allows casting directors or agents reviewing your demo to grasp what you're contributing in each segment.

Crafting a Demo Reel

Creating an impactful demo reel is essential for standing out in the competitive field of video editing. Adobe Premiere Pro offers a robust platform to effectively showcase your skills, creativity, and versatility. Here's a step-by-step guide to help you craft a compelling demo reel using Adobe Premiere Pro:

1. Define Your Purpose

Before you begin, clarify the objective of your demo reel. Are you focusing on a specific niche or industry? Understanding your target audience will help tailor your content to their expectations.

2. Curate Your Best Work

Select a diverse range of your top projects. Choose clips that highlight various editing skills, such as storytelling, pacing, and visual effects. Ensure the clips align with the goals of your reel.

3. Storyboarding and Structure

Plan the layout of your demo reel by creating a storyboard or outline. Organize your clips systematically on the timeline in Adobe Premiere Pro for a coherent flow.

4. Create a Dynamic Intro

Capture your viewer's attention with an engaging intro. Utilize Adobe Premiere Pro's motion graphics template or design a custom animation that reflects your style. Keep it brief yet impactful to set the tone for your reel.

5. Pacing and Variety

Maintain a dynamic pace throughout your demo reel. Avoid lengthy, monotonous segments, and balance different styles and genres to showcase your versatility.

6. Transitions and Effects

Use transition effects in Adobe Premiere Pro to create smooth transitions between clips. Experiment with creative effects, but use them sparingly to enhance, rather than overshadow, your work.

7. Music and Audio

Choose a background music track that complements the mood of your reel. Ensure audio levels are balanced, and utilize Adobe Premiere Pro's audio editing tools to enhance sound quality.

8. Showcase Editing Techniques

Highlight specific editing techniques that set you apart, such as innovative cuts or seamless transitions. Adobe Premiere Pro offers various editing tools to help you express your creativity.

9. Color Grading

Apply color grading to maintain a consistent and polished appearance. Use the Lumetri Color panel in Adobe Premiere Pro for precise control over color correction and grading.

10. Text and Graphics

Incorporate text and graphics to provide context or additional information about each project. Utilize Adobe Premiere Pro's text tools to create visually appealing titles and annotations.

11. Create a Seamless Flow

Ensure a smooth flow between clips. Use Adobe Premiere Pro's timeline tools to refine pacing, timing, and overall coherence, resulting in a polished presentation.

12. Review and Refinement

Regularly review your demo reel and seek feedback from peers or mentors. Make necessary adjustments to ensure every second effectively showcases your skills.

13. Exporting and Delivery

Once you're satisfied with your demo reel, use Adobe Premiere Pro's export settings to create a high-quality video file. Consider exporting in different formats to suit various platforms or delivery needs.

By following these steps, you can create a demo reel that effectively highlights your abilities and leaves a lasting impression.

Building an Online Presence

1. Know Your Audience

Before you start editing videos, it's essential to identify your target audience. Understand their preferences, interests, and the platforms they use. This knowledge will help you create content that resonates with them.

2. Create a Content Strategy

Develop a content strategy that aligns with your goals and appeals to your audience. Decide on the type of content—whether educational, entertaining, or promotional—and establish a consistent theme or style that distinguishes your work.

3. Plan and Script Your Videos

Effective videos start with thorough planning and scripting. Outline the structure of your video, including a captivating introduction, informative or entertaining segments, and a strong call to action. This preparation is vital for a smooth editing experience.

4. Master the Basics of Adobe Premiere Pro

Get familiar with the fundamental features of Adobe Premiere Pro. Learn how to import media, organize clips on the timeline, apply transitions, and use effects. A solid grasp of these basics will streamline your editing process.

5. Enhance Visual Appeal

Adobe Premiere Pro offers various tools to improve your video's visual quality. Experiment with color grading, adjust exposure, and refine your footage for a polished appearance. Consistent visual style helps create a recognizable brand identity.

6. Integrate Graphics and Text

Add graphics and text elements to enrich your video storytelling. Use Adobe Premiere Pro's tools for titles, captions, and other visual elements. Well-designed graphics can enhance your brand and convey information clearly.

7. Focus on Audio Quality

Audio quality is crucial for a positive viewer experience. Utilize Adobe Premiere Pro to clean up audio, incorporate background music, and sync sound with visuals. Clear and balanced audio helps maintain audience engagement.

8. Incorporate Branding Elements

Consistent branding is vital for establishing a recognizable online presence. Include your logo, color scheme, and other brand elements in your videos to reinforce brand identity and create a cohesive visual language.

9. Optimize for Online Platforms

Be aware of the specifications and requirements for different online platforms. Adobe Premiere Pro enables you to export videos in various formats and resolutions. Tailor your content for each platform to enhance visibility and engagement.

10. Engage with Your Audience

Building an online presence involves more than just content creation. Actively interact with your audience through comments, messages, and social media. Creating a sense of community around your content encourages ongoing engagement.

Frequently Asked Questions (FAQs)
What is Premiere Pro?

Adobe Premiere Pro is a video editing software renowned for its robust and unique features. It serves as a comprehensive toolkit, enabling users to produce, edit, and enhance videos with a wide array of advanced tools. With its user-friendly interface and professional-grade editing capabilities, Premiere Pro empowers creators, filmmakers, and video enthusiasts to craft visually stunning and engaging content.

What are the minimum system requirements to run Premiere Pro?

To ensure smooth and optimal performance when using Adobe Premiere Pro, it's crucial to meet the minimum system requirements. You'll need a 64-bit multi-core CPU for effective processing, along with compatibility for Windows 10 (64-bit) version 1809 or later. A minimum of 8 gigabytes of RAM is necessary to support the program's processing needs, and at least 8 gigabytes of free hard disk space is required for installation. Keep in mind that additional free space is needed during installation, and the software cannot be installed on removable flash storage devices.

Additionally, your display should have a resolution of 1920 x 1080 (with a scale factor of 100%), and you'll need a sound card that supports either the ASIO protocol or the Microsoft Windows Driver Model. An Internet connection is also required to activate the product and download any necessary content for the best experience.

Where can I get a trial version of Premiere Pro?

Accessing a trial version of Premiere Pro is easy through the official Adobe website. This trial allows users to explore the software's extensive features and capabilities, providing a hands-on experience before making a commitment to purchase.

How can I purchase Premiere Pro?

Purchasing Premiere Pro through the official Adobe website is a straightforward and hassle-free process. The site ensures secure transactions, allowing customers to buy a software license and gain full access to the program's comprehensive tools and features for their video editing projects.

What is the difference between Premiere Pro and Premiere Elements?

Premiere Pro and Premiere Procater to different editing needs and user groups. Premiere Pro is a sophisticated, professional-grade video editing software primarily used by filmmakers, television broadcasters, and industry professionals. It offers robust tools and features suitable for tackling complex projects. In contrast, Premiere Prois aimed at home users and amateurs, providing a more intuitive interface and simplified tools that are perfect for basic video editing tasks.

What is the cost of Premiere Pro?

Premiere Pro operates on a subscription-based model, allowing users to choose between a monthly plan at $20.99 per month or an annual plan for $239.88 per year. Both options provide full access to the complete range of tools and features available in Premiere Pro.

What are some alternatives to Premiere Pro?

Alternatives to Premiere Pro include several robust video editing software options, such as Final Cut Pro, DaVinci Resolve, and Avid Media Composer. Each of these alternatives offers a unique set of features and functionalities, catering to diverse editing needs and user preferences.

What is the best computer for running Premiere Pro?

Adobe recommends using a machine that meets the minimum system requirements to achieve optimal performance while running Premiere Pro. This includes a CPU with at least 16 gigabytes of RAM, a powerful graphics card (NVIDIA or AMD) with a minimum of 4 gigabytes of VRAM, and a total of at least 16 gigabytes of RAM. Having a computer that fulfills these specifications will ensure a smoother editing experience and improved performance.

What is the difference between Premiere Pro and After Effects?

The primary function of Premiere Pro is to serve as a video editing software focused on organizing, cutting, and enhancing video content. It allows users to assemble video clips and apply various editing techniques. In contrast, After Effects is specifically designed for motion graphics, visual effects, animation, and compositing. When used alongside Premiere Pro, After Effects becomes a powerful tool for advanced post-production tasks, enabling the creation of intricate special effects, animations, and visually captivating elements that enhance videos.

Recommended Plugins and Extensions

Adobe Premiere Pro is an outstanding video editing software, equipped with a variety of tools for both video and audio that cater to users ranging from beginners to seasoned professionals. Despite competition from programs like Final Cut Pro and Avid Media Composer, Premiere Pro remains one of the most popular and widely used video editing solutions.

However, not every editing package includes all the tools you might need. While Premiere Pro is packed with powerful editing features, there may be times when you require additional capabilities that aren't included by default. This is where plugins come into play. Plugins allow you to expand the toolset available within Adobe Premiere Pro, whether you're looking for simple effects or more complex enhancements.

There's a vast selection of third-party plugins available, many of which can be obtained for free or for a fee. These plugins can enhance the quality of your video clips and ensure your audio remains exceptional. While the options for plugins are nearly limitless and diverse, navigating through them to find exactly what you need can be challenging. Additionally, the availability of both free and commercial plugins adds another layer of complexity to the selection process.

Best Plug-ins for Adobe Premiere Pro (Free and Paid)
1. Knoll Light Factory

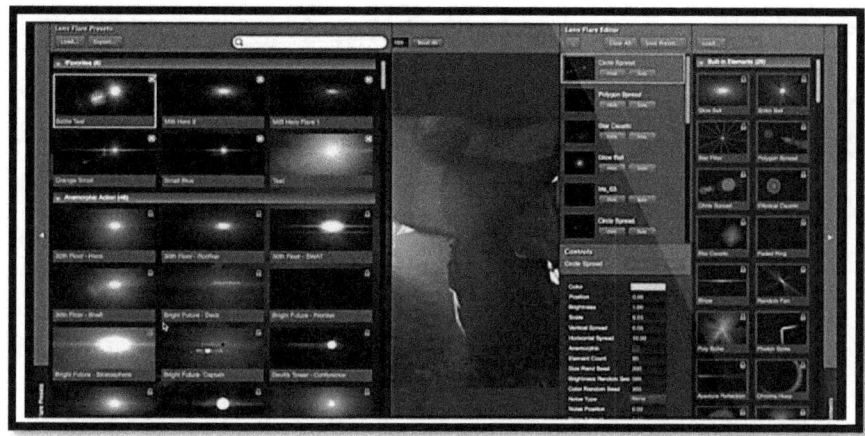

With careful attention to lighting, your videos can transform from merely okay to truly stunning. Knoll Light Factory can be seen as a magical tool that helps you achieve this. It offers a wide array of captivating lighting effects that can elevate the visual appeal of your videos. You can create a variety of impressive lighting effects and flares that make your work stand out, regardless of the video type. These effects possess a natural and powerful look, enhancing your footage beautifully.

The best part? You can customize these effects to fit your specific needs. If you only want one or two, you don't have to purchase a whole bundle. This flexibility allows you to choose and pay for only what you need, helping you save money while achieving the precise aesthetic you're aiming for. Knoll Light Factory functions like a professional tool for crafting stunning lighting effects, delivering extraordinary results.

Pros:

- **Super High-Quality Results**: The effects have a professional studio quality that enhances your videos significantly.
- **Quick Production**: Despite their impressive appearance, creating these effects is a fast process.
- **Variety of Lighting Options**: A broad range of lighting choices lets you select what best suits your video.

- **Pay for What You Need**: You can buy only the specific effects you want, saving you money.

Cons:

- **Costly**: The tool is not inexpensive; it may be a bit pricey for some users.

For $99.00 a month (billed annually), you gain access to all the amazing effects. Fortunately, various pricing plans are available, allowing you to choose one that fits your needs and budget.

2. Motion Array

Motion Array serves as a valuable alternative for those looking for budget-friendly options. Rather than being just a tool, it functions as a comprehensive hub for collaboration in video creation and post-production. While it offers a diverse range of resources—including stock footage, audio, and more—our focus here is on the Adobe Premiere Pro plugins, particularly the video presets.

These presets are collections of pre-saved visual effects designed specifically for video editors, allowing users to quickly apply specific looks or styles to their projects without navigating complex settings. This time-saving feature means you simply select a preset, apply it, and you're ready to go. The presets cater to a wide array of tasks, from basic title graphics to more intricate effects like simulating camera shakes or creating unique transitions. Users can replicate nostalgic film looks, such as early cinematic color processes or the retro aesthetic of VHS tapes, using options from Motion Array's extensive library.

With such a vast collection, users have countless opportunities to experiment with different presets and achieve their desired visual styles, limited only by their creativity.

Pros:

- **Extensive Array of Presets**: A vast selection of presets gives users numerous options for video editing.
- **User-Friendly Interface**: Motion Array's design ensures easy navigation and a seamless user experience.
- **Comprehensive Resource Pool**: In addition to plugins, the platform offers a rich repository of stock footage and music for various creative needs.
- **Regular Updates**: The library is continuously refreshed with new assets, providing users with fresh content.
- **Valuable Investment**: Many users find the subscription worthwhile due to the wealth of resources available.

Cons:

- **Overwhelming Options**: The sheer volume of choices can be daunting, making it hard to know where to begin.

For those interested in pricing, a Motion Array membership can be purchased for $29.99 per month or $19.99 per month when billed annually. Members gain access to all plugins and resources at no additional cost, making it a comprehensive and cost-effective solution for video creators.

3. FilmConvert

FilmConvert stands out among plugins designed to replicate specific film stocks, offering users the ability to add authentic grain and accurate color profiles that reflect their chosen film aesthetics. Its user-friendly interface simplifies the process while still providing a range of parameters for those interested in fine-tuning settings beyond the defaults. Users can adjust various elements, such as lighting levels, gradients, and median tones, allowing for precise customization of their film look.

One of FilmConvert's key advantages is its compatibility with a wide range of camera types, enabling users to create diverse styles—from vintage aesthetics to modern digital looks—ensuring flexibility in visual storytelling. Additionally, its fast-rendering speed is a significant draw; users appreciate the time saved compared to other tools that may keep them waiting for results. FilmConvert proves to be a reliable ally in achieving the desired visual style for any project.

Positives:

- **Extensive Selection of Options**: FilmConvert offers a wide range of choices, allowing for subtle and personalized effects in videos.
- **Rapid Rendering**: Despite its robust capabilities, FilmConvert delivers quick results, minimizing wait times for users.
- **User-Friendly Interface**: The tool strikes a balance between complexity and simplicity, making it accessible for users to navigate and utilize effectively.
- **Diverse Camera Simulation**: Supporting various camera types enables users to replicate multiple looks from different eras and technologies.

Cons:

- **Limited Help Manual**: The available help resources may not provide extensive guidance, but the intuitive interface typically allows users to navigate easily.
- **Higher Price Point, but Justifiable**: While some may find it expensive, the price is reasonable considering the capabilities and value it offers.

Regarding cost, the Adobe Premiere Pro package for FilmConvert is available for $142. Similar packages for DaVinci Resolve and Final Cut Pro are also priced at $142, featuring the same capabilities across all platforms.

4. Neat Video Noise Reduction

In the realm of video capture, digital methods have become the preferred choice for most creators, utilizing portable cameras, smartphones, and various devices. In today's digital landscape, having a reliable noise reduction tool is essential, and **Neat Video Noise Reduction** stands out as an excellent option for producers looking to enhance their films. This plugin effectively removes digital noise and restores images that might otherwise appear overly artificial, transforming footage captured on devices like smartphones into polished, professional visuals.

One of the standout features of Neat Video is its ease of use; getting started requires just a few clicks. The automated profile efficiently handles most tasks, but users who need more control can dive into a wide range of customization options. The plugin offers a "Beginner" mode for novices and an "Advanced" mode for experienced users, each providing various settings that can significantly affect aspects of the video, from background details to subtle elements like skin tones.

Neat Video also includes a collection of presets that simplify the management of common issues, such as light flicker, dust and scratches, and artifact corrections. Users can easily select the appropriate preset, click a button, and resolve these problems, greatly enhancing the quality of the final product. Overall, Neat Video Noise Reduction is a dependable tool for anyone seeking to improve their video content quality.

Pros:

- **User-Friendly Interface**: The software features an intuitive interface, making it accessible to users of all skill levels.

- **Incredible Potency**: Despite its simplicity, the plugin effectively enhances video quality.
- **Wide Array of Presets**: A diverse selection of presets allows users to easily address various video imperfections.
- **Flexibility in Detail Enhancement**: It can manage a broad range of details, even in low-light or shadowy conditions.

Cons:

- **Rendering Time**: While it may not be the fastest in rendering, the preview window aids in decision-making before finalizing changes.

Pricing:

Neat Video offers a free demo version. For Adobe Premiere Pro, the **Home version** costs $74.90, with a resolution limit of 1920×1080, while the **Professional version** is priced at $129.90, providing higher resolution capabilities.

5. FlickerFree

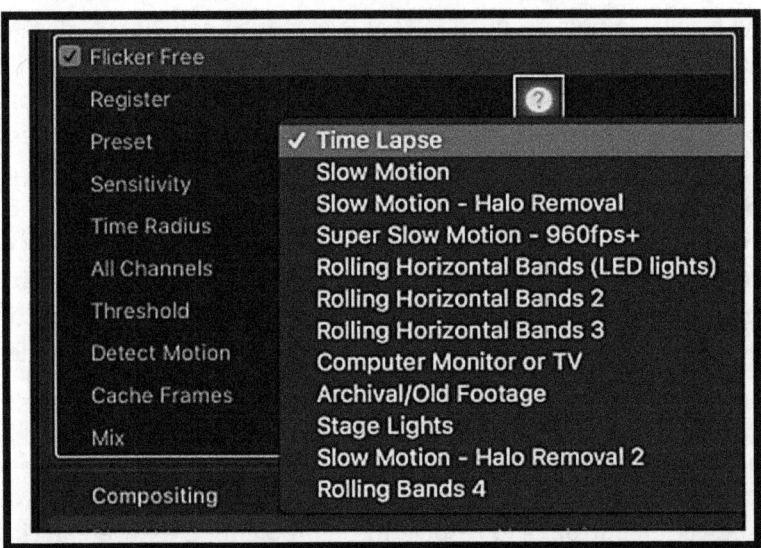

Flicker can be a frustrating challenge for aspiring filmmakers and video editors, often arising from bright lights or TV screens, particularly in drone footage or time-lapse videos. **Digital Anarchy's FlickerFree** has established itself as a go-to solution for these issues. This plugin is effective at addressing most types of flickers, with settings tailored for various scenarios, such as slow-motion footage or stage lighting flickers.

While the range of settings might seem extensive, users can easily explore and adjust them to suit their needs. Additionally, the FlickerFree website offers a wealth of guides to assist in navigating these options. Although FlickerFree cannot resolve every flicker issue, it significantly enhances the usability of footage that might otherwise be discarded. Once you start using FlickerFree, it becomes an invaluable tool for achieving flicker-free videos.

Pros:

- **Simple and Effective**: The tool reliably accomplishes its goal of reducing flicker.
- **Wide Range of Presets**: Users can choose from various presets to address specific flicker types.
- **Easy Fine Control**: Adjustments can be made easily to achieve the desired results.
- **Impressive Outcomes**: The plugin delivers genuinely remarkable improvements to video quality.

Cons:

- **Slow Rendering**: The rendering speed can be slower than ideal.
- **Limitations in High-Contrast Areas**: It may struggle with very high-contrast areas, particularly with fast-moving objects, so it isn't a complete solution for every scenario.

Cost:

FlickerFree offers a free trial version, with the full package available for **$149.00**.

6. Manifesto

If you're looking to present your video project in a captivating way, **Manifesto** is an excellent tool to consider. It enhances visual storytelling by simplifying the creation of engaging title rolls and slides that seamlessly blend opening and end credits. After downloading, you can easily access Manifesto through the Adobe Premiere Pro Effects panel.

Manifesto streamlines the title-making process by offering a wide array of customization options for text and fonts, ensuring that titles align with your desired style. Its intuitive interface features straightforward scroll bars for adjusting the width and placement of elements both horizontally and vertically. For precise control, you can input specific numbers or percentages based on the screen size.

The plugin also boasts numerous animation styles, allowing users to move text in various ways. You can customize fade-in and fade-out effects to add dynamic movement to your titles. The ease of use means that even complex aspects of title design become manageable, empowering users to exercise their creativity without hassle.

Pros:

- **User-Friendly Interface**: Manifesto is designed for simplicity, making it easy to create visually appealing title slides.

- **Extensive Text Options**: Users can modify numerous aspects of text and fonts to achieve their desired look.
- **External Text Compatibility**: It supports RTF files, facilitating the addition of external text and making text management easier.
- **Built-In Features**: The plugin includes motion blurring and de-flickering tools to enhance the overall quality of titles.
- **Text Masking Capability**: Users can easily control the visibility of text for creative effects.

Cons:

- **Simplicity over Complexity**: While its simplicity is advantageous, some users may find the features limited compared to more complex tools.

Best of all, **Manifesto is free**, along with all its title production tools, making it an accessible and cost-effective option for video creators.

7. TimeBolt

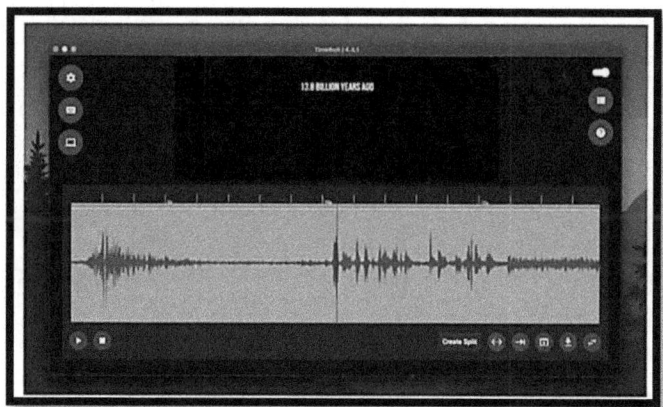

When it comes to the often tedious task of video and audio editing, dealing with dead air—those frustrating moments of silence—can be particularly challenging. **TimeBolt** emerges as an effective solution, designed to simplify and speed up this aspect of the editing process. The software intelligently analyzes your files, identifying and highlighting blank spaces for you. Users can then choose to accept its recommendations, review the identified areas manually, or make adjustments until they're satisfied.

TimeBolt excels in handling complex projects with multiple clips, and it isn't limited to video; it can also remove dead air from audio WAV files effortlessly. Additionally, users can manipulate scenes by speeding them up or slowing them down, as well as add transitions and custom background information. This tool effectively alleviates one of the most time-consuming tasks in editing, streamlining the workflow.

Pros:

- **Easy-to-Use Interface**: TimeBolt features a user-friendly design that makes it accessible for all levels of editors.
- **Thoughtfully Designed Controls**: The controls enhance the overall user experience, making the editing process smoother.
- **Variety of Tools**: While the tools may seem straightforward, they offer significant utility and helpful features.
- **Streamlined Editing Process**: By removing dead air, TimeBolt reduces a major burden for editors.

Cons:

- **Feature Limitations**: While effective, it may not include the comprehensive features found in more advanced editing software.

Cost:

- The basic plan is available for **$17 per month**, with a **60-day money-back guarantee** if you're not satisfied. A free version is also offered, but it only exports video (with no audio) and includes a watermark.

Overall, TimeBolt is a valuable asset for anyone looking to streamline their editing workflow and reduce the hassle of dead air in their projects.

8. PluralEyes

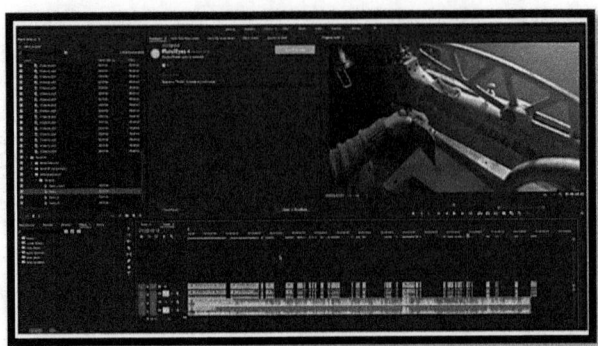

When working with multiple video clips, syncing audio and video can often become a headache, especially during intense editing sessions. **PluralEyes** is an invaluable tool for video creators facing this challenge. It specializes in resyncing audio and video clips, often outperforming any built-in audio sync features found in editing software.

Key Features:

- **Effortless Syncing**: PluralEyes automates much of the syncing process, analyzing your video and audio files to identify and correct any discrepancies.
- **Multi-Camera Support**: It can manage multiple cameras and audio tracks simultaneously, allowing you to sync multiple clips in one go.
- **Flexible Mixing**: Users can mix time-coded and non-time-coded clips without hassle, simplifying complex projects.

Pros:

- **Unmatched Power**: PluralEyes stands out as a highly effective solution, particularly for larger projects.
- **Superior Functionality**: Its capabilities far exceed those of typical built-in sync options.
- **Batch Processing**: The ability to handle numerous audio and video files at once saves significant time and effort.
- **Reliability**: The tool does exactly what it's designed to do, ensuring a stress-free experience.

Cons:

- **Resource Intensive**: PluralEyes can be demanding on system resources, which may affect performance on less powerful machines.

Pricing:

- The standalone package is priced at **$299**, with free trials available for users to explore its capabilities before committing.

Overall, PluralEyes is a powerful ally for video editors looking to streamline their workflow and eliminate the frustration of audio-video syncing issues.

9. Separate RGB

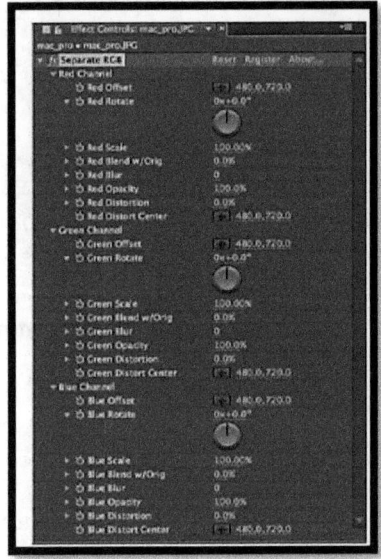

To wrap up our exploration of Adobe Premiere Pro plugins, let's highlight a playful yet impactful tool: **Separate RGB**. This plugin is all about having fun with color by allowing users to separate the red, green, and blue channels of their videos, creating unique visual effects.

Key Features:

- **RGB Channel Manipulation**: Separate RGB allows you to isolate and manipulate each color channel independently.
- **Creative Effects**: You can apply blurs, scaling, fading, and deformations to the RGB channels, resulting in visually striking effects.
- **Chromatic Aberration**: The plugin simplifies the creation of chromatic aberration, a lens distortion effect that adds depth and character to footage.
- **Dynamic Visuals**: You can introduce lens shakes and other camera movements to bring otherwise flat footage to life.

Pros:

- **Endless Creativity**: The freedom to adjust RGB channels opens up a world of creative possibilities.
- **Visually Stunning Effects**: It's easy to create eye-catching visuals that can enhance any project.

- **User-Friendly**: Despite its playful nature, the interface allows for intuitive adjustments without steep learning curves.

Cons:

- **Niche Utility**: While it's fun, the effects might not be suitable for every project, making it more of a specialty tool.

Pricing:

- Available for a **one-time purchase of $39.99**, making it an affordable addition for those looking to experiment with color in their videos.

Overall, Separate RGB is a delightful plugin that adds a layer of creativity and fun to video editing, making it a great tool for anyone looking to explore unique visual styles.

How to Install Audio Plug-ins for Adobe Premiere Pro

Absolutely! While Adobe Premiere Pro is known for its powerful video editing capabilities, enhancing your audio is just as crucial for creating a polished final product. High-quality audio can elevate your video, making it more engaging and professional.

Adding Audio Plug-ins to Adobe Premiere Pro

1. **Choose the Right Plug-ins**: First, identify the audio plug-ins you want to use. They can include effects like equalizers, compressors, reverb, and more. Popular formats include VST, VST3, and AU (for Mac).
2. **Download the Plug-ins**: Obtain the audio plug-ins from the developer's website or a trusted source. Ensure they are compatible with your operating system and Premiere Pro.
3. **Installation Location**: Save the plug-ins to specific folders to ensure Premiere Pro can find them:
   - **For MacOS**:
     - /Users/<user>/Library/Audio/Plug-Ins/VST
     - /Library/Audio/Plug-ins/VST
   - **For Windows**:
     - C:\Program Files\VSTPlugins
4. **Scan for Plug-ins**:
   - Open Adobe Premiere Pro.
   - Navigate to the **Audio** menu.
   - Click on **Audio Plug-in Manager**.
   - Select **Scan for Plug-ins** and point it to the directory where your plugins are saved.

5. **Accessing the Plug-ins**: Once the scan is complete, you can access your newly added audio plug-ins by going to **Effects** > **Audio Effects**.

Benefits of Using Audio Plug-ins:

- **Improved Sound Quality**: Plug-ins can significantly enhance the clarity and richness of your audio.
- **Creative Flexibility**: With various effects at your disposal, you can tailor the audio to suit your video's mood and style.
- **Professional Finish**: High-quality audio contributes to a more polished and immersive viewing experience.

By incorporating audio plug-ins into your workflow, you can ensure that both your video and audio meet high standards, resulting in a more captivating final product.

Troubleshooting

Timeline Panel in Adobe Premiere Pro not working?

You've covered some key reasons for issues with the Timeline Panel in Adobe Premiere Pro. Here are some additional troubleshooting steps and considerations to help resolve these problems:

Common Issues and Solutions

1. **Outdated Software**:
   o Always check for updates through the Adobe Creative Cloud app. New versions often fix bugs and improve performance.
2. **System Specifications**:
   o Verify that your computer meets or exceeds the minimum system requirements for Premiere Pro. Upgrading hardware like RAM or graphics cards can help.
3. **Corrupted Project Files**:
   o Try importing your project into a new project file. This can sometimes bypass corruption issues.
   o Use the "Project Manager" feature to consolidate your project into a new file, which may eliminate problematic media links.
4. **Incompatible Formats**:
   o Ensure that the media files you're using are supported by Premiere Pro. Convert any unsupported formats before importing.
5. **Incorrect Project Settings**:
   o Check the sequence settings and ensure they match your footage settings. Mismatched settings can lead to playback issues.
6. **Reset Preferences**:

- Resetting preferences can resolve various glitches. Hold down **Alt (Windows)** or **Option (Mac)** while launching Premiere Pro to reset preferences.

7. **Clear Media Cache**:
   - Go to **Edit** > **Preferences** > **Media Cache** and clear cache files. This can free up space and improve performance.

8. **Disable Hardware Acceleration**:
   - If you're experiencing crashes or rendering issues, try disabling hardware acceleration in **File** > **Project Settings** > **General**.

9. **Graphics Card Drivers**:
   - Ensure your graphics card drivers are up-to-date, as outdated drivers can cause performance issues.

10. **Reinstall Premiere Pro**:
   - If all else fails, consider uninstalling and then reinstalling Adobe Premiere Pro to ensure a clean installation.

General Tips

- **Backup Your Projects**: Regularly save backups of your projects to avoid losing work in case of corruption.
- **Check for Third-Party Plugins**: Sometimes, plugins can cause conflicts. Try disabling them to see if the issue persists.
- **Consult Adobe Forums**: The Adobe community and forums can be a great resource for troubleshooting specific issues others have encountered.

By systematically going through these steps, you can identify and resolve the issues with your Timeline Panel in Adobe Premiere Pro.

Fix the Premiere Pro Media Pending Error

Great start on addressing the "Media Pending" issue in Premiere Pro! This can definitely be frustrating, but here are additional methods to resolve this problem:

2. Clear Media Cache

Clearing the media cache can often help with various playback and media-related issues.

- **Steps**:
   - Go to **Edit** (Windows) or **Premiere Pro** (Mac) in the top menu.
   - Select **Preferences**, then **Media Cache**.
   - Click on **Delete** under the Media Cache Files section.

       o   Choose to delete unused media cache files or all media cache files, then confirm your choice.

3. Check File Location and Format

Sometimes, the issue arises from files being moved or saved in an unsupported format.

- **Steps**:
    - o   Ensure that the original media files are in their correct locations and haven't been moved or deleted.
    - o   Check the format of your video files. Make sure they're in a supported format (e.g., MOV, MP4).
    - o   If possible, try re-importing the media files into your project.

4. Restart Premiere Pro

If the first two methods don't work, a simple restart might do the trick.

- **Steps**:
    - o   Save your project and close Premiere Pro.
    - o   Reopen Premiere Pro and load your project again.
    - o   Check if the media files now appear correctly.

5. Render the Timeline

Rendering your timeline can help with playback issues and may resolve media pending messages.

- **Steps**:
    - o   Select the sequence you're working on.
    - o   Go to **Sequence** in the top menu.
    - o   Choose **Render In to Out** or press the shortcut **Enter** to render the timeline.

6. Update or Reinstall Premiere Pro

If the issue persists, ensure your software is up to date. Sometimes, reinstalling can fix underlying issues.

- **Steps**:
    - o   Check for updates via the Adobe Creative Cloud app and install any available updates.
    - o   If the problem continues, consider uninstalling and reinstalling Premiere Pro.

7. Use Media Browser for Importing

Instead of dragging and dropping files into the project, use the Media Browser to ensure Premiere Pro reads the files correctly.

- **Steps**:
    - Open the **Media Browser** panel (Window > Media Browser).
    - Navigate to the location of your files and import them from there.

By following these additional methods, you can often resolve the "Media Pending" issue and get back to editing smoothly. If problems persist, consider checking Adobe's support forums or reaching out to Adobe support for further assistance.

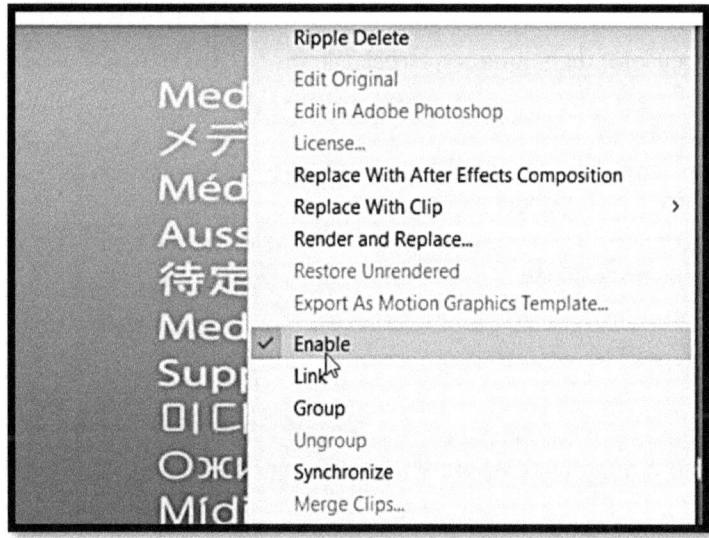

That's a solid workaround! Making a small cut can indeed refresh Premiere Pro's reading of the media and sometimes resolve the "Media Pending" issue. Here are a few more tips to consider alongside your suggestion:

3. Duplicate the Clip

If cutting doesn't resolve the issue, try duplicating the clip:

- **Steps**:
    - Right-click on the clip with the media pending error.
    - Select **Copy** (or use Ctrl+C / Cmd+C).
    - Move to a different spot in the timeline and **Paste** (Ctrl+V / Cmd+V).

<ul>
<li>o Check if the duplicated clip plays correctly.</li>
</ul>

4. Change Clip Properties

Sometimes, changing a property of the clip can prompt Premiere Pro to refresh:

- **Steps**:
  - o Right-click the clip with the issue.
  - o Select **Speed/Duration** and make a slight adjustment (like changing the speed to 100.1%).
  - o Click **OK** and see if this resolves the error.

5. Nest the Sequence

Nesting can also be a useful technique to refresh the timeline.

- **Steps**:
  - o Select the clip (or multiple clips) that are causing issues.
  - o Right-click and select **Nest**.
  - o This creates a new sequence from the selected clips, which can sometimes clear up playback issues.

6. Use Media Cache Again

If you haven't already, it might be worth clearing the media cache again after trying these methods, just to ensure that any temporary files causing conflicts are cleared out.

7. Restart Your System

If all else fails, restarting your computer can sometimes resolve underlying issues that are affecting Premiere Pro.

Conclusion

By trying these additional strategies alongside your initial suggestion, you should be well-equipped to tackle the "Media Pending" issue. Keep experimenting, and hopefully, one of these methods will resolve the problem! If not, checking Adobe's official support or forums may yield more specific guidance based on the project or file type you're working with.

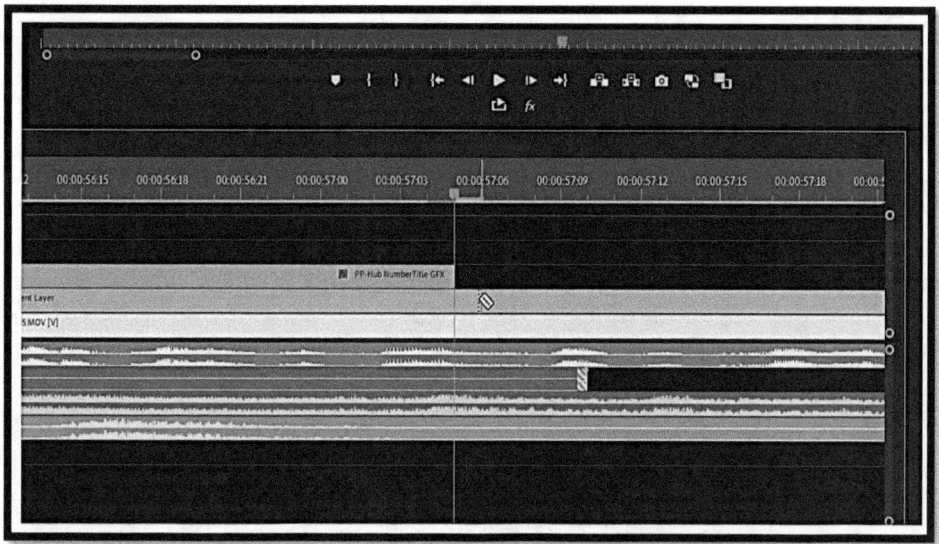

Great addition! Adjusting the duration by one frame can be a very effective way to refresh how Premiere Pro reads the clip. Here's a more detailed breakdown of the process for clarity:

3. Adjust the Duration by One Frame

This method involves making a minimal adjustment to the clip's length, which can prompt Premiere Pro to reprocess the media.

Steps:

1. **Select the Clip**: Click on the clip that has the "media pending" message.
2. **Zoom In**:
    - Use **Ctrl + +** (Windows) or **Cmd + +** (Mac) to zoom in on the timeline. This will help you see the individual frames clearly.
3. **Extend the Clip**:
    - Click and drag the end of the clip outwards by one frame. You can do this by hovering over the end of the clip until you see the trim tool cursor, then dragging to the right.
4. **Zoom Out**:
    - Use **Ctrl + -** (Windows) or **Cmd + -** (Mac) to zoom back out.
5. **Test the Clip**: Play the clip again to see if the "media pending" issue has been resolved.

Additional Tips

- **Snapping**: Ensure that snapping is enabled (the magnet icon in the timeline toolbar) to make it easier to adjust by one frame.
- **Undo Option**: If the adjustment doesn't work, you can always undo the change with **Ctrl + Z** (Windows) or **Cmd + Z** (Mac).

This technique, along with the other methods mentioned, can really help troubleshoot and resolve media-related issues in Premiere Pro. If you have more tips or need assistance with anything else, feel free to ask!

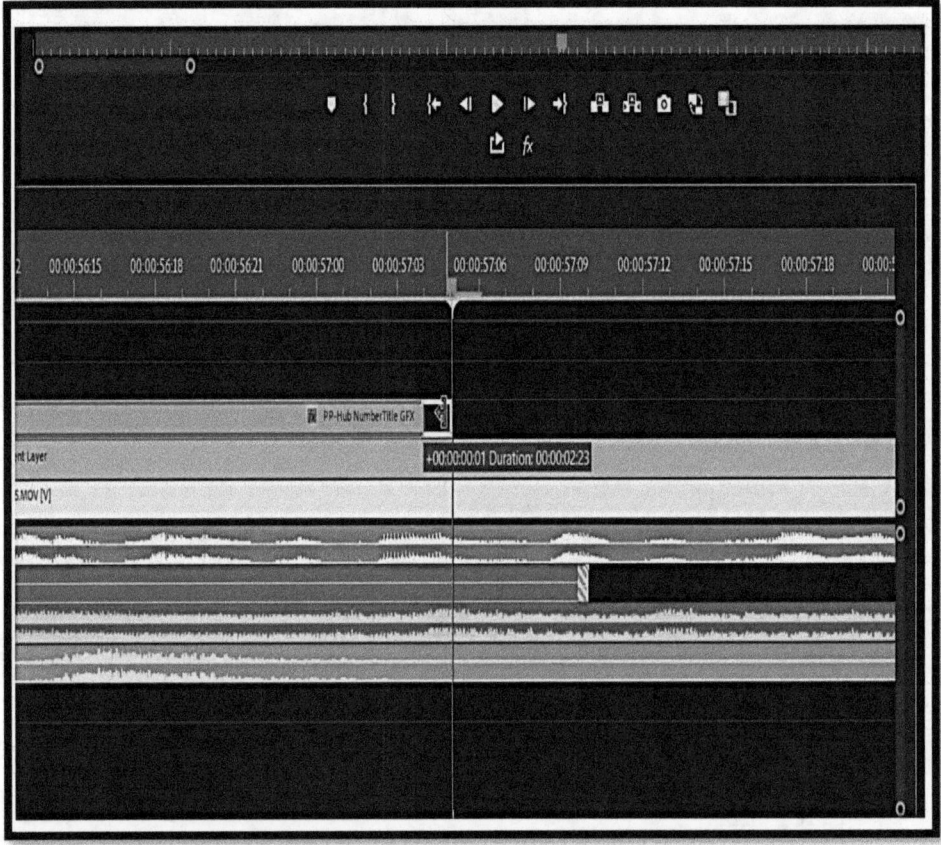

Absolutely! Preventing the "media pending" issue in the future can save you a lot of frustration. Here are some tips to help you avoid encountering this problem again:

Tips to Prevent Media Pending Issues

1. **Organize Your Media**:
   - Keep your project files organized in a structured folder system. This helps Premiere Pro locate the files more efficiently.
   - Avoid moving or renaming files after they've been imported into your project.
2. **Use Proxies for Heavy Files**:
   - If you're working with high-resolution files, consider using proxies. They are lower-resolution versions of your clips that are easier for your system to handle, reducing the chance of media errors.
3. **Ensure System Compatibility**:
   - Make sure your computer meets or exceeds the recommended system requirements for Adobe Premiere Pro. Insufficient hardware can lead to performance issues.
4. **Keep Software Updated**:
   - Regularly check for updates to Premiere Pro and your operating system. Updates often include bug fixes and performance improvements that can mitigate issues.
5. **Clear Media Cache**:
   - Periodically clear your media cache. Go to **Edit > Preferences > Media Cache** (or **Premiere Pro > Preferences > Media Cache** on Mac) and delete unused cache files. This can help with performance.
6. **Avoid Corrupted Files**:
   - Check the integrity of your media files before importing them. Corrupted files can lead to errors during playback.
7. **Use Supported Formats**:
   - Stick to media formats that are fully supported by Premiere Pro. Using unsupported or uncommon formats may lead to reading errors.
8. **Regular Backups**:
   - Regularly back up your projects and media files. This can be helpful in case you encounter any issues that require restoring previous versions.

By following these practices, you can minimize the chances of running into the "media pending" issue in the future. If you encounter any other challenges or have questions, don't hesitate to reach out!

How to Avoid the Media Pending Error

Great point! Understanding the underlying causes of the "media pending" issue can help you address it effectively. Here are some insights and additional steps to troubleshoot and mitigate these issues related to Dynamic Links and Nested Sequences:

Troubleshooting Dynamic Links & Nested Sequences

1. **Dynamic Links**:
   - o **Render and Replace**: As you mentioned, after making changes to dynamically linked footage (like After Effects compositions), using **Render and Replace** can stabilize the link. This renders the footage into a format Premiere can read more reliably.
   - o **Check Link Status**: Ensure that the linked files are intact and accessible. If the original file has been moved or renamed, you'll need to relink it.
2. **Nested Sequences**:
   - o **Simplify Nesting**: Complex nested sequences can lead to confusion and potential errors. If possible, simplify your nesting to reduce the chance of issues.
   - o **Export Nested Sequences**: If you're experiencing persistent problems, consider exporting the nested sequence as a new video file. Then, re-import this file into your project.
3. **Monitor Sequence Settings**:
   - o Ensure that the sequence settings match the media you are using. Mismatched settings can sometimes lead to issues in playback and editing.
   - o Double-check the frame rate, resolution, and audio settings to ensure compatibility.
4. **Clear Dynamic Link Cache**:
   - o If issues persist, clearing the Dynamic Link cache can sometimes resolve lingering problems. Go to **Edit > Preferences > Media Cache** and clear the cache to refresh links.
5. **Regularly Update Software**:
   - o Ensure both Adobe Premiere Pro and After Effects are up to date. Sometimes, compatibility issues between versions can cause problems with dynamic links.
6. **Test Projects**:
   - o Create a simple test project with similar sequences and links. This can help you identify if the issue is specific to your main project or if it's a broader problem.

By keeping these troubleshooting steps in mind, you can better diagnose the reasons behind the "media pending" error and take proactive measures to avoid it in the future. If the issue persists despite these efforts, it may be worth consulting Adobe's support resources or community forums for further assistance.

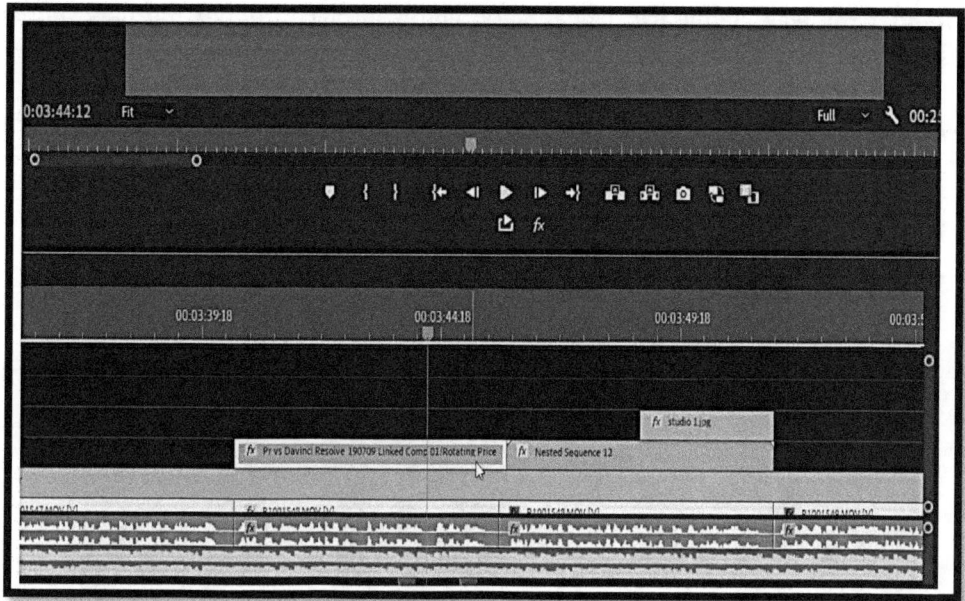

Great advice! Replacing the sequence can often resolve persistent issues related to "media pending." Here's a quick recap of the process to ensure clarity:

Replacing the Sequence

1. **Create a New Sequence**:
   - Right-click on the existing sequence in your Project panel.
   - Select **"New Sequence from Clip"** to create a new sequence with the same settings.
2. **Copy the Clips**:
   - In the timeline of the original sequence (the one with the media pending issue), press **Ctrl+C** (Windows) or **Cmd+C** (Mac) to copy all the clips. You can select all clips by pressing **Ctrl+A** (Windows) or **Cmd+A** (Mac) if needed.
3. **Paste into the New Sequence**:
   - Switch to the newly created sequence.
   - Press **Ctrl+V** (Windows) or **Cmd+V** (Mac) to paste the copied clips into the new timeline.

Additional Tips

- **Check for Effects**: After pasting, ensure that any effects or adjustments from the original sequence are correctly applied. You may need to redo or adjust them if they don't transfer as expected.

- **Render the New Sequence**: Once everything is in place, render the new sequence to ensure smooth playback and check if the media pending issue persists.

By following these steps, you can often sidestep any lingering issues tied to the original sequence, providing a fresh slate for your editing work. If problems continue after this, it may be time to explore other avenues like checking media compatibility or system performance.

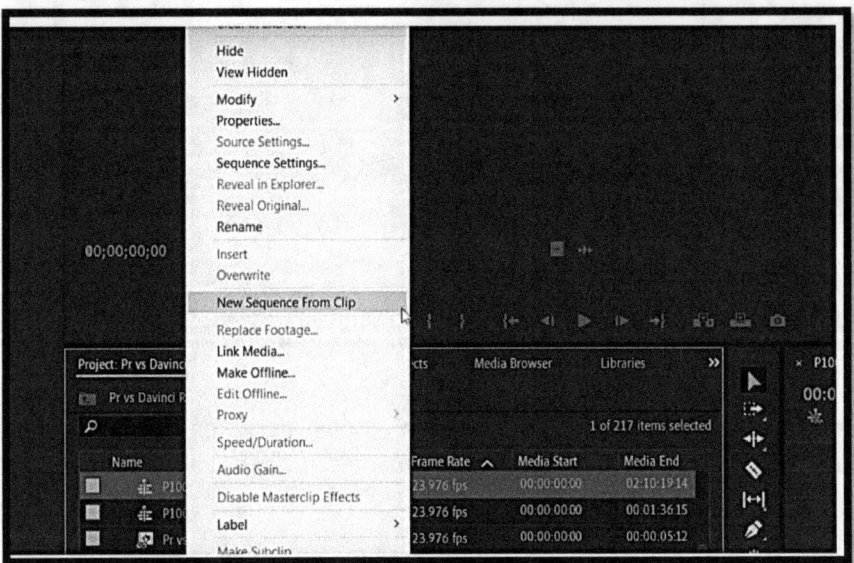

Cleaning up cache files is a great way to resolve persistent "media pending" issues in Adobe Premiere Pro. Here's how to do it step-by-step:

Deleting Cache Files

1. **Access Preferences**:
   - Open Adobe Premiere Pro.
   - Go to the top menu and select **Edit** (Windows) or **Premiere Pro** (Mac).
   - Click on **Preferences** and then select **Media Cache** from the list.
2. **Delete Unused Files**:
   - In the Media Cache preferences window, look for the option that says **Delete Unused Files**.
   - Click this button to remove any cache files that are not currently in use. This can help clear up any potential corruption or errors associated with these files.
3. **Consider Manual Cleanup**:
   - If issues persist, you might want to manually clear out the cache files. You can navigate to the Media Cache folder on your computer (you can find the location in the Media Cache preferences).

○ Delete the contents of the cache folder, but make sure to back up any important files before doing this.

Additional Tips

- **Restart Premiere**: After deleting cache files, it's a good idea to restart Adobe Premiere Pro to allow the software to rebuild any necessary cache as you work.
- **Regular Maintenance**: Periodically clearing cache files can help maintain performance and prevent potential issues. Consider setting a reminder to do this every few weeks or after completing major projects.

By following these steps, you can often alleviate lingering media pending errors and improve the overall responsiveness of your editing environment.

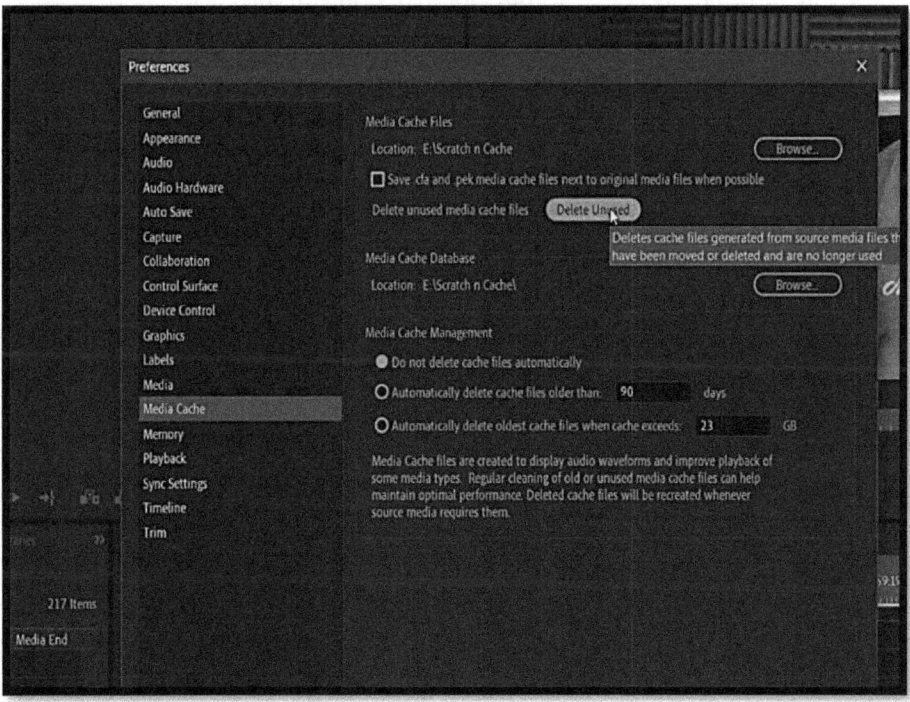

If you're still facing issues with "media pending" messages in Adobe Premiere Pro, manually clearing out preview files can often help. Here's how to do it step-by-step:

Deleting/Removing Preview Files

1. **Close Premiere Pro**:

- o Ensure that Adobe Premiere Pro is completely closed to avoid any file access issues.
2. **Locate Your Project Folder**:
   - o Navigate to the folder where your project file (.prproj) is saved. This is typically where you've been working on your project.
3. **Find the Preview Files Folder**:
   - o Look for a folder named **Adobe Premiere Pro Video Previews**. This folder contains the preview files generated by Premiere Pro.
4. **Delete the Preview Files**:
   - o Select all files in the **Adobe Premiere Pro Video Previews** folder and delete them. You can do this manually, ensuring that only the preview files are removed, not your project files.
5. **Reopen Premiere Pro**:
   - o Open Adobe Premiere Pro again. The software will automatically regenerate new preview files as needed when you work on your project.

Additional Considerations

- **Move Cache Location**: If issues persist, consider changing the cache location to a different hard drive. To do this:
  - o Go to **Edit > Preferences > Media Cache**.
  - o Click on **Browse** to select a new location for your cache files. This can sometimes alleviate performance issues.
- **Regular Maintenance**: Regularly clearing both cache and preview files can help prevent future issues and keep your editing environment running smoothly.

By following these steps, you should be able to resolve lingering "media pending" issues and enhance the overall performance of your projects in Adobe Premiere Pro.

Fix Choppy Playback in Premiere Pro

Absolutely, choppy playback in Adobe Premiere Pro can be frustrating, especially when you're trying to focus on editing. Here are some common reasons for choppy playback and potential solutions to improve performance:

Common Reasons for Choppy Playback

1. **Heavy Effects and Filters**:
   - o Using multiple effects or high-resolution filters can strain your system's resources, leading to choppy playback.
2. **High-Resolution Footage**:

- o Editing 4K or higher resolution footage can be taxing, particularly if your hardware isn't equipped to handle it.
3. **Insufficient System Resources**:
   - o Limited RAM, an outdated graphics card, or a slow hard drive can impede playback smoothness.
4. **Incorrect Playback Settings**:
   - o Your playback resolution settings may be set too high for your system to handle efficiently.
5. **Background Processes**:
   - o Other programs running in the background can consume CPU and memory resources, affecting Premiere's performance.

Solutions to Improve Playback

1. **Lower Playback Resolution**:
   - o In the Program Monitor, reduce the playback resolution. Setting it to 1/2 or 1/4 can significantly enhance playback smoothness without affecting your editing.
2. **Render Effects In to Out**:
   - o Select the timeline section with effects and choose **Sequence > Render In to Out**. This will create preview files for smoother playback.
3. **Use Proxies**:
   - o Create lower-resolution proxy files for editing. Proxies allow you to work with smaller, less resource-intensive files that are easier on your system.
4. **Optimize Media Cache**:
   - o Clear your media cache by going to **Edit > Preferences > Media Cache** and deleting unused files. Consider changing the cache location to a faster drive.
5. **Close Unnecessary Programs**:
   - o Make sure to close any unnecessary applications running in the background that might be using system resources.
6. **Check Sequence Settings**:
   - o Ensure your sequence settings match your footage settings to prevent unnecessary rendering.
7. **Update Graphics Drivers**:
   - o Keeping your graphics card drivers up to date can enhance performance and compatibility.
8. **Upgrade Hardware**:
   - o If you consistently encounter performance issues, consider upgrading your RAM, SSD, or graphics card for better overall performance.

By implementing these strategies, you should see an improvement in playback smoothness in Adobe Premiere Pro, allowing for a more efficient and enjoyable editing experience.

What to Check When Your Premiere Pro Playback Is Choppy

Absolutely, troubleshooting choppy playback in Adobe Premiere Pro can often hinge on identifying the root cause. Here's a deeper look at the steps you can take to diagnose and fix the issue:

Troubleshooting Steps for Choppy Playback

1. **Check Your Hardware**:
   o **System Requirements**: Ensure your computer meets the minimum system requirements for running Premiere Pro, including CPU, RAM, and GPU specifications.
   o **Storage Space**: Make sure you have adequate free space on your hard drive. Premiere Pro requires space for caching and temp files, and low disk space can severely impact performance.
2. **Check for Updates**:
   o **Premiere Pro Updates**: Regularly check for updates to Premiere Pro itself. Adobe frequently releases patches and updates that can improve performance and fix bugs.
   o **Operating System Updates**: Ensure your operating system is up to date, as compatibility issues can sometimes lead to performance problems.
3. **Check Sequence and Clip Settings**:
   o **Match Settings**: Verify that the sequence settings match your clip settings. If you're mixing different resolutions (like 4K and 1080p) or frame rates (such as 60fps clips in a 24fps sequence), it can cause playback issues.
   o **Frame Rate Consistency**: Ensure all clips are recorded at similar frame rates. If not, consider converting clips to match the timeline settings for smoother playback.
4. **Optimize Playback Settings**:
   o **Playback Resolution**: As mentioned, lowering the playback resolution in the Program Monitor can drastically improve performance.
   o **Use the "Render In to Out" Option**: This can help with clips that have heavy effects applied, creating temporary files for smoother playback.
5. **Examine Effects and Plugins**:
   o **Heavy Effects**: Review the effects applied to your clips. Remove or disable any unnecessary effects to see if performance improves.
   o **Third-Party Plugins**: Sometimes, third-party plugins can cause issues. Temporarily disable them to check for conflicts.
6. **Clear Media Cache**:

- o **Cache Management**: Regularly clear your media cache. Go to **Edit > Preferences > Media Cache** and delete unused files. This can resolve issues caused by corrupt cache files.
7. **Test with a New Project**:
   - o **New Project**: Create a new project and import a few clips to see if the playback issue persists. This can help determine if the problem lies within a specific project file.
8. **Hardware Acceleration**:
   - o **Enable Hardware Acceleration**: In Premiere Pro, go to **File > Project Settings > General** and ensure that "Renderer" is set to "Mercury Playback Engine GPU Acceleration" (if your hardware supports it).
9. **Close Background Applications**:
   - o **Resource Management**: Close any unnecessary applications running in the background to free up system resources.

By following these steps, you can systematically identify and address the factors contributing to choppy playback in Premiere Pro, allowing for a smoother editing experience.

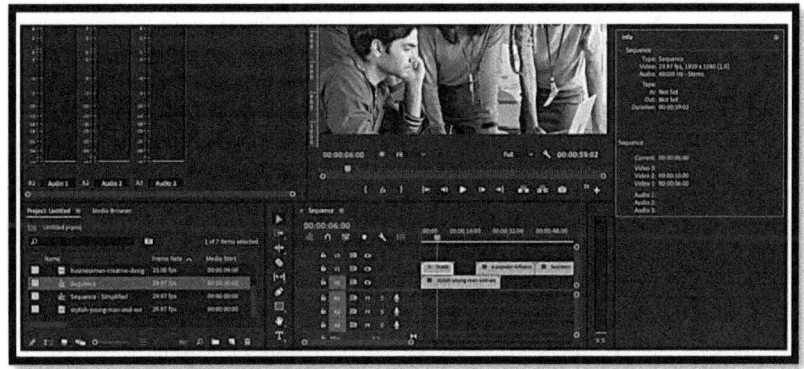

🞂 To review the settings of a clip, select it in the timeline and navigate to the Info tab in the Inspector. The clip may have been recorded with different settings compared to the rest of your sequence. You can create a Proxy clip or isolate the clip and export it to ensure it matches the other footage.

🞂 Too many applications are open: A common issue might be having too many apps running on your device. Even a simple web browser can slow down Premiere Pro on an underperforming computer. Close as many applications as possible, keeping only those essential for your editing work.

⧉ Restarting the program: This is a simple solution that works for most software across devices. Sometimes, Leading Edge can become unresponsive. Restarting the application and your device can help it reset. Remember to save your work before closing the program.

How to Fix Choppy Playback in Premiere Pro

Often, choppy playback in Premiere Pro is due to your project being too large or complex for your device to handle. Fortunately, there are several methods to address these lag issues directly within Premiere.

Consolidate the Project

Maintaining a straightforward file structure for your projects is essential, as Premiere can struggle with complexity behind the scenes. By using the Premiere Consolidation tool, you can keep all your files and videos organized in one location. This tool allows you to select specific sequences and transfer them to a new project in a different location. The consolidation process copies more than just the sequence itself, making it an effective way to streamline and manage your projects during the writing stages.

- Go to "File" and select "Project Manager."
- Choose the sequences you want to duplicate.
- Ensure you include all necessary elements by reviewing the other selection options.

⧉ Click on the file name to specify the new save location.

⬜ Press the "Calculate" button to determine the size of the copied project.

⬜ Once you're finished, click "OK" and wait for Premiere to complete the consolidation.

⬜ Locate your new project and open it to continue making updates.

GPU Acceleration

If your computer is equipped with a dedicated graphics card for video tasks, you can enable GPU Acceleration to enhance playback speed.

⬜ Launch Premiere Pro and open any project to enable GPU acceleration.

⬜ Access the project settings by navigating to File > Project Settings > General.

⬜ In the drop-down menu, select "Mercury Playback Engine GPU Acceleration" as the Renderer.

⬜ Click "OK" to apply the changes.

Get rid of the media cache.

Premiere Pro stores files in the Media Cache folder to enhance your editing experience, making playback smoother. Each time you play a clip in your project, Premiere adds more files to this cache. These "helper files" are designed to optimize playback. However, the Media Cache can fill up quickly and consume significant storage space. Clearing the Media Cache can improve performance, but keep in mind that it will require your project to be rendered again.

Playback Resolution

If you don't make a selection, Premiere will playback your edit using the sequence settings, which are typically set to 1080p or higher. Lowering the playback quality means Premiere has to process less data for each frame, making playback smoother. You can adjust the viewing size using the drop-down menu located in the bottom right corner of your Media Viewer.

Toggle Effects

If your project includes numerous effects, color grades, or adjustments, the added complexity can lead to choppy playback. To quickly assess the playback speed of your edit, you can toggle the effects for the entire sequence on and off.

- Locate the "fx" button in the menu at the bottom of the Media Viewer.

☐ If the Fx icon isn't visible, click the plus sign (+).

☐ In the pop-up window, locate the fx icon and drag it to the Media Viewer menu. Then, close the pop-up.

☐ Click the "fx" button in the menu to toggle the effects on and off in the timeline.

How to Fix Stuttering and Glitches Video in Premiere Pro

Many issues in Premiere can be perplexing and may not have a clear solution. This quick fix is useful when you're unsure of the problem and have exhausted other options.

- Save your work and close the current project.
- Press Alt + Command/Control + N on your keyboard, or go to File > New > Project.
- Save the new project in the same location, giving it a name that indicates it's the latest version.
- Navigate to File > Import or press Command/Control + I, then locate your old Premiere Pro project in the finder window.
- Select the project file and click "Import." This may take some time depending on the project size.
- Keep your new project saved in a secure location.
- Find the sequence in the Media Browser and open it. While the reason for this fix is unclear, it can resolve many issues in Premiere Pro.

Relink Media That Is Missing

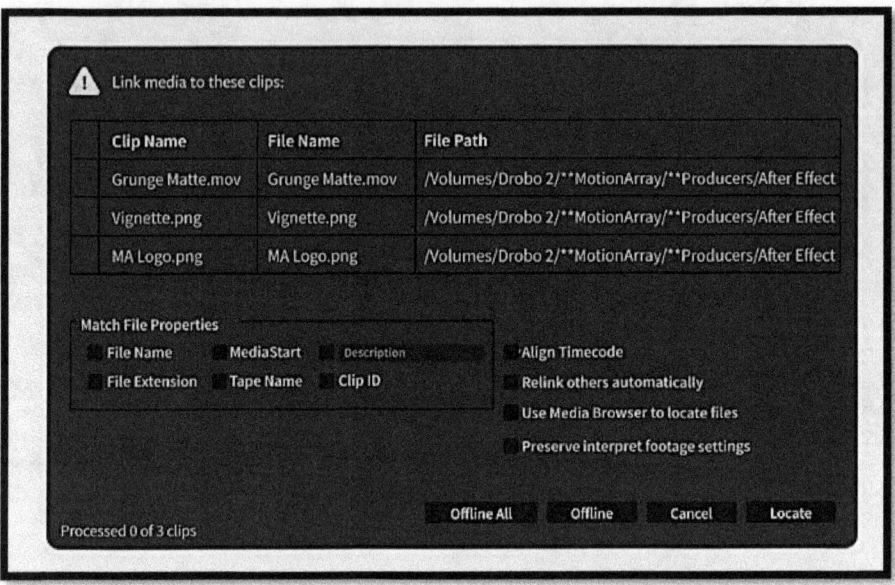

If you encounter a message about missing media when starting a project, don't worry! Here's a step-by-step guide to resolve these issues:

When opening a project, you may see an error indicating that some files are missing.

- In the pop-up window displaying the missing files, click on "Locate."
- On the left side, you'll see several folders. Navigate to your Motion Directory (or the specific name you've assigned it).
- Click "Search" in the bottom right corner of the dialog box. This will scan your video files to locate the desired clip.
- Once you've found the clip, select it and click "OK."
- By clicking "OK," all linked clips will be reconnected.
- As Premiere Pro searches, it may also find other missing files in the same directory. If it successfully locates them all, you should be good to go.
- If not, click "Locate" again and explore the folders until all missing files are found. Repeat this process until you've restored all lost media. You should then be able to continue making your edits without any issues.

Resolve the Offline Error Message

If you see a message indicating that the media is offline while a project is open, you can resolve this issue by following these steps:

- Click on the Project Panel.
- Look for the word "Offline" in the panel; this is the easiest way to identify offline media, and it will display all the offline sources.
- From the results, select all the files that are offline.
- Click a third time and choose "Relink."
- The Find box will appear again.
- As before, click on "Find" and navigate to the main folder containing your media.
- Click "OK" once you've located the file.

This will reconnect all the media, and everything should be back in working order!

Glossary

This book will cover various audio and video technology terms, particularly related to nonlinear post-production. If you're new to this, some concepts may be unfamiliar.

Key Terms:

- **Alpha Channel:** This invisible channel determines a pixel's opacity. It's stored similarly to the three-color channels and can be manipulated through manual adjustments or visual effects. For instance, in a greenscreen effect, Premiere Pro modifies the alpha channel for selected pixels to reveal the background.
- **Aspect Ratio:** This refers to the proportional relationship between a video's width and height. For example, a 1:1 ratio indicates a square, while 16:9 is common for videos. The aspect ratio remains constant regardless of screen size or image quality. Both sequences and images have aspect ratios, and while most pixels are square, some video formats use non-square pixels.
- **Bin:** Bins function like folders in Finder (macOS) or Explorer (Windows), but they exist solely within your current Premiere Pro project.
- **Bit Depth:** This defines the number of gradations between "black" and "white," or "no blue" to "full blue." Bit depth is represented by the number of bits used to store color information. Higher bit depths allow for more detail: 8-bit has 256 levels, while 10-bit offers 1,024. A 16-bit depth allows for 65,536 levels. Understanding bit depth is crucial for maintaining image quality during color corrections.
- **Clip:** In media editing, a clip is a pointer to a specific media file, similar to an alias or shortcut. Clips can include various content types, such as video, audio, and graphics, and

they retain attributes like size and frame rate, acting as integral components of media projects.

- **Codec:** Short for "coder/decoder," a codec is a method for encoding digital data, especially audio and video. It compresses files for more efficient storage and transmission, akin to shorthand. Most videos are recorded using codecs to minimize size while preserving quality, though some cameras capture raw footage without compression.
- **Compression:** This term has two meanings in media. First, it refers to using codecs to reduce the size of audio and video files for easier storage and transfer. Second, it pertains to reducing the dynamic range in audio, making the overall sound seem louder by decreasing the volume variation.
- **Cut:** A cut is a transition marker in a sequence where one clip ends and another begins. Originating from traditional film editing, it represents a straightforward way to switch between clips and is one of the most common editing techniques.
- **Effect:** Effects modify the visual or audio aspects of multimedia content. They can enhance features like brightness, sound levels, and image placement. Effects are essential for enriching storytelling and overall presentation in multimedia projects.
- **Export:** After assembling video clips in Premiere Pro, exporting creates a new media file for distribution. During this process, you can select various parameters, including file format and codec, to ensure compatibility and quality based on the intended platform.
- **Footage:** Originally referring to film length in feet, "footage" now denotes the raw video content captured during recording, measured in hours and minutes, before any editing takes place.
- **Format:** In media, "format" can indicate the file type (e.g., AVI, MOV) and encompasses attributes like frame size, shape, and rate (fps). These characteristics influence how the content is displayed and its overall quality.
- **Frame:** A frame is a single still image that forms the basis of video. Videos consist of rapidly displayed frames, and the frame rate (fps) determines the motion's smoothness.
- **High Dynamic Range (HDR):** HDR measures the brightness levels of displays, with "nits" as a common unit. This technology allows for greater contrast and a wider color spectrum compared to standard displays. HDR enhances the viewing experience by enabling more vivid and realistic imagery.
- **Import:** In Premiere Pro, importing a media file integrates it into a project without physically moving the data. Instead, Premiere Pro creates links (clips) that reference the media, enabling editing without duplicating files.
- **Keyframe:** A keyframe marks a specific moment in a timeline where a property (like position or volume) is set. Multiple keyframes allow editors to create gradual changes over time, with Premiere Pro automatically interpolating between them for smooth transitions.
- **Media:** Media encompasses all content used in a project, including videos, graphics, audio, and animations. It includes both raw and processed elements necessary for creating multimedia projects.

- **Metadata:** Metadata is descriptive information that adds context to main content. For example, video metadata might include camera details, timestamps, and location data, providing insights into the content's creation.
- **Pixel:** A pixel is the smallest unit of a digital image, composed of color values often represented in red, green, and blue (RGB). Pixels combine to form the complete picture displayed on a screen.
- **Project:** In Premiere Pro, a project is a container for all media assets, edits, and creative elements. This file holds the entire creative process and organizes clips, effects, and audio tracks.
- **RGB Color:** RGB stands for Red, Green, and Blue, the primary color model for digital displays. By varying the intensities of these colors, a wide spectrum of hues is created, essential for vibrant visuals in digital media.
- **Sequence:** A sequence is a timeline arrangement of clips in Premiere Pro. It typically consists of multiple layers for integrating various media types, allowing for editing and creativity within the project.
- **Timecode:** Timecode is a standardized method for measuring time in recorded media, using units of hours, minutes, seconds, and frames. It is crucial for precise editing and synchronization in post-production.
- **Timeline:** The Timeline panel in Premiere Pro is a workspace for organizing and adjusting sequences. It visually represents the editing process, allowing editors to manage clips, effects, and transitions effectively.
- **Transition:** A transition is a visual or audio effect facilitating the switch from one clip to another. While a simple cut is common, Premiere Pro offers various transition effects to enhance storytelling and indicate shifts in time or mood.
- **Vector-based Graphics:** Unlike pixel-based images, vector graphics use mathematical formulas to define shapes and lines. This allows them to maintain clarity and sharpness regardless of scaling, making them ideal for designs like logos and illustrations.
- **Virtual Reality Video:** VR video captures 360-degree scenes, creating an immersive experience for viewers. Although not strictly virtual reality, it allows for an engaging viewing experience, especially with VR headsets.
  - **360-degree Video Camera System:** These cameras record footage in all directions simultaneously, producing a panoramic image. The combined recordings allow viewers to explore the environment interactively.
  - **Virtual Reality Headsets:** These headsets provide an immersive experience, allowing users to engage with 360-degree content. They track head movements, enhancing the sense of presence in the virtual space. Premiere Pro supports editing for VR video, making the process more intuitive.

Conclusion

As you conclude this Adobe Premiere Pro guidebook, take a moment to reflect on your transformation from a beginner to a skilled video editor. This guide was designed with your learning journey in mind, making the complex realm of video editing accessible and enjoyable. You've navigated through the basics and advanced features of Adobe Premiere Pro, discovering tools and techniques that empower you to bring your creative ideas to life.

With step-by-step instructions and clear examples, this guide aimed to support you at every stage of your learning process. Remember, video editing is not just about mastering technical skills; it's also about storytelling and self-expression. The guide encouraged you to not only manipulate footage but to weave narratives, evoke emotions, and captivate your audience.

We included troubleshooting tips to acknowledge that challenges are part of learning. Whenever you faced obstacles, this guide aimed to be your supportive companion, offering solutions and fostering your independence as an editor.

Staying updated with the latest features in Adobe Premiere Pro is crucial for your continued growth and innovation. As you close this chapter, keep in mind that learning is an ongoing journey. The skills you've developed here are just the foundation for future experimentation and creativity.

Whether you're editing for personal projects, professional work, or simply for enjoyment, may your upcoming edits be filled with confidence and artistic expression. Thank you for choosing this guidebook as your partner in your Adobe Premiere Pro adventure. Here's to the exciting projects that await you!

INDEX

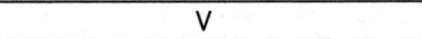

www.ingramcontent.com/pod-product-compliance
Lightning Source LLC
La Vergne TN
LVHW080111070326
832902LV00015B/2518